MW00335283

Apache Solr Enterprise Search Server

Third Edition

Enhance your searches with faceted navigation, result highlighting, relevancy-ranked sorting, and much more with this comprehensive guide to Apache Solr 4

David Smiley
Eric Pugh
Kranti Parisa
Matt Mitchell

[PACKT] open source *
PUBLISHING   community experience distilled

BIRMINGHAM - MUMBAI

Apache Solr Enterprise Search Server
Third Edition

Copyright © 2015 Packt Publishing

All rights reserved. No part of this book may be reproduced, stored in a retrieval system, or transmitted in any form or by any means, without the prior written permission of the publisher, except in the case of brief quotations embedded in critical articles or reviews.

Every effort has been made in the preparation of this book to ensure the accuracy of the information presented. However, the information contained in this book is sold without warranty, either express or implied. Neither the authors, nor Packt Publishing, and its dealers and distributors will be held liable for any damages caused or alleged to be caused directly or indirectly by this book.

Packt Publishing has endeavored to provide trademark information about all of the companies and products mentioned in this book by the appropriate use of capitals. However, Packt Publishing cannot guarantee the accuracy of this information.

First published: August 2009
Second edition: November 2011
Third edition: May 2015

Production reference: 1200515

Published by Packt Publishing Ltd.
Livery Place
35 Livery Street
Birmingham B3 2PB, UK.

ISBN 978-1-78216-136-3

www.packtpub.com

Cover image by Sylvia Smiley (sylvie.zajac@gmail.com)

Credits

Authors
David Smiley
Eric Pugh
Kranti Parisa
Matt Mitchell

Reviewers
Edd Grant
Aamir Hussain
Dmitry Kan

Acquisition Editors
Nikhil Karkal
Rebecca Youé

Content Development Editor
Shubhangi Dhamgaye

Technical Editor
Pankaj Kadam

Copy Editors
Puja Lalwani
Laxmi Subramanian

Project Coordinator
Harshal Ved

Proofreaders
Stephen Copestake
Safis Editing

Indexer
Tejal Soni

Graphics
Jason Monteiro

Production Coordinator
Manu Joseph

Cover Work
Manu Joseph

About the Authors

Born to code, **David Smiley** is a software engineer who's passionate about search, Lucene, spatial, and open source. He has a great deal of expertise with Lucene and Solr, which started in 2008 at MITRE. In 2009, as the lead author, along with the coauthor Eric Pugh, he wrote *Solr 1.4 Enterprise Search Server*, the first book on Solr, published by Packt Publishing. It was updated in 2011, *Apache Solr 3 Enterprise Search Server*, *Packt Publishing*, and again for this third edition.

After the first book, he developed 1- and 2-day Solr training courses, delivered half a dozen times within MITRE, and he has also delivered training on LucidWorks once. Most of his excitement and energy relating to Lucene is centered on Lucene's spatial module to include Spatial4j, which he is largely responsible for. He has presented his progress on this at Lucene Revolution and other conferences several times. He currently holds the status of committer & Project Management Committee (PMC) member with the Lucene/Solr open source project. Over the years, David has staked his career on search, working exclusively on such projects, formerly for MITRE and now as an independent consultant for various clients. You can reach him at dsmiley@apache.org and view his LinkedIn profile here: http://www.linkedin.com/in/davidwsmiley.

> Writing a book is the biggest project I've ever worked on, where I've put time outside of employed working hours; it requires an inordinate amount of time. I have a great deal of respect for the other authors who undertake such projects.
>
> I'm deeply appreciative of my wife, Sylvie, for enduring this time commitment and for taking care of our young daughters, Camille and Adeline. I also thank my coauthors, Eric, Kranti, and Matt, for their share of this herculean effort—it is too much for anyone of us. And finally, I am most appreciative of the compliments I've received from readers about the previous editions. It helps make the effort worthwhile.

Fascinated by the "craft" of software development, **Eric Pugh** has been involved in the open source world as a developer, committer, and user for the past decade. He is an emeritus member of the Apache Software Foundation.

In biotech, financial services, and defense IT, he has helped European and American companies develop coherent strategies to embrace open source software. As a speaker, he has advocated the advantages of Agile practices in search, discovery, and analytics projects.

Eric became involved in Solr when he submitted the patch SOLR-284 to parse rich document types, such as PDF and MS Office formats, that became the single-most popular patch, as measured by votes! The patch was subsequently cleaned up and enhanced by three other individuals, demonstrating the power of the free / open source models to build great code collaboratively. SOLR-284 was eventually refactored into Solr Cell.

He blogs at http://www.opensourceconnections.com/blog/.

Someone once told me the best business card you can have is a book, and I've discovered over the past three editions of this book that this is a very true thing. Of course, I've also learned that printing out 500 business cards is a much easier job than updating a book. Additionally, we wanted some fresh voices in this edition of the book. I'd like to thank Matt and Kranti for jumping feet first into this project. I'd like to thank David for putting so much passion into this book and being our fearless leader through all the twists and turns.

I also want to thank Erik Hatcher once again for his continuing support and mentorship over the past 10 years. Without his encouragement, I wouldn't have spoken at Euro Lucene or become involved in the Solr community.

I also want to thank all of my colleagues at OpenSource Connections. We've come a long way as a company, and I'm excited about SlopBucket, our very own conference this fall! Matt Overstreet, your creativity that you contributed to the content on SolrCloud was critical to my finishing Chapter 10.

My darling wife, Kate, who says, "It can't be that hard to finish, just do it!", I know life continues to be busy, but I couldn't be happier sharing my life with you, Morgan, and Asher. I love you.

Lastly, I want to thank all the adopters of Solr and Lucene! Without you, I wouldn't have this wonderful open source project to be so incredibly proud of! I look forward to meeting more of you at the next conference.

Kranti Parisa has more than a decade of software development expertise and a deep understanding of open source, enterprise software, and the execution required to build successful products.

He has fallen in love with enterprise search technologies, especially Lucene and Solr, after his initial implementations and customizations carried out in early 2008 to build a legal search engine for bankruptcy court documents, docket entries, and cases. He is an active contributor to the Apache Solr community. One of his recent contributions, along with Joel Bernstein, SOLR-4787, includes scalable and nested join implementations.

Kranti is currently working at Apple. Prior to that, he worked as a lead engineer and search architect at Comcast Labs, building and supporting a highly scalable search and discovery engine for the X1/X2 platform—the world's first entertainment operating system.

An entrepreneur by DNA, he is the cofounder and technical advisor of multiple start-ups focusing on cloud computing, SaaS, big data, and enterprise search based products and services. He holds a master's degree in computer integrated manufacturing from the National Institute of Technology, Warangal, India.

You can reach him on LinkedIn: `http://www.linkedin.com/in/krantiparisa`.

First and foremost, many thanks to Albert Einstein for his extraordinary innovations and one of his many inspirational quotes: *I have no special talent. I am only passionately curious.* I'd like to thank and acknowledge all the contributors to the Apache Lucene and Solr projects. You're totally awesome! Completing this work would have been all the more difficult were it not for the support and friendship provided by my coauthors—David, Eric, and Matt. I am indebted to them for their help.

Thanks to my family and friends for believing in me; I couldn't have done this without you. A very special thanks to my darling mother, Nagarani, and my beautiful wife, Pallavi, for their unconditional love, support, and patience as I spent countless weekends working on this book.

And, of course, I want to thank the team at Packt Publishing for their tremendous support in all ways, large and small. There are many more people I would like to thank, but time, space, and modesty compel me to stop here.

Matt Mitchell studied music synthesis and performance at Boston's Berklee College of Music, but his experiences with computers and programming in his younger years inspired him to pursue a career in software engineering. A passionate technologist, he has worked in many areas of software development, is active in several open source communities, and now has over 15 years of professional experience. He had his first experiences with Lucene and Solr in 2008 at the University of Virginia Library, where he became a core contributor to an open source search platform called Backlight. Matt is the author of many open source projects, including a Solr client library called RSolr, which has had over 1 million downloads from `rubygems.org`. He has been responsible for the design and implementation of search systems at several tech companies, and he is currently a senior member of the engineering team at LucidWorks, where he's working on a next generation search, discovery, and analytics platform.

You can contact Matt on LinkedIn at `https://www.linkedin.com/in/mattmitchell4`.

I'd like to thank my amazing wife, Jenny, and our kids, Henry and Dorothy, for their unbelievable patience and support during this journey. My parents, thank you for making my fantastic life possible. Eric, Kranti, and David, for all the blood, sweat, and tears you've put into this book, along with all the time you've spent helping me. My good friend, Anthony Fox, who never seems to stop encouraging and inspiring me. Erik Hatcher and Bess Sadler, for getting me started with all of this search stuff in the first place. The Lucene and Solr communities and committers, for all of their amazing work. Packt Publishing, for their endless patience and exceptional guidance. And, of course, the readers and reviewers of this book — thank you all!

About the Reviewers

Edd Grant is a freelance software engineer who has been building software professionally since 2003. He is passionate about designing first-class, maintainable systems by leveraging agile and TDD principles and has helped his clients adopt and excel at these practices.

Edd is an experienced implementor of cloud-scale web applications and services, continuous delivery, and infrastructure automation. As an open source advocate, he has helped many clients take advantage of a diverse range of such products.

Edd has a website, which he updates when he gets the time (`http://www.eddgrant.com`), and has a passion for mountain biking and tea.

Aamir Hussain is an experienced customer- and business-focused technology leader with rich hands-on engineering, business and management experience. He has over 6 years of experience in software engineering and complex systems design with focus on the Cloud software architecture and design, Software as a Service (SaaS), Platform as a Service (PaaS), monitoring and tools infrastructure, network design, and data center operations.

Starting the journey of his career from the world's most disturbed and heavily militarized zone, Aamir had also been honored and awarded multiple times in the application development programs conducted by Health2con and WHO in USA. He is currently working with one of India's largest e-commerce logistics company (Delhivery) as a senior architect.

Aamir had also managed to get his name on multiple books of Apache Solr and Python published by Packt Publishing.

Dmitry Kan leads the search technology development at AlphaSense, the one-stop financial search engine company. In parallel, he is the founder and CEO of the language intelligence company SemanticAnalyzer. Dmitry enjoys building and blogging about software, in particular, search (Solr/Lucene), machine learning (sentiment detection and machine translation), and tools that make a programmer's life easier. You can find his blogs at `dmitrykan.blogspot.com` and `semanticanalyzer.info/blog`. He developed his fully blown search engine back in 2003 as a university project. The main achievements were beating MySQL full-text search engine in speed by over 5 million records. This is when he introduced himself to the world of skip lists and balanced hash tables. In 2010, Dmitry learned about Lucene and Solr, and since then, he has been an active community member, occasionally taking part (and winning!) in the famous Stump the Chump sessions. Dmitry holds a PhD in CS from the Saint Petersburg State University (Russia) and a master's degree in CS from the University of Kuopio (Finland). In his free time, Dmitry enjoys answering questions on Stack Overflow, building models on kaggle, and cycling.

He is the maintainer and developer of *Lucene Luke*, which can be found at `https://github.com/dmitrykey/luke`. You can reach him on Twitter at `twitter.com/dmitrykan`.

I am immensely grateful to my parents for giving me the support and hunger for knowledge. My wife, Tatiana, is my first kind listener to all the ideas I get around IT, apart from being a loving and supporting wife. She knows how hard it is to be around a programming geek like me. Big thanks to all Luke fans, you help me learn new things around Apache Lucene and search in general.

www.PacktPub.com

Support files, eBooks, discount offers, and more

For support files and downloads related to your book, please visit www.PacktPub.com.

Did you know that Packt offers eBook versions of every book published, with PDF and ePub files available? You can upgrade to the eBook version at www.PacktPub.com and as a print book customer, you are entitled to a discount on the eBook copy. Get in touch with us at service@packtpub.com for more details.

At www.PacktPub.com, you can also read a collection of free technical articles, sign up for a range of free newsletters and receive exclusive discounts and offers on Packt books and eBooks.

https://www2.packtpub.com/books/subscription/packtlib

Do you need instant solutions to your IT questions? PacktLib is Packt's online digital book library. Here, you can search, access, and read Packt's entire library of books.

Why subscribe?

- Fully searchable across every book published by Packt
- Copy and paste, print, and bookmark content
- On demand and accessible via a web browser

Free access for Packt account holders

If you have an account with Packt at www.PacktPub.com, you can use this to access PacktLib today and view 9 entirely free books. Simply use your login credentials for immediate access.

Table of Contents

Preface

If you are a developer building an application today, then you know how important a good search experience is. Apache Solr, built on Apache Lucene, is a wildly popular open source enterprise search server that easily delivers the powerful search and faceted navigation features that are elusive with databases. Solr supports complex search criteria, faceting, result highlighting, query-completion, query spellcheck, relevancy tuning, and more.

Apache Solr Enterprise Search Server, *Third Edition* is a comprehensive resource to almost everything Solr has to offer. It serves the reader right from initiation to development to deployment. It also comes with complete running examples to demonstrate its use and show how to integrate Solr with other languages and frameworks—even Hadoop.

By using a large set of metadata, including artists, releases, and tracks, courtesy of the MusicBrainz.org project, you will have a testing ground for Solr and will learn how to import this data in various ways. You will then learn how to search this data in different ways, including Solr's rich query syntax and boosting match scores based on record data. Finally, we'll cover various deployment considerations to include indexing strategies and performance-oriented configuration that will enable you to scale Solr to meet the needs of a high-volume site.

Solr 4 or Solr 5?
See the *What you need for this book* section further below.

What this book covers

Chapter 1, Quick Starting Solr, introduces Solr to you so that you understand its unique role in your application stack. You'll get started quickly by indexing example data and searching it with Solr's sample / browse UI. This chapter is oriented to Solr 5, but the majority of content applies to Solr 4 too.

Chapter 2, Schema Design, guides you through an approach to modeling your data within Solr into one or more Solr indices and schemas. It covers the schema thoroughly and explores some of Solr's field types.

Chapter 3, Text Analysis, covers how to customize text tokenization, stemming, synonyms, and related matters to have fine control over keyword search matching. It also covers multilingual strategies.

Chapter 4, Indexing Data, explores all of the options Solr offers for importing data, such as XML, CSV, databases (SQL), and text extraction from common documents. This includes important information on commits, atomic updates, and real-time search.

Chapter 5, Searching, covers the query syntax, from the basics to Boolean options to more advanced wildcard and fuzzy searches, join queries, and geospatial search.

Chapter 6, Search Relevancy, explains how Solr scores documents for relevancy ranking. We'll review different options to influence the score, called boosting, and apply it to common examples such as boosting recent documents and boosting by a user vote.

Chapter 7, Faceting, shows you how to use Solr's killer feature — faceting. You'll learn about the different types of facets and how to build filter queries for a faceted navigation interface.

Chapter 8, Search Components, explores how to use a variety of valuable search features implemented as Solr search components. This includes result highlighting, query spellcheck, query suggest / complete, result grouping / collapsing, and more.

Chapter 9, Integrating Solr, explores some external integration options to interface with Solr. This includes some language-specific frameworks for Java, JavaScript, Ruby, and PHP, as well as a web crawler, Hadoop, a quick prototyping option, and more.

Chapter 10, Scaling Solr, covers how to tune Solr to get the most out of it. Then we'll introduce how to scale beyond one instance with SolrCloud.

Chapter 11, Deployment, guides you through deployment considerations to include deploying Solr to Apache Tomcat, to logging, and to security, and setting up Apache ZooKeeper.

Appendix, Quick Reference, serves as a small parameter quick-reference guide you can print to have within reach when you need it.

What you need for this book

The *Getting started* section in *Chapter 1, Quick Starting Solr*, explains what you need in detail. In summary, you should obtain:

- Java 8, a JDK release. Java 7 is fine too. Support for Java 6 was last available in Solr 4.7. More information on this is in *Chapter 1, Quick Starting Solr*.

- Apache Solr 4.8.1 is officially the version of Solr this book was written for. Nonetheless, some of the features are discussed or referenced in the later versions of Solr as far as 5.0. In fact, *Chapter 1, Quick Starting Solr*, orients you to Solr 5, which has a different first-impression experience than its predecessor. Once you get Solr running, you should be able to follow along easily with Solr 5. In *Chapter 10, Scaling Solr*, there are some SolrCloud startup commands that are a little different, and we've pointed out how they change. The only substantial topic not covered in this book that evolved through the Solr 4 point releases is data-driven schemaless mode, and HTTP API calls to make schema changes.

- The code supplement to the book. It's not essential, but you'll want it to try some of the examples or to experiment with a sizable amount of real data. See the *Downloading the example code* section.

Who this book is for

This book is primarily for developers who want to learn how to use Apache Solr in their applications. Only basic programming skills are assumed, although the vast majority of content should be useful to those with a solid technical foundation that have not yet programmed.

Conventions

In this book, you will find a number of styles of text that distinguish between different kinds of information. Here are some examples of these styles, and an explanation of their meaning.

Code words in text, database table names, folder names, filenames, file extensions, pathnames, dummy URLs, user input, and Twitter handles are shown as follows: "Typing `java -version` at a command line will tell you exactly which version of Java you are using, if any."

A block of code is set as follows:

```
"responseHeader": {
    "status": 0,
```

```
      "QTime": 1,
      "params": {
        "q": "lcd",
        "indent": "true",
        "wt": "json"
      }
    }
  ...
```

When we wish to draw your attention to a particular part of a code block, the relevant lines or items are set in bold:

```
    {
        "id": "9885A004",
        "name": "Canon PowerShot SD500",
        "manu": "Canon Inc.",
        "manu_id_s": "canon",
        "cat": [
          "electronics",
          "camera"
        ],
        "features": [
          "3x zoop, 7.1 megapixel Digital ELPH",
          "movie clips up to 640x480 @30 fps",
          "2.0\" TFT LCD, 118,000 pixels",
          "built in flash, red-eye reduction"
        ],
        "includes": "32MB SD card, USB cable, AV cable, battery",
        "weight": 6.4,
        "price": 329.95,
        "price_c": "329.95,USD",
        "popularity": 7,
        "inStock": true,
        "manufacturedate_dt": "2006-02-13T15:26:37Z",
        "store": "45.19614,-93.90341",
        "_version_": 1500358264225792000
      },
    ...
```

Any command-line input or output is written as follows:

```
>> cd example/exampledocs
>> java -Dc=techproducts -jar post.jar *.xml
SimplePostTool version 5.0.0
Posting files to [base] url
http://localhost:8983/solr/techproducts/update using
content-type application/xml...
POSTing file gb18030-example.xml
```

```
POSTing file hd.xml
etc.
14 files indexed.
COMMITting Solr index changes to http://localhost:8983/solr/techproducts/
update...
```

New terms and **important words** are shown in bold. Words that you see on the screen, in menus or dialog boxes for example, appear in the text like this: "Click on the **Core Selector** drop-down menu and select the **techproducts** link."

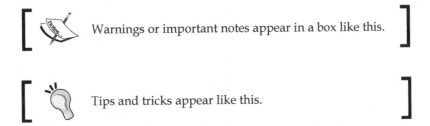

Warnings or important notes appear in a box like this.

Tips and tricks appear like this.

Reader feedback

Feedback from our readers is always welcome. Let us know what you think about this book—what you liked or may have disliked. Reader feedback is important for us to develop titles that you really get the most out of.

To send us general feedback, simply send an e-mail to feedback@packtpub.com, and mention the book title via the subject of your message.

If there is a topic that you have expertise in and you are interested in either writing or contributing to a book, see our author guide on www.packtpub.com/authors.

Customer support

Now that you are the proud owner of a Packt book, we have a number of things to help you to get the most from your purchase.

Downloading the example code

You can download the example code files for all Packt books you have purchased from your account at http://www.packtpub.com. If you purchased this book elsewhere, you can visit http://www.packtpub.com/support and register to have the files e-mailed directly to you.

A copy of the code bundle and possibly other information will also be available at `http://www.solrenterprisesearchserver.com`.

Errata

Although we have taken every care to ensure the accuracy of our content, mistakes do happen. If you find a mistake in one of our books—maybe a mistake in the text or the code—we would be grateful if you could report this to us. By doing so, you can save other readers from frustration and help us improve subsequent versions of this book. If you find any errata, please report them by visiting `http://www.packtpub.com/submit-errata`, selecting your book, clicking on the **Errata Submission Form** link, and entering the details of your errata. Once your errata are verified, your submission will be accepted and the errata will be uploaded to our website or added to any list of existing errata under the Errata section of that title.

To view the previously submitted errata, go to `https://www.packtpub.com/books/content/support` and enter the name of the book in the search field. The required information will appear under the **Errata** section.

Piracy

Piracy of copyright material on the Internet is an ongoing problem across all media. At Packt, we take the protection of our copyright and licenses very seriously. If you come across any illegal copies of our works, in any form, on the Internet, please provide us with the location address or website name immediately so that we can pursue a remedy.

Please contact us at `copyright@packtpub.com` with a link to the suspected pirated material.

We appreciate your help in protecting our authors, and our ability to bring you valuable content.

Questions

You can contact us at `questions@packtpub.com` if you are having a problem with any aspect of the book, and we will do our best to address it.

1
Quick Starting Solr

Welcome to Solr! You've made an excellent choice to power your search needs. In this chapter, we're going to cover the following topics:

- An overview of what Solr and Lucene are all about
- What makes Solr different from databases?
- How to get Solr, what's included, and what is where?
- Running Solr and importing sample data
- A quick tour of the admin interface and key configuration files
- A brief guide on how to get started quickly

An introduction to Solr

Solr is an open source enterprise search server. It is a mature product powering search for public sites such as CNET, Yelp, Zappos, and Netflix, as well as countless other government and corporate intranet sites. It is written in Java, and that language is used to further extend and modify Solr through various extension points. However, being a server that communicates using standards such as HTTP, XML, and JSON, knowledge of Java is useful but not a requirement. In addition to the standard ability to return a list of search results based on a full text search, Solr has numerous other features such as result highlighting, faceted navigation (as seen on most e-commerce sites), query spellcheck, query completion, and a "more-like-this" feature for finding similar documents.

You will see many references in this book to the term **faceting**, also known as **faceted navigation**. It's a killer feature of Solr that most people have experienced at major e-commerce sites without realizing it. Faceting enhances search results with aggregated information over all of the documents found in the search. Faceting information is typically used as dynamic navigational filters, such as a product category, date and price groupings, and so on. Faceting can also be used to power analytics. *Chapter 7, Faceting*, is dedicated to this technology.

Lucene – the underlying engine

Before describing Solr, it is best to start with Apache Lucene, the core technology underlying it. Lucene is an open source, high-performance text search engine library. Lucene was developed and open sourced by Doug Cutting in 2000 and has evolved and matured since then with a strong online community. It is the most widely deployed search technology today. Being just a code library, Lucene is not a server and certainly isn't a web crawler either. This is an important fact. There aren't even any configuration files.

In order to use Lucene, you write your own search code using its API, starting with indexing documents that you supply to it. A **document** in Lucene is merely a collection of **fields**, which are name-value pairs containing text or numbers. You configure Lucene with a text **analyzer** that will **tokenize** a field's text from a single string into a series of **tokens** (words) and further transform them by reducing them to their stems, called **stemming**, substitute synonyms, and/or perform other processing. The final indexed tokens are said to be the **terms**. The aforementioned process starting with the analyzer is referred to as **text analysis**. Lucene *indexes* each document into its **index** stored on a disk. The index is an **inverted index**, which means it stores a mapping of a field's terms to associated documents, along with the ordinal word position from the original text. Finally, you search for documents with a user-provided query string that Lucene parses according to its syntax. Lucene assigns a numeric relevancy **score** to each matching document and only the top scoring documents are returned.

This brief description of Lucene internals is what makes Solr work at its core. You will see these important vocabulary words throughout this book — they will be explained further at appropriate times.

Lucene's major features are:

- An inverted index for efficient retrieval of documents by indexed terms. The same technology supports numeric data with range- and time-based queries too.

- A rich set of chainable text analysis components, such as tokenizers and language-specific stemmers that transform a text string into a series of terms (words).

- A query syntax with a parser and a variety of query types, from a simple term lookup to exotic fuzzy matching.

- A good scoring algorithm based on sound **Information Retrieval (IR)** principles to produce the best matches first, with flexible means to affect the scoring.

- Search enhancing features. There are many, but here are some notable ones:

  - A highlighter feature to show matching query terms found in context.

  - A query spellchecker based on indexed content or a supplied dictionary.

  - Multiple suggesters for completing query strings.

  - Analysis components for various languages, faceting, spatial-search, and grouping and joining queries too.

 To learn more about Lucene, read *Lucene In Action, Second Edition, Michael McCandless, Erik Hatcher, and Otis Gospodneti, Manning Publications.*

Solr – a Lucene-based search server

Apache Solr is an enterprise search server that is based on Lucene. Lucene is such a big part of what defines Solr that you'll see many references to Lucene directly throughout this book. Developing a high-performance, feature-rich application that uses Lucene directly is difficult and it's limited to Java applications. Solr solves this by exposing the wealth of power in Lucene via configuration files and HTTP parameters, while adding some features of its own. Some of Solr's most notable features beyond Lucene are as follows:

- A server that communicates over HTTP via multiple formats, including XML and JSON

- Configuration files, most notably for the index's schema, which defines the fields and configuration of their text analysis

- Several types of caches for faster search responses
- A web-based administrative interface, including the following:
  - ○ Runtime search and cache performance statistics
  - ○ A schema browser with index statistics on each field
  - ○ A diagnostic tool for debugging text analysis
  - ○ Support for dynamic core (indices) administration
- Faceting of search results (note: distinct from Lucene's faceting)
- A query parser called **eDisMax** that is more usable for parsing end user queries than Lucene's native query parser
- Distributed search support, index replication, and fail-over for scaling Solr
- Cluster configuration and coordination using ZooKeeper
- Solritas—a sample generic web search UI for prototyping and demonstrating many of Solr's search features

Also, there are two `contrib` modules that ship with Solr that really stand out, which are as follows:

- **DataImportHandler (DIH)**: A database, e-mail, and file crawling data import capability. It includes a debugger tool.
- **Solr Cell**: An adapter to the Apache Tika open source project, which can extract text from numerous file types.

As of the 3.1 release, there is a tight relationship between the Solr and Lucene projects. The source code repository, committers, and developer mailing list are the same, and they are released together using the same version number. Since Solr is always based on the latest version of Lucene, most improvements in Lucene are available in Solr immediately.

Comparison to database technology

There's a good chance that you are unfamiliar with Lucene or Solr and you might be wondering what the fundamental differences are between it and a database. You might also wonder if you use Solr, do you need a database.

The most important comparison to make is with respect to the data model—the organizational structure of the data. The most popular category of databases is relational databases—**RDBMS**. A defining characteristic of relational databases is a data model, based on multiple tables with lookup keys between them and a *join* capability for querying across them. That approach has proven to be versatile, being able to satisfy nearly any information-retrieval task in one query.

However, it is hard and expensive to scale them to meet the requirements of a typical search application consisting of many millions of documents and low-latency response. Instead, Lucene has a much more limiting *document-oriented* data model, which is analogous to a single table. Document-oriented databases such as MongoDB are similar in this respect, but their documents can be nested, similar to XML or JSON. Lucene's document structure is flat like a table, but it does support multivalued fields—a field with an array of values. It can also be very sparse such that the actual fields used from one document to the next vary; there is no space or penalty for a document to not use a field.

 Lucene and Solr have limited support for *join* queries, but they are used sparingly as it significantly reduces the scalability characteristics of Lucene and Solr.

Taking a look at the Solr feature list naturally reveals plenty of search-oriented technology that databases generally either don't have, or don't do well. The notable features are relevancy score ordering, result highlighting, query spellcheck, and query-completion. These features are what drew you to Solr, no doubt. And let's not forget faceting. This is possible with a database, but it's hard to figure out how, and it's difficult to scale. Solr, on the other hand, makes it incredibly easy, and it does scale.

Can Solr be a substitute for your database? You can add data to it and get it back out efficiently with indexes; so on the surface, it seems plausible. The answer is that *you are almost always better off using Solr in addition to a database*. Databases, particularly RDBMSes, generally excel at *ACID* transactions, insert/update efficiency, in-place schema changes, multiuser access control, bulk data retrieval, and they have second-to-none integration with application software stacks and reporting tools. And let's not forget that they have a versatile data model. Solr falls short in these areas.

 For more on this subject, see our article, *Text Search, your Database or Solr*, at http://bit.ly/uwF1ps, which although it's slightly outdated now, is a clear and useful explanation of the issues. If you want to use Solr as a document-oriented or key-value NoSQL database, *Chapter 4, Indexing Data*, will tell you how and when it's appropriate.

A few differences between Solr 4 and Solr 5

The biggest change that users will see in Solr 5 from Solr 4 is that Solr is now deployed as its own server process. It is no longer a WAR file that is deployed into an existing Servlet container such as Tomcat or Jetty. The argument for this boiled down to "you don't deploy your MySQL database in a Servlet container; neither should you deploy your Search engine". By owning the network stack and deployment model, Solr can evolve faster; for example, there are patches for adding HTTP/2 support and pluggable authentication mechanisms being worked on. While internally Solr is still using Jetty, that should be considered an implementation detail. That said, if you really want a WAR file version, and you're familiar with Java and previous Solr releases, you can probably figure out how to build one.

As part of Solr 5 being it's own server process, it includes a set of scripts for starting, stopping, and managing Solr collections, as well as running as a service on Linux.

The next most obvious difference is that the distribution directory structure is different, particularly related to the old `example` and new `server` directory.

 The rest of this chapter refers to Solr 5, however the remainder of the book was updated for Solr 4, and applies to Solr 5.

Getting started

We will get started by downloading Solr, examining its directory structure, and then finally run it.

This will set you up for the next section, which tours a running Solr 5 server.

1. **Get Solr**: You can download Solr from its website `http://lucene.apache.org/solr/`. This book assumes that you downloaded one of the binary releases (not the src (source) based distribution). In general, we recommend using the latest release since Solr and Lucene's code are extensively tested. For downloadable example source code, and book errata describing how future Solr releases affect the book content, visit our website `http://www.solrenterprisesearchserver.com/`.

2. **Get Java**: The only prerequisite software needed to run Solr is Java 7 (that is, Java Version 1.7). But the latest version is Java 8, and you should use that. Typing `java -version` at a command line will tell you exactly which version of Java you are using, if any.

   Java is available on all major platforms, including Windows, Solaris, Linux, and Mac OS X. Visit `http://www.java.com` to download the distribution for your platform. Java always comes with the **Java Runtime Environment (JRE)** and that's all Solr requires. The **Java Development Kit (JDK)** includes the JRE plus the Java compiler and various diagnostic utility programs. One such useful program is JConsole, which we'll discuss in *Chapter 11, Deployment*, and *Chapter 10, Scaling Solr* and so the JDK distribution is recommended.

    Solr is a Java-based web application, but you don't need to be particularly familiar with Java in order to use it. This book assumes no such knowledge on your part.

3. **Get the book supplement**: This book includes a code supplement available at our website `http://www.solrenterprisesearchserver.com/`; you can also find it on Packt Publishing's website at `http://www.packtpub.com/books/content/support`. The software includes a Solr installation configured for data from MusicBrainz.org, a script to download, and indexes that data into Solr—about 8 million documents in total, and of course various sample code and material organized by chapter. This supplement is not required to follow any of the material in the book. It will be useful if you want to experiment with searches using the same data used for the book's searches or if you want to see the code referenced in a chapter. The majority of the code is for *Chapter 9, Integrating Solr*.

Solr's installation directory structure

When you unzip Solr after downloading it, you should find a relatively straightforward directory structure (differences between Solr 4 and 5 are briefly explained here):

- `contrib`: The Solr `contrib` modules are extensions to Solr:
    - `analysis-extras`: This directory includes a few **text analysis** components that have large dependencies. There are some **International Components for Unicode (ICU)** unicode classes for multilingual support—a Chinese stemmer and a Polish stemmer. You'll learn more about text analysis in the next chapter.

- ° clustering: This directory will have an engine for clustering search results. There is a one-page overview in *Chapter 8, Search Components*.

- ° dataimporthandler: The DataImportHandler (DIH) is a very popular contrib module that imports data into Solr from a database and some other sources. See *Chapter 4, Indexing Data*.

- ° extraction: Integration with Apache Tika — a framework for extracting text from common file formats. This module is also called SolrCell and Tika is also used by the DIH's TikaEntityProcessor — both are discussed in *Chapter 4, Indexing Data*.

- ° langid: This directory contains a contrib module that provides the ability to detect the language of a document before it's indexed. More information can be found on the *Solr's Language Detection* wiki page at http://wiki.apache.org/solr/LanguageDetection.

- ° map-reduce: This directory has utilities for working with Solr from Hadoop Map-Reduce. This is discussed in *Chapter 9, Integrating Solr*.

- ° morphlines-core: This directory contains Kite Morphlines, a document ingestion framework that has support for Solr. The morphlines-cell directory has components related to text extraction. Morphlines is mentioned in *Chapter 9, Integrating Solr*.

- ° uima: This directory contains library for Integration with Apache UIMA — a framework for extracting metadata out of text. There are modules that identify proper names in text and identify the language, for example. To learn more, see *Solr's UIMA integration* wiki at http://wiki.apache.org/solr/SolrUIMA.

- ° velocity: This directory will have a simple search UI framework based on the Velocity templating language. See *Chapter 9, Integrating Solr*.

- dist: In this directory, you will see Solr's core and contrib JAR files. In previous Solr versions, the WAR file was found here as well. The core JAR file is what you would use if you're embedding Solr within an application. The Solr test framework JAR and /test-framework directory contain the libraries needed in testing Solr extensions. The SolrJ JAR and /solrj-lib are what you need to build Java based clients for Solr.

- docs: This directory contains documentation and "Javadocs" for the related assets for the public Solr website, a quick tutorial, and of course Solr's API.

If you are looking for documentation outside of this book, you are best served by the Solr Reference Guide. The docs directory isn't very useful.

- `example`: Pre Solr 5, this was the complete Solr server, meant to be an example layout for deployment. It included the Jetty servlet engine (a Java web server), Solr, some sample data and sample Solr configurations. With the introduction of Solr 5, only the `example-DIH` and `exampledocs` are kept, the rest was moved to a new `server` directory.
  - `example/example-DIH`: These are DataImportHandler configuration files for the example Solr setup. If you plan on importing with DIH, some of these files may serve as good starting points.
  - `example/exampledocs`: These are sample documents to be indexed into the default Solr configuration, along with the `post.jar` program for sending the documents to Solr.

- `server`: The files required to run Solr as a server process are located here. The interesting child directories are as follows:
  - `server/contexts`: This is Jetty's WebApp configuration for the Solr setup.
  - `server/etc`: This is Jetty's configuration. Among other things, here you can change the web port used from the presupplied `8983` to `80` (HTTP default).
  - `server/logs`: Logs are by default output here. Introduced in Solr 5 was collecting JVM metrics, which are output to `solr_gc.log`. When you are trying to size your Solr setup they are a good source of information.
  - `server/resources`: The configuration file for Log4j lives here. Edit it to change the behavior of the Solr logging, (though you can also changes levels of debugging at runtime through the **Admin** console).
  - `server/solr`: The configuration files for running Solr are stored here. The `solr.xml` file, which provides overall configuration of Solr lives here, as well as `zoo.cfg` which is required by SolrCloud. The subdirectory `/configsets` stores example configurations that ship with Solr.
  - `example/webapps`: This is where Jetty expects to deploy Solr from. A copy of Solr's WAR file is here, which contains Solr's compiled code and all the dependent JAR files needed to run it.
  - `example/solr-webapp`: This is where Jetty deploys the unpacked WAR file.

Running Solr

Solr ships with a number of example collection configurations. We're going to run one called *techproducts*. This example will create a collection and insert some sample data.

> The addition of scripts for running Solr is one of the best enhancements in Solr 5. Previously, to start Solr, you directly invoked Java via `java -jar start.jar`. Deploying to production meant figuring out how to migrate into an existing Servlet environment, and was the source of much frustration.

First, go to the `bin` directory, and then run the main Solr command. On Windows, it will be `solr.cmd`, on *nix systems it will be just `solr`. Jetty's `start.jar` file by typing the following command:

```
>>cd bin
>>./solr start -e techproducts
```

The `>>` notation is the command prompt and is not part of the command. You'll see a few lines of output as Solr is started, and then the techproducts collection is created via an API call. Then the sample data is loaded into Solr. When it's done, you'll be directed to the Solr admin at `http://localhost:8983/solr`.

To stop Solr, use the same Solr command script:

```
>>./solr stop
```

A quick tour of Solr

Point your browser to Solr's administrative interface at `http://localhost:8983/`. The admin site is a single-page application that provides access to some of the more important aspects of a running Solr instance.

> The administrative interface is currently being completely revamped, and the below interface may be deprecated.

This tour will help you get your bearings in navigating around Solr.

In the preceding screenshot, the navigation is on the left while the main content is on the right. The left navigation is present on every page of the admin site and is divided into two sections. The primary section contains choices related to higher-level Solr and Java features, while the secondary section lists all of the running Solr cores.

The default page for the admin site is **Dashboard**. This gives you a snapshot of some basic configuration settings and stats, for Solr, the JVM, and the server. The **Dashboard** page is divided into the following subareas:

- **Instance**: This area displays when Solr started.
- **Versions**: This area displays various Lucene and Solr version numbers.
- **JVM**: This area displays the Java implementation, version, and processor count. The various Java system properties are also listed here.
- **System**: This area displays the overview of memory settings and usage; this is essential information for debugging and optimizing memory settings.
- **JVM-Memory**: This meter shows the allocation of JVM memory, and is key to understanding if garbage collection is happening properly. If the dark gray band occupies the entire meter, you will see all sorts of memory related exceptions!

The rest of the primary navigation choices include the following:

- **Logging**: This page is a real-time view of logging, showing the time, level, logger, and message. This section also allows you to adjust the logging levels for different parts of Solr at runtime. For Jetty, as we're running it, this output goes to the console and nowhere else. See *Chapter 11, Deployment,* for more information on configuring logging.

- **Core Admin**: This section is for information and controls for managing Solr cores. Here, you can unload, reload, rename, swap, and optimize the selected core. There is also an option for adding a new core.

- **Java Properties**: This lists Java system properties, which are basically Java-oriented global environment variables. Including the command used to start the Solr Java process.

- **Thread Dump**: This displays a Java thread dump, useful for experienced Java developers in diagnosing problems.

Below the primary navigation is a list of running Solr cores. Click on the **Core Selector** drop-down menu and select the **techproducts** link. You should see something very similar to the following screenshot:

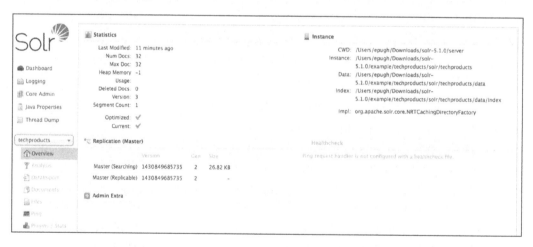

The default page labeled **Overview** for each core shows core statistics, information about replication, an **Admin Extra** area. Some other options such as details about **Healthcheck** are grayed out and made visible if the feature is enabled.

You probably noticed the subchoice menu that appeared below **techproducts**. Here is an overview of what those subchoices provide:

- **Analysis**: This is used for diagnosing query and indexing problems related to text analysis. This is an advanced screen and will be discussed later.

- **Data Import**: Provides information about the DataImport handler (the DIH). Like replication, it is only useful when DIH is enabled. The DataImport handler will be discussed in more detail in *Chapter 4, Indexing Data*.

- **Documents**: Provides a simple interface for creating a document to index into Solr via the browser. This includes a Document Builder that walks you through adding individual fields of data.

- **Files**: Exposes all the files that make up the core's configuration. Everything from core files such as `schema.xml` and `solrconfig.xml` to `stopwords.txt`.

- **Ping**: Clicking on this sends a ping request to Solr, displaying the latency. The primary purpose of the ping response is to provide a health status to other services, such as a load balancer. The ping response is a formatted status document and it is designed to fail if Solr can't perform a search query that you provide.

- **Plugins / Stats**: Here you will find statistics such as timing and cache hit ratios. In *Chapter 10, Scaling Solr*, we will visit this screen to evaluate Solr's performance.

- **Query**: This brings you to a search form with many options. With or without this search form, you will soon end up directly manipulating the URL using this book as a reference. There's no data in Solr yet, so there's no point in using the form right now.

- **Replication**: This contains index replication status information, and the controls for disabling. It is only useful when replication is enabled. More information on this is available in *Chapter 10, Scaling Solr*.

- **Schema Browser**: This is an analytical view of the schema that reflects various statistics of the actual data in the index. We'll come back to this later.

- **Segments Info**: Segments are the underlying files that make up the Lucene data structure. As you index information, they expand and compress. This allows you to monitor them, and was newly added to Solr 5.

 You can partially customize the admin view by editing a few templates that are provided. The template filenames are prefixed with `admin-extra`, and are located in the `conf` directory.

Loading sample data

Solr comes with some sample data found at example/exampledocs. We saw this data loaded as part of creating the *techproducts* Solr core when we started Solr. We're going to use that for the remainder of this chapter so that we can explore Solr more, without getting into schema design and deeper data loading options. For the rest of the book, we'll base the examples on the digital supplement to the book—more on that later.

We're going to re-index the example data by using the post.jar Java program, officially called SimplePostTool. Most JAR files aren't executable, but this one is. This simple program takes a Java system variable to specify the collection: -Dc=techproducts, iterates over a list of Solr-formatted XML input files, and HTTP posts it to Solr running on the current machine —http://localhost:8983/solr/techproducts/update. Finally, it will send a commit command, which will cause documents that were posted prior to the commit to be saved and made visible. Obviously, Solr must be running for this to work. Here is the command and its output:

```
>> cd example/exampledocs
>> java -Dc=techproducts -jar post.jar *.xml
SimplePostTool version 5.0.0
Posting files to [base] url http://localhost:8983/solr/techproducts/
update using
content-type application/xml...
POSTing file gb18030-example.xml
POSTing file hd.xml
etc.
14 files indexed.
COMMITting Solr index changes to http://localhost:8983/solr/techproducts/
update...
```

If you are using a Unix-like environment, you have an alternate option of using the /bin/post shell script, which wraps the SimplePostTool.

 The post.sh and post.jar programs could be used in a production scenario, but they are intended just as a demonstration of the technology with the example data.

Let's take a look at one of these XML files we just posted to Solr, `monitor.xml`:

```xml
<add>
  <doc>
    <field name="id">3007WFP</field>
    <field name="name">Dell Widescreen UltraSharp 3007WFP</field>
    <field name="manu">Dell, Inc.</field>
    <!-- Join -->
    <field name="manu_id_s">dell</field>
    <field name="cat">electronics</field>
    <field name="cat">monitor</field>
    <field name="features">30" TFT active matrix LCD, 2560 x 1600,
    .25mm dot pitch, 700:1 contrast</field>
    <field name="includes">USB cable</field>
    <field name="weight">401.6</field>
    <field name="price">2199</field>
    <field name="popularity">6</field>
    <field name="inStock">true</field>
    <!-- Buffalo store -->
    <field name="store">43.17614,-90.57341</field>
  </doc>
</add>
```

The XML schema for files that can be posted to Solr is very simple. This file doesn't demonstrate all of the elements and attributes, but it shows the essentials. Multiple documents, represented by the `<doc>` tag, can be present in series within the `<add>` tag, which is recommended for bulk data loading scenarios. This subset may very well be all that you use. More about these options and other data loading choices will be discussed in *Chapter 4, Indexing Data*.

A simple query

Point your browser to `http://localhost:8983/solr/#/techproducts/query`—this is the query form described in the previous section. The search box is labeled **q**. This form is a standard HTML form, albeit enhanced by JavaScript. When the form is submitted, the form inputs become URL parameters to an HTTP GET request to Solr. That URL and Solr's search response is displayed to the right. It is convenient to use the form as a starting point for developing a search, but then subsequently refine the URL directly in the browser instead of returning to the form.

Run a query by replacing the `*:*` in the **q** field with the word `lcd`, then clicking on the **Execute Query** button. At the top of the main content area, you will see a URL like this `http://localhost:8983/solr/techproducts/select?q=monitor&wt=j son&indent=true`. The URL specifies that you want to query for the word `lcd`, and that the output should be in indented JSON format.

Below this URL, you will see the search result; this result is the response of that URL.

By default, Solr responds in XML, however the query interface specifies JSON by default. Most modern browsers, such as Firefox, provide a good JSON view with syntax coloring and hierarchical controls. All response formats have the same basic structure as the JSON you're about to see. More information on these formats can be found in *Chapter 4, Indexing Data*.

The JSON response consists of a two main elements: `responseHeader` and `response`. Here is what the header element looks like:

```
"responseHeader": {
    "status": 0,
    "QTime": 1,
    "params": {
      "q": "lcd",
      "indent": "true",
      "wt": "json"
    }
  }
...
```

The following are the elements from the preceding code snippet:

- `status`: This is always zero, unless there was a serious problem.
- `QTime`: This is the duration of time in milliseconds that Solr took to process the search. It does not include streaming back the response. Due to multiple layers of caching, you will find that your searches will often complete in a millisecond or less if you've run the query before.
- `params`: This lists the request parameters. By default, it only lists parameters explicitly in the URL; there are usually more parameters specified in a `<requestHandler/>` in `solrconfig.xml`. You can see all of the applied parameters in the response by setting the `echoParams` parameter to `true`.

 More information on these parameters and many more is available in *Chapter 5, Searching*.

Next up is the most important part, the results:

```
"response": {
    "numFound": 5,
    "start": 0,
```

The numFound value is the number of documents matching the query in the entire index. The start parameter is the index offset into those matching (ordered) documents that are returned in the response below.

Often, you'll want to see the score of each matching document. The document score is a number that represents how relevant the document is to the search query. This search response doesn't refer to scores because it needs to be explicitly requested in the fl parameter—a comma-separated field list. A search that requests the score via fl=*,score will have a maxScore attribute in the "response" element, which is the maximum score of all documents that matched the search. It's independent of the sort order or result paging parameters.

The content of the result element is a list of documents that matched the query. The default sort is by descending score. Later, we'll do some sorting by specified fields.

```
{
            "id": "9885A004",
            "name": "Canon PowerShot SD500",
            "manu": "Canon Inc.",
            "manu_id_s": "canon",
            "cat": [
                "electronics",
                "camera"
            ],
            "features": [
                "3x zoop, 7.1 megapixel Digital ELPH",
                "movie clips up to 640x480 @30 fps",
                "2.0\" TFT LCD, 118,000 pixels",
                "built in flash, red-eye reduction"
            ],
            "includes": "32MB SD card, USB cable, AV cable, battery",
            "weight": 6.4,
            "price": 329.95,
            "price_c": "329.95,USD",
            "popularity": 7,
            "inStock": true,
            "manufacturedate_dt": "2006-02-13T15:26:37Z",
            "store": "45.19614,-93.90341",
            "_version_": 1500358264225792000
        },
    ...
```

The document list is pretty straightforward. By default, Solr will list all of the *stored* fields. Not all of the fields are necessarily stored—that is, you can query on them but not retrieve their value—an optimization choice. Notice that it uses the basic data types of strings, integers, floats, and Booleans. Also note that certain fields, such as features and cat are multivalued, as indicated by the use of [] to denote an array in JSON.

This was a basic keyword search. As you start using more search features such as faceting and highlighting, you will see additional information following the response element.

Some statistics

Let's take a look at the statistics available via the **Plugins / Stats** page. This page provides details on all the components of Solr. Browse to **CORE** and then pick a **Searcher**. Before we loaded data into Solr, this page reported that numDocs was 0, but now it should be 32.

Now take a look at the update handler stats by clicking on the **UPDATEHANDLER** and then expand the stats for the update handler by clicking on the **updateHandler** toggle link on the right-hand side of the screen. Notice that the /update request handler has some stats too:

CACHE	**updateHandler**	
CORE	class:	org.apache.solr.update.DirectUpdateHandler2
HIGHLIGHTING	version:	1.0
	description:	Update handler that efficiently directly updates the on-disk main lucene index
OTHER	src:	null
QUERYHANDLER		
QUERYPARSER	stats:	commits:	4
		autocommit maxTime:	15000ms
UPDATEHANDLER		autocommits:	1
		soft autocommits:	1
Watch Changes		optimizes:	0
Refresh Values		rollbacks:	0
		expungeDeletes:	0
		docsPending:	0
		adds:	0
		deletesById:	0
		deletesByQuery:	0
		errors:	0
		cumulative_adds:	65
		cumulative_deletesById:	0
		cumulative_deletesByQuery:	0
		cumulative_errors:	0
		transaction_logs_total_size:	17563
		transaction_logs_total_number:	3

If you think of Solr as a RESTful server, then the various public end points are exposed under the **QUERYHANDLER** menu. Solr isn't exactly REST-based, but it is very similar. Look at the **/update** to see the indexing performance, and **/select** for query performance.

 These statistics are accumulated since when Solr was started or reloaded, and they are not stored to disk. As such, you cannot use them for long-term statistics. There are third-party SaaS solutions referenced in *Chapter 11, Deployment*, which capture more statistics and persist it long-term.

The sample browse interface

The final destination of our quick Solr tour is to visit the so-called *browse interface*—available at http://localhost:8983/solr/techproducts/browse. It's for demonstrating various Solr features:

- **Standard keyword search**: Here, you can experiment with Solr's syntax.
- **Query debugging**: Here, you can toggle display of the parsed query and document score "explain" information.
- **Query-suggest**: Here, you can start typing a word like enco and suddenly "encoded" will be suggested to you.
- **Highlighting**: Here, the highlighting of query words in search results is in bold, which might not be obvious.
- **More-like-this**: This returns documents with similar words.
- **Faceting**: This includes field value facets, query facets, numeric range facets, and date range facets.
- **Clustering**: This shows how the search results cluster together based on certain words. You must first start Solr as the instructions describe in the lower left-hand corner of the screen.
- **Query boosting**: This influences the scores by product price.
- **Geospatial search**: Here, you can filter by distance. Click on the **spatial** link at the top-left to enable this.

This is also a demonstration of **Solritas**, which formats Solr requests using templates that are based on Apache Velocity. The templates are VM files in example/techproducts/solr/techproducts/conf/velocity. Solritas is primarily for search UI prototyping. It is not recommended for building anything substantial. See *Chapter 9, Integrating Solr*, for more information.

The browse UI as supplied assumes the default example Solr schema. It will not work out of the box against another schema without modification.

Here is a screenshot of the browse interface; not all of it is captured in this image:

Configuration files

When you start up Solr using the `-e techproducts` parameter, it loads the configuration files from `/server/solr/configsets/sample_techproducts_configs`. These configuration files are extremely well documented.

A Solr core's instance directory is laid out like this:

- `conf`: This directory contains configuration files. The `solrconfig.xml` and `schema.xml` files are most important, but it will also contain some other `.txt` and `.xml` files, which are referenced by these two.
- `conf/schema.xml`: This is the schema for the index, including field type definitions with associated analyzer chains.
- `conf/solrconfig.xml`: This is the primary Solr configuration file.

- `conf/lang`: This directory contains language translation `.txt` files that is used by several components.
- `conf/xslt`: This directory contains various XSLT files that can be used to transform Solr's XML query responses into formats such as Atom and RSS. See *Chapter 9, Integrating Solr*.
- `conf/velocity`: This includes the HTML templates and related web assets for rapid UI prototyping using Solritas, covered in *Chapter 9, Integrating Solr*. The previously discussed **browse** UI is implemented with these templates.
- `lib`: Where extra Java JAR files can be placed that Solr will load on startup. This is a good place to put contrib JAR files, and their dependencies. You'll need to create this directory on your own, though; it doesn't exist by default.

> Unlike typical database software, in which the configuration files don't need to be modified much (if at all) from their defaults, you will modify Solr's configuration files extensively—especially the schema. The as-provided state of these files is really just an example to both demonstrate features and document their configuration and should not be taken as the only way of configuring Solr. It should also be noted that in order for Solr to recognize configuration changes, a core must be reloaded (or simply restart Solr).

Solr's schema for the index is defined in `schema.xml`. It contains the index's fields within the `<fields>` element and then the field type definitions within the `<types>` element. You will observe that the names of the fields in the documents we added to Solr intuitively correspond to the sample schema. Aside from the fundamental parts of defining the fields, you might also notice the `<copyField>` elements, which copy an input field as provided to another field. There are various reasons for doing this, but they boil down to needing to index data in different ways for specific search purposes. You'll learn all that you could want to know about the schema in the next chapter.

Each Solr core's `solrconfig.xml` file contains lots of parameters that can be tweaked. At the moment, we're just going to take a peek at the **request handlers**, which are defined with the `<requestHandler>` elements. They make up about half of the file. In our first query, we didn't specify any request handler, so we got the default one:

```
<requestHandler name="/select" class="solr.SearchHandler>
  <!-- default values for query parameters can be specified, these
          will be overridden by parameters in the request
  -->
  <lst name="defaults">
    <str name="echoParams">explicit</str>
    <int name="rows">10</int>
```

```
        <str name="df">text</str>
    </lst>
    <!-- … many other comments … -->
</requestHandler>
```

Each HTTP request to Solr, including posting documents and searches, goes through a particular request handler. Handlers can be registered against certain URL paths by naming them with a leading /. When we uploaded the documents earlier, it went to the handler defined like this, in which /update is a relative URL path:

```
<requestHandler name="/update" class="solr.UpdateRequestHandler"
/>
```

Requests to Solr are nearly completely configurable through URL parameters or POST'ed form parameters. They can also be specified in the request handler definition within the <lst name="defaults"> element, such as how rows is set to 10 in the previously shown request handler. The well-documented file also explains how and when they can be added to appends, or invariants named lst blocks. This arrangement allows you to set up a request handler for a particular application that will be searching Solr, without forcing the application to specify all of its search parameters. More information on request handlers can be found in *Chapter 5, Searching*.

What's next?

You now have an excellent, broad overview of Solr! The numerous features of this tool will no doubt bring the process of implementing a world-class search engine closer to reality. But creating a real, production-ready search solution is a big task. So, where do you begin? As you're getting to know Solr, it might help to think about the main process in three phases: indexing, searching, and application integration.

Schema design and indexing

In what ways do you need your data to be searched? Will you need faceted navigation, spelling suggestions, or more-like-this capabilities? Knowing your requirements up front is the key in producing a well-designed search solution. Understanding how to implement these features is critical. A well-designed schema lays the foundation for a successful Solr implementation.

However, during the development cycle, having the flexibility to try different field types without changing the schema and restarting Solr can be very handy. The dynamic fields feature allows you to assign field types by using field name conventions during indexing. Solr provides many useful predefined dynamic fields. *Chapter 2, Schema Design*, will cover this in-depth.

However, you can also get started right now. Take a look at the stock dynamic fields in `/server/solr/configsets/sample_techproducts_configs/conf/schema.xml`. The dynamicField, XML tags represent what is available. For example, the dynamicField named `*_b` allows you to store and index Boolean data types; a field named `admin_b` would match this field type.

For the stock dynamic fields, here is a subset of what's available from the `schema.xml` file:

- `_i`: This includes the indexed and stored integers
- `_ss`: This includes the stored and indexed, multi-valued strings
- `_dt`: This includes the indexed and stored dates
- `_p`: This includes the indexed and stored `lat/lng` types

To make use of these fields, you simply name your fields using those suffixes — `example/exampledocs/ipod_other.xml` makes good use of the `*_dt` type with its `manufacturedate_dt` field. Copying an example file, adding your own data, changing the suffixes, and indexing (via the SimplePost tool) is all as simple as it sounds. Give it a try!

Text analysis

It's probably a good time to talk a little more about text analysis. When considering field types, it's important to understand how your data is processed. For each field, you'll need to know its data type, and whether or not the value should be stored and/or indexed. For string types, you'll also need to think about how the text is analyzed.

Simply put, text analysis is the process of extracting useful information from a text field. This process normally includes two steps: tokenization and filtering. Analyzers encapsulate this entire process, and Solr provides a way to mix and match analyzer behaviors by configuration.

Tokenizers split up text into smaller chunks called tokens. There are many different kinds of tokenizers in Solr, the most common of which splits text on word boundaries, or whitespace. Others split on regular expressions, or even word prefixes. The tokenizer produces a stream of tokens, which can be fed to an optional series of filters.

Filters, as you may have guessed, commonly remove *noise* — things such as punctuation and duplicate words. Filters can even lower/upper case tokens, and inject word synonyms.

Once the tokens pass through the analyzer processor chain, they are added to the Lucene index. *Chapter 2, Schema Design*, covers this process in detail.

Searching

The next step is, naturally, searching. For most applications processing user queries, you will want to use the [e]dismax query parser, set with defType=edismax. It is not the default but arguably should be in our opinion; [e]dismax handles end-user queries very well. There are a few more configuration parameters it needs, described in *Chapter 5, Searching*.

Here are a few example queries to get you thinking.

 Be sure to start up Solr and index the sample data by following the instructions in the previous section.

Find all the documents that have the phrase hard drive in their cat field:

```
http://localhost:8983/solr/techproducts/select?q=cat:"hard+drive"
```

Find all the documents that are in-stock, and have a popularity greater than 6:

```
http://localhost:8983/solr/techproducts/select?q=+inStock:true+AND+
popularity:[6+TO+*]
```

Here's an example using the eDisMax query parser:

```
http://localhost:8983/solr/techproducts/select?q=ipod&defType=edism
ax&qf=name^3+manu+cat&fl=*,score
```

This returns documents where the user query in q matches the name, manu, and cat fields. The ^3 after the manu field tells Solr to boost the relevancy of the document scores when the manu field matches. The fl param tells Solr what fields to return— The * means return all fields, and score is a number that represents how well the document matched the input query.

Faceting and statistics can be seen in this example:

```
http://localhost:8983/solr/techproducts/select?q=ipod&defType=disma
x&qf=name^3+manu+cat&fl=*,score&rows=0&facet=true&facet.field=manu
_id_s&facet.field=cat&stats=true&stats.field=price&stats.field=wei
ght
```

This builds on the previous, dismax example, but instead of returning documents (rows=0), Solr returns multiple facets and stats field values.

For detailed information on searching, see *Chapter 5, Searching*.

Integration

If the previous tips on indexing and searching are enough to get you started, then you must be wondering how you integrate Solr and your application. By far, the most common approach is to communicate with Solr via HTTP. You can make use of one of the many HTTP client libraries available. Here's a small example using the Ruby library, RSolr:

```
require "rsolr"
client = RSolr.connect
params = {:q => "ipod", :defType => "dismax", :qf => "name^3 manu
cat", :fl => "*,score"}
result = client.select(:params => params)
result["response"]["docs"].each do |doc|
  puts doc.inspect
end
```

Using one of the previous sample queries, the result of this script would print out each document, matching the query `ipod`.

There are many client implementations, and finding the right one for you is dependent on the programming language your application is written in. *Chapter 9, Integrating Solr*, covers this in depth, and will surely set you in the right direction.

Resources outside this book

The following are some Solr resources other than this book:

- *Apache Solr 4 Cookbook*, *Rafał Kuć* is another Solr book published by Packt Publishing. It is a style of book that comprises a series of posed questions or problems followed by their solution. You can find this at `www.packtpub.com/big-data-and-business-intelligence/apache-solr-4-cookbook`.

- *Apache Solr Reference Guide* is a detailed, online resource contributed by Lucidworks to the Solr community. You can find the latest version at `https://cwiki.apache.org/confluence/display/solr/Apache+Solr+Reference+Guide`. Consider downloading the PDF corresponding to the Solr release you are using.

- Solr's Wiki at `http://wiki.apache.org/solr/` has a lot of great documentation and miscellaneous information. For a Wiki, it's fairly organized too. In particular, if you use a particular app-server in production, then there is probably a Wiki page there on specific details.

- Within the Solr installation, you will also find that there are `README.txt` files in many directories within Solr and that the configuration files are very well documented. Read them!

The `solr-user@lucene.apache.org` mailing list contains a wealth of information. If you have a few discriminating keywords, then you can find nuggets of information in there with a search engine. The mailing lists of Solr and other Lucene subprojects are best searched at `http://find.searchhub.org/` or `http://search-lucene.com/solr` or `http://nabble.com`.

> We highly recommend that you subscribe to the Solr-users mailing list. You'll learn a lot and potentially help others, too.

- Solr's issue tracker contains information on enhancements and bugs. It's available at `http://issues.apache.org/jira/browse/SOLR` and it uses Atlassian's JIRA software. Some of the comments attached to these issues can be extensive and enlightening.

> **Notation convention**
>
> Solr's JIRA issues are referenced like this — SOLR-64. You'll see such references in this book and elsewhere. You can easily look these up at Solr's JIRA. You might also see issues for Lucene that follow the same convention, for example, LUCENE-1215.

There are, of course, resources for Lucene, such as *Lucene In Action, Second Edition, Michael McCandless, Erik Hatcher, and Otis Gospodneti, Manning Publications*. If you intend to dive into Solr's internals, then you will find Lucene resources helpful, but that is not the focus of this book.

Summary

This completes a quick introduction to Solr. In the following chapters, you're really going to get familiar with what Solr has to offer. We recommend that you proceed in order from the next chapter through *Chapter 8, Search Components*, because these build on each other and expose nearly all of the capabilities in Solr. These chapters are also useful as a reference to Solr's features. You can, of course, skip over sections that are not interesting to you. *Chapter 9, Integrating Solr*, is one you might peruse at any time, as it may have a section applicable to your Solr usage scenario. Finally, be sure that you don't miss the appendix for a search quick-reference cheat-sheet.

2
Schema Design

The foundation of Solr is based on Lucene's index — the subject of this chapter. In this chapter, you will learn about:

- Schema design decisions in which you map your source data to Lucene's limited structure. In this book, we'll consider the data from www.MusicBrainz.org.

- The structure of the schema.xml file, where the schema definition is defined. This file contains both the definition of field types and the fields of those types that store your data.

The following diagram shows the big picture of how various aspects of working with Solr are related. In this chapter, we will focus on the foundational layer — the index:

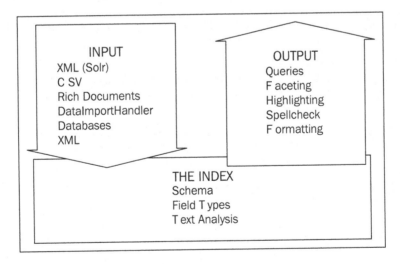

INPUT
XML (Solr)
C SV
Rich Documents
DataImportHandler
Databases
XML

OUTPUT
Queries
F aceting
Highlighting
Spellcheck
F ormatting

THE INDEX
Schema
Field T ypes
T ext Analysis

In a hurry?

This is a fairly important foundational chapter. That said, you can start building your own search engine using the predefined field types provided with Solr's example schema. Eventually, you will want to return to make adjustments.

Is Solr schemaless?

Solr supports a rich schema specification that allows for a wide range of flexibility in dealing with different document fields and has a "free" schema, in that, you don't have to define all of your fields ahead of time using dynamic fields. There are discussions in the search and NoSQL communities questioning the value in a schema. Having the ability to configure the fields in a configuration file, outside the actual code, gives more flexibility and makes us think about the data and business needs, which are key for any successful search engine.

Grant Ingersoll, Lucene and Solr committer, cofounder of the Apache Mahout machine learning project, and a long standing member of the Apache Software Foundation, has the following insightful commentary on the subject:

> *As for the notion of "schemaless", it's a bit of a marketing term, no? ("Less" schema is probably better, but it doesn't roll off the tongue now does it?) What is really meant by it, as far as I can tell, is that the system uses convention over configuration and that it is easy to change it to adapt to business needs. ElasticSearch has a schema, it's just implied by your JSON and its preset configuration. And if you don't like it you can programmatically go change it, thereby embedding your schema into your code. In Solr, you can also have convention over configuration via dynamic fields and by naming your fields accordingly. There is also work under way to be able to use other conventions programmatically. And I don't know about you, but is opening up a config file and making a few edits really that hard, especially when it makes you think about your data?*

You can find the source at http://www.ymc.ch/en/why-we-chose-solr-4-0-instead-of-elasticsearch.

MusicBrainz.org

Instead of continuing to work with the sample data that comes with Solr, we're going to use a large database of music metadata from the MusicBrainz project at `http://musicbrainz.org`. The data is free and is submitted by a large community of users. One way MusicBrainz offers this data is in the form of a large SQL file for import into a PostgreSQL database. In order to make it easier for you to play with this data, the online code supplement to this book includes the data in formats that can readily be imported into Solr. Alternatively, if you already have your own data, then we recommend starting with that, using this book as a guide.

The MusicBrainz database is highly relational. Therefore, it will serve as an excellent instructional dataset to discuss Solr schema choices. The MusicBrainz database schema is quite complex, and it would be a distraction to go over even half of it. We are going to use a subset of it and express it in a way that has a straightforward mapping to the user interface, which can be seen on the MusicBrainz website. Each of these tables that are depicted in the following diagram can be easily constructed through SQL subqueries or views from the actual MusicBrainz tables:

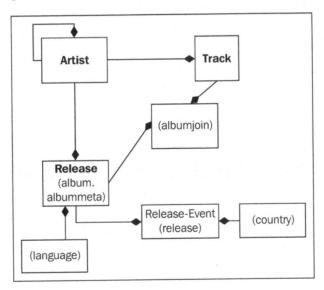

To describe the major tables that we mentioned earlier, we'll use some examples from the band, *The Smashing Pumpkins*:

- The Smashing Pumpkins is an **artist** with a type of *group* (a band). Some artists (groups in particular) have members who are also other artists of type *person*. So this is a self-referential relationship. The Smashing Pumpkins band has Billy Corgan, Jimmy Chamberlin, and others as members.

- An artist is attributed as the creator of a *release*. The most common type of release is an **album** but there are also singles, EPs, compilations, and others. Furthermore, releases have a *status* property that is either official, promotional, or bootleg. A popular official album from The Smashing Pumpkins is titled *Siamese Dream*.

- A release can be published at various times and places, which MusicBrainz calls an **event** (a release-event). Each event contains the date, country, music label, and format (CD or tape).

- A release is composed of one or more **tracks**. *Siamese Dream* has 13 tracks starting with *Cherub Rock* and ending with *Luna*. Note that a track is a part of just one release and so it is not synonymous with a song. For example, the song *Cherub Rock* is not only a track on this release but also on the *Greatest Hits* release, as well as quite a few others in the database. A track has a **PUID** (**PortableUniqueIdentifier**), an audio fingerprinting technology quasi-identifier, based on the actual sound on a track. It's not foolproof as there are collisions, but these are rare. Another interesting bit of data MusicBrainz stores is the PUID lookup count, which is how often it has been requested by their servers—a good measure of popularity.

Note that we'll be using the word **entity** occasionally here in the data modeling sense—it's basically a type of *thing* represented by the data. Artist, release, event, and track are all entity types with respect to MusicBrainz. In a relational database, most tables correspond to an entity type and the others serve to relate them or to provide for multiple values. In Solr, each document will have a primary entity type and may contain other entities as part of it, too.

One combined index or separate indices

The following discussion concerns how to manage the searching of different types of data, such as artists and releases from MusicBrainz. In the MusicBrainz configuration example, each document of each type gets their own index but they all share the same configuration. Although we wouldn't generally recommend it, this approach was done for convenience and to reduce the complexity for this book at the expense of a one-size-fits-all schema and configuration.

A Solr server hosts one or more Solr Cores. A Solr Core is an instance of Solr to include the configuration and index, sometimes the word "core" is used synonymously with "index". Even if you have one type of data to search for in an application, you might still use multiple cores (with the same configuration) and shard the data for scaling. Managing Solr Cores is discussed further in *Chapter 11, Deployment*.

One combined index

A combined index might also be called an *aggregate index*. As mentioned in the first chapter, an index is conceptually like a single-table relational database schema, thus sharing similarities with some NoSQL (non-relational) databases. In spite of this limitation, there is nothing to stop you from putting different types of data (say, artists and releases from MusicBrainz) into a single index. All you have to do is use different fields for the different document types, and use a field to discriminate between the types. An identifier field would need to be unique across all documents in this index, no matter what the type is, you could easily do this by concatenating the field type and the entity's identifier. This may appear ugly from a relational database design standpoint, *but this isn't a database!* More importantly, unlike a database, there is no overhead whatsoever for some documents to not populate some fields. This is where the spreadsheet metaphor can break down, because a blank cell in a spreadsheet takes up space, but not in Solr's index.

Here's a sample `schema.xml` snippet of the fields for a single combined index approach:

```
<field name="id" ... /><!-- example:  "artist:534445"  -->
<field name="type" ... /><!-- example: "artist", "track",
"release",... -->
<field name="name" ... /><!-- (common to various types) -->

<!-- track fields: -->
<field name="PUID" ... />
<field name="num" ... /><!-- i.e. the track # on the release -->
<!-- etc. -->
<!-- artist fields: -->
<field name="startDate" ... /><!-- date of first release -->
<field name="endDate" ... /><!-- date of last release -->
<field name="homeCountry" ... />
<!-- etc. -->
```

 A combined index has the advantage of being easier to maintain, since it is just one configuration. It is also easier to do a search over multiple document types at once, since this will naturally occur, assuming you search on all the relevant fields. For these reasons, it is a good approach to start off with. However, consider the shortcomings to be described shortly.

For the book, we've taken a hybrid approach in which there are separate Solr Cores (indices) for each MusicBrainz data type, but they all share the same configuration, including the schema.

Problems with using a single combined index

Although a combined index is more convenient to set up, there are some problems that you may face:

- There may be namespace collision problems unless you prefix the field names by type such as: `artist_startDate` and `track_PUID`. In the example that we just saw, most entity types have a name. Therefore, it's straightforward for all of them to have this common field. If the type of the fields were different, then you would be forced to name them differently.

- If you share the same field for different entities such as the `name` field in the example that we just saw, then there are some problems that can occur when using that field in a query and while filtering documents by document type. These caveats do not apply when searching across all documents.

- You will get scores that are of lesser quality due to suboptimal **document frequency** and **total document count** values, and components of the IDF part of the score. The document frequency is simply the number of documents in which a queried term exists for a specific field. If you put different types of things into the same field, then what could be a rare word for a track name might not be for an artist name. The total document count ends up being inflated instead of being limited to a specific document type (although the problem isn't as bad as the suboptimal document frequency). Scoring is described further in *Chapter 6, Search Relevancy*.

- Prefix, wildcard, and fuzzy queries will take longer. If you share a field with different types of documents, then the total number of terms to be searched is going to be larger, which takes longer for these query types.

- For a large number of documents, a strategy using multiple indices will prove to be more scalable. Only testing will indicate what "large" is for your data and your queries, but less than a million documents are not likely to benefit from multiple indices. Once you have tens of millions of documents, you would consider multiple indices. There are so many factors involved, so take these numbers as rough guidelines.

- Committing changes to a Solr index invalidates the caches used to speed up querying, and these get rebuilt during the warming phase of a commit. If this happens often, and the changes are usually due to one type of entity in the index, then you will get better performance by using separate indices.

Separate indices

For separate indices, you simply develop your schemas independently. You can use a combined schema as previously described, and use it for all of your cores so that you don't have to manage them separately. It's not an approach for the purist, but it is convenient and it is also what we've done for the book's example code. The rest of the discussion here assumes that the schemas are independent.

 To share the same schema field type definitions (described in the following sections) across your schemas without having to keep them in sync, use the **XInclude** feature. XInclude is described in *Chapter 11, Deployment*.

If you do develop separate schemas and need to search across your indices in one search, then you must perform a distributed search, described in *Chapter 10, Scaling Solr*. A distributed search is usually feature employed for a large corpus, but it applies here too. Be sure to read more about it before using it as there are some limitations. As in the combined-schema, you will need a unique ID across all documents and you will want a field type to differentiate documents in your search results. You don't need commonly named fields to search on, since the query will be processed at each core using the configuration there to determine, for example, what the default search field is.

 You can't go wrong with multiple indices (Solr Cores); it's just a bit more to manage. And just because you have multiple indices doesn't preclude sharing as much of the configuration (including the schema) as you want to among the cores. *Chapter 11, Deployment*, will discuss configuring the cores including sharing them and parameterizing them.

Schema design

A key thing to come to grips with is that the queries you need Solr to support completely drive your Solr schema design. This is very important to understand. Conversely, relational databases typically use standard third normal form decomposition of the data, largely because they have strong SQL relational-join support. Since queries drive the Solr schema design, all the data needed to match a document, that is, the criteria, should be in the document matched, not in a related one. To satisfy that requirement, data that would otherwise exist in one place is copied into related documents that need it to support a search. For example, an artist's name in MusicBrainz will not just exist on an artist document but also in a track document to support searching for tracks by artist. Solr 4's new **Join** support allows this design principle to be relaxed; however, it's not as capable as a SQL join and is often slow, so only consider this as a last resort.

Even if you're not working with a database as your source data, these concepts still apply. So pay close attention to this important subject in any case.

At this point, we're going to outline a series of steps to follow in order to arrive at one or more Solr schemas to power searches for an application of any sort. For specifics, we will consider the www.MusicBrainz.org website and how it could work, hypothetically. It goes as far as listing the fields but not into text analysis or making changes for particular search features, such as faceting. In truth, schema design is somewhat creative and is always evolutional—so consider these steps as a guide for your first time at it, though not a foolproof process.

Step 1 – determine which searches are going to be powered by Solr

Any text search capability is going to be Solr powered. At the risk of stating the obvious, we're referring strictly to those places where a user types in a bit of text and subsequently gets some search results. On the MusicBrainz website, the main search function is accessed through the form that is always present on the top. There is also a more advanced form that adds a few options but is essentially the same capability present on the search menu page, and we treat it as such from Solr's point of view. We can see the MusicBrainz search form in the following screenshot:

Once we look through the remaining steps, we may find that Solr should additionally power some faceted navigation in areas that are not accompanied by text search (that is, the facets are of the entire dataset, not necessarily limited to the search results of a text query alongside it). An example of this at MusicBrainz is the **Top Voters** tally, which we'll address soon.

Step 2 – determine the entities returned from each search

For the MusicBrainz search form, this is easy. The entities are: artists, releases, tracks, labels, and editors. It just so happens that in MusicBrainz, a search will only return one entity type. However, that needn't be the case. Note that internally, each result from a search corresponds to a distinct document in the Solr index and so each entity will have a corresponding document. This entity also probably corresponds to a particular row in a database table, assuming that's where it's coming from.

> The book examples and digital companion data only make use of MusicBrainz's artists, releases, and tracks.

Step 3 – denormalize related data

For each entity type, find all of the data in the schema that will be needed across all searches of it. By "all searches of it", we mean that there might actually be multiple search forms, as identified in *Step 1 – determine which searches are going to be powered by Solr*. Such data includes any data queried for (that is, criteria to determine whether a document matches or not) and any data that is displayed in the search results. The end result of denormalization is to have each document sufficiently self-contained, even if the data is duplicated across the index(es).

> Solr 4 has a new feature called Joins, which allows a query to match a document based on data in another document related by some field in common. It can be used as an alternative to denormalization when denormalization is impractical due to ballooning index size or for some complex one-to-many query scenarios described soon. A Join query is fairly slow, so always prefer denormalization when you can. See *Chapter 5, Searching*, for more information on Joins.

Let's see an example. Consider a search for tracks matching *Cherub Rock*:

Score	Num	Track	Duration	Type	Artist	Album	Tracks
100	1	Cherub Rock	4:58	album	The Smashing Pumpkins	Siamese Dream	13
100	1	Cherub Rock	4:59	single	The Smashing Pumpkins	Cherub Rock	3
100	4	Cherub Rock	4:57	compilation	The Smashing Pumpkins	Greatest Hits (Rotten Apples)	18
100	14	Cherub Rock	4:29	live	The Smashing Pumpkins	Turpentine Kisses	14
100	11	Cherub Rock	5:55	live	The Smashing Pumpkins	Squashed Zucchini	13

The following tracks matched your query. Page 1 of 1114 (Go!)

Denormalizing – one-to-one associated data

A MusicBrainz track's name and duration are definitely in the track table, but the artist and album names are each in their own tables in the MusicBrainz schema. This is a relatively simple case, because each track has no more than one artist or album. Both the artist name and album name would get their own field in Solr's flat schema for a track. They also happen to be elsewhere in our Solr schema, because artists and albums were identified in *Step 2 – determine the entities returned from each search.* Since the artist and album names are not unambiguous references, it is useful to also add the IDs for these tables into the track schema to support linking in the user interface, among other things.

Denormalizing – one-to-many associated data

One-to-many associations can be easy to handle in the simple case of a field requiring multiple values. Unfortunately, databases usually make this harder than it should be if it's just a simple list. However, Solr's fields directly support the notion of multiple values. Remember that in the MusicBrainz schema, an artist of type group can have some number of other artists as members. Although MusicBrainz's current search capability doesn't leverage this, we'll capture it anyway because it is useful for more interesting searches. The Solr schema to store this would simply have a member name field that is multivalued. The member_id field alone would be insufficient, because denormalization requires that the member's name be copied into the artist. This example is a good segue to how things can get a little more complicated.

If we only record the member name, it is problematic to do things such as have links in the UI from a band member to that member's detail page. This is because we don't have that member's artist ID, but only their name. So we'll add a multivalued field for the member's ID. Multivalued fields maintain ordering so that the two fields would have corresponding values at a given index. If one of the values is optional, remember to supply an empty string placeholder to keep the field values aligned. The client code would have to know about this placeholder.

The following diagram represents an example of one-to-many associations:

One-to-many Associations Example: The Smashing Pumpkins (Artist ID: 11650)	
Artist ID	11650
Member ID	102693 102694 102695 102696
Member Name	Billy Corgan James Iha Jimmy Chamberlin Mike Byrne

What you should not do is try to shove different types of data into the same field by putting both the artist IDs and names into one field. It could introduce text analysis problems, as the field would have to satisfy both types, and it would require the client to parse out the pieces. The exception to this is when you are merely storing it for display, not searching for it. Then, you can store whatever you want in a field.

A problem with denormalizing one-to-many data comes into play when multiple fields from the other entity are brought in, and you need to search on more than one of those fields at once. For a hypothetical example, imagine a search for releases that contain a track with a particular word in the name and with a particular minimum duration. Both the track name and duration fields on a release would be multivalued, and a search would have criteria for both. Unfortunately, Solr would erroneously return releases in which one track name satisfies the criteria and a separate track duration satisfies the criteria but not necessarily for the same track. One workaround is to search for the track index instead of the release one, and to use Solr's new feature, **result grouping,** also known as **field collapsing,** to group by release. This solution, of course, depends on an additional index holding entity relationships going the other way. If you are faced with this challenge but can't create this additional index because the index would be prohibitively large for your data, then you will have to use Solr 4's Join feature. See *Chapter 5, Searching,* for more information on Joins.

Step 4 – omit the inclusion of fields only used in search results (optional)

It's not likely that you will actually do this, but it's important to understand the concept. If there is any data shown on the search results that is not queryable, not sorted upon, not faceted on, nor are you using the highlighter feature for, and for that matter you are not using any Solr feature that uses the field except to simply return it in search results, then it is not necessary to include it in the schema for this entity. Let's say, for the sake of argument, that when doing a query for tracks, the only information queryable, sortable, and so on is a track's name. You can opt not to inline the artist name, for example, into the track entity. When your application queries Solr for tracks and needs to render search results with the artist's name, the onus would be on your application to get this data from somewhere—it won't be in the search results from Solr. The application might look these up in a database, in some caching middleware, or perhaps even query our Solr artist index.

This clearly makes generating a search results screen more difficult, because you now have to get the data from more than one place. Moreover, to do it efficiently, you would need to take care to query the needed data in bulk, instead of each row individually. Additionally, it would be wise to consider a caching strategy to reduce the queries to the other data source. It will, in all likelihood, slow down the total render time too. However, the benefit is that you needn't get the data and store it into the index at indexing time. It might be a lot of data, which would grow your index, or it might be data that changes often, necessitating frequent index updates.

If you are using distributed search, as discussed in *Chapter 9, Integrating Solr*, there is some performance gain in not sending too much data around in the requests. Let's say that you have song lyrics for each track, it is distributed on 20 machines, and you get 100 results. This could result in 2,000 records being sent around the network. Just sending the IDs around would be much more network-efficient; however, this leaves you with the job of collecting the data elsewhere before display. The only way to know if this works for you is to test both scenarios. In general, if the data in question is not large, then keep it in Solr.

At the other end of the extreme is storing all data in Solr. Why not? At least in the case of MusicBrainz, it wouldn't be appropriate. Take the **Top Voters** tally, for example. The account names listed are actually editors in MusicBrainz terminology. This piece of the screen tallies an edit, grouped by the editor who performed the edit. It's the edit that is the entity in this case. The following screenshot shows the **Top Voters** (also known as editors), which are tallied by the number of edits:

This data simply doesn't belong in an index, because there's no use case for searching edits, only lookup when we want to see the edits on some other entity like an artist. If you insisted on having the voter's tally (as previously seen) powered by Solr, then you'd have to put all this data (of which there is a lot!) into an index, just because you wanted a simple statistical list of top voters. It's just not worth it!

One objective guide to help you decide on whether to put an entity in Solr or not is to ask yourself whether users will ever be doing a text search on that entity — a feature where index technology stands out from databases. If not, then you probably don't want the entity in your Solr index.

The schema.xml file

Let's finally explore a Solr schema.

Before we continue, find a `schema.xml` file to follow along. This file belongs in the `conf` directory for a Solr Core instance configuration. For simple single-core Solr setups, this is the same as a Solr home directory. We suggest looking at `configsets/mbtype/conf/schema.xml` in the example code distributed with the book, available online. If you are working off of the Solr distribution, you'll find it in `example/solr/collection1/conf/schema.xml`. The example `schema.xml` is loaded with useful field types, documentation, and field definitions used for the sample data that comes with Solr.

We prefer to initialize a Solr configuration by copying the example Solr home directory and liberally modifying it as needed, ripping out or commenting what we don't need (which is often a lot). This is half way between starting with nothing, or starting with the example and making essential modifications. If you do start with Solr's example configuration, be sure to revisit your configuration at some point to clean out what you aren't using. In addition, it's tempting to keep the existing documentation comments, but you can always refer back to what comes with Solr as needed and keep your config file clean.

At the start of the file is the schema opening element:

```
<schema name="musicbrainz" version="1.5">
```

We've set the name of this schema to `musicbrainz`, the name of our application. If we used different schema files, then we should name them differently so as to differentiate them.

Field definitions

The definitions of the fields in the schema are located within the `<fields/>` element. There are many attributes that can be added to configure them, but here are the most important ones:

- `name` (required): This uniquely identifies the field. There aren't any restrictions on the characters used nor any words to avoid, except for score.

- `type` (required): This is a reference to one of the field types defined in the schema.

- `indexed`: This indicates that this field can be searched, sorted, and used in a variety of other Solr features. It defaults to `true` since the only thing you can do with a nonindexed field is return it in search results, assuming it's marked as stored.

- `stored`: This indicates that the field's value will be stored in Solr so that it can be returned in search results verbatim or highlighted for matching query text. By default, fields are stored. Sometimes the same data is copied into multiple fields that are indexed differently (which you'll begin to understand soon), and so the redundant fields should not be marked as stored. As of Solr 4.1, the stored data is internally compressed to save space, and perhaps surprisingly, to improve search performance too.

- `multiValued`: Enable this if a field can contain more than one value. Order is maintained from that supplied at index-time. It's sloppy to have this enabled if the field never has multiple values as some aspects of Solr like faceting are forced to choose less efficient algorithms unnecessarily.

- `default`: This is the default value, if an input document doesn't specify it. A common use of this is to timestamp documents: `<field name="indexedAt" type="tdate" default="NOW/SECOND" />`. For information on specifying dates, see the *Date math* section in *Chapter 5, Searching*.

- `required`: Set this to `true` if you want Solr to fail to index a document that does not have a value for this field.

There are other attributes too that are more advanced; we'll get to them in a bit rather than distract you with them now.

Dynamic field definitions

The very notion of a dynamic field definition highlights the flexibility of Lucene's index, as compared to typical relational database technology. Not only can you explicitly name fields in the schema, but you can also have some defined on the fly based on the name supplied for indexing. Solr's example schema contains some examples of this, as follows:

```
<dynamicField name="*_dt" type="date" indexed="true"
stored="true"/>
```

If at index time a document contains a field that isn't matched by an explicit field definition, but does have a name matching this pattern (that is, ends with _dt, such as updated_dt), then it gets processed according to that definition. A dynamic field is declared just like a regular field in the same section. However, the element is named dynamicField, and it has a name attribute that must either start or end with an asterisk (the wildcard). It can also be just *, which is the final fallback.

> The * fallback is most useful if you decide that all fields attempted to be stored in the index should succeed, even if you didn't know about the field when you designed the schema. It's also useful if you decide that instead of it being an error, such unknown fields should simply be ignored (that is, not indexed and not stored).

In the end, a field is a field, whether explicitly defined or defined dynamically according to a name pattern. Dynamic field definitions are just a convenience that makes defining schemas easier. There are no performance implications of using dynamic field definitions.

Advanced field options for indexed fields

There are additional attributes that can be added to fields marked as indexed to further configure them. These options are all set to false by default:

- sortMissingFirst, sortMissingLast: Sorting on a field with one of these set to true indicates on which side of the search results to put documents that have no data for the specified field, regardless of the sort direction. The default behavior for such documents is to appear first for ascending and last for descending.

- `omitNorms`: Basically, if you don't want the length of a field to affect its scoring (see *Chapter 6, Search Relevancy*) or it isn't used in the score in any way (such as for faceting), and you aren't doing index-time document boosting (see *Chapter 4, Indexing Data*), then enable this. Aside from its effect on scores, it saves a little memory too. It defaults to `true` for primitive field types, such as `int`, `float`, `boolean`, `string`, and so on.

- `omitPositions`: This omits the term position information from the index to save a little space. Phrase queries won't work anymore.

- `omitTermFreqAndPositions`: This omits term frequency and term positions from the index to save a little space. Phrase queries won't work and scores will be less effective.

- `termVectors`: This will tell Lucene to store information that is used in a few cases to improve search performance. If a field is to be used by the MoreLikeThis feature, or for highlighting of a large text field, then try enabling this. It can substantially increase the index size and indexing time, so do a before-and-after measurement. There are two more options, which add more data to term vectors: `termPositions` and `termOffsets`. The `FastVectorHighlighter` class requires these.

- `positionIncrementGap`: For a `multiValued` field, this is the number of (virtual) nonexistent words between each value to prevent inadvertent phrase queries matching across field values. For example, if A and B are given as two values for a field, `positionIncrementGap` of more than 1 prevents the phrase query `"A B"` from matching.

 There is a helpful table on Solr's wiki at `http://wiki.apache.org/solr/FieldOptionsByUseCase`, which shows most of the options with some use cases that need them.

Solr 4.2 introduced a new advanced schema option called DocValues with the `docValues` option in the field type.

The `docValues` is a Boolean that, when enabled, causes Lucene to store the values for this field in an additional way that can be initialized faster than un-inverting indexed data when the field is used for match-only semantics such as term, wildcard, range queries, and so on, and also for faceting, sorting, and other use cases.

DocValues help optimize Solr for meeting real-time search requirements. Unless you have such requirements or you know what you're doing, don't enable DocValues as it uses more disk and the features that use it tend to work slower than without it after it's initialized (as of Solr 4.2). For more information on DocValues, read `https://cwiki.apache.org/confluence/display/solr/DocValues`.

The unique key

After the `<fields>` declarations in the schema, we can have the `<uniqueKey>` declaration specifying which field uniquely identifies each document, if any. This is what we have in our MusicBrainz schema:

```
<uniqueKey>id</uniqueKey>
```

Although it is technically not always required, you should define a unique ID field. In our MusicBrainz schema, the ID is a string that includes an entity type prefix type so that it's unique across the whole corpus, spanning multiple Solr Cores, for example, `Artist:11650`.

If your source data does not have an ID field that you can propagate, then you may want to consider using a **Universally Unique Identifier (UUID)**, according to RFC-4122. Simply have a field with a field type for the class `solr.UUIDField` and either provide a UUID to Solr or use `UUIDUpdateProcessorFactory`, an update processor that adds a newly generated UUID value to any document being added that does not already have a value in the specified field. Solr's UUID support is based on `java.util.UUID`.

The default search field and query operator

There are a couple of schema configuration elements pertaining to search defaults when interpreting a query string:

```
<!-- <defaultSearchField>text</defaultSearchField>
<solrQueryParser defaultOperator="AND"/> -->
```

The `defaultSearchField` parameter declares the particular field that will be searched for queries that don't explicitly reference one. The `solrQueryParser` setting has a `defaultOperator` attribute, which lets you specify the default search operator (that is AND or OR and it will be OR if unspecified) here in the schema. These are essentially defaults for searches that are processed by Solr request handlers defined in `solrconfig.xml`.

We strongly recommend that you leave these commented out in the schema, which is how it comes in the example. It's tempting to set them but it further disperses the configuration relevant to interpreting a query, which already is the URL plus the request handler definition. Its effects are global here and may have unintended consequences on queries you don't want or intend, such as a delete query. Instead, configure the query parser's defaults in a request handler as desired in `solrconfig.xml` — documented in *Chapter 5, Searching*.

Copying fields

Closely related to the field definitions are `copyField` directives. A `copyField` directive copies one or more input field values to another during indexing. A `copyField` directive looks like this:

```
<copyField source="r_name" dest="r_name_sort" maxChars="20" />
```

This directive is useful when a value needs to be copied to additional field(s) to be indexed differently. For example, sorting and faceting require a single indexed value. Another is a common technique in search systems in which many fields are copied to a common field that is indexed without norms and not stored. This permits searches, which would otherwise search many fields, to search one instead, thereby drastically improving performance at the expense of reducing score quality. This technique is usually complemented by searching some additional fields with higher boosts. The `dismax/edismax` query parser, which is described in *Chapter 5, Searching*, makes this easy.

At index-time, each supplied field of input data has its name compared against the `source` attribute of all `copyField` directives. The source attribute might include an * wildcard, so it's possible that the input might match more than one `copyField`. If a wildcard is used in the destination, then it must refer to a dynamic field, and furthermore the source must include a wildcard too—otherwise a wildcard in the destination is an error. A match against a `copyField` directive has the effect of the input value being duplicated, but using the field name of the `dest` attribute of the directive. If `maxChars` is optionally specified, the copy is truncated to these many characters. The duplicate does not replace any existing values that might be going to the field, so be sure to mark the destination field as `multiValued`, if needed.

`<copyField>` is a fundamental and very powerful concept of Solr, which is used more often than not to ensure that data is indexed into several fields based on the type of processing required on them at search time, without needing to include the data in the update command multiple times.

Our MusicBrainz field definitions

What follows is a first cut of our MusicBrainz schema definition. There are additional fields that will be added in other chapters to explore other search features. This is a combined schema defining all core entity types: artists, releases (also known as albums), and tracks. This approach was described earlier in the chapter. Notice that we chose to prefix field names by a character representing the entity type it is on (`a_`, `r_`, `t_`), to avoid overloading the use of any field across entity types.

We also used this abbreviation when we denormalized relationships such as in
`r_a_name` (a release's artist's name).

```xml
<!-- COMMON TO ALL TYPES: -->
<field name="id" type="string" required="true" />
        <!-- Artist:11650 -->
<field name="type" type="string" required="true" />
        <!-- Artist | Release | Label -->
<field name="indexedAt" type="tdate" default="NOW/SECOND" />


<!-- ARTIST: -->
<field name="a_name" type="title" />
        <!-- The Smashing Pumpkins -->
<field name="a_name_sort" type="string" stored="false" />
  <!-- Smashing Pumpkins, The -->
<field name="a_alias" type="title" stored="false" multiValued="true"
/>
<field name="a_type" type="string" />
  <!-- group | person -->
<field name="a_begin_date" type="tdate" />
<field name="a_end_date" type="tdate" />
<field name="a_member_name" type="title" multiValued="true" />
        <!-- Billy Corgan -->
<field name="a_member_id" type="long" multiValued="true" />
        <!-- 102693 -->


<!-- RELEASE -->
<field name="r_name" type="title" />
  <!-- Siamese Dream -->
<field name="r_name_sort" type="string" stored="false" />
  <!-- Siamese Dream -->
<field name="r_a_name" type="title" />
  <!-- The Smashing Pumpkins -->
<field name="r_a_id" type="long" />
  <!-- 11650 -->
<field name="r_attributes" type="int" indexed="false"
multiValued="true" />
  <!-- ex: 0, 1, 100 -->
<field name="r_type" type="rType" stored="false" multiValued="true" />
  <!-- Album | Single | EP |... etc. -->
<field name="r_official" type="rOfficial" stored="false"multiValued="
true" />
  <!-- Official | Bootleg | Promotional -->
<field name="r_lang" type="string" indexed="false" />
  <!-- eng / latn -->
```

```
<field name="r_tracks" type="int" indexed="false" />
<field name="r_event_country" type="string" multiValued="true" />
      <!-- us -->
<field name="r_event_date" type="tdate" multiValued="true" />



  <!-- TRACK -->
<field name="t_name" type="title" />
  <!-- Cherub Rock -->
<field name="t_num" type="int" indexed="false" />
  <!-- 1 -->
<field name="t_duration" type="int"/>
      <!-- 298133 -->
<field name="t_a_id" type="long" />
      <!-- 11650 -->
<field name="t_a_name" type="title" />
  <!-- The Smashing Pumpkins -->
<field name="t_r_name" type="title" />
  <!-- Siamese Dream -->
<field name="t_r_tracks" type="int" indexed="false" />
  <!-- 13 -->
```

Put some sample data in your schema comments

You'll find the sample data helpful and anyone else working on your project will thank you for it! In the preceding examples, we sometimes use actual values, and on other occasions, we list several possible values separated by |, if there is a predefined list.

Also, note that the only fields that we can mark as required are those common to all, which are ID and type, because we're doing a combined schema approach.

In our schema, we're choosing to index most of the fields, even though MusicBrainz's search doesn't require more than the name of each entity type. We're doing this so that we can make the schema more interesting to demonstrate more of Solr's capabilities. As it turns out, some of the other information in MusicBrainz's query results actually are queryable if one uses the advanced search form, checks **use advanced query syntax**, and your query uses those fields (for example, `artist:"Smashing Pumpkins"`).

At the time of this writing, MusicBrainz used Lucene for its text search and so it uses Lucene's query syntax. `http://wiki.musicbrainz.org/TextSearchSyntax`. You'll learn more about the syntax in *Chapter 5, Searching*.

Defining field types

The latter half of the schema is the definition of field types. This section is enclosed in the `<types/>` element and will consume much of the file's content. The field types declare the types of fields, such as `booleans`, `numbers`, `dates`, and various text flavors. They are referenced by the field definitions under the `<fields/>` element. Here is the field type for a Boolean:

```
<fieldType name="boolean" class="solr.BoolField"
sortMissingLast="true" />
```

A field type has a unique name and is implemented by a Java class specified by the `class` attribute.

A fully qualified classname in Java looks like `org.apache.solr.schema.BoolField`. The last piece is the simple name of the class, and the part preceding it is called the package name. In order to make configuration files in Solr more concise, the package name is abbreviated to just `solr` for most of Solr's packages.

Attributes other than the name and class represent configuration options; most are applicable to all types such as those listed earlier and some are specific to the implementing class. They can usually be overridden at the field declaration too. In addition to these attributes, there is also the text analysis configuration that is only applicable to text fields. This will be covered in the next chapter.

Starting from Solr 4.8, both `<fields>` and `<types>` tags have been deprecated and they might be removed completely in the future versions. These tags can be safely removed from the schema file, which allows intermixing of `<fieldType>`, `<field>`, and `<copyField>` definitions, if desired.

Built-in field type classes

There are a number of built-in field types and nearly all are present and documented to some extent in Solr's example schema. We're not going to enumerate all of them here, but instead we will highlight some of ones that are worthy of more explanation.

Numbers and dates

There are no less than five different field types to use to store an integer, perhaps six if you want to count string! It's about the same for `float`, `double`, `long`, and `date`. And to think that you probably initially thought this technology only did text! We'll explain when to use which, using Integer as an example. Most have an analogous name for the other numeric and date types. *The field types with names starting with "Trie" should serve 95 percent of your needs.* To clean up your schema, consider deleting the others. The following is the list of various integer field types that you can use:

- `TrieIntField` (with `precisionStep = 0`) is, commonly named `int`. This is a good default field suitable for most uses, such as an ID field.

- `TrieIntField` (with `precisionStep> 0`), commonly named `tint`. If you expect to do numeric range queries (which include faceted ranges) over many values, then this field type has unbeatable performance at query time at the expense of a little more disk and indexing time cost. The default value configured in Solr's example schema is 8 for numeric and 6 for date; we recommend keeping these defaults. Smaller numbers (but > 0) will increase indexing space and time for better query range performance; although the performance gains rapidly diminish with each step.

- `IntField`, commonly named `pint`. A legacy implementation that encodes integer values as simple strings. The values are evaluated in unicode string order instead of the numeric order. This field type will be removed in future versions; use `TrieIntField` instead.

- `SortableIntField` is commonly named `sint`. `DateField` doesn't follow this naming convention but it also qualifies here. Both `SortableIntField` and `DateField` will be removed in the future versions, use `TrieIntField` and `TrieDateField` instead.

All of these numeric types sort in their natural numeric order instead of lexicographically.

Some other field types

Solr's geospatial support spans multiple parts of Solr from field types to query parsers, to function queries. Instead of having you read relevant parts of three chapters, we've consolidated it into the last part of *Chapter 5, Searching*.

`CurrencyField` (commonly named `currency`) allows us to let Solr calculate the query-time currency conversions and exchange rates and we can also plug in custom implementations of exchange rate providers. The following is the default configuration for `currency` fieldType with `defaultCurrency="USD"` and `currencyConfig="currency.xml"` in which we can list the currencies and their exchange rates.

```
<fieldType name="currency" class="solr.CurrencyField"
precisionStep="8" defaultCurrency="USD"
currencyConfig="currency.xml" />
```

We will discuss this field more in detail in *Chapter 4, Indexing Data*, and the query-time features supported by `currency` fields in *Chapter 5, Searching*. Alternatively, you can read more on Solr wiki at `http://wiki.apache.org/solr/CurrencyField`.

`ExternalFileField` (advanced) reads its float values from a plain text file instead of the index. It was designed for sorting or influencing scores of documents based on data that might change quickly (for example, a rating or click-through) without having to re-index a document. Remember that Lucene fundamentally cannot update just a single field; entire documents need to be re-indexed. This field type is a workaround for this limitation for the aforementioned use cases. This is discussed further in *Chapter 6, Search Relevancy*.

`EnumField` allows us to define a field with a closed set of values and the sort order for these values is predetermined but not lexicographic. Along with the name and the class parameters, which are common to all field types, we need provide two additional parameters:

- `enumsConfig`: This is the configuration (in XML format) filename. The default location of the file is `conf` directory for the collection. The file should contain the `<enum/>` list of field values. You can always add new values to the end of the list, but you can't change the order or existing values in the enum without re-indexing.
- `enumName`: This is the specific enumeration in the `enumsConfig` file to use for the field type.

You can read more about the `EnumField` at `https://cwiki.apache.org/confluence/display/solr/Working+with+Enum+Fields`.

Starting from Solr 4.3, we can configure the
`ManagedIndexSchemaFactory` in the `solrconfig.xml` file, which
enables schema modifications through a REST interface, also known
as the Schema API. You can read more on the wiki page at `https://cwiki.apache.org/confluence/display/solr/Schema+API`.

Summary

At this point, you should have a schema that you believe will suit your needs — for
now anyway. However, do expect to revisit the schema design. It is quite normal
to start with something workable, and then subsequently make modifications to
address issues, and implement features that require changes. The only irritant with
changing the schema is that you probably need to re-index all of the data. The only
exception to this would be an analysis step applied only at query time.

In the next chapter, *Text Analysis*, you'll learn about various text-processing steps such
as tokenization, case normalization, stemming, synonyms, and other miscellaneous
text processing, which are important parts of search engines since the details of the
text have an effect on getting good search results.

3
Text Analysis

Text analysis is a topic that covers text-processing steps such as tokenization, case normalization, stemming, query expansion using synonyms, and other miscellaneous text processing. The analysis is applied to a text field at index time and as part of query string processing at search time. It's an important part of search engines since most of the time business-relevant information is in an unstructured form, primarily text. Also, the details have an effect on getting good search results, especially to *recall*—a dimension of search result quality pertaining to whether all relevant documents are in the search results.

 This chapter is almost completely Lucene-centric and so also applies to any other software built on top of Lucene. For the most part, Solr merely offers XML configuration for the code in Lucene that provides this capability. For information beyond what is covered here, including writing your own analysis components, read *Lucene in Action, Second Edition, Manning Publications*.

Text analysis converts text for a particular field into a sequence of terms. A **term** is the fundamental unit that Lucene actually indexes and searches. The analysis is used on the original incoming value at index time; the resulting terms are ultimately recorded onto disk in Lucene's index structure where it can be searched. The analysis is also performed on words and phrases parsed from the query string; the resulting terms are then searched in Lucene's index. An exception to this is the prefix, wildcard and fuzzy queries, all of which skip text analysis. You'll read about them in *Chapter 5, Searching*.

In a hurry?

As a starting point, you should use the existing field types in Solr's default schema, which includes a variety of text field types for different situations. They will suffice for now and you can return to this chapter later. There will surely come a time when you are trying to figure out why a simple query isn't matching a document that you think it should, and it will quite often come down to your text analysis configuration.

We try to cover Solr in a comprehensive fashion and this chapter mainly focuses on the text analysis for English language.

Non-English text analysis

Text analysis for non-English languages is not straightforward as the rules vary by language. You can refer to the wiki page https://cwiki. apache.org/confluence/display/solr/Language+Analysis for more information. There are 34 language factories available at the time of writing. You'll notice that there is some variation in how to configure Solr for each of them, and that some languages have multiple options. Most language-specific elements are the stemmer and the stop word list, and for Eastern languages, the tokenizer too. There is also a set of **International Components for Unicode (ICU)** related analysis components, some of which you can use for mapping some non-Latin characters to Latin equivalents. We will also discuss the approaches for supporting multilingual search later in this chapter.

Configuring field types

Solr has various field types as we've previously explained, and the most important one is TextField. This is the field type that has an analyzer configuration. Let's look at the configuration for the text_en_splitting field type definition that comes with Solr's example schema. It uses a diverse set of analysis components. We added in a character filter, albeit commented, to show what it looks like. As you read about text analysis in this chapter, you may want to flip back to see this configuration.

```
<fieldType name="text_en_splitting" class="solr.TextField"
           positionIncrementGap="100"
           autoGeneratePhraseQueries="true">
    <analyzer type="index">
<!--<charFilter class="solr.MappingCharFilterFactory"
    mapping="mapping-ISOLatin1Accent.txt"/>-->
        <tokenizer class="solr.WhitespaceTokenizerFactory"/>
```

```
            <filter class="solr.StopFilterFactory"
              ignoreCase="true"
              words="stopwords_en.txt"
              enablePositionIncrements="true"
            />
            <filter class="solr.WordDelimiterFilterFactory"
                generateWordParts="1" generateNumberParts="1"
                catenateWords="1" catenateNumbers="1"
                catenateAll="0" splitOnCaseChange="1"/>
            <filter class="solr.LowerCaseFilterFactory"/>
            <filter class="solr.KeywordMarkerFilterFactory"
                protected="protwords.txt"/>
            <filter class="solr.PorterStemFilterFactory"/>
        </analyzer>
        <analyzer type="query">
          <!--<charFilter class="solr.MappingCharFilterFactory"
                mapping="mapping-ISOLatin1Accent.txt"/>-->
            <tokenizer class="solr.WhitespaceTokenizerFactory"/>
            <filter class="solr.SynonymFilterFactory"
              synonyms="synonyms.txt" ignoreCase="true" expand="true"/>
            <filter class="solr.StopFilterFactory"
              ignoreCase="true"
              words="stopwords_en.txt"
              enablePositionIncrements="true"
            />
            <filter class="solr.WordDelimiterFilterFactory"
                generateWordParts="1" generateNumberParts="1"
                catenateWords="0" catenateNumbers="0" catenateAll="0"
                splitOnCaseChange="1"/>
            <filter class="solr.LowerCaseFilterFactory"/>
            <filter class="solr.KeywordMarkerFilterFactory"
                protected="protwords.txt"/>
            <filter class="solr.PorterStemFilterFactory"/>
        </analyzer>
    </fieldType>
```

The configuration example defines two **analyzers**, each of which specify an ordered sequence of processing steps that convert text into a sequence of terms. The type attribute, which can hold a value of index or query, differentiates whether the analyzer is applied at index time or query time, respectively. If the same analysis is to be performed at both index and query times, you can specify just one analyzer without a type. When both are specified as in the previous example, they usually only differ a little.

Analyzers, tokenizers, filters, oh my!

These are the three main classes in the `org.apache.lucene.` `analysis` package from which all analysis processes are derived, which are about to be defined. They are all conceptually the same—they take in text and spit out text, sometimes filtering, sometimes adding new terms, and sometimes modifying terms. The difference is in the specific flavor of input and output for them—either character based or token based. Also, **term**, **token**, and **word** are often used interchangeably.

An analyzer can optionally begin with one or more **character filters**, which operate at a streaming character level to perform manipulations on original input text. These are most commonly used to normalize characters, such as the removal of accents. Following any optional character filters is the **tokenizer**—the only mandatory piece of the chain. This analyzer takes a stream of characters and tokenizes it into a stream of tokens, perhaps with a simple algorithm, such as splitting on whitespace. The remaining analysis steps, if any, are all **token** filters (often abbreviated to just **filters**), which perform a great variety of manipulations on tokens. The final tokens at the end are referred to as **terms** at this point; they are what Lucene actually indexes and searches. The order of these components is very important and, in most cases, you may want it to be the same at index time and query time. Note that some filters such as `WordDelimiterFilterFactory` actually perform a tokenization action, but they do it on a token, whereas a bonafide tokenizer works from a character stream.

All the class names end with `Factory`. This is a convention followed by all the names of Lucene's Java classes that accept the configuration and instantiate Lucene's analysis components that have the same simple name, minus the `Factory` suffix. References to these analysis components in this book and elsewhere sometimes include the `Factory` suffix and sometimes not; no distinction is intended.

Finally, we want to point out the `autoGeneratePhraseQueries` Boolean attribute—an option only applicable to text fields. If search-time query text analysis yields more than one token, such as `Wi-Fi` tokenizing to `Wi` and `Fi`, then by default these tokens are simply different search terms with no relation to their position. If this attribute is enabled, then the tokens become a phrase query, such as `WiFi` and consequently these tokens must be adjacent in the index. This automatic phrase query generation would always happen prior to Solr 3.1, but it is now configurable and defaults to `false`.

[**We recommend disabling autoGeneratePhraseQueries**

There is conflicting opinion among experts on a suitable setting; setting it to `false` increases recall but decreases precision—two dimensions of search result quality. We favor that choice, since you'll learn in *Chapter 6, Search Relevancy*, how to do automatic phrase boosting to get the most relevant documents (those that match the phrase `Wi Fi`) at the top of the results.]

Experimenting with text analysis

Before we dive into the details of particular analysis components, it's important to become comfortable with Solr's analysis page, which is an experimentation and a troubleshooting tool that is indispensable. You'll use this to try out different configurations to verify whether you get the desired effect, and you'll use this when troubleshooting to find out why certain queries aren't matching certain text that you think they should. In Solr's admin interface, you'll see a link named **Analysis**, which takes you to this screen:

As shown in the preceding screenshot, the option on the form **Analyse Fieldname /
FieldType** is required. You pick whether you want to choose a field type directly by
its name, or if you want to indirectly choose one based on the name of a field. In this
example, we're choosing the `text_en_splitting` field type that has some interesting
text analysis. This tool is mainly for text-oriented field types, not Boolean, date, and
numeric oriented types. You may get strange results if you try those.

At this point, you can analyze index or query text or both at the same time. If you
are troubleshooting why a particular query isn't matching a particular document's
field value, then you'd put the field value into the **Index** box and the query text into
the **Query** box. Technically, that might not be the same thing as the original query
string, because the query string may use various operators to target specified fields,
do fuzzy queries, and so on. You will want to check off **Verbose Output** to take full
advantage of this tool.

The output after clicking on the **Analyse Values** button is a bit verbose with Verbose
Output checked and so we've disabled it for this upcoming screenshot. We encourage
you to try it yourself.

WT	"Quoting,	Wi-Fi"			and	stopword
SF	"Quoting,	Wi-Fi"				stopword
WDF	Quoting	Wi	Fi	WiFi		stopword
LCF	quoting	wi	fi	wifi		stopword
KMF	quoting	wi	fi	wifi		stopword
PSF	quot	wi	fi	wifi		stopword

Each row shown here represents one step in the chain of processing as configured
in the analyzer, for example, the third analysis component is `WordDelimeterFilter`
and the results of its processing are shown in the third row. The columns separate
the tokens, and if more than one token shares the same column, then they share the
same **term position**. The distinction of the term position pertains to how phrase
queries work. One interesting thing to notice about the analysis results is that **Quoting**
ultimately became **quot** after stemming and lowercasing. Also, the word **and** was
omitted by the `StopFilter`, which is the second row.

Character filters

Character filters, declared with the `<charFilter>` element, process a stream of text prior to tokenization. There are only a few. This feature is not commonly used except for the first one described here, which is configured to strip accents:

- `MappingCharFilterFactory`: This maps a character (or string) to another — potentially none. In other words, it's a find-replace capability. There is a `mapping` attribute in which you specify a configuration file. Solr's example configuration includes two such configuration files with useful mappings:

  - `mapping-FoldToASCII.txt`: This is a comprehensive mapping of non-ASCII characters to ASCII equivalents. For further details on the characters mapped, read the comments at the top of the file. This char filter has a token filter equivalent named `ASCIIFoldingFilterFactory` that should run faster and is recommended instead.

  - `mapping-ISOLatin1Accent.txt`: This is a smaller subset covering just the ISO Latin1 accent characters (like ñ to n). Given that `FoldToASCII` is more comprehensive; it's likely to be a better default than this one.

This analysis component and quite a few others have an attribute in which you can specify a configuration file. Usually, you can specify more than one file, separated by a comma but some components don't support that. They are always in the `conf` directory and UTF-8 encoded.

- `HTMLStripCharFilterFactory`: This is used for HTML or XML, and it need not be well formed. Essentially, it removes all markup, leaving just the text content of elements. The text of script and style elements are removed. Entity references (for example, `&amp;`) are resolved.

Instead of stripping markup at the analysis stage, which is very late, consider if this should be done at an earlier point with `UpdateRequestProcessor`, or even before Solr gets it. If you need to retain the markup in Solr's stored value, then you will indeed need to perform this step here.

- `PatternReplaceCharFilterFactory`: This performs a search based on a regular expression given as the `pattern` attribute, replacing it with the `replacement` attribute. Only use this char filter if the replacement should affect tokenization, such as by introducing a space.

The regular expression specification supported by Solr is the one that Java uses: http://docs.oracle.com/javase/7/docs/api/java/util/regex/Pattern.html.

Tokenization

A **tokenizer** is an analysis component declared with the `<tokenizer>` element that takes text in the form of a character stream and splits it into so-called **tokens**, most of the time skipping insignificant bits like whitespace and joining punctuation. An analyzer has exactly one tokenizer. Your tokenizer choices are as follows:

- `KeywordTokenizerFactory`: This tokenizer doesn't actually do any tokenization! The entire character stream becomes a single token. The `string` field type has a similar effect but doesn't allow configuration of text analysis like lower-casing, for example. Any field used for sorting or most uses of faceting will require an indexed field with no more than one term per original value.

- `WhitespaceTokenizerFactory`: Text is tokenized by whitespace: spaces, tabs, carriage returns, line feeds.

- `StandardTokenizerFactory`: This is a general-purpose tokenizer for most Western languages. It tokenizes on whitespace and other points specified by the Unicode standard's annex on word boundaries. Whitespace and punctuation characters at these boundaries get removed. Hyphens are considered a word boundary, making this tokenizer less desirable for use with `WordDelimiterFilter`.

- `UAX29URLEmailTokenizer`: This behaves like `StandardTokenizer` with the additional property of recognizing e-mail addresses and URLs as single tokens.

- `ClassicTokenizerFactory`: (This was formerly the `StandardTokenizer` before Solr 3.) This is a general-purpose tokenizer for English. In English text, it does do a few things better than `StandardTokenizer`. Acronyms using periods are recognized, leaving the final period in place, which would otherwise be removed for example, `I.B.M.`; hyphens don't split words when the token contains a number; and e-mail addresses and Internet hostnames survive as one token.

  Additionally, there is a `ClassicFilter` token filter that is usually configured to follow this tokenizer. It will strip the periods out of acronyms and remove any trailing apostrophes (English possessive). It will only work with `ClassicTokenizer`.

- `LetterTokenizerFactory`: This tokenizer considers each contiguous sequence of letters (as defined by Unicode) as a token and disregards other characters.

- `LowerCaseTokenizerFactory`: This tokenizer is functionally equivalent to `LetterTokenizer` followed by `LowerCaseFilter`, but faster.

- `PatternTokenizerFactory`: This regular expression-based tokenizer can behave in one of the following two ways:
    - To split the text on a separator specified by a pattern, you can use it like this: `<tokenizer class="solr.PatternTokenizerFactory" pattern=";*" />`. This example tokenizes a semi-colon separated list.
    - To match only particular patterns and possibly use only a subset of the pattern as the token, for example, `<tokenizer class="solr.PatternTokenizerFactory" pattern="\'([^\']+)\'" group="1" />`. The `group` attribute specifies which matching group will be the token. If you had input text like `aaa 'bbb' 'ccc'`, this would result in tokens `bbb` and `ccc`.

- `PathHierarchyTokenizerFactory`: This is a configurable tokenizer that tokenizes strings that follow a simple character delimiter pattern, such as file paths or domain names. It's useful in implementing hierarchical faceting, as discussed in *Chapter 7, Faceting*, or simply filtering documents by some root prefix of the hierarchy. As an example, the input string `/usr/local/apache` would be tokenized to these three tokens: `/usr`, `/usr/local`, and `/usr/local/apache`. This tokenizer has four configuration options:
    - `delimiter`: This is a character delimiter; the default is `/`
    - `replace`: This is a replacement character for `delimiter` (optional)
    - `reverse`: This is a Boolean to indicate whether the root of the hierarchy is on the right, such as with a hostname; the default is `false`
    - `skip`: This is a number of leading root tokens to skip; the default is `0`

- `WikipediaTokenizerFactory`: This is an experimental tokenizer for Mediawiki syntax, such as that used in Wikipedia.

There are some other tokenizers that exist for languages such as Chinese and Russian, as well as `ICUTokenizer`, which detects the language (or script) used and tokenizes accordingly. And furthermore, NGram-based tokenizers will be discussed later.

See http://wiki.apache.org/solr/
AnalyzersTokenizersTokenFilters for more information
on some of these tokenizers, or the API documentation.

Filtering

The token filters are declared in the `<filter>` element and consume one stream of
tokens, known as **TokenStream**, and generate another. Hence, they can be chained
one after another indefinitely. A token filter may be used to perform complex analysis
by processing multiple tokens in the stream at once but in most cases it processes each
token sequentially and decides to consider, replace, or ignore the token.

There may only be one official tokenizer in an analyzer; however, the token filter
named `WordDelimiterFilter` is in-effect a tokenizer too:

```
<filter class="solr.WordDelimiterFilterFactory"
generateWordParts="1" generateNumberParts="1"
catenateWords="1" catenateNumbers="1"
catenateAll="0" splitOnCaseChange="1"/>
```

(*Not all options were just shown*) The purpose of this analyzer is to both split and join
compound words with various means of defining compound words. This one is
typically used with `WhitespaceTokenizer`, not `StandardTokenizer`, which removes
punctuation-based intra-word delimiters, thereby defeating some of this processing.
The options for this analyzer have the values `1` to enable and `0` to disable.

This analysis component is the most configurable of all and it can be
a little confusing. Use Solr's Analysis screen, which described in the
Experimenting with text analysis section to validate your configuration.

The `WordDelimiterFilter` will first tokenize the input word, according to the
configured options. Note that the commas on the right-hand side of the following
examples denote separate terms, and options are all `true` by default:

- **Split on intra-word delimiters**: `Wi-Fi` to `Wi, Fi`
- **Split on letter-number transitions**: `SD500` to `SD, 500` (if `splitOnNumerics`)
- **Omit any delimiters**: `/hello--there, dude` to `hello, there, dude`
- **Remove trailing 's**: `David's` to `David` (if `stemEnglishPossessive`)
- **Split on lower to upper case transitions**: `WiFi` to `Wi, Fi`
  (if `splitOnCaseChange`)

At this point, the resulting terms are all filtered out unless some of the following options are enabled. You should always enable at least one of them:

- If `generateWordParts` or `generateNumberParts` is enabled, all-alphabetic terms or all-number terms pass through (meaning, they are not filtered). Either way, they are still considered for the concatenation options.

- To concatenate a consecutive series of alphabetic terms, enable `catenateWords` (for example, `wi-fi` to `wifi`). If `generateWordParts` is also enabled, this example would generate `wi` and `fi` but not otherwise. This will work even if there is just one term in the series, thereby generating a term that disabling `generateWordParts` would have omitted. `catenateNumbers` works similarly but for numeric terms. The `catenateAll` option will concatenate all of the terms together. The concatenation process will take care to not emit duplicate terms.

- To preserve the original word, enable `preserveOriginal`.

Here is an example exercising all the aforementioned options: `WiFi-802.11b` to `Wi`, `Fi`, `WiFi`, `802`, `11`, `80211`, `b`, `WiFi80211b`, `WiFi-802.11b`.

Internally, this filter assigns a type to each character (such as letter or number) before looking for word boundaries. The types are determined by Unicode character categories. If you want to customize how the filter determines what the type of each character is, you can provide one or more mapping files with the `types` option. An example use case would be indexing Twitter tweets in which you want # and @ treated as type `ALPHA`.

> For more details on this esoteric feature, see SOLR-205. You can find sample configuration, about how to customize WordDelimiterFilter's tokenization rules, at `https://issues.apache.org/jira/browse/SOLR-2059`.

Lastly, if there are a certain limited number of known input words that you want this filter to pass through untouched, then they can be listed in a file referred to with the `protected` option. Some other filters share this same feature.

Solr's out-of-the-box configuration for the `text_en_splitting` field type is a reasonable way to use the `WordDelimiterFilter`—generation of word and number parts at both index- and query-time, but concatenating only at index time, since doing so at query time too would be redundant.

Stemming

Stemming is the process of reducing inflected or sometimes derived words to their stem, base, or root form, for example, a stemming algorithm might reduce Riding and Rides, to just Ride. Stemming is done to improve search result *recall*, but at the expense of some *precision*. If you are processing general text, you will improve your search results with stemming. However, if you have text that is mostly proper nouns, such as an artist's name in MusicBrainz, then anything more than light stemming will hurt the results. If you want to improve the precision of search results but retain the recall benefits, you should consider indexing the data in two fields, one stemmed and the other not stemmed. The DisMax query parser, described in *Chapter 5, Searching*, and *Chapter 6, Search Relevancy*, can then be configured to search the stemmed field and boost by the unstemmed one via its bq or pf options.

Many stemmers will generate stemmed tokens that are not correctly spelled words, such as Bunnies becoming Bunni instead of Bunny or stemming Quote to Quot; you'll see this in Solr's Analysis screen. This is harmless since stemming is applied at both index and search times; however, it does mean that a field that is stemmed like this cannot also be used for query spellcheck, wildcard searches, or search term autocomplete—features described in later chapters. These features directly use the indexed terms.

A stemming algorithm is very language specific compared to other text analysis components; remember to visit https://cwiki.apache.org/confluence/display/solr/Language+Analysis as advised earlier for non-English text. It includes information on a Solr token filter that performs *decompounding*, which is useful for certain languages (not English).

Here are stemmers suitable for the English language:

- SnowballPorterFilterFactory: This one lets you choose among many stemmers that were generated by the so-called *Snowball* program, hence the name. It has a language attribute in which you make the implementation choice from a list. Specifying English uses the Porter2 algorithm—regarded as a slight improvement over the original. Specifying Lovins uses the Lovins algorithm for English—regarded as an improvement on Porter but too slow in its current form.

- PorterStemFilterFactory: This is the original English Porter algorithm. It is said to be twice as fast as using Snowball English.

- `KStemFilterFactory`: This English stemmer is less aggressive than Porter's algorithm. This means it will not stem in as many cases as Porter will in an effort to reduce false-positives at the expense of missing stemming opportunities. *We recommend this as the default English stemmer.*

- `EnglishMinimalStemFilterFactory`: This is a simple stemmer that only stems on typical pluralization patterns. Unlike most other stemmers, the stemmed tokens that are generated are correctly spelled words; they are the singular form. A benefit of this is that a single Solr field with this stemmer is usable for both general searches and for query term autocomplete simultaneously, thereby saving index size and making indexing faster.

Correcting and augmenting stemming

These stemmers are algorithmic instead of being based on a vetted Thesaurus for the target language. Languages have so many spelling idiosyncrasies that algorithmic stemmers are imperfect—they sometimes stem incorrectly or don't stem when they should.

If there are particularly troublesome words that get stemmed, you can prevent it by preceding the stemmer with a `KeywordMarkerFilter` with the `protected` attribute referring to a file of newline-separated tokens that should not be stemmed. An `ignoreCase` Boolean option is available too. Some stemmers have, or used to have, a `protected` attribute that worked similarly, but that old approach isn't advised any more.

If you need to augment the stemming algorithm so that you can tell it how to stem some specific words, precede the stemmer with `StemmerOverrideFilter`. It takes a `dictionary` attribute referring to a UTF8-encoded file in the `conf` directory of token pairs, one pair per line, and a tab is used to separate the input token from the output token (the desired stemmed form of the input). An `ignoreCase` Boolean option is available too. This filter will skip tokens already marked by `KeywordMarkerFilter` and it will keyword-mark all the tokens it replaces itself, so that the stemmer will skip them.

Here is a sample excerpt of an analyzer chain showing three filters in support of stemming:

```
<filter class="solr.KeywordMarkerFilterFactory"
  protected="protwords.txt" />
<filter class="solr.StemmerOverrideFilterFactory"
  dictionary="stemdict.txt" />
<filter class="solr.PorterStemFilterFactory" />
```

Processing synonyms

The purpose of synonym processing is straightforward. Someone searches using a word that wasn't in the original document but is synonymous with a word that is indexed, so you want that document to match the query. Of course, the synonym need not be strictly those identified by a Thesaurus, and they can be whatever you want, including terminology specific to your application's domain.

> The most widely known free Thesaurus is WordNet (http://wordnet.princeton.edu/). From Solr 3.4, we have the ability to read WordNet's "prolog" formatted file via a `format="wordnet"` attribute on the synonym filter. However, don't be surprised if you lose precision in the search results—it's not a clear win, for example, "Craftsman" in context might be a proper noun referring to a brand, but WordNet would make it synonymous with "artisan". Synonym processing doesn't know about context—it's simple and dumb.

Here is a sample analyzer configuration line for synonym processing:

```
<filter class="solr.SynonymFilterFactory" synonyms="synonyms.txt"
ignoreCase="true" expand="true"/>
```

The synonym reference is to a file in the `conf` directory. Set `ignoreCase` to `true` for the case-insensitive lookup of synonyms.

Before describing the `expand` option, let's consider an example. The synonyms file is processed line-by-line. Here is a sample line with an explicit mapping that uses the arrow `=>`:

```
i-pod, i pod =>ipod
```

This means that if either `i-pod` (one token) or `i` then `pod` (two tokens) are found in the incoming token stream to this filter, then they are replaced with `ipod`. There could have been multiple replacement synonyms, each of which might contain multiple tokens. Also notice that commas are what separate each synonym, which is then split by whitespace for multiple tokens. To customize the tokenization to be something more sophisticated than whitespace, there is a `tokenizerFactory` attribute, but it's rarely used.

Alternatively, you may have lines that look like this:

```
ipod, i-pod, i pod
```

These lines don't have `=>` and are interpreted differently according to the `expand` parameter. If `expand` is `true`, the line will be translated to the following explicit mapping:

```
ipod, i-pod, i pod =>ipod, i-pod, i pod
```

If `expand` is `false`, the aforementioned line will become this explicit mapping, in which the first source synonym is the replacement synonym:

```
ipod, i-pod, i pod =>ipod
```

It's okay to have multiple lines that reference the same synonyms. If a source synonym in a new rule is already found to have replacement synonyms from another rule, then those replacements are merged.

Multiword (also known as Phrase) synonyms

For multiword synonyms to work, the analysis must be applied at index time and with expansion so that both the original words and the combined word get indexed. The next section elaborates on why this is so. Also, be aware that the tokenizer and previous filters can affect the tokens that the `SynonymFilter` sees. So, depending on the configuration and hyphens, other punctuations may or may not be stripped out.

Synonym expansion at index time versus query time

If you are doing synonym expansion (have any source synonyms that map to multiple replacement synonyms or tokens), do synonym processing at either index time or query time, but not both. Doing it in both places will yield correct results but will perform slower. We recommend doing it at index time because of the following problems that occur when doing it at query time:

- A source synonym containing multiple words (for example, `i pod`) isn't recognized at query time because the query parser tokenizes on whitespace before the analyzer gets it.

- The IDF component of Lucene's scoring algorithm (discussed in *Chapter 6, Search Relevancy*) will be much higher for documents matching a synonym appearing rarely, compared to its equivalents that are common. This reduces the scoring effectiveness.

- Prefix, wildcard, and fuzzy queries aren't analyzed, and thus won't match synonyms.

However, any analysis at index time is less flexible, because any changes to the synonyms will require a complete re-index to take effect. Moreover, the index will get larger if you do index-time expansion—perhaps too large if you have a large set of synonyms such as with WordNet. It's plausible to imagine the aforementioned issues being rectified at some point. In spite of this, we usually recommend index time.

Alternatively, you could choose not to do synonym expansion. This means for a given synonym token, there is just one token that should replace it. This requires processing at both index time and query time to effectively normalize the synonymous tokens. However, since there is query-time processing, it suffers from the problems mentioned earlier (with the exception of poor scores, which isn't applicable). The benefit to this approach is that the index size would be smaller, because the number of indexed tokens is reduced.

You might also choose a blended approach to meet different goals, for example, if you have a huge index that you don't want to re-index often, but you need to respond rapidly to new synonyms, then you can put new synonyms into both a query-time synonym file and an index-time one. When a re-index finishes, you empty the query-time synonym file. You might also be fond of the query-time benefits, but due to the multiple word token issue, you decide to handle those particular synonyms at index time.

Working with stop words

There is a simple filter called `StopFilterFactory` that filters out certain so-called stop words specified in a file in the `conf` directory, optionally ignoring case. The example usage is as follows:

```
<filter class="solr.StopFilterFactory" words="stopwords.txt"
ignoreCase="true"/>
```

When used, it is present in both index and query analyzer chains.

For indexes with lots of text, common uninteresting words such as "the", "a", and so on, make the index large and slow down phrase queries that use them. A simple solution to this problem is to filter them out of the fields in which they often show up. Fields likely to contain more than a sentence are ideal candidates. Our MusicBrainz schema does not have content like this. The trade-off when omitting stop words from the index is that those words are no longer queryable. This is usually fine, but in some circumstances like searching for `To be or not to be`, it is obviously a problem.

The ideal solution to the common word problem is not to remove them. *Chapter 10, Scaling Solr*, discusses an approach called common-grams implemented with `CommonGramsFilterFactory` that can be used to improve phrase search performance, while keeping these words. It is highly recommended.

Solr comes with a decent set of stop words for the English language. You may want to supplement it or use a different list altogether, if you're indexing non-English text. In order to determine which words appear commonly in your index, access the **Schema Browser** menu option in Solr's admin interface. All of your fields will appear in a drop-down list on the form. In case the list does not appear at once, be patient. For large indexes, there is a considerable delay before the field list appears because Solr is analyzing the data in your index. Now, choose a field that you know contains a lot of text. In the main viewing area, you'll see a variety of statistics about the field, including the top 10 terms appearing most frequently. If you can't see the term info by default, click on the **Load Term Info** button and select the **Autoload** checkbox.

You can also manage synonyms and stop words via a REST API using `ManagedSynonymFilterFactory` and `ManagedStopFilterFactory` respectively. You can read more and find sample configurations at `https://cwiki.apache.org/confluence/display/solr/Managed+Resources`.

Phonetic analysis

Another useful text analysis option to enable searches that sound like a queried word is phonetic translation. A filter is used at both index and query time that phonetically encodes each word into a phoneme-based word. There are many phonetic encoding algorithms to choose from: `BeiderMorse`, `Caverphone`, `Cologne`, `DoubleMetaphone`, `Metaphone`, `RefinedSoundex`, and `Soundex`. We suggest using `DoubleMetaphone` for most text, and definitely `BeiderMorse` for names. However, you might want to experiment in order to make your own choice.

Solr has three tools for more aggressive inexact searching: phonetic, query spellchecking, and fuzzy searching. These are all employed a bit differently.

The following code shows how to configure text analysis for phonetic matching using the DoubleMetaphone encoding in the schema.xml file:

```
<!-- for phonetic (sounds-like) indexing -->
<fieldType name="phonetic" class="solr.TextField"
    positionIncrementGap="100">
  <analyzer>
      <tokenizer class="solr.StandardTokenizerFactory"/>
      <filter class="solr.DoubleMetaphoneFilterFactory"
          inject="false" maxCodeLength="8"/>
  </analyzer>
</fieldType>
```

The previous example uses the DoubleMetaphoneFilterFactory analysis filter, which has the following two options:

- inject: This is a Boolean defaulting to true that will cause the original words to pass through the filter. It might interfere with other filter options, querying, and potentially scoring. Therefore, it is preferred to disable this, and use a separate field dedicated to phonetic indexing.

- maxCodeLength: This is the maximum phoneme code (that is, phonetic character or syllable) length. It defaults to 4. Longer codes are truncated. Only DoubleMetaphone supports this option.

Note that the phonetic encoders internally handle both uppercase and lowercase, so there's no need to add a lowercase filter.

In the MusicBrainz schema that is supplied with the book, a field named a_phonetic is declared to use BeiderMorse because that encoding is best for names. The field has the artist name copied into it through a copyField directive. In *Chapter 5, Searching*, you will read about the DisMax query parser that can conveniently search across multiple fields with different scoring boosts. It can be configured to search not only the artist name (a_name) field, but also a_phonetic with a low boost so that regular exact matches will come above those that match phonetically.

Here is how BeiderMorse is configured:

```
<fieldType name="phonetic" class="solr.TextField"
  positionIncrementGap="100">
  <analyzer type="index">
    <tokenizer class="solr.StandardTokenizerFactory"/>
    <!-- ... potentially others ... -->
    <filter class="solr.BeiderMorseFilterFactory"
      ruleType="APPROX"/>
  </analyzer>
```

```
<analyzer type="query">
  <tokenizer class="solr.StandardTokenizerFactory"/>
  <filter class="solr.BeiderMorseFilterFactory"
    ruleType="EXACT"/>
</analyzer>
</fieldType>
```

Notice the difference in `ruleType` between the query and index analyzers. In order to use most of the phonetic encoding algorithms, you must use the following filter:

```
<filter class="solr.PhoneticFilterFactory"
encoder="RefinedSoundex" inject="false"/>
```

The `encoder` attribute must be one of those algorithms listed in the first paragraph of this section, with the exception of `DoubleMetaphone` and `BeiderMorse`, which have dedicated filter factories.

 Try Solr's Analysis admin page to see how variations in text change (or don't change) the phonemes that are indexed and searched.

Substring indexing and wildcards

Usually, the text indexing technology is employed to search entire words. Occasionally, however, there arises a need for a query to match an arbitrary substring of an indexed word or across them. Solr supports wildcards on queries (for example, `mus*ainz`), but there is some consideration needed in the way data is indexed.

It's useful to first get a sense of how Lucene handles a wildcard query at the index level. Lucene internally scans the sorted terms list on disk starting with the nonwildcard prefix (`mus` in the previous example). One thing to note about this is that the query takes exponentially longer for each fewer prefix character. In fact, Solr configures Lucene to not accept a leading wildcard to ameliorate the problem. Another thing to note is that stemming, phonetic, and other trivial text analysis will interfere with these kinds of searches, for example, if `running` is stemmed to `run`, then `runni*` would not match.

 Before employing these approaches, consider whether you really need better tokenization for special codes, for example, if you have a long string code that internally has different parts that users might search in separately, then you can use a `PatternReplaceFilterFactory` with some other analyzers to split them up.

ReversedWildcardFilter

Solr doesn't permit a leading wildcard in a query unless you index the text in a reverse direction in addition to the forward direction. Doing this will also improve query performance when the wildcard is very close to the front. The following example configuration should appear at the end of the index analyzer chain:

```
<filter class="solr.ReversedWildcardFilterFactory" />
```

It has several performance-tuning options you can investigate further at its Javadocs, available at http://lucene.apache.org/solr/api/org/apache/solr/analysis/ReversedWildcardFilterFactory.html, but the defaults are reasonable.

Solr does not support a query with both a leading and trailing wildcard for performance reasons. Given our explanation of the internals, we hope you understand why.

N-gram analysis

N-gram analysis slices text into many smaller substrings ranging between a minimum and maximum configured size, for example, consider the word "Tonight". An NGramFilterFactory configured with minGramSize of 2 and maxGramSize of 5 would yield all of the following indexed terms: (2-grams:) To, on, ni, ig, gh, ht, (3-grams:) Ton, oni, nig, igh, ght, (4-grams:) Toni, onig, nigh, ight, (5-grams:) Tonig, onigh, night. Note that "Tonight" fully does not pass through because it has more characters than the maxGramSize. N-gram analysis can be used as a token filter, and it can also be used as a tokenizer with NGramTokenizerFactory, which will emit n-grams spanning across the words of the entire source text.

The term **n-gram** can be ambiguous. Outside of Lucene, it is more commonly defined as word-based substrings, not character based. Lucene calls this **shingling** and you'll learn how to use that in *Chapter 10, Scaling Solr*.

The following is a suggested analyzer configuration using n-grams to match substrings:

```
<fieldType name="nGram" class="solr.TextField"
        positionIncrementGap="100">
    <analyzer type="index">
        <tokenizer class="solr.StandardTokenizerFactory"/>
        <!-- potentially word delimiter, synonym filter, stop
          words, NOT stemming -->
        <filter class="solr.LowerCaseFilterFactory"/>
```

```
    <filter class="solr.NGramFilterFactory" minGramSize="2"
        maxGramSize="15"/>
  </analyzer>
  <analyzer type="query">
    <tokenizer class="solr.StandardTokenizerFactory"/>
    <!-- potentially word delimiter, synonym filter, stop
      words, NOT stemming -->
    <filter class="solr.LowerCaseFilterFactory"/>
  </analyzer>
</fieldType>
```

Notice that the n-gramming only happens at index time. The range of gram sizes goes from the smallest number of characters you wish to enable substring searches on (2 in this example), to the maximum size permitted for substring searches (15 in this example).

Apply this analysis to a field created solely for the purpose of matching substrings. Another field should exist for typical searches, and configure the DisMax query parser, described in *Chapter 5, Searching*, for searches to use both fields using a smaller boost for this field.

Another variation is EdgeNGramTokenizerFactory and EdgeNGramFilterFactory, which emit n-grams that are adjacent to either the start or end of the input text. For the filter-factory, this input-text is a token, and for the tokenizer, it is the entire input. In addition to minGramSize and maxGramSize, these analyzers take a side argument that is either front or back. If only prefix or suffix matching is needed instead of both, then an EdgeNGram analyzer is for you.

N-gram costs

There is a high price to be paid for n-gramming. Recall that in the earlier example, Tonight was split into 15 substring terms, whereas typical analysis would probably leave only one. This translates to greater index sizes, and thus a longer time to index. Let's look at the effects of this in the MusicBrainz schema. The a_name field, which contains the artist name, is indexed in a typical fashion and is a stored field. The a_ngram field is fed by the artist name and is indexed with n-grams ranging from 2 to 15 characters in length. It is not a stored field because the artist name is already stored in a_name.

	a_name	a_name + a_ngram	Increase
Indexing Time	46 seconds	479 seconds	> 10x
Disk Size	11.7 MB	59.7 MB	> 5x
Distinct Terms	203,431	1,288,720	> 6x

The preceding table shows a comparison of index statistics of an index with just a_name versus both a_name and a_ngram. Note the ten-fold increase in indexing time for the artist name, and a five-fold increase in disk space. Remember that this is just one field!

> Given these costs, n-gramming, if used at all, is generally only done on a field or two of small size where there is a clear requirement for *fast* substring matches.

The costs of n-gramming are lower if minGramSize is raised and to a lesser extent if maxGramSize is lowered. Edge n-gramming costs less too. This is because it is only based on one side. It definitely costs more to use the tokenizer-based n-grammers instead of the term-based filters used in the example before, because terms are generated that include and span whitespace. However, with such indexing, it is possible to match a substring spanning words.

Sorting text

Usually, search results are sorted by relevancy via the score pseudo-field, but it is common to need to support conventional sorting by field values too. And, in addition to sorting search results, there are ramifications to this discussion in doing a range query and when showing facet results in a sorted order.

> **Sorting limitations**
>
> A field needs to be indexed, not be multivalued, and for text, it should not have multiple tokens (either there is no text analysis or it yields just one token).

It just so happens that MusicBrainz already supplies alternative artist and label names for sorting. When different from the original name, these sortable versions move words like "The" from the beginning to the end after a comma. We've marked the sort names as indexed but not stored since we're going to sort on it but not display it—deviating from what MusicBrainz does. Remember that indexed and stored are true by default. Because of the special text analysis restrictions of fields used for sorting, text fields in your schema that need to be sortable will usually be copied to another field and analyzed differently. The copyField directive in the schema facilitates this task. The string type is a type that has no text analysis and so it's perfect for our MusicBrainz case. As we're getting a sort-specific value from MusicBrainz, we don't need to derive something ourselves.

However, note that in the MusicBrainz schema there are no sort-specific release names, so let's add sorting support. One option is to use the `string` type again. That's fine, but you may want to lowercase the text, remove punctuation, and collapse multiple spaces into one (if the data isn't clean). You can even use `PatternReplaceFilterFactory` to move words like "The" to the end. It's up to you. For the sake of variety in our example, we'll be taking the latter route; we're using a type `title_sort` that does these kinds of things.

By the way, Lucene sorts text by the internal Unicode code point. You probably won't notice any problem with the sort order. If you want sorting that is more accurate to the finer rules of various languages (English included), you should try `CollationKeyFilterFactory`. Since it isn't commonly used and it's already well documented, we'll refer you to the wiki page `https://cwiki.apache.org/confluence/display/solr/Language+Analysis#LanguageAnalysis-UnicodeCollation`.

Miscellaneous token filters

Solr includes many more token filters:

- `ClassicFilterFactory`: (It was formerly named `StandardFilter` prior to Solr 3.1.) This filter works in conjunction with `ClassicTokenizer`. It will remove periods in between acronyms and `'s` at the end of terms:

  `"I.B.M. cat's" => "IBM", "cat"`

- `EnglishPossessiveFilterFactory`: This removes the trailing `'s`.

- `TrimFilterFactory`: This removes leading and trailing whitespace. We recommend doing this sort of thing before text analysis, same as using `TrimFieldUpdateProcessorFactory` (see *Chapter 4, Indexing Data*).

- `LowerCaseFilterFactory`: This lowercases all text. Don't put this before `WordDelimeterFilterFactory` if you want to split on case transitions.

- `KeepWordFilterFactory`: This filter omits all of the words, except those in the specified file:

  ```
  <filter class="solr.KeepWordFilterFactory"
  words="keepwords.txt" ignoreCase="true"/>
  ```

  If you want to ensure a certain vocabulary of words in a special field, you might enforce it with this.

- `LengthFilterFactory`: This filters out the terms that do not have a length within an inclusive range. The following is an example:

  ```
  <filter class="solr.LengthFilterFactory" min="2" max="5" />
  ```

- `LimitTokenCountFilterFactory`: This filter caps the number of tokens passing through to that specified in the `maxTokenCount` attribute. Even without any hard limits, you are effectively limited by the memory allocated to Java—reach that and Solr will throw an error.

- `RemoveDuplicatesTokenFilterFactory`: This ensures that no duplicate terms appear at the same position. This can happen, for example, when synonyms stem to a common root. It's a good idea to add this to your last analysis step if you are doing a fair amount of other analysis.

- `ASCIIFoldingFilterFactory`: See `MappingCharFilterFactory` in the earlier *Character filters* section for more information on this filter.

- `CapitalizationFilterFactory`: This filter capitalizes each word according to the rules that you specify. For more information, see the Javadocs at `http://lucene.apache.org/core/4_10_4/analyzers-common/org/apache/lucene/analysis/miscellaneous/CapitalizationFilterFactory.html`.

- `PatternReplaceFilterFactory`: This takes a regular expression and replaces the matches. Take a look at the following example:

```
<filter class="solr.PatternReplaceFilterFactory"
pattern=".*@(.*)"
        replacement="$1" replace="first" />
```

This example is for processing an e-mail address field to get only the domain of the address. This replacement happens to be a reference to a regular expression group, but it might be any old string. If the `replace` attribute is set to `first`, then only the first match is replaced; if `replace` is `all`, the default, then all matches are replaced.

- **Write your own**: Writing your own filter is an option if the existing ones don't suffice. Crack open the source code to Lucene for one of these to get a handle on what's involved. Before you head down this path though, you'd be surprised at what a little creativity with `PatternReplaceFilterFactory` and some of the others can offer you. For starters, check out the `rType` field type in the `schema.xml` that is supplied online with this book.

There are some other miscellaneous Solr filters we didn't mention for various reasons. For common-grams or shingling, see *Chapter 10, Scaling Solr*. See the all known implementing classes section at the top of `http://lucene.apache.org/core/4_10_4/analyzers-common/org/apache/lucene/analysis/util/TokenFilterFactory.html` for a complete list of token filter factories, including documentation.

The multilingual search

If you have text in various languages, the main issues you have to think about are the same issues for working with any one language—how to analyze content, configure fields, define search defaults, and so on. In this section, we present three approaches to integrate linguistic analysis into Solr.

The multifield approach

With this approach, you will need to create one field per language for all the searchable text fields. As part of your indexing process, you can identify the language and apply the relevant analyzers, tokenizers, and token filters for each of those fields. The following diagram represents how each of the documents in your index will have language-specific fields:

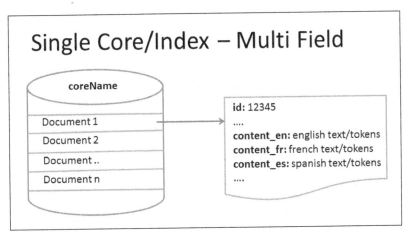

The following are the pros:

- As you have separate fields for each language, searching, filtering, and/or faceting will be easy
- You will have accurate and meaningful relevancy scores (TF/IDF)

The following are the cons:

- The number of fields will increase with the number of languages.
- Query performance will be affected when you search across many languages and fields. However, this may not be a concern if you are searching for a specific language.

The multicore approach

As represented in the following diagram, the second approach uses one core (or shard) per language. Each core will contain documents of the same language. As part of the indexing process, you will need to identify the language of each document and index into the appropriate core. Language-specific analyzers, tokenizers and token filters will still be required.

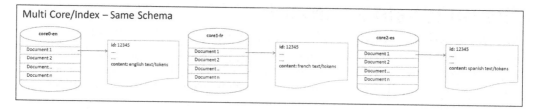

The following are the pros:

- The field names are the same in all the cores, which simplifies query-time processing, and it's easy to search, filter, and facet by language.

- As you have separate cores per language, you will have flexibility in adding or removing specific languages without affecting other cores.

The following are the cons:

- There is overhead in maintaining multiple cores.

- If you make copies of the multilingual documents on every core whose language matches one of the languages of the documents, there is a high possibility that a distributed search query will bring back the same original document from multiple cores, which will show as duplicates to the user.

- **Term frequency** (TF) counts are per core, so if search results are being pulled from multiple queries, you have to decide how to merge the relevancy scores presented by each core. Solr will do a basic merge for you, but it may not be what you expect.

The single field approach

The following diagram represents the third approach, which is to have a single field for all languages that you want to support. The simplest way to implement this as described here is to use `ICUTokenizerFactory` provided by ICU4J in `contrib/analysis-extras`. Alternatively, you can write a custom analyzer that analyzes differently depending on the language of the text, but that is very complex and has its own pros/cons.

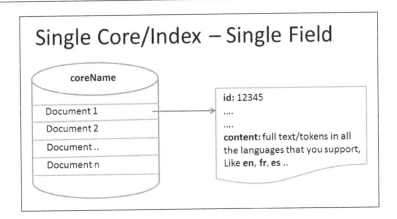

The following are the pros:

- A single universal field makes the indexing and search process easy.
- Having a single field for indexing should keep the indexing throughput high; and likewise for searching.
- Adding languages doesn't require schema changes or additional cores.

The following are the cons:

- You can't use any of the stemmers, as they are language specific. Not stemming hurts recall in search results. You can't remove stop words either, as this is also language specific.
- As all of the languages are in the same field, a document's relevancy (TF/IDF) score (described in *Chapter 6, Search Relevancy*) may be poor.

Summary

Text analysis provides forward-thinking organizations with a framework to maximize the value of information within large quantities of text. It also helps automate the process by extracting relevant information, interpreting, mining, and structuring information to improve findability, reveal patterns, sentiments and relationships among documents.

At this point, you've learned about different types of analyzers, tokenizers, token filters and their configuration settings, which helps us convert unstructured data/text into terms in a Lucene Index. You've also learned about the approaches for supporting multilingual search using Solr.

In the next chapter, you'll learn about the various ways to import data into Solr.

4

Indexing Data

In this chapter, we're going to explore ways to get data into Solr. The process of doing this is referred to as **indexing**, although the term **importing** is also used.

This chapter is structured as follows:

- Communicating with Solr
- Sending data using Solr's Update-XML, JSON, and CSV formats
- Commit, optimize, and rollback the transaction log
- Atomic updates and optimistic concurrency
- Importing content from a database or XML using Solr's **DataImportHandler (DIH)**
- Extracting text from rich documents through Solr's ExtractingRequestHandler (also known as Solr Cell)
- Post-processing documents with UpdateRequestProcessors

You will also find some related options in *Chapter 9, Integrating Solr*, that have to do with language bindings and framework integration, including a web crawler. Most use Solr's Update-XML format.

In a hurry?

There are many approaches to indexing, and you don't need to be well versed in all of them. The section on commit and optimize is important for everyone because it is universal. If you plan to use a Solr integration framework that handles indexing data, such as Sunspot for Ruby on Rails, then you can follow the documentation for that framework and skip this chapter for now. Otherwise, the DataImportHandler will likely satisfy your needs.

Communicating with Solr

There are quite a few options when it comes to importing data into Solr. In this section, we'll examine a few of those, and then follow up with interaction examples. Details on specific formats, such as Solr's Update-XML, will come later.

The following diagram represents the high-level workflow of the indexing process in Solr. In addition to the predefined importing mechanisms, you can also build custom import handlers. Before generating the index, Solr uses the field definitions and other configurations from `schema.xml` and `solrconfig.xml` to process the data for each field.

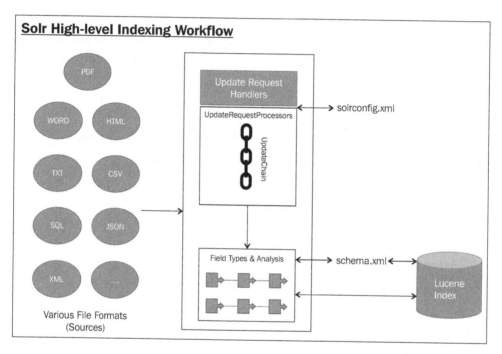

Using direct HTTP or a convenient client API

Most applications interact with Solr over HTTP. This can either be done using a typical HTTP client, or indirectly via a Solr integration API such as SolrJ or Sunspot. Such APIs are discussed in *Chapter 9, Integrating Solr*.

 Another option is to embed Solr into your Java application instead of running it as a server. The SolrJ API is conveniently used for both remote and embedded use. More information about SolrJ and Embedded Solr can be found in *Chapter 9, Integrating Solr*.

Pushing data to Solr or have Solr pull it

Even though an application will be communicating with Solr over HTTP, it does not have to include the documents to be indexed in the request. Solr supports what it calls **remote streaming** in which it's given a URL to the data. It might be an HTTP URL, but it's more likely to be a filesystem-based URL, applicable when the data is already on Solr's machine or a locally accessible filesystem. This option avoids the overhead of sending documents over HTTP. Another way to ask Solr to pull data is to use the DataImportHandler (DIH), which can pull data from a database and other sources. The DIH offers an extensible framework that can be adapted to custom data sources.

Data formats

The following are various data formats for indexing data into Solr:

- **Solr's Update-XML**: Solr accepts documents that are expressed in XML conforming to a simple Solr-specific format. This XML option also has support for commands such as delete, commit, and optimize.

  Other XML: Any arbitrary XML can be given to Solr along with an XSLT file that Solr will use to translate the XML to the Update-XML format for further processing. There is a short example of this in the *Importing XML from a file with XSLT* section, by way of comparison.

- **Solr's Update-JSON**: This is a **JavaScript Object Notation (JSON)** variation of Solr's Update-XML. For more details, see `https://cwiki.apache.org/confluence/display/solr/Indexing+and+Basic+Data+Operations`.

- **Java-Bin**: This is an efficient binary variation of Solr's Update-XML. Officially, only the SolrJ client API supports this, but there is a third-party Ruby port too.

- **CSV**: A comma (or other character) separated value format.

- **Rich documents**: Most user file formats such as PDF, XLS, DOC, and PPT; text; and metadata are extracted from these formats and put into various Solr fields. This is enabled via the Solr Cell contrib module.

The DataImportHandler contrib module is a flexible data import framework. It has out-of-the-box support for dealing with arbitrary XML and even e-mail. It is commonly used for pulling data from relational databases. For some enterprises, it might be more appropriate to integrate **Solr** with **Apache Camel**, a versatile open-source integration framework based on well-known Enterprise Integration Patterns. It provides a nice **Domain Specific Language (DSL)** for wiring together different data sources, performing transformations, and finally sending data to Solr. For more details, see `http://camel.apache.org/solr.html`.

We'll demonstrate Solr's capability to import MusicBrainz data in XML, CSV, and from a database. Other examples will include rich document importing via the DIH and Solr Cell. Most likely, an application would use just one format.

Before these approaches are described, we'll discuss remote streaming—a foundational topic.

Solr's HTTP POST options

Solr receives commands and possibly documents through HTTP POST.

Solr lets you use HTTP GET too, such as direct web browser access. However, this is an inappropriate HTTP verb for anything other than retrieving data and the size of the request is limited in most of the web servers, hence too long requests are not processed correctly. For more information on this concept, read about REST at http://en.wikipedia.org/wiki/Representational_State_Transfer.

One way to send an HTTP POST is through the Unix command-line program curl (also available on Windows through Cygwin: http://www.cygwin.com). An alternative is cross-platform import tool that comes with Solr is post.jar (also known as SimplePostTool) located in Solr's example/solr directory. To get some basic guidance on how to use it, run the following command:

```
>> java -jar example/solr/post.jar -help
```

You'll see in a bit that you can post name-value pair options as HTML form data. However, post.jar doesn't support that, so you'll have to specify the URL and put the options in the query string.

The post.jar tool also has an automode, which guesses the content type for you, and also sets a default ID and filename when sending to Solr. Also, a recursive option lets you automatically post a whole directory (including the subdirectories).

For the next set of examples, we'll use the command-line program curl.

There are several ways to tell Solr to index data, and all of them are through HTTP POST:

- Send the data as the entire POST payload. The curl program can do this with --data-binary (among other ways) and an appropriate content-type header for whatever the format is.

- Send name-value pairs akin to an HTML form submission. With `curl`, such pairs are preceded by `-F`. If you're giving data to Solr to be indexed as opposed to it looking for data in a database, then there are a few ways to do that:

    ○ Put the data into the `stream.body` parameter. If it's small, perhaps less than a megabyte, this approach is fine. The limit is configured with the `multipartUploadLimitInKB` setting in `solrconfig.xml`, defaulting to 2 GB. If you're tempted to increase this limit, you should reconsider your approach.

    ○ Refer to the data through either a local file on the Solr server using the `stream.file` parameter or a URL that Solr will fetch through the `stream.url` parameter. These choices are a feature that Solr calls **remote streaming**.

Here is an example of the first choice. Let's say we have a Solr Update-XML file named `artists.xml` in the current directory. We can post it to Solr using the following command line:

```
>> curl http://localhost:8983/solr/mbartists/update -H
'Content-type:text/xml; charset=utf-8' --data-binary
@artists.xml
```

If it succeeds, you'll have output that looks like this:

```
<?xml version="1.0" encoding="UTF-8"?>
<response>
<lst name="responseHeader">
    <int name="status">0</int><int name="QTime">128</int>
</lst>
</response>
```

To use the `stream.body` feature for the preceding example, do the following:

```
curl http://localhost:8983/solr/mbartists/update -F
stream.body=@artists.xml
```

In both cases, the `@` character instructs `curl` to get the data from the file instead of being `@artists.xml` literally. If the XML is short, you can just as easily specify it, literally, on the command line:

```
curl http://localhost:8983/solr/mbartists/update -F
stream.body=' <commit />'
```

Notice the leading space in the value. This was intentional. In this example, curl treats @ and < to mean things we don't want. In this case, it might be more appropriate to use form-string instead of -F. However, it requires more typing, and we're feeling lazy.

Remote streaming

In the preceding examples, we've given Solr the data to index in the HTTP message. Alternatively, the POST request can give Solr a pointer to the data in the form of either a file path accessible to Solr or an HTTP URL to it.

 The file path is relative to the server running Solr, not the client. Additionally, the files must have the proper filesystem permissions so that Solr can access them.

Just as in the earlier case, the originating request does not return a response until Solr has finished processing it. If the file is of a decent size or is already at some known URL, then you may find remote streaming faster and/or more convenient, depending on your situation.

Here is an example of Solr accessing a local file:

```
curl http://localhost:8983/solr/mbartists/update -F
stream.file=/tmp/artists.xml
```

To use a URL, the parameter would change to stream.url, and we'd specify a URL. We're passing a name-value parameter (stream.file and the path), not the actual data.

 Security risk

Use of remote streaming (stream.file or stream.url) is enabled by default in solrconfig.xml with the enableRemoteStreaming setting. This can be considered a security risk; so only keep it on if Solr is protected. See *Chapter 11, Deployment*, for more information.

Solr's Update-XML format

Using XML, you can send add, `commit`, `optimize`, and `delete` commands
to Solr. Here is an XML sample for sending HTTP POST to Solr; this will add
(or replace) documents:

```
<add overwrite="true">
  <doc boost="2.0">
    <field name="id">Artist:11650</field>
    <field name="type">Artist</field>
    <field name="a_name" boost="0.5">The Smashing Pumpkins</field>
    <!-- the date/time syntax MUST look just like this -->
    <field name="a_begin_date">2007-12-31T09:40:00Z</field>
  </doc>
  <doc>
    <field name="id">Artist:11651</field>
    <field name="type">Artist</field>
    <field name="a_begin_date">2007-12-31T09:40:00Z</field>
  </doc>
  <!-- more doc elements here as needed -->
</add>
```

> A valid XML document has one root element. If you want to send
> multiple XML-based commands to Solr in the same message/file,
> you can wrap the commands in an arbitrarily named root element.

If you have a field in your schema defined as unique, and the `overwrite` attribute is
set to `true` (the default), an incoming document will replace an existing document
when both documents have the same unique field value.

> If you are sure that you will be adding a document that is not a
> duplicate, then you can set `overwrite` to `false` to get a small
> performance improvement, since Solr won't check uniqueness
> of the unique key field.

The `boost` attribute affects the scoring of search results at query time. Providing a
boost value, whether at the document or field level, is optional. The default value is
`1.0`, which is effectively a nonboost. Technically, documents are boosted at the field
level. The effective boost value for a field is the document boost, multiplied by the
field boost value.

Specifying boosts here is called **index-time** boosting, which is rarely done as compared to the more flexible **query-time** boosting. Index-time boosting is less flexible because such boosting decisions must be decided at index-time and will apply to all of the queries. You'll learn more about boosting and scoring in *Chapter 6, Search Relevancy*.

Deleting documents

You can delete a document by its unique field and value. Here, we delete two documents:

```
<delete><id>Artist:11604</id><id>Artist:11603</id></delete>
```

A query can provide a more flexible way to specify which documents are to be deleted:

```
<delete><query>timestamp:[* TO NOW-12HOUR]</query></delete>
```

The previous delete query would delete all documents whose timestamps are *older* than 12 hours from the current time. More info on querying Solr can be found in *Chapter 5, Searching*.

The contents of the delete tag can be any number of id and query tags, so you can batch many deletions into one message to Solr.

 If you want to delete the entire index during development (or perform major schema changes in production), simply delete the data directory while Solr is shut down.

Commit, optimize, and rollback the transaction log

Data sent to Solr is not immediately searchable, nor do deletions take immediate effect. Like a database, changes must be committed. There are two types of commits:

- **Hard commit**: This is expensive because it pushes the changes to the filesystem (making them persistent) and has a significant performance impact. This is performed by the <autoCommit> option in solrconfig.xml or by adding commit=true request parameter to a Solr update URL.

- **Soft commit**: This is less expensive but is not persistent. This is performed by the <autoSoftCommit> option in solrconfig.xml or using the softCommit=true option along with the commit parameter or by using the commitWithin parameter.

The request to Solr could be the same request that contains data to be indexed then committed, or an empty request—it doesn't matter. For example, you can visit this URL to issue a commit on our `mbreleases` core: `http://localhost:8983/solr/mbreleases/update?commit=true`. You can also commit changes using the XML syntax by simply sending this to Solr:

```
<commit />
```

There are three important things to know about commits that are unique to Solr:

- Commits are slow. Depending on the index size and disk hardware, Solr's auto-warming configuration, and Solr's cache state prior to committing, a commit can take a considerable amount of time. With a lot of warming configured, it can take a number of minutes in extreme cases. To learn how to decrease this time, read about real-time search in *Chapter 10, Scaling Solr*.

- There is no *transaction isolation*. This means that if more than one Solr client were to submit modifications and commit them at overlapping times, it is possible for part of one client's set of changes to be committed before that client told Solr to commit. This applies to *rollback* as well. If this is a problem for your application, then consider using one client process that is responsible for updating Solr.

- Simultaneous commits should be avoided, particularly more than two. The problem actually pertains to simultaneous query warming, which is the latter and lengthy part of a commit. Solr will use a lot of resources and it might even yield an error indicating there is too much simultaneous warming—though the commit will eventually still have its effect.

When you are bulk-loading data, these concerns are not an issue since you're going to issue a final commit at the end. But if Solr is asynchronously updated by independent clients in response to changed data, commits could come too quickly and might overlap. To address this, Solr has two similar features, **autoCommit** and **commitWithin**. The first refers to a snippet of XML configuration that is commented in `solrconfig.xml`, in which Solr will automatically commit at a document-count threshold or time-lapse threshold (time of oldest uncommitted document). In this case, Solr itself handles committing and so your application needn't send commits. `commitWithin` is a similar time-lapse option that is set by the client on either the `<add commitWithin="...">` element or the `<commit commitWithin="..."/>` element of an XML formatted update message or a request parameter by the same name. It will ensure a commit occurs within the specified number of milliseconds. Here's an example of a 30-second commit window:

```
<commit commitWithin="30000"/>
```

Since Solr 4.0, the `commitWithin` performs a soft-commit, which prevents the slaves from replicating the changes in a master/slave configuration. However, this default behavior can be overwritten in `solrconfig.xml` by enabling the `forceHardCommit` option to allow `commitWithin` to perform hard commits.

Don't overlap commits

During indexing, you may find that you are starting to see this error message:

```
<h2>HTTP ERROR: 503</h2><pre>Error opening new searcher. exceeded
limit of maxWarmingSearchers=2, try again later.</pre>
```

Every time a commit happens, a new searcher is created, which invokes the searcher warm up process for populating the cache, and that can take a while. While you can bump up the `maxWarmingSearchers` parameter in `solrconfig.xml`, *you shouldn't* since you could still hit the new limit, but worse is that memory requirements can soar and the system will slow down when multiple searchers are warming. So, you need to ensure commits aren't happening concurrently – or, if you must, that there are no more than two. If you see this problem, you should use the **autoCommit** or **commitWithin** parameter when issuing commits. In both cases, you need to choose a time window that is long enough for a commit to finish.

> **commitWithin is preferable to autoCommit**
>
> The commitWithin feature is preferable to the autoCommit feature in `solrconfig.xml` because the latter is global and can't be disabled.

Index optimization

Lucene's index is internally composed of one or more **segments**. When a buffer of indexed documents gets flushed to the disk, it creates a new segment. Deletes get recorded in another file, but they go to disk too. Sometimes, after a new segment is written, Lucene will merge some of them together. When Lucene has just one segment, it is in an **optimized** state. The more segments there are, the more query performance will degrade. Of course, optimizing an index comes at a cost; the larger your index is, the longer it will take to optimize. Finally, an `optimize` command implies commit semantics. You may specify an `optimize` command in all the places you specify a commit. So, to use it in a URL, try this: `http://localhost:8983/solr/mbreleases/update?optimize=true`. For the XML format, simply send this:

```
<optimize />
```

We recommend explicitly optimizing the index at an opportune time, such as after a bulk load of data and/or a daily interval in off-peak hours, if there are low-volume sporadic updates to the index. *Chapter 10, Scaling Solr* has a tip on optimizing to more than one segment if the optimizes are taking too long.

Both commit and optimize commands take two additional Boolean options that default to `true`:

```
<optimize waitFlush="true" waitSearcher="true"/>
```

If you were to set these to `false`, then commit and optimize commands return immediately, even though the operation hasn't actually finished yet. So, if you write a script that commits with these at their false values and then executes a query against Solr, you might find that the search does not reflect the changes yet. By waiting for the data to flush to the disk (`waitFlush`) and waiting for a new searcher to be ready to respond to changes (`waitSearcher`), this circumstance is avoided. These options are useful for executing an optimize command from a script that simply wants to optimize the index and otherwise doesn't care when newly added data is searchable.

 No matter how long a commit or optimize command takes, Solr still executes searches concurrently — there is no read lock. However, query latency may be impacted.

Rolling back an uncommitted change

There is one final indexing command to discuss — `rollback`. All uncommitted changes can be canceled by sending Solr the `rollback` command either via a URL parameter such as `http://localhost:8983/solr/mbreleases/update?rollback=true` or with the following XML code:

```
<rollback />
```

The transaction log

When the transaction log (tlogs) are enabled via the `updateLog` feature in `solrconfig.xml`, Solr writes the raw documents into the tlog files for recovery purposes. Transaction logs are used for **near real-time (NRT)** get, durability, and SolrCloud replication recovery.

To enable tlogs, simply add the following code to your `updateHandler` configuration:

```
<updateLog>
  <str name="dir">${solr.ulog.dir:}</str>
</updateLog>
```

Here, `dir` represents the target directory for transaction logs. This defaults to the Solr `data` directory.

> If you don't need NRT get feature and you are not using SolrCloud, you can safely comment-out the `updateLog` section in `solrconfig.xml`. For more details about NRT get, see `https://cwiki.apache.org/confluence/display/solr/RealTime+Get`.

Atomic updates and optimistic concurrency

Atomic updates allow you to update an already indexed document by giving a new field value, adding a value to the existing values on a multivalued field, or by incrementing a numeric field. Instead of giving an entire document, you supply a document that only has the fields that are to be modified in some way, and with a special modifier (described next). If Solr sees these modifiers on any field in an incoming document, then it knows this is an atomic-update to an existing document versus a new or replacement document. This is both a convenience feature, and with optimistic concurrency (described soon), allows Solr to be a credible NoSQL option.

We'll show you how this is used by way of a succinct example, and we'll use JSON this time. Note that, most fields don't just have a value but are structured to include one of several mutation modifiers. In the XML syntax, these are specified with attributes.

```
{"id":"mydoc",
 "price":{"set":99},
 "popularity":{"inc":20},
 "categories":{"add":["toys","games"]},
 "promo_ids":{"remove":"a123x"},
 "tags":{"remove":["free_to_try","on_sale"]}
}
```

The following are the key points to remember while using atomic updates:

- The core functionality of atomically updating a document requires that all fields in your SchemaXml must be configured as `stored="true"` except for fields that are `<copyField/>` destinations, which must be configured as `stored="false"`. This is because the atomic updates are applied to the document represented by the existing stored field values.

- An `<updateLog/>` must be configured in your `solrconfig.xml` in order for atomic document updates to be used. This is necessary to ensure that the update instructions are applied to the most recently indexed version of the document even if that version has not yet been committed.

Optimistic concurrency can be used by applications that update or replace documents to ensure that the document they are updating or replacing has not been concurrently modified by another application. This feature works by requiring a _version_ field on all documents in the index, and comparing that to a _version_ specified as part of the `update` command. By default, Solr's `schema.xml` includes a _version_ field, and this field is automatically added to each new document. Along with NRT get and atomic updates, this feature allows Solr to be used as a NoSQL database.

For examples of using atomic updates and optimistic concurrency, see `https://cwiki.apache.org/confluence/display/solr/Updating+Parts+of+Documents`.

Sending CSV-formatted data to Solr

If you have data in a CSV format or if it is more convenient for you to get CSV than XML or JSON, then you may prefer the CSV option. Solr's CSV support is fairly flexible. You won't be able to specify an index-time boost but that's an uncommon need.

CSV is uniquely the only format that Solr supports for _round-tripping_ data. As such, you can query for CSV-formatted data that is suitable to be added right back into Solr (for stored fields only, of course). The XML and JSON query output formats are structured differently than their input formats, so they don't count.

To get CSV data out of a local PostgreSQL database for the MusicBrainz tracks, we ran this command:

```
psql -U postgres -d musicbrainz_db -c "COPY (\
select 'Track:' || t.id as id, 'Track' as type, t.name as t_name,
t.length/1000 as t_duration, a.id as t_a_id, a.name as t_a_name,
albumjoin.sequence as t_num, r.id as t_r_id, r.name as t_r_name,
array_to_string(r.attributes,' ') as t_r_attributes, albummeta.tracks
as t_r_tracks \
from (track t inner join albumjoin on t.id = albumjoin.track \
 inner join album r on albumjoin.album = r.id left join albummeta on
albumjoin.album = albummeta.id) inner join artist a on t.artist =
a.id \
) to '/tmp/mb_tracks.csv' CSV HEADER"
```

And it generated about 7 million lines of output that looks like this (the first three lines):

```
id,type,t_name,t_duration,t_a_id,t_a_name,t_num,t_r_id,t_r_name,t_r_a
ttributes,t_r_tracks
Track:183326,Track,In the Arms of Sleep,254,11650,The Smashing
Pumpkins,4,22471,Mellon Collie and the Infinite Sadness (disc 2:
Twilight to Starlight),0 1 100,14
Track:183328,Track,Tales of a Scorched Earth,228,11650,The Smashing
Pumpkins,6,22471,Mellon Collie and the Infinite Sadness (disc 2:
Twilight to Starlight),0 1 100,14
...
```

This CSV file is provided with the code supplement to the book. To get Solr to import the CSV file, type this at the command line:

```
curl http://localhost:8983/solr/update/csv -F
f.t_r_attributes.split=true -F f.t_r_attributes.separator=' ' -F
overwrite=false -F commit=true -F stream.file=/tmp/mb_tracks.csv
```

The CSV options were specified via form values (-F) here; you can alternatively encode them into the query portion of the URL—it doesn't matter.

> **Consider the Unix mkfifo command**
>
> When we actually did this, we had PostgreSQL on one machine and Solr on the other. We've used the Unix mkfifo command to create an in-memory data pipe mounted at /tmp/mb_tracks.csv. This way, we didn't have to actually generate a huge CSV file. We could essentially stream it directly from PostgreSQL into Solr. Details on this approach and PostgreSQL are beyond the scope of this book.

Configuration options

The following are the names of each configuration option with an explanation. For the MusicBrainz track CSV file, the defaults were used with the exception of specifying how to parse the multivalued `t_r_attributes` field and disabling unique key processing for performance.

- `separator`: This is the character that separates each value on a line. It defaults to a comma.

 If you're using curl and need to specify a tab character or some other character that isn't visible other than a space, then the easiest way to do this is to specify this parameter on the URL as a query parameter instead of with `-F`. Remember to URL encode it, for example, `.../update/csv?separator=%09` `-F` ... and so on.

- `header`: Set this to `true` if the first line lists the field names (the default).

- `fieldnames`: If the first line doesn't have the field names, you'll have to use this instead to indicate what they are. They are comma separated. If no name is specified for a column, then its data is skipped.

- `skip`: This specifies which fields to not import in the CSV file.

- `skipLines`: This is the number of lines to skip in the input file. It defaults to `0`.

- `trim`: If this is `true`, it removes the leading and trailing white space as a final step, even if quoting is used to explicitly specify a space. It defaults to `false`. Solr already does an initial pass trim, but quoting may leave spaces.

- `encapsulator`: This character is used to encapsulate (that is surround, quote) values in order to preserve the field separator as a field value instead of mistakenly parsing it as the next field. This character itself is escaped by doubling it. It defaults to the double quote, unless escape is specified. Consider the following example:

  ```
  11604, foo, "The ""second"" word is quoted.", bar
  ```

- `escape`: If this character is found in the input text, then the next character is taken literally in place of this escape character, and it isn't otherwise treated specially by the file's syntax; for example, consider the following code:

  ```
  11604, foo, The second\, word is followed by a comma., bar
  ```

- `keepEmpty`: This specifies whether blank (zero length) fields should be indexed as such or omitted. It defaults to `false`.

- `literal`: This adds a fixed field name and value to all the documents. For example, `literal.datasource=artists` adds the `datasource` field with the value `artists` to every document.

- `rowid`: This adds a field to every document where the passed in parameter name is the field name and the current line number is the value. This is very helpful when there is no unique ID for each row and also for debugging purposes. It defaults to `null` and is optional.

- `rowidOffset`: This works with the `rowid` parameter; this integer value will be added to the actual rowid / current line number before adding it to the specified `rowid` field in the index.

- `overwrite`: This indicates whether to enforce the unique key constraint of the schema by overwriting existing documents with the same ID. It defaults to `true`. Disable this to increase performance, if you are sure you are passing new documents.

- `split`: This is a field-specific option used to split what would normally be one value into multiple values. Another set of CSV configuration options (separator, and so on) can be specified for this field to instruct Solr on how to do that. See the previous track's MusicBrainz example on how this is used.

- `map`: This is another field-specific option used to replace input values with another. It can be used to remove values too. The value should include a colon, which separates the left side that is replaced with the right side. If we were to use this feature on the tracks of the MusicBrainz data, then it could be used to map the numeric code in `t_r_attributes` to more meaningful values. Here's an example of such an attempt:

```
-F keepEmpty=false -F f.t_r_attributes.map=0:  -F
f.t_r_attributes.map=1:Album -F
f.t_r_attributes.map=2:Single
```

This causes 0 to be removed, because it seems to be useless data, as nearly all tracks have it, and we map 1 to `Album` and 2 to `Single`.

The DataImportHandler framework

Solr includes a very popular contrib module for importing data known as the DataImportHandler. It's a data processing pipeline built specifically for Solr. Here's a list of the notable capabilities:

- It imports data from databases through **JDBC (Java Database Connectivity)**. This supports importing only changed records, assuming a last-updated date

- It imports data from a URL (HTTP GET)

- It imports data from files (that is, it *crawls* files)

- It imports e-mail from an IMAP server, including attachments

- It supports combining data from different sources

- It extracts text and metadata from rich document formats

- It applies XSLT transformations and XPath extraction on XML data

- It includes a diagnostic/development tool

Furthermore, you could write your own data source or transformation step once you learn how by seeing how the existing ones are coded.

Consider DIH alternatives

The DIH's capabilities really have little to do with Solr itself, yet the DIH is tied to Solr (to a Solr core, to be precise). Consider alternative data *pipelines* such as those referenced here: `http://wiki.apache.org/solr/SolrEcosystem` — this includes building your own. Alternatives can run on another machine to reduce the load on Solr when there is significant processing involved. And in being agnostic of where the data is delivered, your investment in them can be re-used for other purposes independent of Solr. With that said, the DIH is a strong choice because it is integrated with Solr and it has a lot of capabilities.

The complete reference documentation for the DIH is available at `https://cwiki.apache.org/confluence/display/solr/Uploading+Structured+Data+Store+Data+with+the+Data+Import+Handler`. It's rather thorough. In this chapter, we'll demonstrate some of its features, but you'll need to turn to the wiki for further details.

Configuring the DataImportHandler framework

The DIH is not considered a core part of Solr, even though it comes with the Solr download. Consequently, you must add its Java JAR files to your Solr setup in order to use it. If this isn't done, you'll eventually see a `ClassNotFoundException` error. The DIH's JAR files are located in Solr's `dist` directory: `solr-dataimporthandler-4.x.x.jar` and `solr-dataimporthandler-extras-4.x.x.jar`. The easiest way to add JAR files to a Solr configuration is to copy them to the `<solr_home>/lib` directory; you may need to create it. Another method is to reference them from `solrconfig.xml` via `<lib/>` tags — see Solr's example configuration for examples of that. *You will probably need some additional JAR files as well.* If you'll be communicating with a database, you'll need to get a JDBC driver for it. If you will be extracting text from various document formats, you'll need to add the JARs in `/contrib/extraction/lib`. Finally, if you'll be indexing an e-mail, you'll need to add the JARs in `/contrib/dataimporthandler/lib`.

The DIH needs to be registered with Solr in `solrconfig.xml` as follows:

```
<requestHandler name="/dih_artists_jdbc"
class="org.apache.solr.handler.dataimport.DataImportHandler">
    <lst name="defaults">
        <str name="config">mb-dih-artists-jdbc.xml</str>
    </lst>
</requestHandler>
```

This reference `mb-dih-artists-jdbc.xml` is located in `<solr-home>/conf`, which specifies the details of a data import process. We'll get to that file in a bit.

The development console

Before describing a DIH configuration file, we're going to take a look at the DIH development console. Visit the URL `http://localhost:8983/solr/#/mbartists/dataimport/` (modifications may be needed for your host, port, core, and so on).

If there is more than one request handler registered, then you'll see a simple page listing them with links to get to the development console for that handler. The development console looks like the following screenshot:

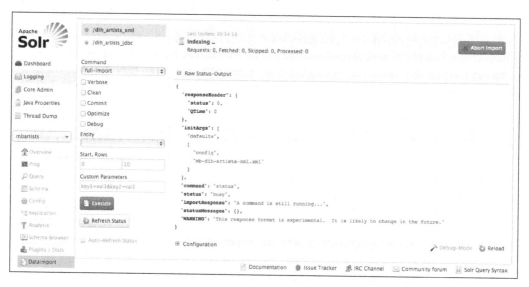

The screen is divided into two panes: on the left is the DIH control form and on the right is the command output as JSON.

The editable configuration, via Debug-Mode option, highlighted in the preceding screenshot, is not saved to the disk! It is purely for live trial-and-error debugging. Once you are satisfied with any changes, you'll need to save them back to the file yourself and then take some action to get Solr to reload the changes, such as by clicking on the **Reload** button, and then reload the page to pick up the changes on the screen.

The last section on the DIH in this chapter goes into more detail on submitting a command to the DIH.

Writing a DIH configuration file

The key pieces of a DIH configuration file includes a data source, an entity, some transformers, and a list of fields. Sometimes they can be omitted. At first, we'll list the various types of these DIH components with a simple description. Each has further details on usage, for which you'll need to see the Solr Reference Guide. Then we'll show you a few sample configuration files to give you a sense of how it all comes together.

Data sources

A `<dataSource/>` tag specifies, as you might guess, the source of data referenced by an entity. This is the simplest piece of the configuration. The `type` attribute specifies the type, which defaults to `JdbcDataSource`. Depending on the type, there are further configuration attributes (not listed here). There could be multiple data sources but not usually. Furthermore, with the exception of `JdbcDataSource`, each type handles either binary or text but not both. The following is a listing of available data source types. They all have a name ending with `DataSource`.

- `JdbcDataSource`: This is a reference to a database via JDBC; usually relational

- `FieldStreamDataSource` and `FieldReaderDataSource`: These are for extracting binary or character data from a column from `JdbcDataSource`.

- `BinFileDataSource` and `FileDataSource`: This is to specify a path to a binary or text file

- `URLDataSource`: This is to specify a URL to a text resource

- `BinContentStreamDataSource` and `ContentStreamDataSource`: These receive binary or text data posted to the DIH instead of the DIH pulling it from somewhere.

ContentStreamDataSource is very interesting because it lets you use the DIH to receive asynchronous, on-demand data processing instead of the typical scheduled batch-process mode. It could be used for many things, even a Web Hook: http://www.webhooks.org/.

If you were looking for a MailDataSource, then there isn't one. The MailEntityProcessor was coded to fetch the e-mail itself instead of decoupling that function to a data source.

Entity processors

Following the data sources is a <document/> element, which contains one or more <entity/> elements referencing an Entity Processor via the processor attribute; the default is SqlEntityProcessor. An entity processor produces documents when it is executed. The data to produce the documents typically comes from a referenced data source. An entity that is an immediate child of <document> is by default a **root entity**, which means its documents are indexed by Solr. If the rootEntity attribute is explicitly set to false, then the DIH recursively traverses down until it finds one that doesn't have this marking. There can be sub-entities, which execute once for each parent document and which usually reference the parent document to narrow a query. Documents from a sub-entity are merged into its root entity's document, producing multivalued fields when more than one document with the same field is produced by the sub-entity.

This explanation is surely quite confusing without having seen several examples. You might want to read this again once you get to some examples.

The entity processors have some common configuration attributes and some that are unique to each one.

Entity processors all have a name ending with EntityProcessor. The following are a list of them:

- SqlEntityProcessor: This references a JdbcDataSource and executes a specified SQL query. The columns in the result set, map to fields by the same name. This processor uniquely supports delta import.

- CachedSqlEntityProcessor: This is like SqlEntityProcessor, but caches every record in memory for future lookups instead of running the query each time. This is only an option for sub-entities of a root entity.

- `XPathEntityProcessor`: This processes XML from a text data source. It separates the XML into separate documents according to an XPath expression. The fields reference a part of the XML via an XPath expression.

- `PlainTextEntityProcessor`: This takes the text from a text data source putting it into a single field.

- `LineEntityProcessor`: This takes *each line* of text from a text data source, creating a document from each one. A suggested use is for an input file of URLs that are referenced by a sub-entity such as Tika.

- `FileListEntityProcessor`: This finds all files meeting the specified criteria, creating a document from each one with the file path in a field. A sub-entity such as Tika could then extract text from the file.

- `TikaEntityProcessor`: This extracts text from a binary data source, using Apache Tika. Tika supports many file types such as HTML, PDF, and Microsoft Office documents. Recent Tika versions allow specifying that the HTML not be stripped out (it is by default). From Solr 4.3, you can specify this via `IdentityHtmlMapper` in the DIH configuration. This is an alternative approach to Solr Cell, which is described later.

- `MailEntityProcessor`: This fetches e-mail from an IMAP mail server, including attachments processed with Tika. It doesn't use a data source. You can specify a starting date, but, unfortunately, it doesn't support DIH's delta import.

> Solr supports a pluggable cache for DIH so that any entity can be made cacheable by adding the `cacheImpl` parameter. For additional information, check SOLR-2382.

Fields and transformers

Within an `<entity/>` tag are `<field/>` elements that declare how the columns in the query map to Solr. A field element must have a `column` attribute that matches the corresponding named column in the SQL query. Its `name` attribute is the Solr schema field name that the column is going into. If it is not specified, then it defaults to the column name. When a column in the result can be placed directly into Solr without further processing, there is no need to specify the field declaration, because it is implied.

> When importing from a database, use the SQL `AS` keyword to use the same names as the Solr schema instead of the database schema. This reduces the number of `<field/>` elements and shortens the existing ones.

An attribute of the entity declaration that we didn't mention yet is the transformer. This declares a comma-separated list of transformers that create, modify, and delete fields and even entire documents. The transformers are evaluated in order, which can be significant. Usually, the transformers use attributes specific to them on a given field to trigger that it should take some action, whether it be splitting the field into multiple values or formatting it. The following is a list of transformers:

- TemplateTransformer: This overwrites or modifies a value based on a string template. The template can contain references to other fields and DIH variables.

- RegexTransformer: This either performs a string substitution, splits the field into multiple values, or splits the field into separately named fields. This transformer is very useful!

- DateFormatTransformer: This parses a date-time format according to a specified pattern. The output format is Solr's date format.

- NumberFormatTransformer: This parses a number according to a specified locale and *style* (that is number, percent, integer, currency). The output format is a plain number suitable for one of Solr's numeric fields.

- HTMLStripTransformer: This removes the HTML markup according to HTMLStripCharFilter (documented in the previous chapter). By performing this step here instead of a text analysis component, the stored value will also be cleansed, not just the indexed (that is, searchable) data.

- ClobTransformer: This transforms a CLOB value from a database into a plain string.

- LogTransformer: This logs a string for diagnostic purposes, using a string template such as TemplateTransformer. Unlike most transformers, this is configured at the entity since it is evaluated for each entity output document, not for each field.

- ScriptTransformer: This invokes user-defined code in-line that is defined in a <script/> element. This transformer is specified differently within the transformers attribute — use ..., script:myFunctionName, ... where myFunctionName is a named function in the provided code. The code is written in JavaScript by default, but most other languages that run on the JVM can be used too.

By the way, DIH transformers are similar to Solr UpdateRequestProcessors described at the end of this chapter. The former operates strictly within the DIH framework, whereas the latter is applicable to any importing mechanism.

Example DIH configurations

A DIH configuration file tends to look different depending on whether the source is a database, the content is XML, or if text is being extracted from documents.

 It's important to understand that the various data sources, data formats, and transformers, are mostly independent. The next few examples pick combinations to demonstrate a variety of possibilities for illustrative purposes. You should pick the pieces that you need.

Importing from databases

The following is the mb-dih-artists-jdbc.xml file with a rather long SQL query:

```
<dataConfig>
  <dataSource name="jdbc" driver="org.postgresql.Driver"
    url="jdbc:postgresql://localhost/musicbrainz_db"
    user="musicbrainz" readOnly="true" autoCommit="false" />
  <document>
    <entity name="artist" dataSource="jdbc" pk="id" query="
      select
        a.id as id,
        a.name as a_name, a.sortname as a_name_sort,
        a.begindate as a_begin_date, a.enddate as a_end_date,
        a.type as a_type,
        array_to_string(
          array(select aa.name from artistalias aa
            where aa.ref = a.id ),
          '|') as a_alias,
        array_to_string(
          array(select am.name from v_artist_members am
            where am.band = a.id order by am.id),
          '|') as a_member_name,
        array_to_string(
          array(select am.id from v_artist_members am
            where am.band = a.id order by am.id),
          '|') as a_member_id,
        (select re.releasedate from release re inner join
          album r on re.album = r.id where r.artist = a.id
          order by releasedate desc limit 1)
          as a_release_date_latest
      from artist a
          "transformer="RegexTransformer,DateFormatTransformer,
            TemplateTransformer">
```

```
        <field column = "id" template="Artist:${artist.id}" />
        <field column = "type" template="Artist" />
        <field column = "a_begin_date"
          dateTimeFormat="yyyy-MM-dd" />
        <field column = "a_end_date"
          dateTimeFormat="yyyy-MM-dd" />
        <field column = "a_alias" splitBy="\|" />
        <field column = "a_member_name" splitBy="\|"/>
        <field column = "a_member_id" splitBy="\|" />
      </entity>
    </document>
  </dataConfig>
```

If the `type` attribute on `dataSource` is not specified (it isn't here), then it defaults to `JdbcDataSource`. Those familiar with JDBC should find the attributes in this example familiar, and there are also others available. For a reference to all of them, see the Solr Reference Guide.

Efficient JDBC configuration

Many database drivers in the default configurations (including those for PostgreSQL and MySQL) fetch all of the query results into memory instead of on-demand or using a batch/fetch size! This may work well for typical database usage, in which a relatively small amount of data needs to be fetched quickly, but is completely unworkable for ETL (**Extract, Transform, and Load**) usage such as this. Configuring the driver to stream the data will sometimes require driver-specific configuration settings. Settings for some specific databases are at `http://wiki.apache.org/solr/DataImportHandlerFaq`.

The main piece of an `<entity/>` used with a database is the `query` attribute, which is the SQL query to be evaluated. You'll notice that this query involves some subqueries, which are made into arrays and then transformed into strings joined by spaces. The particular functions used to do these sorts of things are generally database specific. This is done to shoehorn multivalued data into a single row in the results. It may create a more complicated query, but it does mean that the database does all of the heavy lifting so that all of the data Solr needs for an artist is in one row.

Sub-entities

There are numerous examples on the DIH wiki depicting entities within entities (assuming the parent entity is a `root` entity). This is an approach to the problem of getting multiple values for the same Solr field. It's also an approach for spanning different data sources. We advise caution against that approach because it will generate a separate query in response to each source record, which is very inefficient. It can be told to cache just one query to be used for future lookups, but that is only applicable to data shared across records that can also fit in memory. If all required data is in your database, we recommend the approach illustrated earlier instead.

Importing XML from a file with XSLT

In this example, we're going to import an XML file from the disk and use XSLT to do most of the work instead of DIH transformers.

Solr supports using XSLT to process input XML without requiring use of the DIH as we show in this simple example. The following command would have the same effect:

```
curl
'http://localhost:8983/solr/mbartists/update/xslt?tr=art
ists.xsl&commit=true' -H 'Content-type:text/xml' --data-
binary @downloads/artists_veryshort.xml
```

```
<dataConfig>
  <dataSource name="artists" type="FileDataSource" encoding="UTF-8"
    />
  <document name="artists">
    <entity name="artist" dataSource="artists"
      url="downloads/artists_veryshort.xml"
      processor="XPathEntityProcessor"
      xsl="cores/mbtype/conf/xslt/artists.xsl"
      useSolrAddSchema="true">
    </entity>
  </document>
</dataConfig>
```

This `dataSource` of type `FileDataSource` is for text files. The entity URL is relative to the `baseUrl` on the data source; since it's not specified then, it defaults to the current working directory of the server. To see the referenced XSLT file, download the code supplement for the book.

An interesting thing about this example is not just the use of XSLT, but the use of useSolrAddSchema, which signifies that the resulting XML structure follows Solr's XML <add><doc><field name=... structure. Our input file is an HTML table and the XSLT file transforms it. These two options are best used together.

 There are some other examples at the DIH wiki illustrating XML processing. One of them shows how to process a Wikipedia XML file dump, which is rather interesting.

Importing multiple rich document files – crawling

In this example, we have a configuration that crawls all PDF files in a directory and then extracts text and metadata from them:

```
<dataConfig>
  <dataSource type="BinFileDataSource" />
  <document>
    <entity name="f" dataSource="null" rootEntity="false"
      processor="FileListEntityProcessor"
      baseDir="/my/file/path" fileName=".*pdf"
      recursive="true">
    <entity name="tika-test" processor="TikaEntityProcessor"
      url="${f.fileAbsolutePath}" format="text">
      <field column="Author" name="author" meta="true"/>
      <field column="title" name="title" meta="true"/>
      <field column="text" name="text"/>
    </entity>
    </entity>
  </document>
</dataConfig>
```

The FileListEntityProcessor is the piece that does the file crawling. It doesn't actually use a data source but it's required. Because this entity is not a root entity, thanks to rootEntity="false", it's the sub-entity within it that is a root entity, which corresponds to a Solr document. The entity is named f and the sub-entity tika-test refers to the path provided by f via f.fileAbsolutePath in its url. This example uses the variable substitution syntax ${...}.

 Speaking of which, there are a variety of variables that the DIH makes available for substitution, including those defined in solr.xml and solrconfig.xml. Again, see the DIH wiki for further details.

The TikaEntityProcessor part is relatively straightforward. Tika makes a variety of metadata available about documents; this example just used two.

Importing commands

The DIH is issued one of several different commands to do different things. Importing all data is called a full import, in contrast to a delta import that will be described shortly. Commands are given to the DIH request handler with the command attribute. We could tell the DIH to do a full import just by going to this URL: http://localhost:8983/solr/mbartists/dataimport?command=full-import. On the command line, we will use the following code:

```
curl http://localhost:8983/mbartists/solr/dataimport -F
command=full-import
```

It uses HTTP POST, which is more appropriate than GET, as discussed earlier.

Unlike the other importing mechanisms, the DIH returns an HTTP response immediately while the import continues asynchronously. To get the current status of the DIH, go to this URL http://localhost:8983/solr/mbartists/dataimport, and you'll get an output like the following:

```
<response>
    <lst name="responseHeader">
        <int name="status">0</int>
        <int name="QTime">15</int>
    </lst>
    <lst name="initArgs">
        <lst name="defaults">
            <str name="config">mb-dih-artists-jdbc.xml</str>
        </lst>
    </lst>
    <str name="status">idle</str>
    <str name="importResponse"/>
    <lst name="statusMessages"/>
    <str name="WARNING">This response format is experimental.
       It is likely to change in the future.</str>
</response>
```

The command attribute defaults to status, which is what this output shows. When an import is in progress, it shows statistics on that progress along with a status state of busy.

Other Boolean parameters named clean, commit, and optimize may accompany the command. clean is specific to the DIH, and it means that before running the import, it will delete all the documents first. To customize exactly which documents are deleted, you can specify a preImportDeleteQuery attribute on a root entity. You can even specify documents to be deleted after an import by using the postImportDeleteQuery attribute. The query syntax is documented in *Chapter 5, Searching*.

Beware that these defaults are inconsistent with other Solr importing mechanisms. No other importing mechanism will delete all documents first, and none will commit or optimize by default.

Two other useful commands are `reload-config` and `abort`. The first will reload the DIH configuration file, which is useful for picking up changes without having to restart Solr. The second will cancel any existing imports in progress.

Delta imports

The DIH supports what it calls a **delta import**, which is a mode of operation in which only data that has changed since the last import is retrieved. A delta import is only supported by the `SqlEntityProcessor` and it assumes that your data is time-stamped. The official DIH approach to this is prominently documented on the wiki. It uses a `deltaImportQuery` and `deltaQuery` pair of attributes on the entity, and a `delta-import` command. That approach is verbose, hard to maintain, and slow compared to a novel alternative documented at `http://wiki.apache.org/solr/DataImportHandlerDeltaQueryViaFullImport`.

Essentially, what you can do is introduce a timestamp check in your SQL's WHERE clause using variable substitution, along with another check if the `clean` parameter was given to the DIH in order to control whether or not a delta or full import should happen. Here is a concise `<entity/>` definition on a fictitious schema and dataset showing the relevant WHERE clause:

```
<entity name="item" pk="ID"
   query="SELECT * FROM item
     WHERE '${dataimporter.request.clean}' != 'false'
       OR last_modified > '${dataimporter.last_index_time}'">
```

Notice the `${...}` variable substitution syntax. To issue a full import, use the `full-import` command with `clean` enabled: `/dataimport?command=full-import&clean=true`. And for a delta import, we still use the `full-import` command, but we set `clean` to `false`: `/dataimport?command=full-import&clean=false&optimize=false`. We also disabled the index optimization since it's not likely that this is desired for a delta import.

Indexing documents with Solr Cell

While most of this book assumes that the content you want to index in Solr is in a neatly structured data format of some kind, such as in a database table, a selection of XML files, or CSV, the reality is that we also store information in the much messier world of binary formats such as PDF, Microsoft Office, or even images and music files.

One of the coauthors of this book, Eric Pugh, first became involved with the Solr community when he needed to ingest the thousands of PDF and Microsoft Word documents that a client had produced over the years. The outgrowth of that early effort is Solr Cell providing a very powerful and simple framework for indexing rich document formats.

Solr Cell is technically called the `ExtractingRequestHandler`. The current name came about as a derivation of *Content Extraction Library*, which appeared more fitting to its author, Grant Ingersoll. Perhaps a name including Tika would have been most appropriate considering that this capability is a small adapter to Tika. You may have noticed that the DIH includes this capability via the appropriately named `TikaEntityProcessor`.

The complete reference material for Solr Cell is available at `https://cwiki.apache.org/confluence/display/solr/Uploading+Data+with+Solr+Cell+using+Apache+Tika`.

Extracting text and metadata from files

Every file format is different and all of them provide different types of metadata, as well as different methods of extracting content. The heavy lifting of providing a single API to an ever-expanding list of formats is delegated to Apache Tika.

> *Apache Tika is a toolkit for detecting and extracting metadata and structured text content from various documents using existing parser libraries.*

Tika supports a wide variety of formats, from the predictable to the unexpected. Some of the most commonly used formats supported are Adobe PDF, Microsoft Office, including Word, Excel, PowerPoint, Visio, and Outlook. The other formats that are supported include extracting metadata from images such as JPG, GIF, and PNG, as well as from various audio formats such as MP3, MIDI, and Wave audio. Tika itself does not attempt to parse the individual document formats. Instead, it delegates the parsing to various third-party libraries, while providing a high-level stream of XML SAX events as the documents are parsed. A full list of the supported document formats supported by the 1.5 version that are used by Solr 4.8 is available at `http://tika.apache.org/1.5/formats.html`.

Solr Cell is a fairly thin adapter to Tika consisting of a SAX ContentHandler that consumes the SAX events and builds the input document from the fields that are specified for extraction.

Some not-so-obvious things to keep in mind when indexing binary documents are:

- You can supply any kind of supported document to Tika, and Tika will attempt to discover the correct MIME type of the document in order to use the correct parser. If you know the correct MIME type, you can specify it via the stream.type parameter.

- The default SolrContentHandler that is used by Solr Cell is fairly simplistic. You may find that you need to perform extra massaging of the data being indexed beyond what Solr Cell offers to reduce the junk data being indexed. One approach is to implement a custom Solr UpdateRequestProcessor, described later in this chapter. Another is to subclass ExtractingRequestHandler and override createFactory() to provide a custom SolrContentHandler.

- Remember that during indexing, you are potentially sending large binary files over the wire that must then be parsed by Solr, which can be very slow. If you are looking to only index metadata, then it may make sense to write your own parser using Tika directly, extract the metadata, and post that across to the server. See the *Indexing with SolrJ* section in *Chapter 9, Integrating Solr* for an example of parsing out metadata from an archive of a website and posting the data through SolrJ.

You can learn more about the Tika project at http://tika.apache.org/.

Configuring Solr

A sample request handler for parsing binary documents, in solrconfig.xml, looks like the following code:

```
<requestHandler name="/update/extract"
class="org.apache.solr.handler.extraction.ExtractingRequestHandler
">
    <lst name="defaults">
      <str name="map.Last-Modified">last_modified</str>
      <str name="uprefix">metadata_</str>
    </lst>
</requestHandler>
```

Here, we can see that the Tika metadata attribute `Last-Modified` is being mapped to the Solr field `last_modified`, assuming we are provided that Tika attribute. The `uprefix` parameter specifies the prefix to use when storing any Tika fields that don't have a corresponding matching Solr field.

Solr Cell is distributed as a contrib module and is made up of the `solr-cell-4.x.x.jar` and roughly 25 more JARs that support parsing individual document formats. In order to use Solr Cell, you will need to place the Solr Cell JAR and supporting JARs in the `lib` directory for the core, as it is not included by default in `solr.war`. To share these libs across multiple cores, you would add them to `./examples/cores/lib/`.

Solr Cell parameters

Before jumping into examples, we'll review Solr Cell's configuration parameters, all of which are optional. They are organized here and are ordered roughly by their sequence of use internally.

At first, Solr Cell (or, more specifically, Tika) determines the format of the document. It generally makes good guesses, but it can be assisted with these parameters:

- `resource.name`: This is an optional parameter for specifying the name of the file. This assists Tika in determining the correct MIME type.

- `stream.type`: This optional parameter allows you to explicitly specify the MIME type of the document being extracted to Tika, taking precedence over Tika guessing.

Tika converts all input documents into a basic XHTML document, including metadata in the `head` section. The metadata becomes fields and all text within the body goes into the `content` field. The following parameters further refine this:

- `capture`: This is the XHTML element name (for example, `"p"`) to be copied into its own field; it can be set multiple times.

- `captureAttr`: This is set to `true` to capture XHTML attributes into fields named after the attribute. A common example is for Tika to extract `href` attributes from all the `<a/>` anchor tags for indexing into a separate field.

- xpath: This allows you to specify an XPath query to filter which element's text is put into the content field. To return only the metadata, and discard all the body content of the XHMTL, you would use xpath=/xhtml:html/ xhtml:head/descendant:node(). Notice the use of the xhtml: namespace prefix for each element. Note that only a limited subset of the XPath specification is supported. See http://tika.apache.org/0.8/api/org/ apache/tika/sax/xpath/XPathParser.html. The API fails to mention that it also supports /descendant:node().

- literal.[fieldname]: This allows you to supply the specified value for this field, for example, for the unique key field.

At this point each resulting field name is potentially renamed in order to map into the schema. These parameters control this process:

- lowernames: This is set to true to lowercase the field names and convert nonalphanumeric characters to an underscore. For example, Last-Updated becomes last_updated.

- fmap.[tikaFieldName]: This maps a source field name to a target field name. For example, fmap.last_modified=timestamp maps the metadata field last_modified generated by Tika to be recorded in the timestamp field defined in the Solr schema.

- uprefix: This prefix is applied to the field name, if the unprefixed name doesn't match an existing field. It is used in conjunction with a dynamic field for mapping individual metadata fields separately:

```
uprefix=meta_
<dynamicField name="meta_*" type="text_general"
indexed="true" stored="true" multiValued="true"/>
```

- defaultField: This is a field to use if uprefix isn't specified, and no existing fields match. This can be used to map all the metadata fields into one multivalued field:

```
defaultField=meta
<field name="meta" type="text_general" indexed="true"
stored="true" multiValued="true"/>
```

Ignoring metadata fields

If you don't want to index unknown metadata fields, you can throw them away by mapping them to the ignored_ dynamic field by setting uprefix="ignore_" and using the ignored field type: <dynamicField name="ignored_*" type="ignored" multiValued="true"/>.

The other miscellaneous parameters:

- `boost.[fieldname]`: Boost the specified field by this factor, a float value, to affect scoring. For example, `boost="2.5"`, default value is `1.0`.

- `extractOnly`: Set this to `true` to return the XHTML structure of the document as parsed by Tika without indexing the document. This is typically done in conjunction with `wt=json&indent=true` to make the XHTML easier to read. The purpose of this option is to aid in debugging.

- `extractFormat`: This defaults to `xml` (when `extractOnly=true`) to produce the XHMTL structure. Can be set to `text` to return the raw text extracted from the document.

Update request processors

No matter how you choose to import data, there is a final configuration point within Solr that allows manipulation of the imported data before it gets indexed. The Solr request handlers that update data put documents on an `update` request processor chain. If you search `solrconfig.xml` for `updateRequestProcessorChain`, then you'll see an example.

You can specify which chain to use on the update request with the `update.chain` parameter. It could be useful, but you'll probably always use one chain. If no chain is specified, you get a default chain of `LogUpdateProcessorFactory` and `RunUpdateProcessorFactory`. The following are the possible update request processors that you can choose from. Their names all end in `UpdateProcessorFactory`.

- `SignatureUpdateProcessorFactory`: This generates a hash ID value based on the field values you specify. If you want to deduplicate your data (that is, you don't want to add the same data twice accidentally), then this will do that for you. For further information, see `http://wiki.apache.org/solr/Deduplication`.

- `UIMAUpdateProcessorFactory`: This hands the document off to the **Unstructured Information Management Architecture (UIMA)**, a Solr contrib module that enhances the document through **natural language processing (NLP)** techniques. For further information, see `http://wiki.apache.org/solr/SolrUIMA`.

 Although it's nice to see an NLP integration option in Solr, beware that NLP processing tends to be computationally expensive. Instead of using UIMA in this way, consider performing this processing external to Solr and cache the results to avoid re-computation as you adjust your indexing process.

- `LogUpdateProcessorFactory`: This is the one responsible for writing the log messages you see when an update occurs.

- `RunUpdateProcessorFactory`: This is the one that actually indexes the document; don't forget it or the document will vanish! To decompose this last step further, it hands the document to Lucene, which will then process each field according to the analysis configuration in the schema.

- `FieldMutatingUpdateProcessorFactory`: This allows you to manipulate the field values when adding the documents to the index. You can configure for what fields the processor should act on by name, type, name regex, or type class. The following are the useful extensions of the `FieldMutatingUpdateProcessorFactory` implementation:

  - `TrimFieldUpdateProcessorFactory`: This trims leading and trailing white spaces from any CharSequence values found in fields matching the specified conditions and returns the resulting string. By default, this processor matches all fields.

  - `RemoveBlankFieldUpdateProcessorFactory`: This removes any values found, which are CharSequence with a length of 0. (that is, empty strings). By default, this processor applies itself to all fields.

  - `FieldLengthUpdateProcessorFactory`: This replaces any CharSequence values found in fields matching the specified conditions with the lengths of those CharSequences (as an integer). By default, this processor matches no fields.

  - `ConcatFieldUpdateProcessorFactory`: This concatenates multiple values for fields matching the specified conditions using a configurable delimiter that defaults to ", ". By default, this processor concatenates the values for any field name, which according to the schema is `multiValued="false"` and uses TextField or StrField.

  - `FirstFieldValueUpdateProcessorFactory`: This trims leading and trailing white spaces from any CharSequence values found in fields matching the specified conditions and returns the resulting String.

  - `LastFieldValueUpdateProcessorFactory`: This keeps only the last value of fields matching the specified conditions. By default, this processor matches no fields.

  - `MinFieldValueUpdateProcessorFactory`: This keeps only the minimum value from any selected fields where multiple values are found. By default, this processor matches no fields.

  - `MaxFieldValueUpdateProcessorFactory`: This keeps only the maximum value from any selected fields where multiple values are found. By default, this processor matches no fields.

- ○ `TruncateFieldUpdateProcessorFactory`: This truncates any CharSequence values found in fields matching the specified conditions to a maximum character length. By default, this processor matches no fields.

- ○ `IgnoreFieldUpdateProcessorFactory`: This ignores and removes fields matching the specified conditions from any document being added to the index. By default, this processor ignores any field name that does not exist according to the schema.

- ○ `CountFieldValuesUpdateProcessorFactory`: This replaces any list of values for a field matching the specified conditions with the count of the number of values for that field. By default, this processor doesn't match any fields. The typical use case for this processor would be in combination with the `CloneFieldUpdateProcessorFactory` so that it's possible to query by the quantity of values in the source field.

- ○ `HTMLStripFieldUpdateProcessorFactory`: This strips all HTML markup in any CharSequence values found in fields matching the specified conditions. By default, this processor matches no fields.

- ○ `RegexReplaceProcessorFactory`: This applies a configured regex to any CharSequence values found in the selected fields, and replaces any matches with the configured replacement string. By default, this processor applies itself to no fields.

- ○ `PreAnalyzedUpdateProcessorFactory`: This parses configured fields of any document being added using `PreAnalyzedField` with the configured format parser. Fields are specified using the same patterns as in `FieldMutatingUpdateProcessorFactory`. They are then checked to see whether they follow a pre-analyzed format defined by the parser. The valid fields are then parsed. The original SchemaField is used for initial creation of IndexableField, which is then modified to add the results from parsing (token stream value and/or string value) and then it will be directly added to the final Lucene Document to be indexed. Fields that are declared in the patterns list but are not present in the current schema will be removed from the input document.

- • `CloneFieldUpdateProcessorFactory`: This is used to clone the values found in any matching `source` field into the configured `dest` field. If the `dest` field already exists in the document, the values from the `source` fields will be added to it. The *boost* value associated with the `dest` will not be changed, and any boost specified on the `source` fields will be ignored.

- `StatelessScriptUpdateProcessorFactory`: This enables custom update processing code to be written in several scripting languages (such as JavaScript, Ruby, Groovy, or Python). In the script, you have access to several Solr objects, allowing you, for instance, to modify a document before it's indexed by Solr, or to add custom info to the Solr log. It can be a very useful feature to centralize logic when using multiple clients, or to modify requests when you have no control over all clients.

>
> The `ScriptUpdateProcessor` is powerful!
> You should certainly use the other update processors as appropriate, but there is nearly nothing you can't do with this one. A sample script file (`update-script.js`) can be found in the `conf` directory. For more details, see `http://wiki.apache.org/solr/ScriptUpdateProcessor`.

- `DocExpirationUpdateProcessorFactory`: Introduced in Solr 4.8, this is used to automatically delete documents from the index. This is executed via a background thread. There are two options available related to the *expiration* of documents, periodically delete documents from the index based on an expiration field and computing expiration field values for documents from a **time to live** (TTL). The `expirationFieldName` value is the name of the expiration field, and `autoDeletePeriodSeconds` specifies how often the timer thread should trigger a `deleteByQuery` to remove the documents. This factory can also be configured to look for a `_ttl_` request parameter, as well as a `_ttl_` field in each document that is indexed. Refer to the Solr wiki or the API docs for more information.

- `DocBasedVersionConstraintsProcessorFactory`: Introduced in Solr 4.6, this is used to enforce the version constraints based on per-document version numbers using a configured name of a `versionField`. It should be configured on the *default* update processor before the `DistributedUpdateProcessorFactory`. Using this, if a document with the same unique key already exists in the index and its value of the `versionField` is not less than the value in the new document, then the new document will be rejected with a 409 version conflict error.

- `RegexpBoostProcessorFactory`: This update processor is used to read the `inputField`, match its content against the regular expressions found in `boostFilename`, and if it matches, return the corresponding boost value into the `boostField` as a double value from the file. If more than one patterns match, then the boost values are multiplied.

- `TikaLanguageIdentifierUpdateProcessorFactory` and `LangDetectLanguageIdentifierUpdateProcessorFactory`: This identifies the language of a document before indexing and then makes appropriate decisions about analysis, and so on. For further info about language detection, see `http://wiki.apache.org/solr/LanguageDetection`.

> There are many other processors available and you can also write your own. It's a recognized extensibility point in Solr that consequently doesn't require modifying Solr itself. For further information, see `http://wiki.apache.org/solr/UpdateRequestProcessor`.

Summary

At this point, you should have a schema that you believe will suit your needs, and you should know how to get your data into it. From Solr's native XML to JSON to CSV to databases to rich documents, Solr offers a variety of possibilities to ingest data into the index. *Chapter 9, Integrating Solr*, will discuss some additional language and framework integration choices for importing data. In the end, usually one or two mechanisms will be used. In addition, you can usually expect the need to write a little code, perhaps just a simple bash or Ant script to implement the automation of getting data from your source system into Solr.

Now that we've got data in Solr, we can finally start searching through it.

The next chapter will describe Solr's query syntax in detail, which includes phrase queries, range queries, wildcards, boosting, as well as the description of Solr's `DateMath` syntax. The chapters after that will get to more interesting searching topics that of course depend on having data to search on!

5
Searching

At this point, you have Solr running and some data indexed, and you're finally ready to put Solr to the test. Searching with Solr is arguably the most fun aspect of working with it, because it's quick and easy to do. While searching your data, you will learn more about its nature than before. It is also a source of interesting puzzles to solve when you troubleshoot why a search didn't find a document, or conversely, why it did, or even why a document wasn't scored sufficiently high.

In this chapter, you are going to learn about the following topics:

- Request handlers
- Query parameters
- Solr's query syntax
- The DisMax query parser – part 1
- Filtering
- Sorting
- Joins
- Geospatial

The subject of searching will progress into the next chapter for debugging queries, relevancy (that is, scoring) matters, function queries—an advanced capability used commonly in relevancy but also used in sorting and filtering—and geospatial search.

In a hurry?

This chapter has a lot of key information on searching. That said, if you're in a hurry, you can skim/skip query parsers, `local-params`, and the query syntax—you'll use DisMax instead. And you can skip DisMax's "min-should-match" too. Read about geospatial if it's applicable.

Your first search – a walk-through

We've got a lot of data indexed, and now it's time to actually use Solr for what it is intended to do—**searching**, also known as querying. When your application interacts with Solr, it will more than likely use HTTP, either directly via common APIs or indirectly through one of Solr's client APIs. However, as we demonstrate Solr's capabilities in this chapter, we'll use Solr's web-based admin interface. In *Chapter 1, Quick Starting Solr*, we covered the basics of Solr's admin interface. To use the admin query interface, click on the **mbartists** core link in the left navigation column, and then click **Query**.

You will see a window as shown in the following screenshot, after clicking on the **Query** link:

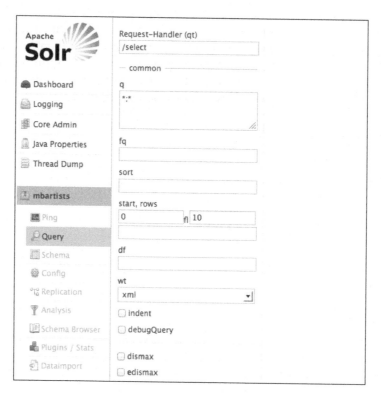

The URL is `http://localhost:8983/solr/#/mbartists/query`. This form has a subset of the options you might specify to run a search. Let's do a quick search. In the **q** box, we'll leave the default of `*:*` (an asterisk, colon, and then another asterisk). Admittedly, that is cryptic if you've never seen it before, but it basically means "match anything in any field", which is to say, it matches all documents. Much more about the query syntax will be discussed soon enough.

Click on the **Execute Query** button and you'll see XML output appear in the main content area. Now click on the URL at the top of this area to view the full response. You should now see something like this:

```xml
<?xml version="1.0" encoding="UTF-8"?>
<response>
  <lst name="responseHeader">
    <int name="status">0</int>
    <int name="QTime">0</int>
    <lst name="params">
      <str name="q">*:*</str>
      <str name="wt">xml</str>
    </lst>
  </lst>
  <result name="response" numFound="399182" start="0">
    <doc>
      <str name="type">Artist</str>
      <str name="id">Artist:272344</str>
      <str name="a_name">F.D. Project</str>
      <date name="a_release_date_latest">2004-11-
        30T00:00:00Z</date>
      <date name="indexedAt">2013-01-24T01:05:29Z</date>
    </doc>
    <doc>
      <str name="type">Artist</str>
      <str name="id">Artist:274969</str>
      <str name="a_name">Tempradura</str>
      <date name="indexedAt">2013-01-24T01:05:29Z</date>
    </doc>
    <doc>
      <str name="type">Artist</str>
      <str name="id">Artist:143163</str>
      <str name="a_name">Future Pilot A.K.A. vs. Two Lone
        Swordsmen</str>
      <date name="indexedAt">2013-01-24T01:05:29Z</date>
    </doc>
    <!--… 7 more documents omitted for brevity -->
  </result>
</response>
```

Browser note

You can use any browser, but Firefox has worked best for every Solr release. Solr 4.1 broke Safari and IE support, which was fixed in Solr 4.2.

A note on response format types

In *Chapter 1, Quick Starting Solr*, we mentioned that XML is not the only response type supported by Solr. The types supported are XML, JSON, Python, Ruby, PHP, and CSV. The parameter responsible for controlling the response type is named wt — the response *writer*. This parameter accepts the previously mentioned formats as lowercased values. For example, to specify JSON, the wt param would be wt=json. Solr's admin query interface provides control of this parameter as a select box. Changing this select box to json and clicking **Execute Query** again would result in a JSON response similar to this:

```
{
    "responseHeader": {
        "status": 0,
        "QTime": 38,
        "params": {
            "indent": "true",
            "q": "*:*",
            "wt": "json"
        }
    },
    "response": {
        "numFound": 399182,
        "start": 0,
        "docs": [
            {"type": "Artist",
             "id": "Artist:272344",
             "a_name": "F.D. Project",
             "a_release_date_latest": "2004-11-30T00:00:00Z",
             "indexedAt": "2013-01-24T01:05:29Z"},
    ....
```

As you have probably noticed, the response structure is the same as the XML format. The keys and values are also the same. The main difference between the JSON and XML is that the data type information is not present in the JSON response. This is a limitation present in all of the non-XML formats supported by Solr.

Solr's generic XML structured data representation

Solr has its own generic XML representation of typed and named data structures. This XML is used for most of the response XML, and it is also used in parts of solconfig. xml. The XML elements involved in this partial XML schema are as follows:

- `<lst>`: This is a named list. Each of its child nodes should have a name attribute. The `<doc>` element is in effect equivalent to lst but is used only for result documents.

- `<arr>`: This is an array of values. Each of its child nodes is a member of this array.

The following elements represent simple values with the text of the element storing the value. The numeric ranges match that of the Java language. They will have a name attribute if they are underneath lst (or doc), but not otherwise.

- `<str>`: A string of text

- `<int>`: An integer in the range -2^{31} to $2^{31}-1$

- `<long>`: An integer in the range -2^{63} to $2^{63}-1$

- `<float>`: A floating point number in the range 1.4e–45 to about 3.4e38

- `<double>`: A floating point number in the range 4.9e–324 to about 1.8e308

- `<bool>`: A Boolean value represented as true or false; when supplying values in a configuration file: on, off, yes, and no are also supported

- `<date>`: A date in the ISO-8601 format such as: 1965-11-30T05:00:00Z; times are always in the UTC time zone represented by Z

Solr's XML response format

The `<response/>` element wraps the entire response. The first child element is `<lst name="responseHeader">`, which is intuitively the response header that captures some basic metadata about the response. Some of the fields you'll find in the responseHeader include:

- status: This is always 0. If a Solr error occurs, then the HTTP response status code will reflect it and a plain HTML page will display the error.

- `QTime`: This refers to the number of milliseconds Solr takes to process the entire request on the server. Due to internal caching, you should see this number drop to a couple of milliseconds or so for subsequent requests of the same query. If subsequent identical searches are much faster, yet you see the same `QTime`, then your web browser (or intermediate HTTP proxy) has cached the response. Solr's HTTP caching configuration will be discussed in *Chapter 10, Scaling Solr*.

- Other data may be present depending on query parameters.

The main body of the response is the search result listing enclosed by `<result name="response" numFound="399182" start="0">`, and it contains a `<doc>` child node for each returned document. Some of the fields have been explained here:

- `numFound`: This is the total number of documents matched by the query. This is not impacted by the `rows` parameter, and as such may be larger (but not smaller) than the number of child `<doc>` elements.

- `start`: This is the same as the `start` request parameter (described shortly), which is the offset of the returned results into the query's result set.

- `maxScore`: Of all documents matched by the query (`numFound`), this is the highest score. If you didn't explicitly ask for the score in the field list using the `fl` request parameter (described shortly), then this won't be here. Scoring will be described in the next chapter.

The contents of the `<result>` element are a list of `doc` elements. Each of these elements represents a document in the index. The child elements of a `doc` element represent fields in the index and are named correspondingly. The types of these elements use Solr's generic data representation, which was described earlier. They are simple values if they are not multi-valued in the schema. For multi-valued values, the field would be represented by an ordered array of simple values.

There was no data following the `results` element in our demonstration query. However, there can be, depending on the query parameters enabling features such as faceting and highlighting. When we cover those features, the corresponding XML will be explained.

Parsing the URL

When the admin **Query** page form is submitted, the form parameters become the query string component of the URL. This URL can be seen at the top of the search results section. Take a good look at the URL; understanding the URL's structure is very important to grasp how searching Solr works:

```
http://localhost:8983/solr/mbartists/select?q=*%3A*&wt=xml
```

- The /solr/ is the web application context where Solr is installed on the Java servlet engine. If you have a dedicated server for Solr, then you might opt to install it at the root. This would make it just /. How to do this is beyond the scope of this book, but letting it remain at /solr/ is fine.

- After the web application context is a reference to the Solr core named mbartists. If you are experimenting with Solr's example setup, you won't see a core name because it has a default one. We'll see more about configuring Solr cores in *Chapter 11, Deployment*.

- The /select is a reference to the Solr **request handler**. More on this is covered next in the *Understanding request handlers* section.

- Following the ? is a set of unordered URL parameters, also known as **query parameters** in the context of Solr. The format of this part of the URL is an & that separates sets of unordered name-value pairs. As the form doesn't have an option for all query parameters, you will manually modify the URL in your browser to add query parameters as needed.

Text in the URL must be UTF-8 encoded then URL-escaped so that the URL complies with its specification. This concept should be familiar to anyone who has done web development. Depending on the context in which the URL is actually constructed, there are API calls you should use to ensure that this escaping happens properly. For example, in JavaScript, you could use encodeURIComponent(). In the previous URL, Solr interpreted %3A as a colon. The most common escaped character in URLs is a space, which is escaped as either + or %20. Fortunately, when experimenting with URLs, browsers are lenient and will permit some characters that should be escaped. For more information on URL encoding, see http://en.wikipedia.org/wiki/Percent-encoding.

Understanding request handlers

Most interactions with Solr, including indexing and searching, are processed by what Solr calls **request handlers**. Request handlers are configured in the solrconfig.xml file and are clearly labeled as such. Many of them exist for special purposes, such as handling a CSV import, for example. Here is how the default request handler is configured:

```
<requestHandler name="/select" class="solr.SearchHandler">
  <!-- default values for query parameters can be specified, these
     will be overridden by parameters in the request -->
  <lst name="defaults">
    <str name="echoParams">explicit</str>
    <int name="rows">10</int>
```

```
      <str name="df">text</str>
    </lst>
  ...
```

The request handlers that perform searches allow configuration of two things:

- Establishing default parameters and making some unchangeable
- Registering Solr search components such as faceting and highlighting

Create a request handler configuration for your application

Instead of using /select for all your application's searches, we recommend that you create a request handler for each type of search that your application requires (for example, separate out a standard search from auto-complete). In doing so, you can more easily change search options through the request handler configuration and reduce hard-wired configuration in the application. This approach gives you better granularity of search statistics on Solr's **Plugins / Stats** screen and it makes your web server logs more discernable.

Let's say that in the MusicBrainz search interface, we have a search form that searches for bands. We have a Solr core just for artists named mbartists, but this contains not only bands but also individual band members. When the field named a_type is *group*, we have a band. To start, copy the default configuration, and give it a name such as /bands. We can now use this request handler with /bands in the URL as follows:

```
/solr/mbartists/bands&q=Smashing&.....
```

An older alternative *that we don't recommend* is to name the handler without a leading / and then use the qt parameter to reference it, but still use the /select path. This requires a change in solrconfig, where you set <requestDispatcher handleSelect="true"> earlier in the file. The URL then looks like this:

```
/solr/mbartists/select?qt=bands&q=Smashing&.....
```

Let's now configure this request handler to filter searches to find only the bands, without the search application having to specify this. We'll also set a few other options as follows:

```
<requestHandler name="/bands" class="solr.SearchHandler">
  <lst name="defaults">
    <str name="echoParams">none</str>
    <int name="rows">20</int>
  </lst>
  <lst name="appends">
```

```
    <str name="fq">a_type:group</str>
  </lst>
  <lst name="invariants">
    <str name="facet">false</str>
  </lst>
</requestHandler>
```

Request handlers have several lists to configure. These use Solr's generic XML data structure, which was described earlier.

- `defaults`: These simply establish default values for various request parameters. Parameters in the request will override them.

- `appends`: For parameters that can be set multiple times, such as `fq`, this section specifies values that will be set in addition to any that may be specified by the request.

- `invariants`: This sets defaults that cannot be overridden. It is useful for security purposes—a topic for *Chapter 11, Deployment*. It can also be used to override what the client sends when you don't have control over the client application; for instance, if the application is deployed and you can't easily re-deploy a new client.

- `first-components`, `components`, `last-components`: These list the Solr **search components** to be registered for possible use with this request handler. By default, a set of search components is already registered to enable functionality such as querying and faceting. Setting `first-components` or `last-components` prepends or appends to this list respectively, whereas setting `components` overrides the list completely. For more information about search components, read *Chapter 8, Search Components*.

Solr 4.2 contains a new query parser named **switch** that is useful when the defaults and appends options above are insufficiently flexible. Consult Solr's new reference guide on it for more information.

Query parameters

There are a great number of request parameters to configure Solr searches, especially when considering all of the components such as faceting and highlighting. Only the core search parameters that aren't specific to any query parser are listed here. Furthermore, in-depth explanations for some lie further in the chapter.

 For the Boolean parameters, a true value can be any one of `true`, `on`, or `yes`. False values can be any of `false`, `off`, and `no`.

Search criteria related parameters

The parameters affecting the query are as follows:

- q: This refers to the *user query* or just *query* for short. This typically originates directly from user input. The query syntax is determined by the defType parameter.

- defType: This is a reference to the query parser for the user query in q. The default is lucene with the syntax to be described shortly. You'll most likely use dismax or edismax discussed later in the chapter.

> **Prefer DisMax or eDisMax for user queries**
>
> For processing queries from users, you should use dismax or edismax, which is described later in the chapter. It supports several features that enhance relevancy, and more limited syntax options that prevent a user from getting unexpected results or an error if they inadvertently use the lucene native syntax.

- fq: This is a filter query that limits the scope of the user query, similar to a WHERE clause in SQL. Unlike the q parameter, it has no effect on scoring. This parameter can be repeated as desired. Filtering has been described later in the chapter.

- qt: This is a reference to the request handler described earlier. By default, it doesn't work anymore with Solr's default configuration.

Result pagination related parameters

A query could match any number of the documents in the index, perhaps even all of them, such as in our first example of *:*. Solr doesn't generally return all the documents. Instead, you indicate to Solr with the start and rows parameters to return a contiguous series of them. The start and rows parameters are explained as follows:

- start (default: 0): This is the zero-based index of the first document to be returned from the result set. In other words, this is the number of documents to skip from the beginning of the search results. If this number exceeds the result count, then it will simply return no documents; but this is not considered an error.

- rows (default: 10): This is the number of documents to be returned in the response XML, starting at index start. Fewer rows will be returned if there aren't enough matching documents. This number is basically the number of results displayed at a time on your search user interface.

In versions 4.6 and earlier, Solr had performance issues when querying with very high **start** parameter values (deep paging). At least for the first thousand documents or so, this shouldn't be noticeable. The good news is that version 4.7.0 fixes the problem, tracked by SOLR-5463.

Output-related parameters

The output-related parameters are explained as follows:

- fl: This parameter accepts a comma- and/or space-delimited list of values that determine which fields will be present in the response documents. This parameter can be specified multiple times. We'll cover the fl parameter details next.

- sort: This refers to a comma-separated field listing to sort on, with a directionality specifier of asc or desc after each field; for example: r_name asc, score desc. The default is score desc. You can also sort by functions, which is a more advanced subject for the next chapter. There is more to sorting than meets the eye; read more about it later in this chapter.

- wt: This is the response format, also known as **writer type** or **query response writer**, defined in solrconfig.xml. Since the subject of picking a response format has to do with how you will integrate with Solr, further recommendations and details are left to *Chapter 9, Integrating Solr*. For now, here is the list of options by name: xml (the default and aliased to standard), json, python, php, phps, ruby, javabin, csv, xslt, velocity.

- version: This refers to the requested version of Solr's response structure, if different than the default. Solr's response format hasn't changed in years. However, if Solr's response structure changes, then it will do so under a new version. By using this in the request from client code, a best practice, you reduce the chances of your client code breaking if Solr is updated.

More about the fl parameter

As noted in the preceding section, the fl parameter is used to specify which fields are included in each of the response documents. The fl parameter accepts a wide range of value types, all of which can be freely mixed together in any order:

- **Field names**: These are simply document field names. Fields added to the fl parameter cause the same fields to be present in the response documents; for example, fl=a_name.

- **Functions**: Any valid Solr **function query** can be included as a document field value (see the next chapter for more on these functions); for example, `fl=sum(1,2,sum(3,4))`.

- **Aliases**: Fields can be renamed (aliased) using the `fl=new_name:original_name` syntax. The result of a function call can also be aliased with `fl=ten:product(2,5)`.

- **Score**: The score for each document can be included in the response by adding `score` to the `fl` parameter.

- **Glob**: Use `*` to refer to all fields and/or partially matching field names. For example, if you want only fields that start with `a_`, you would use `fl=a_*`.

- **Document transformers**: This is an *experimental* feature that allows documents to be modified before being returned to the client. The syntax for transformers uses square brackets around a transformer name with arguments as required: `fl=[explain style=text]`. Custom transformers can be created using Java, and there are several built-in transformers available:

  - `docid`: This adds the Lucene internal document ID to each document.
  - `shard`: This adds the name of the SolrCloud shard that produced the result to each document (*Chapter 10*, *Scaling Solr*, documents SolrCloud).
  - `explain`: This embeds *explain* information for each document. This transformer accepts an optional style argument set to one of these values: `nl`, `text`, or `html`. Solr's explain is covered in the following section on debugging.
  - `value`: This adds static values to each document. This transformer has one required parameter, `v`, which sets the value of the field. An optional type parameter `t` can be set to one of these values: `int`, `double`, `float`, and `date`. An example is `[value v=1 t=double]`.

Each of the types aforementioned can be combined and aliased as needed. Here's an example URL that makes use of the many valid `fl` values: `http://localhost:8983/solr/mbartists/select?q=*:*&fl=type,a_*&fl=theScore:score,three:sum(1,2),luceneID:[docid]`.

And here is a sample document from that query response:

```
<doc>
  <str name="type">Artist</str>
  <str name="a_name">F.D. Project</str>
  <date name="a_release_date_latest">2004-11-30T00:00:00Z</date>
  <float name="theScore">1.0</float>
  <float name="three">3.0</float>
  <int name="luceneID">0</int>
</doc>
```

Diagnostic parameters

These diagnostic parameters are helpful during development with Solr. Obviously, you'll want to be sure NOT to use these, particularly debugQuery, in a production setting because of performance concerns.

- indent: This is a Boolean option that will indent the output to make it easier to read. It works for most of the response formats.

- debugQuery: If true, then following the search results is <lst name="debug"> with diagnostic information. It contains voluminous information about the parsed query string, how the scores were computed, and timings for all of the Solr components to perform their part of the processing such as faceting. You may need to use the View Source function of your browser to preserve the formatting used in the score computation section. Debugging queries and enhancing relevancy is documented further in the next chapter.

  explainOther: If you want to determine why a particular document wasn't matched by the query or why it wasn't scored highly enough, then you can set a query for this parameter, such as id:"Release:12345", and output of the debugQuery will be sure to include the first document matching this query in its output.

- debug: This is a parameter to specify individual debugging features—add a debug parameter pair for each of these values as desired:
  - query: Returns information about how the query was parsed
  - results: Returns scoring information for each matching document
  - timing: Returns component timing information
  - true: Equivalent to debugQuery=true

- echoHandler: If true, then this emits the Java class name identifying the Solr request handler.

- echoParams: This controls whether or not query parameters are returned in the response header, as seen verbatim earlier. This is used to debug URL encoding issues, or to verify the complete set of parameters in effect—those present in the request (the URL plus HTTP post data) and those defined in the request handler. Specifying none disables this, which is appropriate for production real-world use. The default value is explain, which causes Solr to include only the parameters present in the request. Finally, you can use all to include those parameters configured in the request handler in addition to those in the URL.

- debug.explain.structured: When true, the result of the score explanation is returned as structured data.

Finally, there is another parameter that is not easily categorized called `timeAllowed`. This parameter accepts a value in milliseconds, which is a threshold used as the maximum time for a query to complete. If the query does not complete by this time limit, intermediate results are returned. Long-running queries should be very rare, but this allows you to cap them so that they don't overburden your production server.

Query parsers and local-params

A **query parser** parses a string into an internal Lucene query object, potentially considering request parameters and so-called **local-params**. Only a few parsers actually do real string parsing; some parsers—like those for geospatial—don't even use the query string. The default query parser is named `lucene`, and it has a special leading syntax to switch the parser to another and/or to specify parameters. Here's an example using the `dismax` parser along with two local-params and a query string of `billy corgan`:

```
{!dismax qf="a_name^2 a_alias" tie=0.1}billy corgan
```

 It's not common to see this syntax in the user query, `q`, since its parser is conveniently set via `defType`.

There are a few things to know about the local-params syntax:

- The leading query parser name (for example, DisMax) is optional. Without it, the parser remains as lucene. Furthermore, this syntax is a shortcut to put the query parser name in the `type` local-param.

- Usually, a query parser treats local-params as an override to request parameters in the URL.

- A parameter value can refer to a request parameter via a leading $, for example, `v=$qq`. This is useful to decompose a larger query, and to define parts of the query in different places between the request and the request handler's configuration.

- The special parameter `v` can be used to hold the query string as an alternative to it following `}`. The `query()` function query requires this approach. That will be shown later.

- A parameter value doesn't have to be quoted if there are no spaces. There wasn't any for the `tie` parameter in the preceding example.

For an interesting example, see the subquery syntax later in the Subqueries section.

Solr includes quite a few different query parsers. In the next section, you'll learn all about `lucene`. To process user queries, you should typically use `dismax` or `edismax` (short for extended-DisMax), which are described afterwards. The other query parsers are for special things, such as geospatial search, also described at the end of this chapter. This book only explores the most useful parsers; for further information, see `https://cwiki.apache.org/confluence/display/solr/ Query+Syntax+and+Parsing`.

Query syntax (the lucene query parser)

The query parser named `lucene` is Solr's most expressive and capable. With the benefit of hindsight, it should have been named "solr". It is based on Lucene's classic syntax with some additions that will be pointed out explicitly. In fact, you've already seen the first addition, which is local-params.

The `lucene` query parser does have a couple of query parameters that can be set. These parameters aren't normally specified though; Lucene's query syntax is easily made explicit to not need these options.

- `q.op`: This is the default query operator, either AND or OR to signify if all of the search terms or just one of the search terms need to match. If this isn't present, then the default is specified in `schema.xml` near the bottom in the `defaultOperator` attribute. If that isn't specified, then the default is OR.

- `df`: This is the default field that will be searched by the user query. If this isn't specified, then the default is specified in `schema.xml` near the bottom in the `<defaultSearchField>` element. If that isn't specified, then a query that does not explicitly specify a field to search will cause an error.

We recommend not using these parameters, unless they are used with local-params, such as, `{! df=text q.op=AND}my query`. Similarly, we recommend not setting the global defaults in the schema. One reason is that they affect all queries in the same request that you perhaps didn't intend, such as a facet query. Another is that it makes a query that depends on it ambiguous without knowing what these parameters are.

To play along with the examples in the book, go to `http://localhost:8983/ solr/#/mbartists/query` and set the `df` parameter to a_name. We advise you not to use that parameter, but this is for experimentation. The default query operator remains at OR and doesn't need changing. You may find it easier to scan the results if you set `fl` (the field list) to a_name, score.

To see a normalized string representation of the parsed query tree, enable debugQuery or set debug=query (conveniently via the **Raw Query Parameters** input). Then look for parsedquery in the debug output. See how it changes, depending on the query.

Matching all the documents

Lucene doesn't natively have a query syntax to match all documents. Solr enhances Lucene's query syntax to support this with the following syntax:

    :

In Solr 4.2, the syntax is as follows:

    *

When using dismax, it's common to set q.alt to this match-everything query so that a blank query returns all results.

Mandatory, prohibited, and optional clauses

Lucene has a unique way of combining multiple clauses in a query string. It is tempting to think of this as a mundane detail that is common to Boolean operations in programming languages, but Lucene doesn't quite work that way.

A query expression is decomposed into a set of unordered clauses of three types:

- A clause can be **mandatory**: +Smashing

  This matches only artists containing the word Smashing.

- A clause can be **prohibited**: -Smashing

  This matches all artists except those with Smashing. You can also use an exclamation mark as in !Smashing but that's rarely used.

- A clause can be **optional**: Smashing

Spaces must not come between +, ! or - and the search word for it to work as described here, otherwise the operator itself is treated like a separate word and the word to its right will default to **optional**. Typically, the operator won't actually be searched for since text analysis usually removes it.

The term *optional* deserves further explanation. If the query expression contains at least one mandatory clause, then any optional clause is just that—optional. This notion may seem pointless, but it serves a useful function in scoring documents that match more of them higher. If the query expression does not contain any mandatory clauses, then *at least one* of the optional clauses must match. The next two examples illustrate optional clauses.

Here, Pumpkins is optional, and the well-known band will surely be at the top of the list, ahead of bands with names like Smashing Atoms:

    +Smashing Pumpkins

In this example, there are no mandatory clauses and so documents with Smashing or Pumpkins are matched, but not Atoms. The Smashing Pumpkins is at the top because it matched both, followed by other bands containing only one of those words:

    Smashing Pumpkins -Atoms

If you would like to specify that a certain number or percentage of optional clauses should match or should not match, you can instead use the DisMax query parser with the min-should-match feature, described later in the chapter.

Boolean operators

The Boolean operators AND, OR, and NOT can be used as an alternative syntax to arrive at the same set of mandatory, optional, and prohibited clauses that were mentioned previously. Use the debugQuery feature and observe that the parsedquery string normalizes away this syntax into the previous (clauses being optional by default, such as OR).

 Case matters! At least this means that it is harder to accidentally specify a Boolean operator.

When the AND or && operator is used between clauses, then both the left and right sides of the operand become mandatory, if not already marked as prohibited. Let's consider this search result:

    Smashing AND Pumpkins

It is equivalent to:

    +Smashing +Pumpkins

Similarly, if the OR or || operator is used between clauses, then both the left and right sides of the operand become optional, unless they are marked mandatory or prohibited. If the default operator is already OR, then this syntax is redundant. If the default operator is AND, then this is the only way to mark a clause as optional.

To match artist names that contain Smashing or Pumpkins, try:

    Smashing || Pumpkins

The NOT operator is equivalent to the - syntax. So to find artists with Smashing but not Atoms in the name, you can do this:

    Smashing NOT Atoms

We didn't need to specify a + on Smashing. This is because it is the only optional clause and there are no explicit mandatory clauses. Likewise, using AND or OR would have no effect in this example.

It may be tempting to try to combine AND with OR such as:

    Smashing AND Pumpkins OR Green AND Day

However, *this doesn't work as you might expect!* Remember that AND is equivalent to both sides of the operand being mandatory, and thus each of the four clauses becomes mandatory. Our dataset returned no results for this query. In order to combine query clauses in some ways, you will need to use *subqueries*.

Subqueries

You can use parenthesis to compose a query of smaller queries, referred to as subqueries or **nested queries**. The following example satisfies the intent of the previous example:

    (Smashing AND Pumpkins) OR (Green AND Day)

Using what we know previously, this could also be written as:

    (+Smashing +Pumpkins) (+Green +Day)

But this is *not* the same as:

    +(Smashing Pumpkins) +(Green Day)

The preceding subquery is interpreted as documents that must have a name with Smashing or Pumpkins and either Green or Day in its name. So if there were a band named Green Pumpkins, then it would match.

Solr added another syntax for subqueries to Lucene's old syntax, which allows the subquery to use a different query parser, including local-params. This is an advanced technique, so don't worry if you don't understand it at first.

As an example, suppose you have a search interface with multiple query boxes, whereas each box is to search a different field. You could compose the query string yourself, but you would have some query-escaping issues to deal with. And if you wanted to take advantage of the dismax parser, then with what you know so far, that isn't possible. Here's an approach using this new syntax:

```
+{!dismax qf=a_name v=$q.a_name} +{!dismax qf=a_alias
v=$q.a_alias}
```

This example assumes that request parameters of q.a_name and q.a_alias are supplied for the user input for these fields in the schema. Recall from the local-params definition that the parameter v can hold the query and that the $ refers to another named request parameter.

 With versions of Solr earlier than 4.1, the syntax is slightly different and more complicated. The syntax uses a magic field named _query_ with its value being the subquery, which practically speaking, needs to be quoted. Here's the query from the preceding example, using the old syntax:

```
+_query_:"{!dismax qf=a_name v=$q.a_name}"
+_query_:"{!dismax qf=a_alias v=$q.a_alias}"
```

Limitations of prohibited clauses in subqueries

Lucene doesn't actually support a *pure negative query*; for example:

```
-Smashing -Pumpkins
```

Solr enhances Lucene to support this, but only at the top-level query, such as in the preceding example. Consider the following, admittedly strange, query:

```
Smashing (-Pumpkins)
```

This query attempts to ask the question: Which artist names contain either Smashing or do not contain Pumpkins? However, it doesn't work and only matches the first clause—(four documents). The second clause should essentially match most documents resulting in a total for the query that is nearly every document. The artist named Wild Pumpkins at Midnight is the only one in the index that does not contain Smashing but does contain Pumpkins, and so this query should match every document *except* that one.

To make this work, you have to take the subexpression containing only negative clauses, and add the all-documents query clause: *:*, as shown here:

```
Smashing (-Pumpkins *:*)
```

Interestingly, this limitation is fixed in the edismax query parser. Hopefully, a future version of Solr will fix it universally, thereby making this workaround unnecessary.

Querying specific fields

To have a clause explicitly search a particular field, you need to precede the relevant clause with the field's name, and then add a colon; spaces may be used in between, but that is generally not done:

```
a_member_name:Corgan
```

This matches bands containing a member with the name Corgan. To match Billy and Corgan, do the following:

```
+a_member_name:Billy +a_member_name:Corgan
```

Or use this shortcut to match multiple words:

```
a_member_name:(+Billy +Corgan)
```

The content of the parenthesis is a subquery, but with the default field being overridden to be a_member_name, instead of what the default field would be otherwise. By the way, we could have used AND instead of +, of course. Moreover, in these examples, all of the searches were targeting the same field, but you can certainly match any combination of fields needed.

Phrase queries and term proximity

A clause may be a phrase query: a contiguous series of words to be matched in order. In the previous examples, we've searched for text containing multiple words such as Billy and Corgan, but let's say we wanted to match Billy Corgan (that is, the two words adjacent to each other in that order). This further constrains the query. Double quotes are used to indicate a phrase query, as shown in the following query:

```
"Billy Corgan"
```

Related to phrase queries is the notion of the **term proximity**, also known as the **slop factor** or a **near query**. In our previous example, if we wanted to permit these words to be separated by no more than say three words in between, we could do this:

```
"Billy Corgan"~3
```

For the MusicBrainz dataset, this is probably of little use. For larger text fields, this can be useful in improving search relevance. The dismax query parser, which is described in the next chapter, can automatically turn a user's query into a phrase query with a configured slop.

For advanced requirements such as wildcards and Booleans within a phrase query, ComplexPhraseQueryParser can be used. For more information on this parser, its options and performance considerations, visit https://cwiki. apache.org/confluence/display/solr/Other+Parsers#OtherParsers-ComplexPhraseQueryParser.

Wildcard queries

A plain keyword search will look in the index for an exact match, subsequent to text analysis processing on both the query and input document text (for example, tokenization and lowercasing). But sometimes you need to express a query for a partial match expressed using wildcards.

 There is a highly relevant section in *Chapter 3, Text Analysis*, on partial/substring indexing. In particular, read about ReversedWildcardFilterFactory. N-grams is a different approach that does not work with wildcard queries.

There are a few points to understand about wildcard queries:

- Wildcard queries are a type of **multiterm** query, which means that the input is expanded into multiple terms during analysis. By default, multiterm query analyzer chains are in lowercase. Prefix, regex, and range queries are also forms of multiterm queries. For more information on multiterm query analysis, see the wiki page at http://wiki.apache.org/solr/ MultitermQueryAnalysis.

- If the field that you want to use the wildcard query on is stemmed in the analysis, then smashing* might not find the original text Smashing. The Porter stemmer will transform this word to smash, whereas EnglishMinimalStemmer (used in a_name) won't touch this word. Consequently, don't stem or use a minimal stemmer.

- Wildcard queries are one of the slowest types you can run. Use of ReversedWildcardFilterFactory helps with this a lot. But if you have an asterisk wildcard on both ends of the word, then this is the worst-case scenario.

To find artists containing words starting with `Smash`, you can use:

```
smash*
```

Or perhaps to find those starting with `sma` and ending with `ing`, use:

```
sma*ing
```

The asterisk matches any number of characters (perhaps none). You can also use `?` to force a match of any character at that position:

```
sma??*
```

That would match words that start with `sma` that have at least two more characters, but potentially more.

As far as scoring is concerned, each matching term gets the same score regardless of how close it is to the query pattern. Lucene can support a variable score at the expense of performance, but you would need to do some hacking to get Solr to do that.

Fuzzy queries

Fuzzy queries are useful when your search term needn't be an exact match, but the closer the better. The fewer the number of character insertions, deletions, or exchanges relative to the search term length, the better the score. The algorithm used is known as the **Levenshtein Distance** algorithm, also known as the **edit distance**. Fuzzy queries have the same need to avoid stemming, just as wildcard queries do. For example:

```
smashing~
```

Notice the tilde character at the end. Without this notation, simply `smashing` matches only four documents because only that many artist names contain that word. The search term `smashing~` matched 26 documents. The default edit distance is 2, but you can reduce it to 1 like so for less fuzzy matching:

```
smashing~1
```

That results in six matched documents—two more than a non-fuzzy search. Prior to Lucene 4, the edit distance was specified as a fraction of the number of characters in the word, and Lucene could search based on whatever edit distance this came to, albeit slowly. Lucene 4 is much faster but is limited to an edit distance no greater than 2, so you are now best off simply specifying 1 or 2 instead of using the fractional syntax.

Regular expression queries

There may be scenarios where you need to match documents using a specific pattern that can't be expressed using wildcard or fuzzy queries. For these cases, a regular expression query might be the answer.

The Solr regular expression syntax is simple and straightforward. Here's an example that matches documents that contain a possible 5-digit zip code, somewhere in the `a_address` field:

```
a_address:/[0-9]{5}/
```

As you can see, the pattern is enclosed in forward slashes (delimiters). Solr implicitly applies the pattern matching the full indexed value. There is no need to anchor to the beginning or end of the input string.

Regular expression queries are constant scoring—the scores of any matching documents will always be 1.0.

Range queries

Lucene lets you query for numeric, date, and even text ranges. The following query matches all of the bands formed in the 1990s:

```
a_type:2 AND a_begin_date:[1990-01-01T00:00:00.000Z TO 1999-12-
31T24:59:99.999Z]
```

Observe that the date format is the full ISO-8601 date-time in UTC, which Solr mandates (the same format used by Solr to index dates and that which is emitted in search results). The `.999` milliseconds part is optional. The [and] brackets signify an inclusive range, and, therefore, it includes the dates on both ends. To specify an exclusive range, use { and }. In Solr 3, both sides must be inclusive or both exclusive; Solr 4 allows both. The workaround in Solr 3 is to introduce an extra clause to include or exclude a side of the range.

Use the right field type

To get the fastest numerical/date range query performance, particularly when there are many indexed values, use a `trie` field (for example, `tdate`) with `precisionStep`. This was discussed in *Chapter 2, Schema Design*.

For most numbers in the MusicBrainz schema, we only have identifiers, and so it made sense to use the plain `long` field type, but there are some other fields. For the track duration in the tracks data, we could do a query such as the following one to find all of the tracks that are longer than 5 minutes (300 seconds, 300,000 milliseconds):

```
t_duration:[300000 TO *]
```

In this example, we can see Solr's support for *open-ended* range queries by using `*`.

Although uncommon, you can also use range queries with text fields. For this to have any use, the field should have only one term indexed. You can control this either by using the `string` field type, or by using the `KeywordTokenizer`. You may want to do some experimentation. The following example finds all documents where `somefield` has a term starting with `B`:

```
somefield:[B TO C}
```

Both sides of the range `B` and `C` are not processed with text analysis that could exist in the field type definition. If there is any text analysis such as lowercasing, you will need to do the same to the query or you will get unexpected results.

Date math

Solr extended Lucene's old query parser to add date literals as well as some simple math that is especially useful in specifying date ranges. In addition, there is a way to specify the current date-time using `NOW`. The syntax offers addition, subtraction, and rounding at various levels of date granularity, such as years, seconds, and so on down to milliseconds. The operations can be chained together as needed, in which case they are executed from left to right. Spaces aren't allowed. For example:

```
r_event_date:[* TO NOW-2YEAR]
```

In the preceding example, we searched for documents where an album was released over two years ago. `NOW` has millisecond precision. Let's say what we really wanted was precision to the day. By using `/`, we can round down (it never rounds up):

```
r_event_date:[* TO NOW/DAY-2YEAR]
```

The units to choose from are `YEAR`, `MONTH`, `DAY`, `DATE` (synonymous with `DAY`), `HOUR`, `MINUTE`, `SECOND`, `MILLISECOND`, and `MILLI` (synonymous with `MILLISECOND`). Furthermore, they can be pluralized by adding an `S`, as in `YEARS`.

This so-called **DateMath** syntax is not just for querying dates; it is for supplying dates to be indexed by Solr too! An index-time common usage is to timestamp added data. Using the NOW syntax as the `default` attribute of a timestamp field definition makes this easy. Here's how to do that: `<field name="indexedAt" type="tdate" default="NOW/SECOND" />`.

Score boosting

You can easily modify the degree to which a clause in the query string contributes to the ultimate relevancy score by adding a multiplier. This is called **boosting**. A value between 0 and 1 reduces the score, and numbers greater than 1 increase it. You'll learn more about scoring in the next chapter. In the following example, we search for artists that either have a member named `Billy`, or have a name containing the word `Smashing`:

```
a_member_name:Billy^2 OR Smashing
```

Here, we search for an artist name containing `Billy`, and optionally `Bob` or `Corgan`, but we're less interested in those that are also named `Corgan`:

```
+Billy Bob Corgan^0.7
```

Existence and nonexistence queries

This is actually not a new syntax case, but an application of range queries. Suppose you wanted to match all of the documents that have an indexed value in a field. Here, we find all of the documents that have something in `a_name`:

```
a_name:[* TO *]
```

As `a_name` is the default field, just `[* TO *]` will do.

This can be negated to find documents that *do not* have a value for `a_name`, as shown in the following code:

```
-a_name:[* TO *]
```

Just `a_name:*` is usually equivalent, and similarly, `-a_name:*` for negation. This was an accidental feature that users discovered. However, for some non-text fields such as numbers and dates, it is much slower, as it uses a completely different code path that was designed for wildcard text matching, not the nature of the actual field type. Consequently, we recommend avoiding this syntax. See SOLR-1982.

Like wildcard and fuzzy queries, these are expensive, slowing down as the number of distinct terms in the field increases.

Performance tip

If you need to perform these frequently, consider adding this to your schema: `<field name="field_name_ss" type="string" stored="false" multiValued="true" />`. Then, at index time, add the name of fields that have a value to it. There's JavaScript code for this commented in the `update-script.js` file invoked by an `UpdateRequestProcessor`. The query would then simply be `field_name_ss:a_name`, which is as fast as it gets.

Escaping special characters

The following characters are used by the query syntax as described in this chapter:

```
+ - && || ! ( ) { } [ ] ^ " ~ * ? : \ /
```

In order to use any of these without their syntactical meaning, you need to escape them by a preceding \ such as seen here:

```
id:Artist\:11650
```

This also applies to the field name part. In some cases, such as this one, where the character is part of the text that is indexed, the double-quotes phrase query will also work, even though there is only one term:

```
id:"Artist:11650"
```

If you're using SolrJ to interface with Solr, the `ClientUtils.escapeQueryChars()` method will do the escaping for you.

A common situation in which a query needs to be generated, and thus escaped properly, is when generating a simple filter query in response to choosing a field-value facet when faceting. This syntax and suggested situation is getting ahead of us, but I'll show it anyway since it relates to escaping. The query uses the `term` query parser as `{!term f=a_type}group`. What follows } is not escaped at all; even a \ is interpreted literally, and so with this trick, you needn't worry about escaping rules.

The DisMax query parser – part 1

The `lucene` query parser we've been using so far for searching offers a rich syntax, but it doesn't do anything more. A notable problem with using this parser is that the query must be well formed according to the aforementioned syntax rules, such as having balanced quotes and parentheses. Users might type just about anything for a query, not knowing anything about this syntax, possibly resulting in an error or unexpected results. The **DisMax** query parser, named after Lucene's `DisjunctionMaxQuery`, addresses this problem and adds many features to enhance search relevancy (good scoring). The features of this query parser that have a more direct relationship to scoring are described in the *The DisMax query parser – part 2* section in the next chapter. Use of this parser is so important that we need to introduce it here.

You'll see references here to **eDisMax**, whereby the *e* stands for *extended*. This is a forked evolution of DisMax that adds features. It hasn't yet replaced the original DisMax query parser because it enables more support for Lucene's syntax at the expense of a user inadvertently using it. So if you don't care about eDisMax's extra features and don't have users that want the more advanced syntax support, then stick with the venerable DisMax. In a future Solr version, perhaps as soon as the next release, we expect `dismax` to refer to the enhanced version while the older one will likely exist under another name.

Almost always use defType=edismax or dismax

The `dismax` (or `edismax`) query parser should almost always be chosen for parsing user queries q. Set it in the request handler definition for your app. Furthermore, we recommend the use of `edismax`. The only consideration against this is whether it will be a problem for users to be able to use Solr's full syntax, inadvertently or maliciously. This will be explained shortly.

Here is a summary of the features that the `dismax` query parser has over the `lucene` query parser:

- Searches across multiple fields with different score boosts through Lucene's `DisjunctionMaxQuery`.

- Limits the query syntax to an essential subset. The `edismax` query parser permits Solr's full syntax, assuming it parses correctly.

- Automatic phrase boosting of the entire search query. The `edismax` query parser boosts contiguous portions of the query too.

- Convenient query boosting parameters, generally for use with function queries.

- Can specify the minimum number of words to match, depending on the number of words in a query string.
- Can specify a default query to use when no user query is specified.

The `edismax` query parser was only mentioned a couple of times in this list, but it improves on the details of how some of these features work.

Use debugQuery=on or debug=query

Enable query debugging to see a normalized string representation of the parsed query tree, considering all value-add options that `dismax` performs. Then, look for `parsedquery` in the debug output. See how it changes depending on the query.

These features will subsequently be described in greater detail. But first, let's take a look at a request handler we've set up to search for artists. Solr configuration that is not related to the schema is located in `solrconfig.xml`. The following definition is a simplified version of the one in this book's code supplement:

```
<requestHandler name="/mb_artists" class="solr.SearchHandler">
    <lst name="defaults">
        <str name="defType">edismax</str>
        <str name="qf">a_name a_alias^0.8 a_member_name^0.4</str>
        <str name="q.alt">*:*</str>
        <str name="mm">100%</str>
    </lst>
</requestHandler>
```

In Solr's admin **Query** interface screen, we can refer to this by setting **Request-Handler** to `/mb_artists`. You can observe the effect in the URL when you submit the form. It wasn't necessary to set up such a request handler, because Solr is fully configurable from a URL, but it's a good practice and it's convenient for Solr's search form.

Searching multiple fields

You use the `qf` parameter to tell the `dismax` query parser which fields you want to search and their corresponding score boosts. As explained in the section on request handlers, the query parameters can be specified in the URL or in the request handler configuration in `solrconfig.xml`—you'll probably choose the latter for this one. Here is the relevant configuration line from our `dismax` based handler configuration earlier:

```
<str name="qf">a_name a_alias^0.8 a_member_name^0.4</str>
```

This syntax is a space-separated list of field names that can each have optional boosts applied using the same syntax that is used in the query syntax for boosting. This request handler is intended to find artists from a user's query. Such a query would ideally match the artist's name, but we'll also search for aliases as well as bands that the artist is a member of. Perhaps the user didn't recall the band name but knew the artist's name. This configuration would give them the band in the search results, most likely towards the end.

> The score boosts do not strictly order the results in a cascading fashion. An exact match in a_alias that matched only part of a_name will probably appear on top. If in your application you are matching identifiers of some sort, then you may want to give a boost to that field which is very high, such as 1,000, to virtually assure it will be on top.

One detail involved in searching multiple fields is the effect of stop words (for example, "the", "a", and so on) in the schema definition. If qf refers to some fields using stop words and others that don't, then a search involving stop words will usually return no results. The edismax query parser fixes this by making them all optional in the query unless the query is entirely stop words. With dismax, you can ensure the query analyzer chain in queried fields filters out the same set of stop words.

Limited query syntax

The edismax query parser will first try to parse the user query with the full syntax supported by the lucene query parser, with a couple tweaks. If it fails to parse, it will fall back to the limited syntax of the original dismax in the next paragraph. Someday, this should be configurable, but it is not at this time. The aforementioned "tweaks" to the full syntax are that or and and Boolean operators can be used in a lowercase form, and pure-negative subqueries are supported.

When using dismax (or edismax, when the user query failed to parse with the lucene query parser), the parser will restrict the syntax permitted to terms, phrases, and use of + and - (but not AND, OR, &&, | |) to make a clause mandatory or prohibited. Anything else is escaped if needed to ensure that the underlying query is valid. The intention is to never trigger an error, but unless you're using edismax, you'll have to code for this possibility due to outstanding bugs (SOLR-422, SOLR-874).

The following query example uses all of the supported features of this limited syntax:

```
"a phrase query" plus +mandatory without -prohibited
```

Min-should-match

With the `lucene` query parser, you have a choice of the default operator being OR, thereby requiring just one query clause to match, or choosing AND to make all clauses required. This, of course, only applies to clauses not otherwise explicitly marked required or prohibited in the query using + and -. But these are two extremes, and sometimes it is preferable to find some middle ground. The `dismax` parser uses a method called **min-should-match**, a feature which describes how many clauses should match, depending on how many there are in the query—required and prohibited clauses are not included in the numbers. This allows you to quantify the number of clauses as either a percentage or a fixed number. The configuration of this setting is entirely contained within the `mm` query parameter using a concise syntax specification, which I'll describe in a moment.

Always set `mm`. When in doubt what to set it to, use 100 percent. If it is not set, it uses the same defaulting rules as the `lucene` query parser, most likely resulting in an `mm` value equivalent to 0 percent, which is probably not what you want.

This feature is more useful if users use many words in their queries—at least three. This in turn suggests a text field that has some substantial text in it but that is not the case for our MusicBrainz dataset. Nevertheless, we will put this feature to good use.

Basic rules

The following are the four basic `mm` specification formats expressed as examples:

- 3: This specifies that three clauses are required, the rest are optional.

- -2: This specifies that two clauses are optional, the rest are required.

- 66%: This specifies that 66 percent of the clauses (rounded down) are required, the rest are optional.

- -25%: This specifies that 25 percent of the clauses (rounded down) are optional, the rest are required.

Notice that - inverses the required/optional definition. It does not make any number negative from the standpoint of any definitions herein.

Note that 75% and -25% may seem the same but are not due to rounding. Given five queried clauses, the first requires three, whereas the second requires four. This shows that if you desire a round-up calculation, then you can invert the sign and subtract it from 100.

Two additional points about these rules are as follows:

- If the mm rule is a fixed number n, but there are fewer queried clauses, then n is reduced to the queried clause count so that the rule will make sense. For example, if mm is -5 and only two clauses are in the query, then all are optional. Sort of!

- Remember that in all circumstances across Lucene (and thus, Solr); at least one clause in a query must match, even if every clause is optional. So, in the preceding example and for 0 or 0%, one clause must still match, assuming that there are no required clauses present in the query.

Multiple rules

Now that you understand the basic mm specification format, which is for one simple rule, I'll describe the final format, which allows for multiple rules. This format is composed of an ordered space-separated series of number<basicmm. This can be read as, "If the clause count is greater than number, then apply rule basicmm". Only the right-most rule that meets the clause count threshold is evaluated. As they are ordered in an ascending order, the chosen rule is the one that requires the greatest number of clauses. If none match because there are fewer clauses, then all clauses are required—a basic specification of 100 percent.

An example of the mm specification is given here:

```
2<75% 9<-3
```

This reads as follows:

If there are over nine clauses, then all but three are required (three are optional, and the rest are required). If there are over two clauses, then 75 percent are required (rounded down). Otherwise (one or two clauses) all clauses are required, which is the default rule.

 I find it easier to interpret these rules if they are read right to left.

What to choose

A simple configuration for min-should-match is to require all clauses:

```
100%
```

For MusicBrainz searches, I do not expect users to be using many terms, but I expect most of them to match. If a user searches for three or more terms, then I'll let one be optional. Here is the mm spec:

```
2<-1
```

 You may be inclined to require all of the search terms; and that's a good common approach. However, if just one word isn't found, then there will be no search results — an occurrence that most search software tries to minimize. Even if you make some of the words optional, the matching documents that have more of the search words will be towards the top of the search results, assuming score-sorted order (you'll learn why in the next chapter). There are other ways to approach this problem, for example, by performing a secondary search if the first returns none or too few. Solr doesn't do this for you, but it's easy for the client to do. This approach could even tell the user that this was done, which would yield a better search experience.

A default query

The dismax query parser supports a *default query*, which is used in the event the user query q is not specified. This parameter is q.alt, and it is not subject to the limited syntax of dismax. Here's an example of it used to match all documents from within the request handler defaults in solrconfig.xml:

```
<str name="q.alt">*:*</str>
```

This parameter is usually set to *:* to match all documents and is often specified in the request handler configuration in solrconfig.xml. You'll see with faceting in the next section that there will not necessarily even be a keyword search, and so you'll want to display facets over all of the data.

The uf parameter

The **DisMax** and **eDisMax** query parsers support fielded queries within the q parameter. This means that a user can explicitly search any valid field using this syntax: field_name:value. The **uf (user fields)** parameter makes it possible to restrict the set of fields the user can search against. The value of this parameter can be a space-delimited list of field names. A wildcard (*) can be used for field name globing. Dashes can be used to negate fields. For example, to allow user queries to search in the id field, all fields starting with a_ except a_id, the **uf** parameter value would be id a_* -a_id.

Filtering

Separate from the q parameter (the user query), you can specify additional so-called **filter queries** that will filter the search results. Arguably, the user query is also a filter, but you instead see the word "search" used for that. Filter queries don't affect scoring, unlike the user query. To add a filter, simply use the fq parameter. This parameter can be added multiple times for additional filters. A document must match *all* filter queries and the user query for it to be in the results.

As an example, let's say, we wanted to make a search form for MusicBrainz that lets the user search for bands, not individual artists, and those that released an album in the last 10 years. Let's also say that the user's query string is Green. In the index, a_type is either person for an individual or group for a band, or 0 if unknown. Therefore, a query that would find non-individuals would be this, combined with the user's query:

```
+Green -a_type:person +a_release_date_latest:[NOW/YEAR-10YEARS TO *]
```

However, you should *not* use this approach. Instead, use multiple fq query parameters:

```
q=Green&fq=-a_type:person&fq=a_release_date_latest:[NOW/YEAR-
10YEARS+TO+*]
```

A query that an application submits should appear slightly different due to URL Encoding special characters, such as the colon.

Filter queries have some tangential benefits:

- They improve performance, because each filter query is cached in Solr's **filter cache** and can be applied extremely quickly.
- They clarify the logs, which show what the user searched for without it being confused with the filters.

In general, raw user input doesn't wind up being part of a filter query. Instead, the filters are either known by your application in advance or are generated based on your data, for example, in faceted navigation.

You can disable caching of a filter by setting a cache local-param to false. This is useful to avoid pollution of the filter cache when you know the query is not likely to be used again. And if the query is the frange query parser (discussed in *Chapter 6, Search Relevancy*) or the geofilt query parser referencing a LatLonType field (discussed later), there is a potential performance benefit. Non-cached filter queries can be ordered too. For further details on this advanced technique, see https://cwiki.apache.org/confluence/display/solr/Common+Query+Parameters, under the *The cache=false Parameter* section.

Sorting

The sorting specification is specified with the `sort` query parameter. The default is `score desc`. Here, `score` is not a field but a special reference to a relevancy number, described in detail in the next chapter. Whereas, `desc` means descending order; use `asc` for ascending order. Before Solr 4.2, it needed to be lowercase. In the following example, suppose we search for artists that are not individuals (a previous example in the chapter), and then we might want to ensure that those that are surely bands get top placement ahead of those that are unknown. Secondly, we want the typical descending score search. This would simply be:

```
sort=a_type desc,score desc
```

> Pay attention to the field types and text analysis you're using in your schema for fields that you sort on. Basically, fields need to be single valued, indexed, and not tokenized. Some, but not all, support `sortMissingFirst` and `sortMissingLast` options. See the section on sorting in *Chapter 2, Schema Design*, for further information.

In addition to sorting on field values and the score, Solr supports sorting on a function query. Function queries are usually mathematical in nature and used for things like computing a geospatial distance or a time difference between now and some field value. Function queries have been discussed in detail in the next chapter, but here's a simple example sorting by the difference between the artist's begin and end date:

```
sort=sub(a_end_date,a_begin_date) desc
```

An interesting usecase that has nothing to do with math is a trick to sort based on multivalued field data in limited circumstances. For example, what if we wanted to sort on MusicBrainz releases which are declared to be of type `Album` (`r_type` is a multivalued field, remember)? We would use the following:

```
sort=query({!v="r_type:Album"}) desc
```

To understand this admittedly complicated expression, read the earlier section on query parsers and local-params, and read the definition of the `query()` function query in the next chapter. When using the `query()` function query in a sort expression, you must specify use local-params `v` parameter to specify the query string, instead of simply using the query string itself because of syntax restrictions in the context of how the `sort` parameter value is parsed.

Sorting and memory usage

When you ask Solr to sort on a field, every indexed value is put into an array in memory in Lucene's field cache. Text consumes a lot more memory than numbers. Also, the first time it's needed, it takes a noticeable amount of time to bring in all the values from disk. You should add a query that sorts on the fields your app might sort on into `newSearcher` in `solrconfig.xml`.

Joining

In most real world applications, models share relationships of some kind, either directly through their attributes or through an association "table". Traditional database engines make use of foreign keys to describe relationships, and SQL joins are used to merge the record sets together.

Solr has limited support for joining via its join query parsers (*join* and *block-join*). These query parsers use the local-params syntax to describe relationships between documents—local-params was described earlier in this chapter.

These parsers are not equal to SQL joins. The main difference between SQL and Solr in regard to joins is that the Solr joins do not merge related documents together in the search results. Solr joins are analogous to an SQL inner query in a WHERE clause.

The join query parser

The `join` query syntax takes two attributes, `to` and `from`, both of which accept field names as their values. The `from` field is used to link matching documents (those that matched the `join` query) to documents that match the `to` field. Not surprisingly, the join parser also requires a query. This query parser also supports joining across cores through its `fromIndex` option. As an example, let's say we'd like to fetch a set of documents from the `mbartists` core, where the artist has a certain release from the `mbreleases` core:

```
http://localhost:8983/solr/mbartists/select?q={!join from=r_a_id
to=a_id fromIndex=mbreleases}r_id:139850&fl=type,a_id
```

The following is the syntax:

```
{!join from=r_a_id to=a_id fromIndex=mbreleases}r_id:139850
```

The resulting documents would be something like:

```
<result name="response" numFound="1" start="0">
  <doc>
    <str name="type">Artist</str>
    <long name="a_id">11650</long>
  </doc>
</result>
```

For completeness, here's the same query using SQL:

```
SELECT type,a_id FROM mbartists a where a.a_id IN (SELECT r.r_a_id
FROM mbreleases r where r.r_id = 139850);
```

The field type of the from and to fields should be the same.

Here's another example showing a join between more than one core/index within the same query. This also makes use of the special local-params v attribute (the query):

```
fq={!join from=childId1 to=primaryCoreId fromIndex=childCore1
v=$childQ1} AND {!join from=childId2 to=primaryCoreId
fromIndex=childCore2 v=$childQ2}&childQ1=(field1:abc AND field2:[0
TO 1234])&childQ2=(field3:xyz)
```

 If there's a fair chance the same join query will occur again, put it in a filter query (the fq parameter) if you can, so that it will be cached.

One use of the Solr join is to put your volatile data in one core, and the more static in another core, using joins to associate records at query time.

Join queries have no influence on relevancy or document scores. If you're up for customizing Solr though, the Lucene *join* module contains a scoring join query, which could be used with little effort.

It should be noted that join queries can be slow; the more matching IDs there are, the longer the response time will become. In many cases, a carefully designed schema can satisfy most requirements by making good use of denormalization instead of joining.

Block-join query parsers

Block-join is called as such because it requires subdocuments to be indexed together in one *block* with the parent, which trickles down to the underlying index. You can even have a nested hierarchy. But this index requirement is a big limitation—you can't update any one document without updating an entire tree from a parent, and you can't use atomic updates. But for this trade-off, you get very fast joins.

Chapter 4, Indexing Data, covers the details on nested documents, but we'll provide a simple example here. Our sample `nested-docs.json` file contains the following JSON:

```
{
  "add": [{
    "id": "1",
    "title_t": "Node A",
    "relType_s": "parent",
    "_childDocuments_": [{
      "id": "2",
      "title_t": "Node A:A"
    }]
  }, {
    "id": "3",
    "title_t": "Node B",
    "relType_s": "parent",
    "_childDocuments_": [{
      "id": "4",
      "title_t": "Node B:B"
    }]
  }]
}
```

As you can see, the relationships are all self-contained within the special `childDocuments_` array field. To index, we can simply use `curl`:

```
curl -H 'content-type: application/json' -X POST
"http://127.0.0.1:8983/solr/collection1/update?commit=true" --
data-binary @nested-docs.json
```

Now that we have our nested documents indexed, we can query them using the block-join query parsers. There are actually two: block-join-parent and block-join-children. These parsers are quite different from the aforementioned join parser. Instead of returning documents matching a field-based foreign key, we use a query to identify parent/child documents to which we then apply a query to fetch the related results.

The block-join-children parser

The block-join-children parser is to find child documents given a query for parent documents. The syntax requires one attribute called of, the value being a simple Solr query that will be used to identify all valid parent documents. The primary query will be used to find specific parent documents within this set. Matching child documents will then be returned in the result set. For example, to find the child documents of Node A, we use the block-join-children parser as follows:

```
http://localhost:8983/solr/collection1/select?q={!child
of="relType_s:parent"}title_t:"Node A"&wt=json&omitHeader=true
```

The following is the syntax:

```
{!child of="relType_s:parent"}title_t:"Node A"
```

That query yields this response:

```
{
    "response": {
        "numFound": 1,
        "start": 0,
        "docs": [
            {
                "id": "2",
                "title_t": "Node A:A"
            }
        ]
    }
}
```

This returns exactly what you'd expect: one child of Node A, Node A:A.

The block-join-parent parser

To query for parent documents given a query for child documents, use the block-join-parent parser. This parser syntax requires one attribute called which. The value of this attribute is a Solr query that will be used to identify all valid parent documents. The primary query will be used to find specific child documents. Matching parent documents will then be returned in the result set. Here's an example:

```
http://localhost:8983/solr/collection1/select?q={!parent
which="relType_s:parent"}title_t:"Node
A:A"&wt=json&omitHeader=true
```

The following is the syntax:

```
{!parent which="relType_s:parent"}title_t:"Node A:A"
```

The yielded response for this query is as follows:

```
{
  "response": {
    "numFound": 1,
    "start": 0,
      "docs": [
        {
            "id": "1",
            "title_t": "Node A",
            "relType_s": "parent",
            "_version_": 1492571473528750000
        }
      ]
    }
}
```

This is what was expected; one parent document, `Node A`.

> There are other `join` implementations currently available as patch files on SOLR-4787: `PostFilterJoin`, to join records that match the main query and `ValueSourceJoin`, to return values from the second core based on the join query.

Spatial search

> This section was written by David Smiley, a committer on Lucene/Solr specializing in spatial search.

Spatial search is the ability to find geometric information in a multidimensional space. Most information retrieval systems that support spatial data, including Solr, are limited to a two-dimensional Cartesian plane, with additional support for **geospatial search** in which two dimensions reference the location on the surface of a sphere.

That description is a bit abstract, so let's now review some common spatial requirements of an application. If your Solr documents represent businesses and you know where the business resides in terms of a latitude and a longitude, then you probably want to show search results (businesses) filtered to the vicinity of where the user is looking. The user interface might have a map centered at a region of interest, and/or you know approximately where the user is from the GPS of their mobile device, or you might even have a GeoIP database at your disposal to map their IP address to an approximate location. Beyond filtering, you then might want to sort or relevancy-boost by the distance between the center of where the user's search area is and where the business is. Indexing points, filtering them by a rectangle or circle, getting the distance to sort or boost, and displaying that distance to the user, are the most common user requirements.

Spatial in Solr is confusing because there are basically two implementations to pick from: **LatLonType** (since Solr 3) and **SpatialRecursivePrefixTreeFieldType** also known as **RPT** (since Solr 4), and they are quite different. I'll describe the internal workings of both, and then how to use them, pointing out differences along the way.

Spatial in Solr 3 – LatLonType and friends

Solr 3 was the first release to have spatial support, and its implementation is still appropriate for common requirements. It is principally comprised of the `LatLonType` and `PointType` field types, the `geofilt` and `bbox` query parsers, and the `geodist`, `dist`, and `sqedist` functions. There are some other lesser used functions too.

`LatLonType` is geospatially oriented: latitude and longitude with geodetic math—notably the Haversine distance formula. `PointType` holds x and y coordinates on a classic 2D Cartesian plane with faster and simpler Euclidean geometry calculations, such as the Pythagorean Theorem for distance. `PointType` uniquely supports a variable number of dimensions; it's an obscure feature.

The underlying implementation resides in Solr itself, not Lucene-spatial. The overall approach is straightforward, notwithstanding some optimization tricks. The latitude and longitude (or x and y) are internally indexed into separate numeric fields. This approach doesn't support multivalued data, such as modeling businesses with multiple locations. If the query is just a rectangular filter, then it's pretty fast since it just needs to do a couple simple numeric range queries. If, on the other hand, the query shape is a point-distance (circle) shape, then the distance is calculated to potentially all points, depending on the circumstances; consequently, it isn't very scalable. Another thing to be aware of is that the FieldCache is used whenever the distance is required, which is for a point-distance query shape, and/or to sort by distance. The FieldCache holds all coordinate values in memory.

Some of the key characteristics have been summarized here:

- Single-valued point indexed field
- Point-radius (circle) query shape, or a rectangle
- Good implementation for small datasets; bbox is scalable but geofilt (circle) is not

Configuration

Configuring LatLonType and PointType is easy. In the following excerpt taken from Solr's example schema, given the field name store, there will be two automatically generated fields named store_0_coordinate and store_1_coordinate, which you'll see in Solr's schema browser:

```
<field name="store" type="location" indexed="true"
   stored="true"/>
<fieldType name="location" class="solr.LatLonType"
   subFieldSuffix="_coordinate"/>
<dynamicField name="*_coordinate" type="tdouble"
   indexed="true" stored="false"/>
```

> **Use floats instead of doubles**
>
> Change the *_coordinate dynamic field to use type tfloat to use half the memory. Using a 32-bit float for latitude and longitude has precision no worse than 2.37 meters—plenty accurate for most use cases.

We'll show you how to index and search for LatLonType further in this chapter.

Spatial in Solr 4 – SpatialRecursivePrefixTreeFieldType

Solr 4 introduced SpatialRecursivePrefixTreeFieldType, referred to as RPT because it's a mouthful. This one field type can be configured for either geodetic or Euclidean math. The Solr code is not much more than an adapter to the technology that mostly lives in the Lucene spatial module, plus a dependency on Spatial4j for the shape implementations. Additionally, the third-party JTS Topology Suite is required for some shapes, such as polygons. The implementation scheme is based on a variable-depth hierarchical grid in which the world is decomposed into grid cells, which are in turn recursively decomposed into smaller grid cells, until the desired precision is reached.

Indexed shapes of basically any kind are represented completely on the grid, and there are scalable algorithms to find them in relation to a query shape at search time. It's more powerful and often faster at filtering than the comparatively simple LatLonType. For distance sorting/boosting, it includes a custom point cache, but this feature should be avoided as it doesn't scale well.

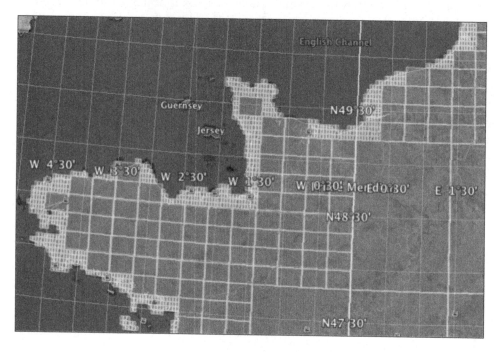

This picture shows how a polygon of France is decomposed into geohash grid cells of varying sizes. This was easily generated using a utility in the web demo of *Spatial Solr Sandbox* on GitHub that generates a KML file that Google Earth can render.

Its key characteristics can be summarized as follows:

- Indexes basically any shape, not just points:
  - ○ Shapes are approximated to a grid of configurable precision
  - ○ Multivalued fields

- Query by basically any shape, and with configurable precision—fast!
- Query by Intersects, Contains, and IsWithin predicates
- Multivalued point cache for distance sorting and relevancy
  - ○ The implementation is not scalable

If you need the distance and you have more than perhaps a million documents, or if you have real-time search requirements, then you should use *both* spatial implementations: RPT for its fast filtering and LatLonType to get the distance. On the other hand, if RPT's features aren't useful to you and you have a million or less documents, then I recommend using LatLonType alone. In a future Solr release, see LUCENE-4698.

Configuration – basic

The RPT field type has many configuration options; we're going to stick to the ones needed for basic geospatial search requirements right now and address other options later. A basic configuration exists in Solr's example schema:

```
<fieldType name="location_rpt"
  class="solr.SpatialRecursivePrefixTreeFieldType"
  geo="true" distErrPct="0.025" maxDistErr="0.000009"
  units="degrees" />
```

To use this field type, you need to declare a field that references this field type.

- geo: This is a Boolean that specifies whether this spatial mathematical model is based on a spherical earth model using latitude and longitude coordinates, or a flat 2D plane.

- units: *Ignore this*; it must be set to degrees. In Solr 5, it will be renamed to distanceUnits and support values like kilometers. In Solr 4, it has no effect. When you see a reference to a measurement in degrees (such as maxDistErr below), know that it refers to 1/360th of the circumference of a sphere when geo=true. Assuming the earth is that sphere, this works out to 111.2 kilometers per degree ($2\pi R/360$, R=6,353km).

The distance (d) parameter used by the geofilt and bbox parsers and the distances returned by the geodist function remain kilometers even if it's used with this field. Those parsers will be described shortly.

- maxDistErr: This refers to the precision of the spatial data in terms of the maximum distance error, as measured in degrees. For example, if the greatest precision you care about is a meter (0.001km), set it as measured in degrees (0.001/111.2 = 0.000009). The actual maximum distance error will be smaller than this, since it's used to choose a grid level that meets or exceeds this precision.

- `distErrPct`: If this number is non-zero, then non-point shapes will be approximated as a function of their overall size. This value is a fraction of a shape's approximate radius to be the allowable error, which in turn indicates to what grid level the shape will be maximally represented as. Under no circumstance can you have more precision than what `maxDistErr` yields. It applies to both indexed non-point shapes and query non-point shapes. There is a way to use a different value for a query shape if desired.

 If that's confusing, look again at the gridded map of France and look at the edge. If `distErrPct` is raised higher, the edge will eventually be even blockier. There are obviously scalability limitations if you attempt to index non-point shapes with a `distErrPct` of 0. Query shapes can handle it fine.

Indexing points

The simplest and most common spatial data to index is a point.

 If you have named locations (for example, Boston, MA) or addresses, then the data needs to be resolved to latitudes and longitudes using a **geocoder**. You can run your own with Gisgraphy—found at `http://www.gisgraphy.com`—or use a hosted service from Google, Yahoo, or others. Most hosted services have caps and/or fees.

When providing data to this field, it is formatted as a string with the latitude then the longitude, separated by a comma. Here's an example in Solr's Update-XML format:

```
<field name="store">43.17614,-90.57341</field>
```

Whether you use SolrJ, the DIH, or any other client/format, it appears as a string going in and coming out of Solr. If you have multiple points to index, simply supply them as additional values, as you would for any other multivalued field. `LatLonType` can't handle this but RPT will.

If the field type is `PointType`, then the dimension order is `x,y`. If the field type is RPT and geo is `false`, then you should supply points as `x y` (a space in between). If you use a comma in this circumstance, then the dimensions will be flipped. This is probably a bug, so don't rely on that behavior.

Filtering by distance or rectangle

Perhaps the most common geospatial need is to filter search results to those documents within a distance radius from a center point. If you are building an application in which the user is presented with a map, perhaps using Google Maps, then the center point is the center of the map the user is looking at and the distance radius is the distance from the center to the nearest map edge. Such a query is generally specified using a Solr filter query (fq parameter) leaving q open for the possibility of a combined keyword search if desired. Both the geofilt and bbox query parsers perform geospatial filtering. The geofilt query parser implements a point-distance based filter, a circle shape, whereas bbox uses the minimum bounding latitude-longitude box surrounding that circle. You can also specify an arbitrary rectangle using Solr's standard range syntax but using points.

LatLonType tuning

If you are using LatLonType, bbox and the rectangle range query syntax are faster than geofilt because they are able to make simple/scalable latitude and longitude numeric range searches, whereas geofilt computes the distance to every point it sees. If you need geofilt and if your spatial queries aren't very cacheable (tend to not be in your filter cache), then try adding these local-params: cache=false cost=100.

Here is a quick example based on Solr's example schema and dataset, showing the URL parameters needed to do the search:

```
q=*:*&fq={!bbox}&sfield=store&pt=45.15,-93.85&d=5
```

The parameters that geofilt and bbox require can be specified as either local-params (between the parser name and closing bracket) or standard request parameters, as shown above. To be clear, here's the same query using local-params:

```
q=*:*&fq={!bbox sfield=store pt=45.15,-93.85 d=5}
```

The advantage of *not* using local-params is that a combined distance sort can reuse the same parameters, as you'll see in a bit. Here are geofilt and bbox's parameters:

- sfield: The name of the spatial field
- pt: A latitude-comma-longitude pair for the center point of the query
- d: The query distance from pt in kilometers (see sphere_radius)
- sphere_radius: The radius of the sphere (Earth) in desired units for d. It defaults to the Earth's mean radius in kilometers.

To query by an arbitrary latitude-longitude rectangle, use a range query between the lower-left corner (smallest latitude and longitude) to the upper-right like so:

```
q=*:*&fq=store:[43.2,-94.1 TO 46.3,-92.0]
```

 If you use this syntax with LatLonType, it won't work if the dateline is crossed (bug SOLR-2609). RPT does not have that limitation.

Sorting by distance

Solr can sort search results by the distance between a document's point and another point supplied at query time. That point is typically the center point of a combined spatial filter. The typical way to spatially sort is to use Solr's ability to sort by a **function query**—a spatial function, geodist() in particular. The geodist() function calculates the geospatial distance (the "great circle distance") as calculated using the Haversine formula between a pair of points. The points are each taken from the first available of an argument, the pt parameter, or the sfield parameter. Any of these might be absent, but at least two must be specified. When a point is specified as an argument (within the parenthesis), it can either be a geospatial field name or a pair of arguments that are in latitude then longitude order. The latitude or longitude can be constants, or they may reference numeric fields' names. Here's an example of this:

```
&sort=geodist(store,42.4,-71.1) asc
```

 By design, these parameter names align with those for the geofilt and bbox query parsers, which pair well with geodist(). Consequently, it is rare to supply arguments if you are also spatially filtering.

Before the RPT field supported geodist() in Solr 4.5, a different, more awkward syntax was needed. You used to have to add a score=distance local-param to the spatial query and then put the spatial query into q to sort by score and filter at the same time. Or, even more awkwardly, you could sort by the query() function query. You can find examples of that syntax, if you must, online.

Returning the distance

It's often desirable to show the distance to users in search results. The most straightforward way to do this is to use a new Solr 4 feature that allows putting a function query into the field list: the `fl` param. Doing this is independent of any filtering or sorting that may exist, and so it's easy to use.

```
&fl=*,score,dist:geodist()&sfield=store&pt=45.15,-93.8
```

That example also gave a label of `dist` to this number in the search results; another label could have been chosen. Without a label, it is named by the actual function query itself in the results.

Boosting by distance

Perhaps you don't want to sort by distance, but you want to influence the relevancy (so-called boosting) by distance. Relevancy tuning is covered in the next chapter, so you will need to read that to better understand this section. The base formula to use for distance-based boosting should be the reciprocal. A Solr function query for the reciprocal used for boosting in this way should look like `recip(x,1,c,c)`, where x is the distance and c is 1/10th of what I call the *horizon distance*. If you have a spatial filter in place, then use the radius of the query shape (center to edge or corner) as the horizon. Otherwise, pick an approximate distance at which any greater distance is unlikely to be relevant to the user. The result of the reciprocal function used in this way will range from 1.0 at the center of the query point to 0.1 at the horizon distance; and it approaches 0 further away.

For example, let's say you have a spatial filter of a 100-kilometer radius at 42.15° N, 93.85° W; you have a keyword search in place using the `edismax` query parser; and you want to multiply the distance boost to the score:

```
&defType=edismax&q=...&qf=...&sort=score desc
&fq={!geofilt}&sfield=store&pt=45.15,-93.85&d=100
&boost=recip(geodist(),1,10,10)
```

Memory and performance of distance sorting and boosting

Sorting or boosting by distance will require all indexed points to be in memory. Use floats instead of doubles, if possible, to reduce this footprint with `LatLonType`. The RPT field type still has a sub-par point cache implementation that has a high memory overhead on a per-point and per-document basis. If you can, use `LatLonType` for sorting instead of RPT, until that is rectified.

Sorting and boosting on a search that matches a great many documents can be slow. This is because the distance needs to be computed to each matching point, even if you only return the top 10 of them. Furthermore, the Haversine formula involves a fair amount of trigonometry that can computationally really add up when computed between many points. What can be done to help is use a cheaper distance function that is less accurate in a geospatial sense but is faster to compute. For example, if all the indexed data is just in one region of the world, then you could project the data onto a 2D plane with minimal distortion around the edges. The data would go in a pair of float fields and then you could replace use of `geodist()` with `sqedist()` — squared Euclidean distance. It takes four arguments, the x and y of the indexed fields, and another pair for the query point. Projecting data is well beyond the scope of this book. For further information, visit `http://trac.osgeo.org/proj4j/`.

Advanced spatial

This book sets aside a fair amount of space to cover spatial search in Solr for the needs of most applications, but there's more that couldn't be included:

- Non-geodetic (for example, Euclidean) spatial such as `PointType` and `dist()`, and the implications of `geo="false"` on RPT.

- Spatial **Well Known Text (WKT)** syntax: WKT is a standard for expressing a variety of shapes, including Polygons. Lucene/Solr can index and search by them. Related to this is including JTS with Solr.

- Spatial predicates that include `Intersects`, `Contains`, `IsWithin`, and `IsDisjointTo`. When indexing non-point shapes, there are more applicable relations than what can occur with just points.

- The `BBoxField` field type supports nearly every predicate and has area-overlap relevancy. It is new in Solr 4.10.

- Indexing and searching on multi-value time durations: If you want to index time or other numeric durations in Solr, particularly when there's a variable number of them per document, then the only way to do this is to express the times as points in spatial. I bet you'll find this fascinating: `http://wiki.apache.org/solr/SpatialForTimeDurations`.

For more coverage of these spatial topics, see the Solr Reference Guide at `https://cwiki.apache.org/confluence/display/solr/Spatial+Search`.

Summary

At this point, you've learned the essentials of searching in Solr, from request handlers to the full query syntax, to DisMax, joins, geospatial, and more. We spent a lot of time on the query syntax because you'll see the syntax pop up in several places across Solr, not just in the user's query. Such places include filter queries, delete queries, boost queries, facet queries, embedded within certain function queries, and query warming (discussed in later chapters).

The subject of searching continues in the next chapter with a focus on relevancy/scoring matters. This starts with an explanation of Lucene/Solr's scoring model, and then various tools Solr gives you to influence the score, such as function queries, which are also useful in sorting and filtering.

6

Search Relevancy

At this point, you've learned the basics of Solr. You've undoubtedly seen your results sorted by score in descending order, the default, but have no understanding as to where those scores came from. This chapter is all about search relevancy, which basically means it's about scoring; but it's also about other non-trivial methods of sorting to produce relevant results. A core Solr feature enabling these more advanced techniques, called **function queries**, will be introduced. The major topics covered in this chapter are as follows:

- Factors influencing the score
- Troubleshooting queries to include scoring
- DisMax part 2—features that enhance relevancy
- Function queries

In a hurry?
Use the `edismax` query parser for user queries by setting the `defType` parameter. Configure the `qf` (query fields), as explained in the previous chapter, set `pf` (phrase fields) considering the call-out tip in this chapter, and set `tie` to `0.1`. If at any point you need help troubleshooting a query (and you will), then return to read the *Troubleshooting queries and scoring* section of this chapter.

Scoring

Scoring in Lucene is an advanced subject, but it is important to at least have a basic understanding of it. We will discuss the factors influencing Lucene's default scoring model and where to look for diagnostic scoring information. If this overview is insufficient for your interest, then you can get the full details at `http://lucene.apache.org/core/4_8_1/core/org/apache/lucene/search/package-summary.html#scoring`.

The important thing to understand about scores is not to attribute much meaning to a score by itself; it's *almost* meaningless. The relative value of an individual score to the max score is much more meaningful. A document scored as 0.25 might be a great match or not, there's no telling, while in another query a document scoring 0.80 may actually not be a great match. But if you compare a score to another from the very same search and find it to be twice as large, then it is fair to say that the query matched this document twice as well. The factors influencing the score are as follows:

- **Term frequency (tf)**: The more times a term is found in a document's field, the higher the score it gets. This concept is most intuitive. Obviously, it doesn't matter how many times the term may appear in some other field, it's the searched field that is relevant (whether explicit in the query or the default).

- **Inverse document frequency (idf)**: The rarer a term is in the entire index, the higher its score is. The document frequency is the number of documents in which the term appears for a given field. It is the *inverse* of the document frequency that is positively correlated with the score.

- **Co-ordination factor (coord)**: The greater the number of query clauses that match a document, the greater the score will be. Any mandatory clauses must match and the prohibited ones must not match, leaving the relevance of this piece of the score to situations where there are optional clauses.

- **Field length (fieldNorm)**: The shorter the matching field is, measured in number of indexed terms, the greater the matching document's score will be. For example, if there was a band named Smashing, and another named Smashing Pumpkins, then this factor in the scoring would be higher for the first band upon a search for just Smashing, as it has one word in the field while the other has two. Norms for a field can be marked as omitted in the schema with the `omitNorms` attribute, effectively neutralizing this component of the score and index-time boosts too.

 A score *explain* will show `queryNorm`. It's derived from the query itself and not the indexed data; it serves to help make scores more comparable for different queries, but not for different documents matching the same query.

These factors are the *intrinsic* components contributing to the score of a document in the results. If your application introduces other components to the score, then that is referred to as **boosting**. Usually, boosting is a simple multiplier to a field's score, either at index or query time, but it's not limited to that.

Alternative scoring models

The scoring factors that have just been described relate to Lucene's default scoring model. It's known as the **Vector Space Model**, also referred to as simply **TF-IDF** due to its most prominent components. This venerable model is well known in the information retrieval community, and it has been the only model Lucene supported since the beginning. Lucene/Solr 4 supports four more models, including a well-known one called **BM25**. BM25 has been the subject of many research papers including those from recognized search experts at Google and Microsoft. It's often pitted against the Vector Space Model portrayed as an improvement, provided its parameters are tuned appropriately.

In Lucene, the relevance model is implemented by a `Similarity` subclass, and Solr provides `SimilarityFactory` for each one. Naturally, they have their own unique tuning parameters. In order to use BM25, simply add the following to your `schema.xml`:

```
<similarity class="solr.BM25SimilarityFactory">
  <float name="k1">1.2</float>
  <float name="b">0.75</float>
</similarity>
```

Don't forget to re-index. The preceding excerpt will have a global effect on relevancy for the schema. It's also possible to choose a different similarity per field. Beware that doing so is problematic if you are using TF-IDF at all; you'll see different scores for TF-IDF depending on whether the similarity is configured at the field level or as the global default, with regard to the query norm and coordination factor.

For more information on configuring scoring models (similarities) in Solr, see the wiki at `http://wiki.apache.org/solr/SchemaXml#Similarity` and Solr's Javadoc API for the factories. But for real guidance on the specific models, you'll have to start Googling.

The default Vector Space Model is a good default

Do not choose a relevancy model and its tuning parameters based solely on a small sampling of anecdotal searches; choose them after a real evaluation, such as from A/B testing.

Query-time and index-time boosting

At index-time boosting, you have the option to boost a particular document specified at the document level or at a specific field. *Chapter 4, Indexing Data*, shows the syntax; it's very simple to use for the XML and JSON formats. The document-level boost is the same as boosting each field by that value. This is internally stored as part of the norms number. Norms must not be omitted in the relevant fields in the schema. It's uncommon to perform index-time boosting because it is not as flexible as query time. That said, index-time boosting tends to have a more predictable and controllable influence on the final score, and it's faster.

At query-time boosting, we described in the previous chapter how to explicitly boost a particular clause of a query higher or lower, if needed, using the trailing ^ syntax. We also showed how the DisMax query parser's qf parameter not only lists the fields to search but allows a boost for them as well. There are a few more ways DisMax can boost queries that you'll read about shortly.

Troubleshooting queries and scoring

An invaluable tool in diagnosing scoring behavior (or why a document isn't in the result or is but shouldn't be) is enabling query debugging with the debugQuery query parameter. There is no better way to describe it than with an example. Consider the fuzzy query on the artists' index:

```
a_name:Smashing~
```

We would intuitively expect that documents with fields containing Smashing would get the top scores, but that didn't happen. Execute the preceding query mentioned with debugQuery=on.

 Depending on the response format and how you're interacting with Solr, you might observe that this information isn't indented. If you see that, switch to another response format. Try Ruby with wt=ruby.

In the following code, the fourth document has Smashing as part of its name but the top three don't:

```
<doc>
  <float name="score">3.999755</float>
  <str name="a_name">Smashin'</str>
</doc>
<doc>
  <float name="score">3.333129</float>
  <str name="a_name">Mashina</str>
```

```
    </doc>
    <doc>
      <float name="score">2.551927</float>
      <str name="a_name">Slashing Funkids</str>
    </doc>
    <doc>
      <float name="score">2.5257545</float>
      <str name="a_name">Smashing Atoms</str>
    </doc>
```

The first and third documents have words that differ from smashing by only one character, the second by two. What's going on here? Let's look at the following debug output, showing just the second and fourth docs for illustrative purposes:

```
<lst name="explain">
  <str name="Artist:227132">
    3.333129 = (MATCH) sum of:
      3.333129 = (MATCH) weight(a_name:mashina^0.71428573 in
      166352) [DefaultSimilarity], result of:
        3.333129 = score(doc=166352,freq=1.0 = termFreq=1.0 ),
        product of:
          0.2524328 = queryWeight, product of:
            0.71428573 = boost
            13.204025 = idf(docFreq=1, numDocs=399182)
            0.026765013 = queryNorm
          13.204025 = (MATCH) fieldWeight(a_name:mashina in
          286945),
          product of:
            1.0 = tf(termFreq(a_name:mashina)=1)
            13.204025 = idf(docFreq=1, numDocs=399182)
            1.0 = fieldNorm(field=a_name, doc=286945)
  </str>
<!--... skip ...-->
  <str name="Artist:93855">
    2.5257545 = (MATCH) sum of:
      2.5257545 = (MATCH) weight(a_name:smashing in 9796)
      [DefaultSimilarity], result of:
        2.5257545 = score(doc=9796,freq=1.0 = termFreq=1.0 ),
        product of:
          0.32888138 = queryWeight, product of:
            12.287735 = idf(docFreq=4, numDocs=399182)
            0.026765013 = queryNorm
          7.6798344 = fieldWeight in 9796, product of:
            1.0 = tf(freq=1.0), with freq of:
              1.0 = termFreq=1.0
```

```
12.287735 = idf(docFreq=4, maxDocs=399182)
0.625 = fieldNorm(doc=9796)
```
```
</str>
```

What we see here is the mathematical breakdown of the various components of the score. We see that `mashina` (the term actually in the index) was given a query-time boost of `0.75` (under-boosted), whereas `smashing` wasn't. We expected this because fuzzy matching gives higher weights to stronger matches, and it did. However, other factors pulled the final score in the other direction. Notice that the `fieldNorm` for `Mashina` is `1.0`, whereas `Smashing Atoms` has a `fieldNorm` of `0.625`. This is because the document we wanted to score higher has a field with two indexed terms versus just the one that `Mashina` has. Another factor is that the IDF for `mashina`, `13.2`, is higher than for `smashing`, `12.3`. Upper/lower case plays no role. So, arguably, `Mashina` is a closer match than `Smashing Atoms` to the fuzzy query `Smashing~`.

How might we fix this? Well, it's not broken, and the number four spot in the search results isn't bad. So this result is arguably in no need of fixing. This is also a fuzzy query that is fairly unusual and arguably isn't a circumstance to optimize for. For the fuzzy query case seen here, you could use DisMax's `bq` parameter (to be described very soon) and give it a non-fuzzy version of the user's query. That will have the effect of boosting an exact match stronger. Another idea is to enable `omitNorms` on `a_name` in the schema; however, that might reduce scoring effectiveness for other queries.

Tools – Splainer and Quepid

If you find the *explain* output hard to wrap your head around, you might want to use an open source tool called **Splainer** that dresses up Solr's raw output in a way that is easier to understand. Splainer is a browser-side web application, and as such, you can try it online against your local Solr instance without having to install or configure anything. Try it at `http://splainer.io`. Be sure to view the tour, which will show more of what it has to offer.

If you want to take search relevancy seriously, then you're going to invest significant time into it. Solr exposes a lot of power and reasonable defaults, but each application is different and it's all too easy to make a change that has a net negative effect across the searches users make. You'll need to do things such as keep track of a set of sample queries and their results, and monitor it over time. You could do this manually with a hodge-podge of spreadsheets and scripts, but a tool such as **Quepid** can help a ton. The most important thing Quepid does is assist you in curating a set of important queries with their search results that have human-entered quality judgments against them. As you tweak Solr's relevancy knobs, you can see the effect. Quepid is available at `https://quepid.com`.

The DisMax query parser – part 2

In the previous chapter, you were introduced to the `dismax` query parser as the preferred choice for user queries. The parser for user queries is set with the `defType` parameter. The syntax, the fields that are queried (with boosts) – `qf`, the min-should-match syntax – `mm`, and the default query – `q.alt`, were already described. We're now going to cover the remaining features: the ones that most closely relate to scoring.

>
>
> Any mention herein to `dismax` applies to the `edismax` query parser too, unless specified otherwise. As explained in the previous chapter, `edismax` is the extended DisMax parser. It is generally superior to `dismax`, as you'll see in the upcoming section.

Lucene's DisjunctionMaxQuery

The ability to search across multiple fields with different boosts in this query parser is a feature powered by Lucene's **DisjunctionMaxQuery** query class. Let's start with an example. If the query string is simply `rock`, then DisMax might be configured to turn this into a `DisjunctionMaxQuery` *similar* to this Boolean query:

```
fieldA:rock^2 OR fieldB:rock^1.2 OR fieldC:rock^0.5
```

The difference between that Boolean OR query and `DisjunctionMaxQuery` (we will call it just DisMax henceforth) is only in the scoring. Without getting into the details, if the intention is to search for the same text across multiple fields, then it's better to use the maximum subclause score rather than the sum. DisMax will take the max, whereas Boolean uses the sum.

The `dismax` query parser has a `tie` parameter, which is between zero (the default) and one. By raising this value above zero, it serves as a tie-breaker to give an edge to a document that matched a term in multiple fields versus one. At the highest value of `1`, it scores very similarly to that of a Boolean query.

>
>
> In practice, setting `tie` to a small value like `0.1` is effective.

Boosting – automatic phrase boosting

Suppose a user searches for `Billy Joel`. This is interpreted as two terms to search for, and depending on how the request handler is configured, either both must be found in the document or just one. Perhaps for one of the matching documents, `Billy` is the sole name of a band, and it has a member named `Joel`. Solr will match this document and perhaps it is of interest to the user since it contained both words the user typed. However, it's a fairly intuitive observation that a document field containing the entirety of what the user typed, `Billy Joel`, represents a closer match to what the user is looking for. Solr would certainly find such a document too, without question, but it's hard to predict what the relative scoring might be. To improve the scoring, you might be tempted to automatically quote the user's query, but that would omit documents that don't have the adjacent words. What the DisMax handler can do is add a phrased version of the user's query onto the original query as an *optional* clause. So, in a nutshell, it rewrites the following query:

```
Billy Joel
```

It then turns it into:

```
+(Billy Joel) "Billy Joel"
```

 The queries here illustrate phrase boosting in its most basic form. It doesn't depict the `DisjunctionMaxQuery` that dismax uses, because there's no query syntax for it.

The rewritten query depicts that the original query is mandatory by using +, and it shows that we've added an *optional* phrase. A document containing the phrase `Billy Joel` not only matches that clause of the rewritten query, but it also matches `Billy` and `Joel` — three clauses in total. If in another document the phrase didn't match, but it had both words, then only two clauses would match. Lucene's scoring algorithm would give a higher **coordination factor** to the first document, and would score it higher, all other factors being equal.

Configuring automatic phrase boosting

Automatic phrase boosting is not enabled by default. In order to use this feature, you must use the `pf` parameter, which is an abbreviation of **phrase fields**. The syntax is identical to `qf`. You should start with the same value and then make adjustments. Common reasons to vary `pf` from `qf` are as follows:

- To use different (typically lower) boost factors so that the impact of phrase boosting isn't overpowering. Experimentation will guide you to make these adjustments.

- To omit fields that are always one term, such as an identifier, because there's no point in searching the field for phrases.

- To omit some of the fields that have lots of text since that *might* slow down search performance too much.

- To substitute a field for another that has the same data but is analyzed differently. For example, you might choose to speed up these phrase searches by **shingling** (a text analysis technique described in *Chapter 10, Scaling Solr*) into a separate field, instead of shingling the original field. Such a shingling configuration would be a little different than described in that chapter; you would set outputUnigrams to false.

> **pf tips**
> Start with the same value used as qf, but with boosts cut in half.
> Remove fields that are always one term, such as an identifier.
> Use **common-grams** or **shingling**, as described in *Chapter 10, Scaling Solr*, to increase performance.

Phrase slop configuration

The previous chapter described phrase **slop**, also known as term proximity. The syntax follows a phrase with a tilde and a number, as follows:

```
"Billy Joel"~1
```

The dismax query parser adds two parameters to automatically set the slop: qs for any *explicit* phrase queries that the user entered and ps for the phrase boosting mentioned previously. If slop is not specified, then there is no slop, which is equivalent to a value of zero. For more information about slop, see the corresponding discussion in the previous chapter. Here is a sample configuration of both slop settings:

```
qs=1&ps=0
```

Partial phrase boosting

In addition to boosting the entire query as a phrase, edismax supports boosting consecutive word pairs if there are more than two queried words, and consecutive triples if there are more than three queried words. Setting pf2 and pf3, respectively, in the same manner that the pf parameter is defined, configures these. For example, consider the following query:

```
how now brown cow
```

It would now become:

```
+(how now brown cow) "how now brown cow" "how now" "now brown"
"brown cow" "how now brown" "now brown cow"
```

This feature is not affected by the `ps` (phrase slop) parameter, which only applies to the entire phrase boost; there's `ps2` and `ps3` to set these slops.

 You can expect the relevancy to improve for longer queries, but of course, these queries are going to be even slower now. To speed up such queries, use common-grams or shingling, described in *Chapter 10, Scaling Solr*. If you are using `pf2` or `pf3`, consider a `maxShingleSize` of 3 (but monitor its impact on index size), and consider omitting larger text fields from `pf2` or `pf3`.

Boosting – boost queries

Continuing with the boosting theme is another way to affect the score of documents: boost queries. The dismax parser lets you specify multiple additional queries using `bq` parameter(s), which, like the automatic phrase boost, get added onto the user's query in a similar manner. Remember that boosting only serves to affect the scoring of documents that already matched the user's query in the `q` parameter. If a matched document *also* matches a `bq` query, then it will be scored higher than if it didn't.

For a realistic example of using a boost query, we're going to look at MusicBrainz releases data. Releases have an `r_type` field containing values such as `Album`, `Single`, `Compilation`, and others, and an `r_official` field containing values such as `Official`, `Promotion`, `Bootleg`, and `Pseudo-Release`. We don't want to sort search results based on these, since it's most important to consider search relevancy of the query. However, we might want to influence the score based on these fields. For example, let's say albums are the most relevant release type, whereas a compilation is the least relevant. And let's say that an official release is more relevant than bootleg or promotional or pseudo-releases. We might express this using a boost query like this (defined in the request handler):

```
bq=r_type:Album^2 (*:* -r_type:Compilation)^2
r_official:Official^2
```

Searching releases for "the aeroplane flies high" (quoted and not a typo) showed that this boost query did what it should by breaking a score tie in which the release names were the same but these attributes varied. In reality, the boosting on each term would not all be 2; they would be tweaked to have the relevancy boost desired by carefully examining the debugQuery output. One oddity in this query is (*:* -r_type:Compilation)^2, which boosts all documents *except* compilations. Using r_type:Compilation^0.5 would not work since it would still be added to the score and only when the document is a compilation—exactly what we *don't* want. Put another way, you can't under-boost, but you can indirectly do it by boosting the inverse set of documents. To understand why *:* is needed, read the previous chapter on the limitations of pure negative queries.

Boosting – boost functions

Boost functions offer a powerful way to either add or multiply the result of a user-specified formula to a document's score. By *formula*, I refer to a composition of Solr **function queries**, which have been described in detail next in this chapter. To add to the score, specify the function query with the bf parameter. The edismax query parser adds support to multiply the result to the score in which you specify the function query with the boost parameter. You can specify bf and boost each as many times as you wish.

> For a thorough explanation of function queries including instructional MusicBrainz examples, see the next section.

An example of boosting MusicBrainz tracks by how recently they were released is:

```
boost=
recip(abs(ms(NOW/DAY,r_event_date_earliest)),1,6.3E10,6.3E10)
```

There cannot be any spaces within the function. The bf and boost parameters are actually not parsed in the same way. The bf parameter allows multiple boost functions within the same parameter, separated by space, as an alternative to using additional bf parameters. You can also apply a multiplied boost factor to the function in bf by appending ^100 (or another number) to the end of the function query. This is equivalent to using the mul() function query, described later.

> Ensure newSearcher in solrconfig.xml has a sample query using the boost functions you're using. In doing so, you ensure that any referenced fields are loaded into Lucene's field cache instead of penalizing the first query with this cost. *Chapter 10, Scaling Solr*, has more information on performance tuning.

Add or multiply boosts

In a nutshell, if you can tame the difficulty in additive boosting (the `bf` param), then you'll probably be more satisfied with the scoring. Multiplicative boosting (the `boost` param) is easier to use, especially if the intended boost query is considered less than or equal to the user query, which is usually true.

If you describe how you'd like the scoring to work as, "I'd like two-thirds of the document score to come from the user query and the remainder one-third to be from my formula," (or whatever ratios) then additive scores are for you. The trick is that you need to know the top score for an excellent match on the user query in order to balance out the proportions right. Try an exact match on a title (a highly boosted field in the query) and see what the top score is. Do this a number of times for a variety of documents, looking for reasonable consistency. So if, for example, the top end of the user query ends up being 1.5, and you want the function query to make up about half as much as the user query does in the final score, then adjust the function query so its upper bound is 0.75. Simply multiply by that if you already have the function query in the 0-1 nominal range. Even if these instructions don't seem too bad, in practice tuning additive scores is tricky since Lucene will react to every change you make by changing the `queryNorm` part of the score out from under you, which you have no control over. As it does this, keep your eye on the overall ratios that you want between the added boost part and the user query part, not the final score values. Another bigger problem is that your experiments in gauging the maximum score of the user query will change as your data changes, which will mean some ongoing monitoring of whatever values you choose. And another complication is that DisMax's `tie` parameter tends to interfere with this way of boosting.

The other way of thinking about your boost function is as a user query score multiplier (a factor). With multiplication you don't need to concern yourself with whatever a "good" user query score is — it has no bearing here. The tricky part of multiplicative boosts is weighting your boost, so it has the relative impact you want. If you simply supply your nominal range (0-1) function directly as the boost, then it has the same weight as the user query. As you shift the function's values above 0, you reduce the influence it has relative to the user query. For example, if you add 1 to your nominal 0-1 range so that it goes from 1-2, then it is weighted roughly half as much [formula: $(2-1)/2 = 0.5$].

It's possible to use multiplicative boosts that are weighted as more relevant than the user query, but I haven't fully worked out the details. A place to start experimenting with this is boosting the boost function by a power, say 1.7, which appeared to about double the weight.

Functions and function queries

Functions, known internally as **ValueSources**, are typically mathematical in nature; they take constants and references to single-valued fields and other functions as input to compute an output number. Functions complement typical queries by enabling you to boost by a function, to sort by a function, to return a value from a function in search results, to filter by a range of values from a function, and they can be used in clever ways wherever Solr accepts a query, such as `facet.query`. They are very versatile, though they are usually only used for custom relevancy boosting.

 A function is often referred to as a *function query* although that is a little confusing, as it makes no distinction with actual function queries that `func` and `frange` produce.

There are quite a few ways in which you can incorporate a function into your searches in Solr:

- **Dismax query parser using the bf or boost parameters**: These two parameters add or multiply the function to the score of the user's query for boosting. They were previously described in the chapter, but you'll see in-depth examples coming up.

- **Boost query parser**: Like DisMax's `boost` parameter, this query parser lets you specify a function that is multiplied to another query. The query string is parsed by the Lucene query parser. Here's an example query:

  `q={!boost b=log(t_trm_lookups)}t_name:Daydreaming`

- **Func query parser**: Wherever a query is expected, such as the `q` param, you can put a function query with this query parser. The `func` query parser will parse the function and expose it as a query matching all documents and return the function's output as the score. Here is an example URL snippet:

  `q={!func}log(t_trm_lookups)&fl=t_trm_lookups,score`

- **Frange (function range) query parser**: This query parser is similar to the `func` query parser, but it also *filters* documents based on the resulting score being in a specified range, instead of returning all documents. It takes a `l` parameter for the lower bound, a `u` parameter for the upper bound, and `incl` and `incu` Boolean parameters to specify whether the lower or upper bounds are inclusive—which they are by default. The parameters are optional, but you will specify at least one of `u` or `l` for meaningful effect. Here's an example URL snippet from its documentation:

  `fq={!frange l=0 u=2.2}sum(user_ranking,editor_ranking)`

Unfortunately, the resulting score from an `frange` query is always 1.

- **Sorting**: In addition to sorting on field values, as mentioned in the previous chapter, you can sort on functions too. Here's an example URL snippet sorting by geospatial distance. This `geodist` function can get its parameters from the URL as other parameters, and we do that here:

```
sort=geodist() asc&pt=…&sfield=…
```

 Despite the multitude of options, you'll most likely just use function queries in boosting with the DisMax parser. It's good to know about other possibilities, though.

The preceding list enumerates the places where you can place a function directly. From this list, `func` and `frange` are query parsers that wrap the function as a query. Using them, you can in turn use functions wherever Solr accepts a query. There are many such places in Solr, so this opens up more possibilities.

For example, Solr's default query parser can switch to another query parser, even just for a subclause. You can then use `func` or `frange` as part of the overall query. Here is an example:

```
q=t_name:Daydreaming AND {!func v=log(t_trm_lookups)}^0.01
```

The function query portion of it will match all documents, so we combine it with other required clauses to actually limit the results. The score is added to the other parts of the query such as `bf`. Note that this feature is unique to Solr; Lucene does *not* natively do this.

 Before Solr 4.1, this was possible but required a rather ugly syntax hack in which the function is prefixed, as if you were searching for it in a pseudo-field named `_val_`, such as `_val_:"log(t_trm_lookups)"`. Similarly, the `_query_` pseudo-field was used to enter a different query parser than `func`. *Don't use this old syntax any more.*

Field references

For fields used in a function query, the constraints are the same as sorting. Essentially, this means the field must be indexed or have DocValues, not multi-valued, and if text fields are used, then they must analyze down to no more than one token. And like sorting, all values get stored in the **field cache** (it's internal to Lucene, not found in `solrconfig.xml`), unless the field has DocValues. *We recommend you set* `docValues="true"` *on these fields.*

The field cache will store all the field values in memory upon first use for sorting or functions. You should have a suitable query in `newSearcher` in `solrconfig.xml` so that the first search after a commit isn't penalized with the initialization cost. If you want to use fast-changing data, consider managing the data externally and using `ExternalFileField`, described a little later. Finally, if your field name has problematic characters, such as a space, you can refer to the field as `field("my field")`.

> If you have a multivalued field you hoped to use, you'll instead have to put a suitable value into another field during indexing. This might be a simple minimum, maximum, or average calculation. There are `UpdateRequestProcessors` that can do this; see *Chapter 4, Indexing Data*.

If there is no value in the field for the document, then the result is zero; otherwise, numeric fields result in the corresponding numeric value. But what about other field types? For `TrieDateField`, you get the `ms()` value, which will be explained shortly. Note that `0` ambiguously means the date might be 1970 or blank. For older date fields, you get the `ord()` value, also explained shortly. For Boolean fields, true is `1` and false is `0`. For text fields, you get the `ord()` value. Some functions can work with the text value—in such cases, you'll need to explicitly use the `literal()` function.

Function references

This section contains a reference of the majority of functions in Solr.

An argument to a function can be a literal constant, such as a number, a field reference, or an embedded function. String constants are quoted. One interesting thing you can do is pull out any argument into a separate named request parameter (in the URL) of your choosing and then refer to it with a leading `$`:

```
&defType=func&q=max(t_trm_lookups,$min)&min=50
```

The parameter might be in the request URL or configured into the request handler configuration. If this parameter dereferencing syntax is familiar to you, then that's because it works the same way in **local-params** too, as explained in *Chapter 5, Searching*.

> Not all arguments can be of any type. For the function definitions below, any argument named x, y, or z can be any expression: constants, field references, or functions. Other arguments such as a or min *require* a literal constant, unless otherwise specified. If you attempt to do otherwise, then you will get a parsing error, as it fails to parse the field name as a number.

Mathematical primitives

These functions cover basic math operations and constants:

- `sum(x,y,z,...)`, aliased to `add` sums up, that is adds, all of the arguments.
- `sub(x,y)` subtracts y from x as in the expression `x-y`.
- `product(x,y,z,...)`, aliased to `mul` multiplies the arguments together.
- `div(x,y)` divides x by y as in the expression `x/y`.
- `log(x)` and `ln(x)` refers to the base-10 logarithm and the natural logarithm.
- For the `sqrt(x)`, `cbrt(x)`, `ceil(x)`, `floor(x)`, `rint(x)`, `pow(x,y)`, `exp(x)`, `mod(x,y)`, and `e()` operations, see the `java.lang.Math` API at `http://docs.oracle.com/javase/7/docs/api/java/lang/Math.html`.

The following are Geometric/Trigonometric operations:

- `rad(x)` and `deg(x)` converts degrees to radians, and radians to degrees.
- For `sin(x)`, `cos(x)`, `tan(x)`, `asin(x)`, `acos(x)`, `atan(x)`, `sinh(x)`, `cosh(x)`, `tanh(x)`, `hypot(x,y)`, `atan2(y,x)`, and `pi()`, see the `java.lang.Math` API.
- Geospatial functions will be covered later.

Other math

These are useful and straightforward mathematical functions:

- `map(x,min,max,target,def?)`: If x is found to be between `min` and `max` inclusive, then `target` is returned. Otherwise, if `def` (an optional parameter) is supplied then that is returned. Else, x is returned. This is useful to deal with default values or to limit x to ensure that it isn't above or below some threshold. The `map()` function is a little similar to `if()` and `def()`.
- `min(x,y,...)` and `max(x,y,...)`: This returns the smallest and greatest parameters, respectively.
- `scale(x,minTarget,maxTarget)`: This returns x scaled to be between `minTarget` and `maxTarget`. For example, if the value of x is found to be one-third from the smallest and largest values of x across all documents, then x is returned as one-third of the distance between `minTarget` and `maxTarget`.

 `scale()` will traverse the entire document set and evaluate the function to determine the smallest and largest values for each query invocation, and it is not cached. This makes it impractical for most uses, as it is too slow.

- `linear(x,m,c)`: A macro for `sum(product(m,x),c)`, for convenience and speed.
- `recip(x,m,a,c)`: A macro for `div(a,linear(x,m,c))`, for convenience and speed.

Boolean functions

Solr 4.0 includes new Boolean functions. When evaluating an expression as a Boolean, 0 is false and any other value is true. `true` and `false` are Boolean literals.

- `and(x,y,...)`, `or(x,y,...)`, `xor(x,y,...)`, `not(x)`: These are primitive Boolean functions with names that should be self-explanatory.
- `if(x,y,z)`: If x is true then y is returned, else z; a little similar to `map()`.
- `exists(x)`: If x is a field name, then this returns true if the current document has a value in this field. If x is a query, then this returns true if the document matches it. Constants and most other value sources are always true.

Relevancy statistics functions

Solr 4.0 includes new functions that expose statistics useful in relevancy. They are fairly advanced, so don't worry if you are new to Solr and these definitions seem confusing. In the following list of functions, *field* is a field name reference, and *term* is an indexed term (a word):

- `docfreq(field,term)`, `totaltermfreq(field,term)` —aliased to `ttf`, `sumtotaltermfreq(field)` —aliased to `sttf`, `idf(field,term)`, `termfreq(field,term)` —aliased to `tf`, `norm(field)`, `maxdoc()`, and `numdocs()`: These functions have names that should be recognizable to anyone who might already want to use them. The earlier part of this chapter defined several of these terms.
- `joindf(idField,linkField)`: This returns the document frequency of the current document's `idField` value in `linkField`. Consider the use case where Solr is storing crawled web pages with the URL in `idField` (need not be the unique key) and `linkField` is a multivalued field referencing linked pages. This function would tell you how many other pages reference the current page.

Ord and rord

 Before ms() was introduced in Solr 1.4, ord() and rord()
were mediocre substitutes. You probably won't use them.
The ms() function will be described soon.

As mentioned earlier, ord(fieldReference) is implied for references to text fields
in the function query. The following is a brief description of ord() and rord():

- ord(field): Given a hypothetical ascending sorted array of all unique
  indexed values for field, this returns the array position; in other words,
  the *ordinal* of a document's indexed value. The field parameter is of course
  a reference to a field. The order of the values is in an ascending order and
  the first position is 1. A non-existent value results in 0.

- rord(field): This refers to the reverse ordinal, as if the term ordering
  was reversed.

Miscellaneous functions

Not every function falls into a neat category; this section covers a few.

The def(x,y,...) function returns the first parameter found that *exists*; otherwise,
the last parameter is returned. def is short for default.

There are multiple ways to use the ms() function to get a date-time value, since its
arguments are all optional. Times are in milliseconds, since the commonly used time
epoch of 1970-01-01T00:00:00Z, which is zero. Times before then are negative. Note
that any field reference to a time will be ambiguous to a blank value, which is zero.

If no arguments are supplied to the ms(date1?,date2?) function, you get the
current time. If one argument is supplied, its value is returned; if two are supplied,
the second is subtracted from the first. The date reference might be the name of a
field or Solr's *date math*; for example, ms(NOW/DAY,a_end_date/DAY).

Interestingly, there are a couple of function queries that return the score results of *another query*. It's a fairly esoteric feature but they have their uses, described as follows:

- `query(q,def?)`: This returns the document's score, as applied to the query given in the first argument. If it doesn't match, then the optional second parameter is returned if supplied, otherwise 0 is returned. Due to the awkward location of the query during function query parsing, it sometimes can't be entered plainly. The query can be put in another parameter and referenced as `query($param)&param=t_trm_attributes:4`. Else, it can be specified using local-params with the query in v, as `query({!v="t_trm_attributes:4"})`. We've used this function to sort by another query, one that returns the distance as its score.

- `boost(q,boost)`: This is similar to `query(q)`, but with the score multiplied by the `boost` constant.

Another interesting function query is one that calculates the *string distance* between two strings based on a specified algorithm. The values are between 0 and 1.

In `strdist(x,y,alg)`, the first two arguments are strings to compute the string distance on. Next is one of `jw` (Jaro Winkler), `edit` (Levenshtein), or `ngram` in quotes. The default `ngram` size is 2, but you can supply an additional argument for something else. For the field references, remember the restrictions listed earlier. In particular, you probably shouldn't reference a tokenized field.

This concludes the Function references section of the chapter. For a potentially more up-to-date source, check out the wiki at `http://wiki.apache.org/solr/FunctionQuery`. The source code is always definitive; see `ValueSourceParser.java`.

 There are some functions related to geospatial search, such as `geodist()`. They have been covered in the previous chapter.

External field values

As you may recall from *Chapter 4, Indexing Data*, if you update a document, Solr internally re-indexes the whole thing, not just the new content. If you were to consider doing this just to increase a number every time a user clicked on a document or clicked some "thumbs-up" button, and so on, then there is quite a bit of work Solr is doing just to ultimately increase a number. For this specific use case, Solr has a specialized field type called `ExternalFileField`, which gets its data from a simple text file containing the field's values. This field type is very limited — the values are limited to floating point numbers and the field can only be referenced within Solr in a function. Changes are only picked up on a commit.

And if you are using Solr 4.1 or later, register `ExternalFileFieldReloader` in `firstSearcher` and `newSearcher` in `solrconfig.xml`. An application using this feature should generate this file on a periodic basis, possibly aligning it with the commit frequency. For more information on how to use this advanced feature, consult the API docs at `http://lucene.apache.org/solr/api/org/apache/solr/schema/ExternalFileField.html` and search Solr's mailing list.

Function query boosting

The overall process to function query boosting is as follows:

1. Pick a formula that has the desired plotted shape.

2. Plug in values specific to your data.

3. Decide the relative weighting of the boost relative to the user query (for example, 1/3).

4. Choose additive or multiplicative boosting and then apply the relative weighting according to the approach you have chosen (see the *Add or multiply boosts* section).

The upcoming examples address common scenarios with readymade formulas for you.

If you want to work on formulas instead of taking one provided here as is, I recommend a tool such as a graphing calculator or other software to plot the functions. If you are using Mac OS X, as I am, then your computer already includes `Grapher`, which generated the charts in this chapter. I highly recommend it. You might be inclined to use a spreadsheet, such as Microsoft Excel, but that's really not the right tool. With luck, you may find some websites that will suffice, perhaps `http://www.wolframapha.com`.

If your data changes in ways that cause you to alter the constants in your function queries, then consider implementing a periodic automated test of your Solr data to ensure that the data fits within expected bounds. A **Continuous Integration (CI)** server might be configured to do this task. An approach is to run a search simply sorting by the data field in question to get the highest or lowest value.

Formula – logarithm

The logarithm is a popular formula for inputs that grow without bounds, but the output is also unbounded. However, the growth of the curve is stunted for larger numbers. This in practice is usually fine, even when you ideally want the output to be capped. An example is boosting by a number of likes or a similar popularity measure.

Here is a graph of our formula, given inputs from a future example:

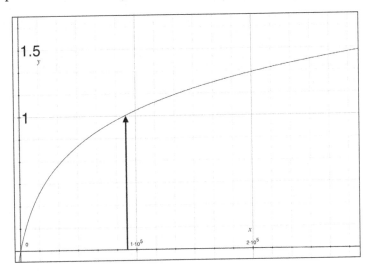

And here is the formula:

$$\log_x\big((c-1)mx+1\big)$$

In this formula, *c* is a number greater than 1 and is a value of your choosing that will alter how the curve bends. I recommend 10 as seen in the preceding graph. Smaller values make it too linear and greater values put a knee bend in the curve that seems too early. In this formula, *m* is the inverse of what I'll call the *horizon*. At this value, the result is 1. With the logarithm, further values advance the output steadily but at a shallow slope that slowly gets shallower. Here is the Solr function query to use, simplified for when *c* is 10: `log(linear(x,m,1))`; where:

- x refers to the input; typically a field reference. It must **not** be negative.
- m refers to *9/horizon* where *horizon* is as described earlier.

Verify your formula by supplying 0, which should result in 0, and then supply *horizon*, which should result in 1. Now that you have your formula, you are ready to proceed with the other function query boosting steps.

Formula – inverse reciprocal

In general, the reciprocal of a linear function is favorable because it gives results that are bounded as the input grows without bounds.

Here is a sample graph to show the curve. The inputs are from a later how-to. The arrow in the following graph shows where the "horizon" (*1/m*) lies:

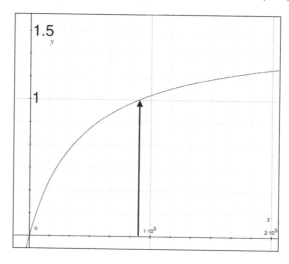

Here is the formula:

$$\frac{-\text{max}^2 + \text{max}}{m - x + \text{max} - 1} + \text{max}$$

Here, `max` is the value that this function approaches, but never quite reaches. It should be greater than 1 and less than 2; 1.5 works well. You can experiment with this to see how it changes the bend in the curve shown next. In the formula, m is the inverse of what I'll call the *horizon*. At this value, the result is 1, and larger inputs only increase it negligibly.

Here is the Solr function query to use: `sum(recip(x,m,a,c),max)`; where:

- x refers to the input; typically a field reference. It must **not** be negative.
- m refers to *1/horizon*, where *horizon* is as described earlier.
- a refers to *max-max*max*.
- c refers to *max – 1*.
- max is *1.5*, or otherwise as defined earlier.

Verify your formula by supplying 0, which should result in 0, to *horizon*, which should result in 1. Now that you have your formula, you are ready to proceed with the other function query boosting steps.

Formula – reciprocal

The reciprocal is an excellent formula to use when you want to maximally boost at input 0 and boost decreasingly less as the input increases. It is often used to boost newly added content by looking at how old a document is.

Here is a sample graph to show the curve. The inputs are from a later how-to. The arrow roughly shows where the *horizon* input value is.

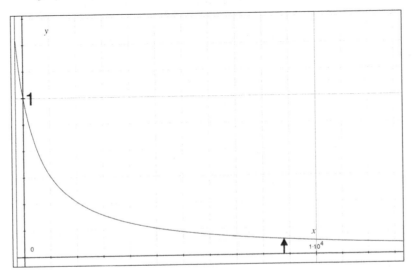

The formula is simply:

$$\frac{c}{x+c}$$

This translates easily to a Solr function query as `recip(x,1,c,c)`; where:

- x refers to the input—a field or another function referencing a field. It should **not** be negative.
- c is roughly 1/10th of the *horizon* input value. As larger values are supplied, the boost effect is negligible.

Verify your formula by supplying 0, which should result in 1, and then *horizon* (as defined earlier), which should result in a number very close to 0.09. Now that you have your formula, you are ready to proceed with the other function query boosting steps.

Formula – linear

If you have a value in your schema (or a computed formula) that you are certain will stay within a fixed range, then the formula to scale and shift this to the 0-1 nominal range is easy. We're also assuming that there is a linear relationship between the desired boost effect and the input.

Simply use the `linear(x,m,c)` function with appropriate values. Below, *a* refers to the end of the range that will have the least significant boost. So if your input ranges from 5 to 10 and if 5 is least relevant compared to 10, then *a* is 5; *b* takes the other side of the input range:

- `x` refers to the input, which is typically a field
- `m` computes *1/(b – a)* and plug in
- `c` computes *a/(a - b)* and plug in

Verify your formula by supplying a value from each end of the range and verify the result is 0 or 1 with 1 being the biggest boost. Now that you have your formula, you are ready to proceed with the other function query boosting steps.

How to boost based on an increasing numeric field

In this section, I'm going to describe a few ways to boost a document based on one of its numeric fields. The greater this number is for a document, the greater boost this document should receive. This number might be a count of likes or thumbs-up votes by users, or the number of times a user accessed (for example, clicked) the referenced document, or something else.

In the MusicBrainz database, there are TRM and PUID lookup counts. TRM and PUID are MusicBrainz's audio fingerprint technologies. These identifiers roughly correspond to a song, which, in MusicBrainz, appears as multiple tracks due to various releases that occur as singles, compilations, and so on. By the way, audio fingerprints aren't perfect, and so a very small percentage of TRM IDs and PUIDs refer to songs that are completely different. Since we're only using this to influence scoring, imperfection is acceptable.

MusicBrainz records the number of times one of these IDs are looked up from its servers, which is a good measure of popularity. A track that contains a higher lookup count should score higher than one with a smaller value, with all other factors being equal. This scheme could easily be aggregated to releases and artists, if desired. In the data loading, I've arranged for the sum of TRM and PUID lookup counts to be stored into our track data as t_trm_lookups with the following field specification in the schema:

```
<field name="t_trm_lookups" type="tint" />
```

About 25 percent of the tracks have a non-zero value. The maximum value is nearly 300,000 but further inspection shows that only a handful of records exceed a value of 90,000.

Step by step...

The first step is to pick a formula. Since this is a classic case of an increasing number without bound in which the greater the number is, the greater the boost should be, the **inverse reciprocal** is a very good choice. Next, we plug in our data into the formula specified earlier and we end up with this function query:

```
sum(recip(t_trm_lookups,0.0000111,-0.75,0.5),1.5)
```

We verify the formula by plugging in 0 and 90,000, which maps to 0 and 1.

The next step is to choose between additive boosts versus multiplicative boosts. Multiplicative boost with edismax is easier, so we'll choose that. And let's say this function query should weigh one-third of the user query. According to earlier instructions, adding to our function query will reduce its weight counter-intuitively. Adding 2 shifts the 0 to 1 range to 2 to 3 and (3 - 2)/3 results in the one-third boost we're looking for. Since our function query conveniently has sum() as its outer function, we can simply add another argument of 2. Here is a URL snippet that shows the relevant parameters:

```
q=cherub+rock&defType=edismax&qf=t_name
&boost=sum(recip(t_trm_lookups,0.0000111,-0.75,0.5),1.5,2)
```

This boost absolutely had the desired effect, altering the score order as we wanted. One unintended outcome is that the top document scores used to be ~8.6 and now they are ~21.1, but *don't worry about it!* The actual scores are irrelevant—a point made in the beginning of the chapter. The goal is to change the relative order of score-sorted documents.

To better illustrate the difference, here is the query before boosting and with CSV output (with spaces added for clarity): `http://localhost:8983/solr/mbtracks/select?q=cherub+rock&defType=edismax&qf=t_name&fl=id,t_name,t_trm_lookups,score&wt=csv&rows=5`:

```
id,t_name,t_trm_lookups,score
Track:2528226, Cherub Rock,     0, 8.615694
Track:2499080, Cherub Rock,     0, 8.615694
Track:2499119, Cherub Rock,     0, 8.615694
Track:2492995, Cherub Rock, 1036, 8.615694
Track:2492999, Cherub Rock,  105, 8.615694
```

And here is the boosted query and the new results: `http://localhost:8983/solr/mbtracks/select?q=cherub+rock&defType=edismax&qf=t_name&boost=sum(recip(t_trm_lookups,0.0000111,-0.75,0.5),1.5,2)&fl=id,t_name,t_trm_lookups,score&wt=csv&rows=5`:

```
id,t_name,t_trm_lookups,score
Track:749561,  Cherub Rock, 19464, 21.130745
Track:183137,  Cherub Rock, 17821, 20.894897
Track:2268634, Cherub Rock,  9468, 19.47599
Track:2203149, Cherub Rock,  9219, 19.426989
Track:7413518, Cherub Rock,  8502, 19.28334
```

If you're wondering why there are so many tracks with the same name, it's because popular songs like this one are published as singles and as part of other collections.

How to boost based on recent dates

Using dates in scores presents some different issues. Suppose when we search for releases, we want to include a larger boost for more recent releases. At first glance, this problem may seem just like the previous one, because dates increase as the scores are expected to, but in practice, it is different. Instead of the data ranging from zero to some value that changes occasionally, we now have data ranging from a non-zero value that might change rarely to a value that we always know, but changes continuously—the current date. Instead, approach this from the other side, that is, by considering how much time there is between the current date and the document's date. So at $x=0$ in the graph (x representing time delta), we want 1 for the greatest boost, and we want it to slope downward towards 0, but not below it.

Step by step…

The first step is to pick a formula. The **reciprocal** is perfect for this scenario. The function query form as detailed earlier is `recip(x,1,c,c)`.

Based on this scenario, *x* is the age—a time duration from the present. Our MusicBrainz schema has `r_event_date`, which is a promising candidate; however, multivalued fields are not supported by function queries. I made a simple addition to the schema and index to record the earliest release event date: `r_event_date_earliest`. With that done, now we can calculate the age with the two-argument variant of `ms()`. As a reminder to show how to run these function queries while debugging, here's a URL snippet:

```
q={!func}ms(NOW,r_event_date_earliest)
&fl=id,r_name,r_event_date_earliest,score&sort=score+asc
```

The book's dataset hasn't markedly changed since the first edition, but when I first obtained it, I noticed that some of the releases were in the future! What I saw then is reproducible by substituting NOW-6YEARS to get to 2008 as I write this in 2014, instead of just NOW in the function. The first documents (score ascending) have negative values, which means they are from the future. We can't have negative inputs, so instead we'll wrap this function with the absolute value using `abs()`.

The other aspect of the inputs to the reciprocal function is finding out what the *horizon* is. This should be a duration of time such that any longer durations have a negligible boost impact. Without too much thought, 20 years seems good. Here's a query to have Solr do the math so we can get our millisecond-count: q={!func} ms(NOW,NOW-20YEARS), which is about 6.3E11. In the documentation for the reciprocal formula, we take one-tenth of that for c. Here is our function query:

```
recip(abs(ms(NOW/DAY,r_event_date_earliest)),1,6.3E10,6.3E10)
```

An important performance tip when using NOW is to round it to an acceptable interval. Instead of using NOW, using NOW/DAY makes this query cacheable within Solr with subsequent requests for a 24-hour period.

At this point, you can follow the final steps in the previous how-to.

Summary

In this chapter, we covered the most advanced topics the book has to offer—scoring and function queries. We began with a fundamental background on Lucene scoring. Next, we saw a real-world example of using the `debugQuery` parameter to diagnose a scoring issue. That exercise might be the most important exercise in the chapter, since it gives you the tools to diagnose why a document matched or didn't match a query. Next, we concluded the coverage of the DisMax query parser. Even if you aren't inclined to use fancy boosting function queries, you can improve your search relevancy simply by configuring phrase boosting. The DisMax query parsers's boost function parameters were segue to the second half of the chapter: function queries. Even if you aren't a math whiz, you should be able to use formulas provided here, especially if you worked through the how-tos.

You might say this is the last of the foundational chapters. The next two chapters cover specific search-value adds that are each fairly compartmentalized. The standout feature that contributes to much of Solr's popularity is faceting, which is covered next in its own chapter.

7
Faceting

Faceting is Solr's killer feature. It's a must-have feature for most search implementations, especially those with structured data like in e-commerce. Yet there are few products that have this capability, especially in open source. Of course, search fundamentals, including highlighting, are critical too, but they tend to be taken for granted. **Faceting** enhances search results with aggregated information over all documents matching the search query. It can answer questions about the MusicBrainz data such as:

- How many releases are official, bootleg, or promotional?
- What were the top five most common countries in which the releases occurred?
- Over the past ten years, how many were released in each year?
- How many releases have names in the ranges A-C, D-F, G-I, and so on?
- How many tracks are < 2 minutes long, 2-3 long minutes, 3-4 minutes long, or longer?

In a hurry?

Faceting is a key feature. Look through the upcoming example, which demonstrates the most common type of faceting, and review the faceting types.

Faceting in the context of the user experience is often referred to as faceted navigation, but also faceted search, faceted browsing, guided navigation, or parametric search. The facets are typically displayed with clickable links that apply Solr filter queries to a subsequent search. Endeca's excellent UX Design Pattern Library contains many screenshots worth viewing. Visit http://www.oracle.com/webfolder/ux/applications/uxd/endeca/content/library/en/home.html and click on **Faceted Navigation**.

If we revisit the comparison of search technology to databases, then faceting is more or less analogous to SQL's GROUP BY feature on a column with count (*). However, in Solr, facet processing is performed subsequent to an existing search as part of a single request-response, with both the primary search results and the faceting results coming back together. In SQL you would need to perform a series of separate queries to get the same information. Furthermore, faceting works so fast that its search response time overhead is often negligible. For more information on why implementing faceting with relational databases is hard and doesn't scale, visit this old article at http://web.archive.org/web/20090321120327/http://www.kimbly.com/blog/000239.html.

A quick example – faceting release types

Observe the following search results. The echoParams parameter is set to explicit (defined in solrconfig.xml) so that the search parameters are seen here. This example is using the default lucene query parser. The dismax query parser is more typical, but it has no bearing on these examples. The query parameter q is *:*, which matches all documents. In this case, the index only has releases, so there is no need to apply filters. Filter queries are used in conjunction with faceting a fair amount, so be sure you are familiar with them; see *Chapter 5, Searching*. To keep this example brief, we set rows to 2. Sometimes when using faceting, you only want the facet information and not the main search, so you would set rows to 0.

```
{"responseHeader":{
  "status":0,
  "QTime":3,
  "params":{
    "facet":"true",
    "f.r_official.facet.method":"enum",
    "f.r_official.facet.missing":"true",
    "facet.field":"r_official",
    "fq":"type:Release",
    "fl":"r_name",
    "q":"*:*",
    "wt":"json",
    "rows":"2"}},
  "response":{"numFound":603090,"start":0,"docs":[
      {"r_name":"Texas International Pop Festival 11-30-69"},
      {"r_name":"40 Jahre"}]},
  "facet_counts":{
    "facet_queries":{},
    "facet_fields":{
```

```
  "r_official":[
    "Official",519168,
    "Bootleg",19559,
    "Promotion",16562,
    "Pseudo-Release",2819,
    null,44982]},
"facet_dates":{},
"facet_ranges":{}}}
```

 It's critical to understand that faceting numbers are computed over the entire search result—603,090 releases, which is all of the releases in this example—and not just the two rows being returned.

The facet-related search parameters are highlighted at the top. The `facet.missing` parameter was set using the field-specific syntax, which will be explained shortly.

Notice that the facet results (highlighted) follow the main search result and are given the name `facet_counts`. In this example, we only faceted on one field, `r_official`, but you'll learn in a bit that you can facet on as many fields as you desire. Within `"r_official"` lie the facet counts for this field—value and count pairs. The first value in a pair, such as `"Official"`, holds a facet value, which is simply an indexed term, and the integer following it is the number of documents in the search results containing that term—the **facet count**. The last facet has the count but no corresponding name. It is a special facet to indicate how many documents in the results don't have any indexed terms.

Field requirements

The principal requirement of a field that will be faceted on is that it must be indexed; it *does not* have to be stored. And for text fields, tokenization is usually undesirable. For example, if the value `Non-Album Track` was tokenized, faceting on a field with that value would show tallies for `Non-Album` and `Track` separately. On the other hand, tag-clouds, some approaches to hierarchical faceting, and term-suggest are faceting use cases that handle tokenization just fine. Keep in mind that with faceting, the facet values returned in search results are the actual indexed terms, and not the stored value, which isn't used.

 If you have conflicting indexing needs for a field, which is common, you will find it necessary to have a copy of a field just for faceting.

Types of faceting

Solr's faceting is broken down into five types. They are as follows:

- `field`: This is the most common type of faceting which counts the number of occurrences of each indexed term in a field. The facet counts are grouped in the output under the name `facet_fields`.

- `range`: Given a numeric or date field, this creates facets for a set of ranges. The facet counts are grouped in the output under the name `facet_ranges`.

> Solr 3 deprecated date faceting with the introduction of the generic range faceting. We won't document it further.

- `query`: This is a very flexible type of faceting which counts the number of documents matching each specified query. The facet counts are grouped in the output under `facet_queries`.

- `pivot`: Also known as decision tree faceting, this type of faceting allows recursive faceting across a set of fields. Results are grouped under `facet_pivot`.

- `interval`: A Solr 4.10-only feature, an interval facet is similar to a query facet with range queries. While the same results can be achieved using query facets with range queries, interval facets are implemented differently and, therefore, have different performance characteristics.

In the rest of this chapter, we will describe how to do these different types of facets. But before that, there is one common parameter to enable faceting:

- `facet`: It defaults to `false`. In order to enable faceting, you must set this to `true` or `on`. If this is not done, then the faceting parameters will be ignored.

In all of the examples in this chapter, we always set `facet=true`.

Faceting field values

Field value faceting is the most common type of faceting. The first example in this chapter demonstrated it in action. Solr, in essence, iterates over all of the indexed terms for the field and tallies a count for the number of searched documents that include the term. Sophisticated algorithms and caching makes this so fast that its overhead is usually negligible.

The following are the request parameters to use it:

- `facet.field`: You must set this parameter to a field's name in order to facet on that field. Repeat this parameter for each field to be faceted on. See the previous Field requirements section.

> The remaining faceting parameters can be set on a per-field basis, otherwise they apply to all faceted fields that don't have a field-specific setting. You will usually specify them per field, especially if you are faceting on more than one field, so that you don't get your faceting configuration mixed up. For example: `f.r_type.facet.sort=index` (`r_type` is a field name, `facet.sort` is a facet parameter).

- `facet.limit`: This limits the number of facet values returned in the search result of a field. As these are usually going to be displayed to the user, it doesn't make sense to have a large number of these in the response. If you need all of them, then disable the limit with a value of `-1`. It defaults to `100`.

- `facet.sort`: This is set to either `count` to sort the facet values by descending totals, or to `index` to sort lexicographically, as if you sorted on the field. If `facet.limit` is greater than zero (typical), then Solr picks `count` as the default, otherwise `index` is chosen.

- `facet.offset`: This is the offset into the facet value list from which the values are returned. It enables paging of facet values when used with `facet.limit` and defaults to `0`.

- `facet.mincount`: This tells Solr to exclude facet values whose counts are less than the number given. It is applied before `limit` and `offset` so that paging works as expected. It is common to set this to 1 since 0 is almost useless. This defaults to `0`.

- `facet.missing`: When enabled, this causes the response to include the number of searched documents that have no indexed terms. The first facet example in the chapter demonstrates this. It defaults to `false` and is set to `true` or `on`.

- `facet.prefix`: This filters the facet values to those starting with this value. This is applied before `limit` and `offset` so that paging works as expected. At the end of this chapter, you'll see how this can be used for hierarchical faceting. In the next chapter, you'll see how faceting with this prefix can be used to power query-term suggests.

- `facet.threads` (advanced): When this parameter is set, Solr loads the fields related to faceting concurrently. The value (an integer) specifies the number of threads to use. Solr will use the Java `Interger.MAX_VALUE` if this parameter is set to a negative number. No threads are spawned if this parameter is not set.

- `facet.method` (advanced): This parameter tells Solr which of its three different field-value faceting algorithms to use in order to influence memory use, query performance, and commit speed. Solr usually makes good choices by default. You can specify one of `enum`, `fcs` or `fc`, or neither, and Solr will, under the right circumstances, choose the third, known as `UnInvertedField`. `fc` refers to the field cache which is only for single-valued fields that are not tokenized. Trie-based fields that are configured for fast range queries (for example, `tint`, not `int`) are only facetable with `UnInvertedField`. If you set `facet.method` incorrectly, then Solr will ignore it.

When to specify facet.method

Normally, you should not specify `facet.method`, thereby letting Solr's internal logic choose an appropriate algorithm. However, if you are faceting on a multi-valued field that only has a small number of distinct values (less than 100, but ideally perhaps 10), then we suggest setting this to `enum`. Solr will use a filter cache entry for each value, so keep that in mind when optimizing that cache's size. Solr uses `enum` by default for Boolean fields only, as it knows there can only be two values. Another parameter we'll mention for completeness is `facet.enum.cache.minDf`, which is the minimum document frequency for filter cache entries (0 − no minimum by default). If the field contains rarely used values occurring less than ~30 times, then setting this threshold to `30` makes sense.

Alphabetic range bucketing

Solr does not directly support alphabetic range bucketing (A-C, D-F, and so on). However, with a creative application of text analysis and a dedicated field, we can achieve this with little effort. Let's say we want to have these range buckets on the release names. We need to extract the first character of `r_name`, and store this into a field that will be used for this purpose. We'll call it `r_name_facetLetter`. Here is our field definition:

```
<field name="r_name_facetLetter" type="bucketFirstLetter"
stored="false" />
```

And here is the `copyField`:

```
<copyField source="r_name" dest="r_name_facetLetter" />
```

The definition of the `bucketFirstLetter` type is the following:

```
<fieldType name="bucketFirstLetter" class="solr.TextField"
sortMissingLast="true" omitNorms="true">
  <analyzer type="index">
    <tokenizer class="solr.PatternTokenizerFactory"
    pattern="^([a-zA-Z]).*" group="1" />
    <filter class="solr.SynonymFilterFactory"
            synonyms="mb_letterBuckets.txt"
            ignoreCase="true"
            expand="false"/>
  </analyzer>
  <analyzer type="query">
    <tokenizer class="solr.KeywordTokenizerFactory"/>
  </analyzer>
</fieldType>
```

The `PatternTokenizerFactory` class, as configured, plucks out the first character, and the `SynonymFilterFactory` class maps each letter of the alphabet to a range such as A-C. The mapping is in `conf/mb_letterBuckets.txt`. The field types used for faceting generally have a `KeywordTokenizerFactory` class for the query analysis to satisfy a possible filter query on a given facet value returned from a previous faceted search. After validating these changes with Solr's analysis admin screen, we then re-index the data. For the facet query, we're going to advise Solr to use the `enum` method, because there aren't many facet values in total. Here's the URL to search Solr:
`http://localhost:8983/solr/mbreleases/select?indent=on&wt=json&q=*:*&facet=on&facet.field=r_name_facetLetter&facet.sort=lex&facet.missing=on&facet.method=enum`.

The URL produces results containing the following facet data:

```
{"facet_counts": {
  "facet_queries": {},
  "facet_fields": {
  "r_name_facetLetter": [
    "a-c", 99005,
    "d-f", 68376,
    "g-i", 60569,
    "j-l", 49871,
    "m-o", 59006,
    "p-r", 47032,
    "s-u", 143376,
```

```
    "v-z", 33233,
    null, 42622]},
  "facet_dates": {},
  "facet_ranges": {}}}
```

Faceting numeric and date ranges

Solr has built-in support for faceting numeric and date fields by a range and a divided interval. You can think of this as a convenience feature that calculates the ranges for you with succinct input parameters and output, rather than you calculating and submitting a series of facet queries — facet queries are described after this section.

Range faceting is particularly useful for dates. We'll demonstrate an example against MusicBrainz release dates and another against MusicBrainz track durations, and then describe the parameters and their options.

 Date faceting is the date-specific predecessor of range faceting and is deprecated as of Solr 3. Date faceting uses similar parameters starting with facet.date and has similar output under facet_dates.

Here's the URL:

```
http://localhost:8983/solr/mbreleases/mb_releases?indent=on&wt=jso
n&omitHeader=true&rows=0&facet=true&facet.range.other=all&f.r_even
t_date_earliest.facet.range.start=NOW/YEAR-
10YEARS&facet.range=r_event_date_earliest&facet.range.end=NOW/YEAR
&facet.range.gap=+1YEAR&q=smashing
```

And here's the response:

```
{"response":{"numFound":248,"start":0,"docs":[]},
  "facet_counts":{
    "facet_queries":{},
    "facet_fields":{},
    "facet_dates":{},
    "facet_ranges":{
      "r_event_date_earliest":{
        "counts":[
          "2003-01-01T00:00:00Z",2,
          "2004-01-01T00:00:00Z",1,
          "2005-01-01T00:00:00Z",1,
          "2006-01-01T00:00:00Z",3,
```

```
        "2007-01-01T00:00:00Z",11,
        "2008-01-01T00:00:00Z",0,
        "2009-01-01T00:00:00Z",0,
        "2010-01-01T00:00:00Z",0,
        "2011-01-01T00:00:00Z",0,
        "2012-01-01T00:00:00Z",0],
      "gap":"+1YEAR",
      "start":"2003-01-01T00:00:00Z",
      "end":"2013-01-01T00:00:00Z",
      "before":93,
      "after":0,
      "between":18}}}}
```

This example demonstrates a few things, not only range faceting:

- /mb_releases is a request handler using dismax to query appropriate release fields.

- q=smashing indicates that we're faceting on a keyword search instead of all the documents. We kept the rows at zero, which is unrealistic, but not pertinent as the rows setting does not affect facets.

- The facet start date was specified using the field specific syntax for demonstration purposes. You would do this with every parameter if you need to do a range facet on other fields; otherwise, don't bother.

- The "start" and "end" part below the facet counts indicates the upper bound of the last facet count. It may or may not be the same as facet.range.end (see facet.range.hardend explained in the next section).

- The before, after, and between counts are to specify facet.range.other. We'll see shortly what this means.

The results of our facet range query show that there were three releases in 2006 and eleven in 2007. There is no data after that, since the data is out of date at this point.

Here is another example, this time using range faceting on a number — MusicBrainz track durations (in seconds). The URL is http://localhost:8983/solr/mbtracks/mb_tracks?wt=json&omitHeader=true&rows=0&facet.range.other=after&facet=true&q=Geek&facet.range.start=0&facet.range=t_duration&facet.range.end=240&facet.range.gap=60.

This is the response:

```
{"response":{"numFound":552,"start":0,"docs":[]},
  "facet_counts":{
    "facet_queries":{},
    "facet_fields":{},
```

```
"facet_dates":{},
"facet_ranges":{
  "t_duration":{
    "counts":[
      "0",128,
      "60",64,
      "120",111,
      "180",132],
    "gap":60,
    "start":0,
    "end":240,
    "after":117}}}}
```

Taking the first facet, we see that there are 128 tracks that are 0–59 seconds long, given the keyword search "Geek".

Range facet parameters

All of the range faceting parameters start with `facet.range`. As with most other faceting parameters, they can be made field specific in the same way. The parameters are explained as follows:

- `facet.range`: You must set this parameter to a field's name to range-facet on that field. The trie-based numeric and date field types (those starting with `t`, as in `tlong` and `tdate`) perform best, but others will work. Repeat this parameter for each field to be faceted on.

 The remainder of these range faceting parameters can be specified on a per-field basis in the same fashion as field-value faceting parameters can. For example, `f.r_event_date_earliest.facet.range.start`.

- `facet.range.start`: This is mandatory. It is a number or date to specify the start of the range to facet on. For dates, see the *Date math* section in *Chapter 5, Searching*. Using NOW with some Solr date math is quite effective as in this example: NOW/YEAR-5YEARS, interpreted as five years ago, starting at the beginning of the year.

- `facet.range.end`: This is mandatory. It is a number or date to specify the end of the range. It has the same syntax as `facet.range.start`. Note that the actual end of the range may be different (see `facet.range.hardend`).

- `facet.range.gap`: This is also mandatory. It specifies the interval to divide the range. For dates, it uses a subset of Solr's *Date Math* syntax, as it's a time *duration* and not a particular time. It should always start with a +. For example, +1YEAR or +1MINUTE+30SECONDS. Note that after URL encoding, + becomes %2B.

   Note that for dates, the `facet.range.gap` is not necessarily a fixed length of time. For example, +1MONTH is different depending on the month.

- `facet.range.hardend`: This parameter instructs Solr on what to do when `facet.range.gap` does not divide evenly into the facet range (start | end). If this is `true`, then the last range will be shortened. Moreover, you will observe that the end value in the facet results is the same as `facet.range.end`. Otherwise, by default, the end is essentially increased sufficiently so that the ranges are all equal according to the gap value. The default value is `false`.

- `facet.range.other`: This parameter adds more faceting counts depending on its value. It can be specified multiple times. See the example using this at the start of this section. It defaults to `none`.

  - `before`: Count of documents before the faceted range
  - `after`: Count of documents following the faceted range
  - `between`: Count of documents within the faceted range
  - `none` (disabled): The default
  - `all`: Shortcut for all three (`before`, `between`, and `after`)

- `facet.range.include`: This specifies which range boundaries are inclusive. The choices are `lower`, `upper`, `edge`, `outer`, and `all` (all being equivalent to all the others). This parameter can be set multiple times to combine choices and defaults to `lower`. Instead of defining each value, we will describe when a given boundary is inclusive:

  - The lower boundary of a gap-based range is included if `lower` is specified. It is also included if it's the first gap range and `edge` is specified.
  - The upper boundary of a gap-based range is included if `upper` is specified. It is also included if it's the last gap range and `edge` is specified.
  - The upper boundary of the `before` range is included if the boundary is not already included by the first gap-based range. It's also included if `outer` is specified.

    °   The lower boundary of the `after` range is included if the boundary is not already included by the last gap-based range. It's also included if `outer` is specified.

Avoid double counting

The default `facet.range.include` of `lower` ensures that an indexed value occurring at a range boundary is counted in exactly one of the adjacent ranges. This is usually desirable, but your requirements may differ. To ensure you don't double count, don't choose both `lower` and `upper` together and don't choose `outer`.

Facet queries

This is the final type of faceting, and it offers a lot of flexibility. Instead of choosing a field to facet its values on or faceting a specified range of values, we specify some number of Solr queries so that each itself becomes a facet. For each facet query specified, the number of documents matching the facet query that also match the main search is counted. Each facet query with its facet count is returned in the results under the `facet_queries` section. Facet queries are each cached in the filter cache.

There is only one parameter to configure facet queries:

- `facet.query`: This is a Solr query to be evaluated over the search results. The number of matching documents (the facet count) is returned as an entry in the results next to this query. Specify this multiple times to have Solr evaluate multiple facet queries.

In general, if field value faceting or range faceting don't do what you want, you can probably turn to facet queries. For example, if range faceting is too limiting because `facet.range.gap` is fixed, then you could specify a facet query for each particular range you need. Let's use that scenario for our example. Here are search results showing a few facet queries on MusicBrainz release dates, using the `/mb_artists` request handler. I've used `echoParams` to make the search parameters clear instead of showing a lengthy URL:

```
{"responseHeader":{
  "status":0,
  "QTime":80,
  "params":{
    "facet":"on",
    "facet.query":[
      "a_release_date_latest:[NOW/DAY-1YEAR TO *]",
```

```
          "a_release_date_latest:[NOW/DAY-5YEAR TO *]",
          "a_release_date_latest:[NOW/DAY-20YEAR TO *]"
      ],
      "wt":"json",
      "rows":"0",
      "echoParams":"explicit",
      "indent":"on"}},
  "response":{"numFound":399182,"start":0,"docs":[]},
  "facet_counts":{
      "facet_queries":{
        "a_release_date_latest:[NOW/DAY-1YEAR TO *]":0,
        "a_release_date_latest:[NOW/DAY-5YEAR TO *]":33,
        "a_release_date_latest:[NOW/DAY-20YEAR TO *]":80009},
      "facet_fields":{},
      "facet_dates":{},
      "facet_ranges":{}}}
```

In this example, the `facet.query` parameter was specified three times showing releases released in the past 1 year, 5 years, and 20 years. An interesting thing to note about the facet query response is that the name of each of these facets is the query itself.

> Query facets with range queries allow arbitrary "bucket" value sizes. Solr 4.10 supports a new interval facet that also provides this capability. In some cases, this facet type may perform better than query/range faceting. Details can be found in the reference guide at `https://cwiki.apache.org/confluence/display/solr/Faceting#Faceting-IntervalFaceting`.

Building a filter query from a facet

When faceting is used, it is usually used in the context of faceted navigation, in which a facet value becomes a navigation choice for the user to filter on. In Solr, that becomes an additional filter query in a subsequent search. The total matching documents of that search should be equal to the facet value count. In this section, we'll review how to build the filter queries. We won't show an example for facet query faceting because there's nothing to do—the facet query is a query and can be supplied directly as an `fq` parameter.

> To keep the filter queries easier to read, we won't show them URL encoded.

Field value filter queries

For the case of field value faceting, consider the first example in the chapter where `r_official` has a value `Bootleg`. Generating a filter query for this couldn't be simpler: `fq=r_official:Bootleg`. But what if the value contained a space or some other problematic character? You'd have to escape it using quotes or backslash escaping as explained in *Chapter 5, Searching*. This is a separate issue from URL encoding, which we're omitting here for clarity; this pertains to the query syntax. Another potential problem relates to the fact that the value, even if escaped, still might have to go through text analysis in the field type configuration, which could modify the value resulting in a failed match. This is a rare circumstance and it's impossible with the `string` field type, but nonetheless it's something to watch out for, particularly for tag-cloud-like use cases. A solution to both problems is to use the `term` query parser, in this manner, `fq={!term f=r_official}Bootleg`. Here, the value needs no escaping as it sidesteps text analysis.

 Consider using the `term` query parser for all text field value faceting as it avoids escaping problems.

You might be wondering how to generate a filter query for the `facet.missing` facet, as there is no value to filter on. *Chapter 5, Searching*, covered a little-known trick to query for a field with no indexed data involving a range query. Here it is for `r_official`, without URL encoding:

```
fq=-r_official:[* TO *].
```

Facet range filter queries

Range faceting is the most complicated to generate filter queries for. Consider the first date range example. The first facet returned is as follows:

```
"2003-01-01T00:00:00Z",2
```

The gap is `+1YEAR`. The facet's quoted date value is the start of the range. The end of the range is the next facet date value. If there are no more, then the final range's end point depends on `facet.range.hardend`—if it is `false`, the default, then you add `facet.range.gap`. For numbers, you calculate this math yourself. For dates, you can conveniently concatenate the string like this, `2006-01-01T00:00:00Z+1YEAR`. On the other hand, if there is a hard end, then the last range end point is simply `facet.range.end`.

At this point, you might think the filter query for the first range is `fq=r_event_date_earliest:[2006-01-01T00:00:00Z TO 2007-01-01T00:00:00Z]`. However, that is incorrect! You must now consider the implications of `facet.range.include`. If you set this parameter to both `lower` and `upper`, then the aforementioned filter query would be correct, but by default it's just `lower` (which is generally a good default that doesn't double count). If a date falls on precisely New Year's Eve of 2014, then we don't want to count that date. The solution is to use this range query, `fq=r_event_date_earliest:[2006-01-01T00:00:00Z TO 2007-01-01T00:00:00Z}`—note the curly bracket (exclusivity) at the end of the range query. Varying exclusivity and inclusivity in a range query like this is a new feature as of Solr 4.

Generating filter queries for the `before` and `after` ranges isn't too hard. Here is the filter query for the `before` range, which is exclusive of the `facet.range.start` point:

```
fq=r_event_date_earliest:{* TO 2006-01-01T00:00:00Z}
```

Pivot faceting

Pivot facets enable Solr to return facet counts across sets of fields. This means that the facet results are multi-level, where each level is a different Solr field. Pivot facets are great for hierarchical or tree faceting.

 Pivot facets are not supported in distributed mode until Solr 4.10.

Pivot faceting is simple to use. The feature itself introduces only two new parameters:

- `facet.pivot`: This field is similar to `facet.field`, but instead of giving it a single field, it expects an ordered comma-delimited list of fields. Each field is recursively faceted from the field listed before it in the list.

- `facet.pivot.mincount`: This is similar to `facet.mincount`, but only for pivot facets. The default value is 1.

It's important to know that the `facet.pivot` parameter only accepts field names. It won't handle functions, for example. Additionally, the `facet.pivot` parameter can be specified multiple times.

Time for an example! Let's query the mbtracks core to show artist name, release name and the length of each track using pivot facets.

As mentioned in the beginning of this chapter, it's important that you choose the right field types. The example we're about to show you mostly works because we've explicitly chosen fields that contain only single words. You'll see though, that the values are lowercased as a result of tokenizing/lower-casing — this is for demonstration purposes only.

The query is `http://localhost:8983/solr/mbtracks/mb_tracks?omitHeader=true&wt=json&q=t_r_id:116747&rows=0&facet=true&facet.pivot=t_a_name,t_r_name,t_duration`.

And here's the resulting response:

```
{"response":{"numFound":12,"start":0,"docs":[]},
  "facet_counts":{
    "facet_queries":{},
    "facet_fields":{},
    "facet_dates":{},
    "facet_ranges":{},
    "facet_pivot":{
      "t_a_name,t_r_name,t_duration":[{
        "field":"t_a_name",
        "value":"nirvana",
        "count":12,
        "pivot":[{
          "field":"t_r_name",
          "value":"nevermind",
          "count":12,
          "pivot":[
            {"field":"t_duration",
             "value":142,
             "count":1},
            {"field":"t_duration",
             "value":156,
             "count":1},
            {"field":"t_duration",
             "value":176,
             "count":1},
            ...]}]}]}}}
```

The relevant request and response values are highlighted. The `facet.pivot` parameter contains the list of fields. Here, we're querying on a release ID of `116747`, which happens to be the album `"nevermind"` by `"nirvana"`. The pivot facets contextually show the artist name, the release name, and the length of each track.

> Solr 5.0 introduces an extremely useful enhancement to pivot facets—pivot facet stats. With this new feature, you can attach stats to each leaf node in the pivot tree. We cover the stats component in *Chapter 5, Searching*, and more details on the pivot stats feature can be found at `https://cwiki.apache.org/confluence/display/solr/Faceting#Faceting-Pivot(DecisionTree)Faceting`.

Hierarchical faceting

Pivot facets lend themselves quite well to hierarchical faceting. You could easily imagine a dataset where documents have geographical attributes, such as continent, country, region, and city. On the indexing side, these fields would need to be nontokenized, stored, and indexed string types. This would allow the values to be searched as well as displayed properly. On the output and query side, building a navigational tree with counts is trivial using pivot facets. You'd simply specify your list of fields as described previously `facet.pivot=continent,country,region,city`. The `facet_pivot` object in the response would contain all the data needed to build the UI component.

It's worth noting that pivot facets only work when the nodes within a tree have only one parent. The dataset described above works with pivot facets because there's a single path from child to parent. Datasets that have more than one parent (a family tree, and so on) will require a different solution. The Solr Wiki contains a good amount of information on hierarchical faceting and can be found at `https://wiki.apache.org/solr/HierarchicalFaceting`.

Excluding filters – multiselect faceting

Consider a scenario where you are implementing faceted navigation and you want to let the user pick several values of a field to filter on instead of just one. Typically, when an individual facet value is chosen, this becomes a filter. The filter makes subsequent faceting on that field almost pointless because the filter filters out the possibility of seeing other facet choices—assuming a single-valued field. In this scenario, we'd like to exclude this filter for this facet field.

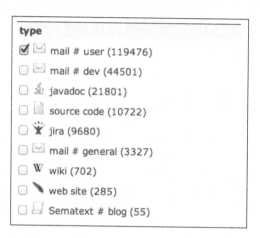

The preceding screenshot is from `http://search-lucene.com`, in which you can search across the mailing lists, API documentation, and other places that have information about Lucene, Solr, and other related projects. This screenshot shows that it lets users choose more than one type of information to filter results on at the same time, by letting users pick as many check boxes as they like.

We'll demonstrate the problem that multiselect faceting solves with a MusicBrainz example and then show how to solve it.

Here is a search for releases containing `smashing` and faceting on `r_type`. We'll leave rows at 0 for brevity, but observe the `numFound` value nonetheless. At this point, the user has not chosen a filter (therefore no `fq`):`http://localhost:8983/solr/mbreleases/mb_releases?indent=on&wt=json&omitHeader=true&rows=0&q=smashing&facet=on&facet.field=r_type&facet.mincount=1&facet.sort=index`.

The output of the preceding URL is as follows:

```
{"response":{"numFound":248,"start":0,"docs":[]},
  "facet_counts":{
    "facet_queries":{},
    "facet_fields":{
```

```
    "r_type":[
      "Album",29,
      "Compilation",41,
      "EP",7,
      "Interview",3,
      "Live",95,
      "Other",19,
      "Remix",1,
      "Single",45,
      "Soundtrack",1]},
  "facet_dates":{},
  "facet_ranges":{}}}
```

Now the user chooses the Album facet value. This adds a filter query. As a result, now the URL is as before but has &fq=r_type%3AAlbum at the end and has this output:

```
{"response":{"numFound":29,"start":0,"docs":[]},
  "facet_counts":{
    "facet_queries":{},
    "facet_fields":{
      "r_type":[
        "Album",29]},
    "facet_dates":{},
    "facet_ranges":{}}}
```

Notice that the other r_type facet counts are gone because of the filter, yet in this scenario, we want these to show the user what their counts would be if the filter wasn't there. The reduced numFound of 29 is good though, because at this moment, the user did indeed filter on a value.

Solr can solve this problem with some additional metadata on both the filter query and the facet field reference using local-params. The local-params syntax was described in *Chapter 5, Searching*, where it appears at the beginning of a query to switch the query parser and to supply parameters to it. As you're about to see, it can also be supplied at the start of facet.field—a bit of a hack, perhaps, to implement this feature. The previous example would change as follows:

- fq would now be {!tag=foo}r_type:Album
- facet.field would now be {!ex=foo}r_type

> Remember to URL encode this added syntax when used in the URL. The only problem character is =, which becomes %3D.

Now, we will explain each parameter of the previous example:

- The `tag` parameter is a local parameter to give an arbitrary label to this filter query.

- The tag name `foo` was an arbitrarily chosen name to illustrate that it doesn't matter what it's named. If multiple fields and filter queries are to be tagged correspondingly, then you would probably use the field name as the tag name to differentiate them consistently.

- The `ex` parameter is a local parameter on a facet field that refers to tagged filter queries to be *excluded* in the facet count. Multiple tags can be referenced with commas separating them. For example, `{!ex=t1,t2,t3}r_type`.

- The advanced usage is not shown here, which is an optional facet field `local-param` called `key` that provides an alternative label to the field name in the response. By providing an alternative name, the field can be faceted on multiple times with varying names and filter query exclusions.

The new complete URL is `http://localhost:8983/solr/mbreleases/mb_release s?indent=on&wt=json&omitHeader=true&rows=0&q=smashing&facet=on&facet. field={!ex=foo}r_type&facet.mincount=1&facet.sort=index&fq={!tag=foo} r_type:Album`.

And here is the output. The facet counts are back, but `numFound` remains at the filtered `29`:

```
{"response":{"numFound":29,"start":0,"docs":[]},
  "facet_counts":{
   "facet_queries":{},
   "facet_fields":{
     "r_type":[
       "Album",29,
       "Compilation",41,
       "EP",7,
       "Interview",3,
       "Live",95,
       "Other",19,
       "Remix",1,
       "Single",45,
       "Soundtrack",1]},
   "facet_dates":{},
   "facet_ranges":{}}}
```

At this point, if the user chooses additional values from this facet, then the filter query would be modified to allow for more possibilities, such as `fq={!tag=foo}` `r_type:Album r_type:Other` (not URL escaped for clarity). This filters for releases that are either of type `Album` or `Other`, as the default query parser Boolean logic is `OR`.

Summary

Faceting is possibly the most valuable and popular Solr search component. We've covered the five types of faceting, how to build filter queries from them, and some interesting use cases, such as alphabetic range bucketing and hierarchical faceting. Now you have the essential knowledge to put it to use in faceted navigation-based user interfaces and other uses like analytics.

In the next chapter, we'll cover Solr Search Components. You've actually been using them already because performing a query, enabling debug output, and faceting are each actually implemented as search components. But there's also search result highlighting, spelling correction, term-suggest, suggesting similar documents, collapsing/rolling up search results, editorially elevating or evicting results, and more!

8
Search Components

Many of Solr's major capabilities are internally organized into **search components**. You've actually been using several of them already: `QueryComponent` performs the actual searching, `DebugComponent` gathers invaluable query debugging information when setting `debugQuery`, and `FacetComponent` performs the faceting we used in *Chapter 7, Faceting*. In addition, there are many more that do all sorts of useful things that can really enhance your search experience:

- **Highlighting**: This returns highlighted text snippets of matching text in the original data
- **Spell checking**: This suggests alternative queries, often called *Did you mean?*
- **Suggester**: This suggests complete queries based on partially typed input; often called *query autocomplete*
- **Query elevation**: This manually modifies search results for certain queries.
- **More-like-this**: This helps to find documents similar to another document or provided text
- **Stats**: This is used for mathematical statistics of indexed numbers
- **Clustering**: This organizes search results into statistically similar clusters
- **Collapse and Expand / Grouping**: These group search results by a field and limit the number of results per group
- **Terms and TermVector**: These retrieve raw indexed data

And there are a few others we won't go into. For example, `ResponseLogComponent` adds document IDs and scores to Solr's log output—a feature useful for debugging and for relevancy analysis.

In a hurry?

Search features, such as search result highlighting, query spell-checking, and auto-completing queries are of high value for most search applications; don't miss them. Take a peek at the others to see if they are applicable to you.

About components

At this point, you should be familiar with the `<requestHandler/>` definitions defined in `solrconfig.xml` — this was explained in *Chapter 5, Searching*. Any request handlers with `class="solr.SearchRequestHandler"` are intuitively related to searching. The Java code implementing `SearchRequestHandler` doesn't actually do any searching! Instead, it maintains a list of `SearchComponents` that are invoked in sequence for a request. The search components used and their order are configurable.

What follows is our request handler for MusicBrainz releases but modified to explicitly configure the components for the purpose of illustration:

```
<requestHandler name="mb_releases" class="solr.SearchHandler">
  <!-- default values for query parameters -->
  <lst name="defaults">
    <str name="defType">edismax</str>
    <str name="qf">r_name r_a_name^0.4</str>
    <str name="pf">r_name^0.5 r_a_name^0.2</str>
    <str name="qs">1</str>
    <str name="ps">0</str>
    <str name="tie">0.1</str>
    <str name="q.alt">*:*</str>
  </lst>
  <!-- note: these components are the default ones -->
  <arr name="components">
    <str>query</str>
    <str>facet</str>
    <str>mlt</str>
    <str>highlight</str>
    <str>stats</str>
    <str>debug</str>
  </arr>
  <!-- INSTEAD, "first-components" and/or
    "last-components" may be specified. -->
</requestHandler>
```

The named search components are the default ones that are automatically registered if you do not specify the `components` section. To specify additional components, you can either re-specify `components` with changes, or you can add it to the `first-components` or `last-components` lists, which are prepended and appended respectively to the standard component list.

 Many components depend on other components being executed first, especially the query component, so you will usually add components to `last-components`.

Search components must be registered in `solrconfig.xml` so that they can then be referred to in a components list. The components in the default set are pre-registered, and some like highlighting will be registered explicitly anyway because they have configuration settings that aren't request parameters. Here's an example of how the search component named `elevator` is registered in `solrconfig.xml`:

```
<searchComponent name="elevator"
class="solr.QueryElevationComponent">
  <str name="queryFieldType">string</str>
  <str name="config-file">elevate.xml</str>
</searchComponent>
```

The functionality in `QueryComponent`, `FacetComponent`, and `DebugComponent` have been described in previous chapters. The rest of this chapter describes other search components that come with Solr.

Doing a distributed-search?

A Solr **distributed-search** has Solr search across multiple Solr cores/servers (*shards* in distributed-search lingo) as if it were one logical index. It will be discussed in *Chapter 11, Deployment*. An internal sharded request will by default go to the default request handler, *even if your client issued a request to another handler*. To ensure that the relevant search components are still activated on a sharded request, you can use the `shards.qt` parameter, just as you would `qt`. Solr 5.1 changed the default behavior for the better.

The highlight component

You are probably most familiar with search highlighting when you use an Internet search engine such as Google. Most search results come back with a snippet of text from the site containing the word(s) you search for, highlighted. Solr can do the same thing. In the following screenshot, we see Google highlighting a search including **Solr** and **search** (in bold):

Introduction to The **Solr** Enterprise **Search** Server 🔼 ❌
Solr is a standalone enterprise **search** server with a web-services like API. You put documents in it (called "indexing") via XML over HTTP. ...
lucene.apache.org/**solr**/features.html - 13k - Cached - Similar pages - 💬

To conserve screen space, you might even use this feature to simply tell the user that there was a match in certain fields without showing a highlighted value. This could make sense if there are many metadata fields. Nevertheless you would still likely highlight some.

A highlighting example

Admittedly the MusicBrainz dataset does not make an ideal example to show off highlighting because there's no substantial text, but it can still be useful, nonetheless.

The following is a sample use of highlighting on a search for `Corgan` in the MusicBrainz's artist dataset. Recall that the `/mb_artists` request handler is configured to search against the artist's name, alias, and members fields:
`http://localhost:8983/solr/mbartists/ mb_artists?indent=on&q=`
`corgan&rows=3&hl=true`.

And here is the result of that search:

```
<?xml version="1.0" encoding="UTF-8"?>
<response>
<lst name="responseHeader">
    <int name="status">0</int>
    <int name="QTime">89</int>
</lst>
<result name="response" numFound="5" start="0">
    <doc>
        <date name="a_begin_date">1967-03-17T05:00:00Z</date>
        <str name="a_name">Billy Corgan</str>
        <date name="a_release_date_latest">
                2005-06-21T04:00:00Z</date>
        <str name="a_type">1</str>
```

```
            <str name="id">Artist:102693</str>
            <str name="type">Artist</str>
        </doc>
        <doc>
            <str name="a_name">Billy Corgan &amp; Mike Garson</str>
            <str name="a_type">2</str>
            <str name="id">Artist:84909</str>
            <str name="type">Artist</str>
        </doc>
        <doc>
            <arr name="a_member_id"><str>102693</str></arr>
            <arr name="a_member_name"><str>Billy Corgan</str></arr>
            <str name="a_name">Starchildren</str>
            <str name="id">Artist:35656</str>
            <str name="type">Artist</str>
        </doc>
    </result>
    <lst name="highlighting">
        <lst name="Artist:102693">
            <arr name="a_name">
            <str>Billy &lt;em&gt;Corgan&lt;/em&gt;</str>
            </arr>
        </lst>
        <lst name="Artist:84909">
            <arr name="a_name">
            <str>Billy &lt;em&gt;Corgan&lt;/em&gt; &amp; Mike
                Garson</str>
            </arr>
        </lst>
        <lst name="Artist:35656">
            <arr name="a_member_name">
            <str>Billy &lt;em&gt;Corgan&lt;/em&gt;</str>
            </arr>
        </lst>
    </lst>
    </response>
```

What should be noted in this example is the manner in which the highlighting results appear in the response data. Also note that not all of the result highlighting was against the same field.

 It is possible to enable highlighting and discover that some of the results are not highlighted. Sometimes this can be due to complex text analysis; although more likely, it could simply be that there is a mismatch between the fields searched and those highlighted.

Choose the Standard, FastVector, or Postings highlighter

Before jumping into the highlighting parameters and configuration, it's important to be aware that Lucene has three highlighter implementations, all of which are exposed through Solr. All of them require that the field you highlight on be marked as stored in the schema, for obvious reasons. If you've at least done that, then you can skip choosing among them for early prototyping/experimentation and proceed to the next section using the venerable standard highlighter. The primary reason there are multiple implementations is performance—particularly for lengthy text. The faster ones make trade-offs either in features or additional index size. Many (but not all) highlighting request parameters apply to all highlighters, but frustratingly, most of the `solrconfig.xml` based settings vary between the highlighters.

The Standard (default) highlighter

Lucene's original highlighter was simply called the highlighter, but it's now referred to as either the default or standard highlighter. This is the one you get if you take no action to choose the others. This highlighter has the fewest index requirements— simply make sure that the field is stored. For lengthier text fields, it's the slowest since it re-analyzes the text, and if you want phrase queries to highlight correctly (`hl.usePhraseHighlighter`), then it will index it in-memory on the fly for that feature. But this highlighter is the most accurate, particularly if you are using **SpanQueries**. The **ComplexPhrase** and **Surround** query parsers are the only out-of-the-box query parsers that can produce such queries, but plenty of Solr users write their own that make use of SpanQueries.

 The performance is much faster if you index term vectors, which spares the need to re-analyze the text and to index on the fly for phrase queries. Use the same schema options as required for the FastVector highlighter, which will be described next. If you are using Solr 5 in particular, then the difference can be dramatic.

Unlike the other two highlighters, this one's snippet fragmenting options do *not* include one based on Java's BreakIterator. **BreakIterator** has better internationalization support and some overall nice features versus using a regular expression.

The FastVector highlighter

The **FastVector highlighter** (FVH) was the second highlighter to come about and is fundamentally based on term vector information in the index—something that isn't there unless you enable it. Term vectors are hefty, usually consuming almost as much space on-disk as the stored content does, which is the biggest part of the index. They're fairly accurate with the exception of SpanQueries, as mentioned previously. Also, this highlighter has the unique feature of being able to highlight each query term with different markup, such as a distinct color.

The schema field requirements are `indexed="true" stored="true" termVectors="true" termPositions="true" termOffsets="true"`. To tell Solr to use the FVH, set `hl.useFastVectorHighligher=true` in your request parameters.

 If a field to highlight doesn't have term vectors enabled, the standard/default highlighter will be used even if this FVH request parameter has been set. This is a good thing as it allows you to use term vectors where they have the most benefit: on long text fields, not short ones.

The Postings highlighter

This new highlighter was introduced in Solr 4.1 and uses Lucene's newfound ability to store offset information with the postings data in the index. This extra information takes up much less space than term vectors do. The Postings highlighter was also written to be as fast as can be, compromising on matching phrase queries or any other query that is position-sensitive accurately. In other words, if the query is a quoted phrase, the highlighter will not honor the adjacency requirement; all words in the phrase will be highlighted, no matter where they lie. And even though it's generally the fastest highlighter, it's markedly slower with wildcard, fuzzy, and other so-called multiterm queries. So, with these points in mind, choose this highlighter when there is a lot of text to be highlighted and speed/efficiency is the top requirement over accuracy.

The schema field requirements are `indexed="true" stored="true" storeOffsetsWithPositions="true"`. If you attempt to use this highlighter in a field that doesn't meet this requirement, it will appear as an error. Now, unlike the standard and FastVector highlighters, you must modify `solrconfig.xml` to register `HighlightComponent` configured to use this highlighter, like so:

```
<searchComponent class="solr.HighlightComponent" name="highlight">
  <highlighting
  class="org.apache.solr.highlight.PostingsSolrHighlighter"/>
</searchComponent>
```

Only one search component can be registered with a specific name: `highlight` in this case. If you want to also highlight with the standard and FVH highlighters for different search requests, then you can register both under separate names and configure separate request handlers to use each.

A final caveat to this highlighter is that it may work incorrectly when the index analysis configuration has token filters that emit tokens in the wrong order with respect to the offsets. The other highlighters have workarounds, but not the postings highlighter. This used to pose more problems in earlier 4.x releases, but they are rarer now, so you might just accept this as a low risk.

Highlighting configuration

Highlighting, like most parts of Solr searching, is largely configured through request parameters. The standard and FastVector highlighters also contain configuration options in `solrconfig.xml`, while the postings highlighter was designed to be completely configured via request parameters. You can specify these in the URL, but it is more appropriate to specify the majority of these in your application's request handler in `solrconfig.xml` because they are unlikely to change between requests. Furthermore, it can be convenient to tweak/tune settings on the Solr end versus your application for most of these parameters, since most wouldn't require a change in processing by the application.

What follows are common parameters observed by the highlighter search component. Understand that like faceting, nearly all highlighter parameters can be overridden on a per-field basis. The syntax looks like `f.fieldName.paramName=value`; for example, `f.allText.snippets=0`.

- `hl`: This is set to `true` in order to enable search highlighting. Without this, the other parameters are ignored, and highlighting is effectively disabled.

- `hl.fl`: This will highlight a comma or space separated list of fields. It is important for a field to be marked as stored in the schema in order to highlight it. Sometimes, this parameter can be omitted, but the highlighter often has difficulty ascertaining which fields are in the query, so you are advised to just set it. You may use an asterisk wildcard, such as `*` or `r_*`, to conveniently highlight on all of the text fields. If you use a wildcard, then consider enabling the `hl.requireFieldMatch` option.

- `hl.requireFieldMatch`: If set to `true`, a field will not be highlighted for a result unless the query also matched against that field. This is set to `false` by default, meaning that it's possible to query one field and highlight another and get highlights back, as long as the terms searched for are found within the highlighted field. If you use a wildcard in `hl.fl`, then you will probably enable this. However, if you query against an all-text catch-all field (probably using copy-field directives) then leave this as `false`, so that the search results can indicate from which field the query text was found. The postings highlighter doesn't support this; the field must match (`true`).

- `hl.snippets`: This is the maximum number of highlighted snippets (also known as fragments) that will be generated per field. It defaults to `1`, which you will probably not change. By setting this to `0` for a particular field (for example, `f.allText.hl.snippets=0`), you can effectively disable highlighting for that field. You might do that if you used a wildcard for `hl.fl` and want to make an exception.

- `hl.fragsize`: This is the maximum number of characters returned in each snippet (fragment), which is measured in characters. The default is `100`. If `0` is specified, then the field is not fragmented and whole field values are returned. Obviously, be wary of doing this for large text fields.

- `hl.mergeContiguous`: If set to `true`, then overlapping snippets are merged. The merged fragment size is not limited by `hl.fragsize`. The default is `false`, but you will probably set this to `true` when `hl.snippets` is greater than zero and `fragsize` is non-zero.

> In this edition of the book, *we only document some common parameters.* See the Solr Reference Guide for definitive information on all of the rest (there are a lot more) at `https://cwiki.apache.org/confluence/display/solr/Highlighting`.

The SpellCheck component

One of the best ways to enhance the search experience is by offering spelling corrections. This is sometimes presented at the top of search results with such text as "Did you mean ...". Solr supports this with the `SpellCheckComponent`.

> A related technique is to use fuzzy queries using the tilde syntax. However, fuzzy queries don't tell you what alternative spellings were used; the case is similar for phonetic matching.

For spelling corrections to work, Solr must clearly have a corpus of words (a dictionary) to suggest alternatives to those in the user's query. "Dictionary" is meant loosely as a collection of words, and not their definitions. Typically, you configure an appropriately indexed field as the dictionary or instead, you supply a plain text file. Solr can be configured to use one or more of the following spellcheckers:

- **DirectSolrSpellChecker**: This uses terms from a field in the index. It computes suggestions by working directly off the main index. A configurable distance-measure computes similarities between words. By working off of the main index, this choice is very convenient, especially when getting started. For more performance or more options, choose another.

- **IndexBasedSpellChecker**: This uses terms from a field in the index. It builds a **parallel index** and computes suggestions from that. A configurable distance-measure computes similarities between words.

- **FileBasedSpellChecker**: This uses a simple text file of words. It's otherwise essentially the same as `IndexBasedSpellChecker`.

- **WordBreakSolrSpellChecker**: This detects when a user has inadvertently omitted a space between words or added a space within a word. It computes suggestions directly off the main index. It's often used in conjunction with one of the other SpellChecker components.

There is also a **Suggester** SpellChecker that implements auto-suggest / query completion. That choice is deprecated as of Solr 4.7, which introduced a dedicated SearchComponent for suggestions. We'll describe that feature later in this chapter.

The notion of a **parallel index**, also known as a **side-car index**, is simply an additional internal working index for a dedicated purpose. These must be 'built', which takes time, and they can get out of sync with the main index.

 Before reading on about configuring spell checking in `solrconfig.xml`, you may want to jump ahead and take a quick peek at an example towards the end of this section, and then come back.

The schema configuration

Assuming your dictionary is going to be based on indexed content instead of a file, a field should be set aside exclusively for this purpose. This is so that it can be analyzed appropriately and so that other fields can be copied into it, as the spellcheckers use just one field. Most Solr setups would have one field; our MusicBrainz searches, on the other hand, are segmented by the data type (artists, releases, and tracks), and so one for each would be best. For the purposes of demonstrating this feature, we will only do it for artists.

In `schema.xml`, we need to define the field type for spellchecking. This particular configuration is one we recommend for most scenarios:

```
<fieldType name="textSpell" class="solr.TextField"
      positionIncrementGap="100" stored="false" multiValued="true">
  <analyzer type="index">
    <tokenizer class="solr.StandardTokenizerFactory"/>
    <filter class="solr.LowerCaseFilterFactory"/>
    <filter class="solr.SynonymFilterFactory"
            synonyms="synonyms.txt" ignoreCase="true"
            expand="true"/>
    <filter class="solr.StopFilterFactory" ignoreCase="true"
            words="stopwords.txt"/>
    <filter class="solr.RemoveDuplicatesTokenFilterFactory"/>
  </analyzer>
  <analyzer type="query">
    <tokenizer class="solr.StandardTokenizerFactory"/>
    <filter class="solr.LowerCaseFilterFactory"/>
    <filter class="solr.StopFilterFactory" ignoreCase="true"
            words="stopwords.txt"/>
    <filter class="solr.RemoveDuplicatesTokenFilterFactory"/>
  </analyzer>
</fieldType>
```

A field type for spellchecking is not marked as stored because the spellcheck component only uses the indexed terms. The important thing is to ensure that the text analysis does *not* perform stemming, as the corrections presented would suggest the stems, which would look very odd to the user for most stemmer algorithms. It's also hard to imagine a use case that doesn't apply lowercasing.

Now, we need to create a field for this data:

```
<field name="a_spell" type="textSpell" />
```

And we need to get data into it with some `copyField` directives:

```
<copyField source="a_name" dest="a_spell" />
<copyField source="a_alias" dest="a_spell" />
```

Arguably, a_member_name may be an additional choice to copy as well, as the `dismax` search we configured (seen in the following code) searches it too, albeit at a reduced score. This, as well as many decisions with search configuration, is subjective.

Configuration in solrconfig.xml

To use any search component, it needs to be in the components list of a request handler. The spellcheck component is not in the standard list, so it needs to be added:

```
<requestHandler name="/mb_artists" class="solr.SearchHandler">
  <!-- default values for query parameters -->
  <lst name="defaults">
    <str name="defType">edismax</str>
    <str name="qf">a_name a_alias^0.8 a_member_name^0.4</str>
    <!-- etc. -->
  </lst>
  <arr name="last-components">
    <str>spellcheck</str>
  </arr>
</requestHandler>
```

This component should already be defined in `solrconfig.xml`. Within the spellchecker search component, there is one or more XML blocks named `spellchecker`, so that different dictionaries and other options can be configured. These might also be loosely referred to as the dictionaries, because the parameter that refers to this choice is named that way (more on that later). We have two spellcheckers configured as follows:

- `a_spell`: This is an index-based spellchecker that is a typical recommended configuration using `DirectSolrSpellChecker` on the `a_spell` field.
- `file`: This is a sample configuration where the input dictionary comes from a file (not included).

A complete MusicBrainz implementation would have a different spellchecker for each MB data type, with all of them configured similarly.

Following the excerpt given here is an example configuration of the key options available in the spellchecker component:

```
<searchComponent name="spellcheck"
    class="solr.SpellCheckComponent">
  <str name="queryAnalyzerFieldType">textSpell</str><!-- 'q'
    only -->

  <lst name="spellchecker">
    <str name="name">a_spell</str>
    <str name="field">a_spell</str>
    <str name="classname">solr.DirectSolrSpellChecker</str>
    <str name="distanceMeasure">internal</str>
    <float name="accuracy">0.5</float>
    <int name="maxEdits">1</int>
    <int name="minPrefix">1</int>
    <int name="maxInspections">5</int>
    <int name="minQueryLength">4</int>
    <float name="maxQueryFrequency">0.01</float>
    <float name="thresholdTokenFrequency">.01</float>
  </lst>
  <!-- just an example -->
  <lst name="spellchecker">
    <str name="name">file</str>
    <str name="classname">solr.FileBasedSpellChecker</str>
    <str name="sourceLocation">spellings.txt</str>
    <str name="characterEncoding">UTF-8</str>
  </lst>
</searchComponent>
```

Configuring spellcheckers – dictionaries

The double layer of spellchecker configuration is perhaps a little confusing. The outer one just names the search component—it's just a container for configuration(s). The inner ones are distinct configurations to choose at search time.

The following options are common to all spellcheckers, unless otherwise specified:

- name: This refers to the name of the spellcheck configuration. It defaults to default. Be sure not to have more than one configuration with the same name.

- classname: This refers to the implementation of the spellchecker. It's optional *but you should be explicit*. The choices are solr.DirectSolrSpellChecker, solr.IndexBasedSpellChecker, solr.WordBreakSolrSpellChecker, and solr.FileBasedSpellChecker. Further information on these is just ahead.

- `accuracy`: This sets the minimum spelling correction accuracy to act as a threshold. It falls between 0 and 1 with a default of 0.5. The higher this number is, the simpler the corrections are. The accuracy is computed by the `distanceMeasure`. This option doesn't apply to `WordBreakSolrSpellChecker`.

- `distanceMeasure`: This Java class computes how similar a possible misspelling and a candidate correction are. It defaults to `org.apache.lucene.search.spell.LevensteinDistance`, which is the same algorithm used in fuzzy query matching. Alternatively, `org.apache.lucene.search.spell.JaroWinklerDistance` works quite well. This option doesn't apply to `WordBreakSolrSpellChecker`.

- `field`: This refers to the name of the field within the index that contains the dictionary. It's mandatory except when using `FileBasedSolrSpellChecker` where it's not applicable, since its data comes from a file, not an index. The field must be indexed as the data is taken from there and not from the stored content, which is ignored. Generally, this field exists expressly for spell correction purposes and other fields are copied into it.

- `fieldType`: This is a reference to a field type in `schema.xml` to perform text-analysis on words to be spellchecked by the `spellcheck.q` parameter (not q). If this isn't specified, then it defaults to the field type of the `field` parameter, and if not specified, it defaults to a simple whitespace delimiter, which most likely would be a misconfiguration. When using the file-based spellchecker with `spellcheck.q`, be sure to specify this.

Technically, `buildOnCommit` and `buildOnOptimize` should be in the preceding list, but it's only worthwhile for the Index- or file-based spellcheckers, since they maintain a parallel index.

DirectSolrSpellChecker options

The `DirectSolrSpellChecker` component works directly off the Solr index without needing to maintain a parallel index to generate suggestions that might get out of sync. It's a great choice to start with.

- `maxEdits`: This is the number of changes to allow for each term; the default value is 2. Since most spelling mistakes are only one letter off, setting this to 1 will reduce the number of possible suggestions.

- `minPrefix`: This refers to the minimum number of characters that the terms should share. If you want the spelling suggestions to start with the same letter, set this value as 1.

- `maxInspections`: This defines the maximum number of possible matches to review before returning the results; the default is 5.

- `minQueryLength`: This specifies how many characters must be in the input query before suggestions are returned; the default is 4.

- `maxQueryFrequency`: This is the maximum threshold for the number of documents a term must appear in before being considered as a suggestion. This can be a percentage (such as .01 percent for 1 percent) or an absolute value (such as 2). A lower threshold is better for small indexes.

- `thresholdTokenFrequency`: This specifies a document frequency threshold, which will exclude words that don't occur sufficiently often. This can be expressed as a fraction in the range 0-1, defaulting to 0, which effectively disables the threshold, letting all words through. It can also be expressed as an absolute value.

> If there is a lot of data and lots of common words, as opposed to proper nouns, then this threshold should be effective. If testing shows spelling candidates including strange fluke words found in the index, then introduce a threshold that is high enough to weed out such outliers. The threshold will probably be less than 0.01 — one percent of documents.

IndexBasedSpellChecker options

The `IndexBasedSpellChecker` component gets the dictionary from the indexed content of a field in a Lucene/Solr index, and it loads it into its own private parallel index to perform spellcheck searches on. The options are explained as follows:

- `buildOnCommit` and `buildOnOptimize`: These Boolean options (defaulting to `false`) enable the spellchecker's internal index to be built automatically when either Solr performs a commit or optimize. This can make keeping the spellchecker in sync easier than building manually, but beware that commits or optimizes will subsequently be hit with a long delay.

- `spellcheckIndexDir`: This is the directory where the spellchecker's internal dictionary is *built*, not its source. It is relative to Solr's data directory. This is actually optional, which results in an in-memory dictionary.

> For a high-load Solr server, an in-memory index is appealing. Until SOLR-780 is addressed, you'll have to take care to tell Solr to build the dictionary whenever the Solr core gets loaded. This happens at startup or if you tell Solr to reload a core.

- sourceLocation: If specified, it refers to a directory containing Lucene index files, such as a Solr data directory. This is an unusual expert choice, but shows that the source dictionary does not need to come from Solr's main index; it could be from another location, perhaps from another Solr core. If you are doing this, then you'll probably also need to use the spellcheck. reload command mentioned later.

Warning

This option name is common to both IndexBasedSpellChecker and FileBasedSpellChecker but is defined differently.

- thresholdTokenFrequency: This has the same definition as in DirectSolrSpellChecker

FileBasedSpellChecker options

The FileBasedSpellChecker component is very similar to IndexBasedSpellChecker, except that it gets the dictionary from a plain text file instead of the index. It maintains its own private parallel index to perform spellcheck searches on. This can be useful if you are using Solr as a spelling server, or if you don't need spelling suggestions to be based on actual terms in the index. The file format is one word per line. You can find an example file (spellings.txt) in the conf directory.

- buildOnCommit, buildOnOptimize, and, spellcheckIndexDir: For more on these, see the *IndexBasedSpellChecker options* section

- sourceLocation: This is mandatory and references a plain text file with each word on its own line. Note that an option by the same name but different meaning exists for IndexBasedSpellChecker.

For a freely available English word list, check out **Spell Checker Oriented Word Lists (SCOWL)** at http://wordlist. sourceforge.net. In addition, see the dictionary files for OpenOffice, which supports many languages at http://wiki. services.openoffice.org/wiki/Dictionaries.

- characterEncoding: This is optional, but should be set. It is the character encoding of sourceLocation, defaulting to UTF-8.

WordBreakSolrSpellChecker options

The `WordBreakSolrSpellChecker` component offers suggestions by combining adjacent query terms and/or breaking terms into multiple words from the Solr index. It can detect spelling errors resulting from misplaced whitespace without the use of shingle-based dictionaries and provides collation support for word-break errors, including cases where the user has a mix of single-word spelling errors and word-break errors in the same query. The following are options specific to this spellchecker:

- `combineWords`: This defines whether words should be combined in a dictionary search; default is `true`

- `breakWords`: This defines whether words should be broken during a dictionary search; default is `true`

- `maxChanges`: This defines how many times the spell checker should check collation possibilities against the index; default is `10` (can be any integer)

For more advanced options, see the Javadocs at `http://lucene.apache.org/solr/4_8_0/solr-core/org/apache/solr/spelling/WordBreakSolrSpellChecker.html`.

> If you use this spellchecker, you'll probably want to combine its suggestions with one of the other spellcheckers. All you need to do is reference multiple dictionaries at search time (more on that later) and Solr will merge them. Pretty cool!

You can find an example of this spellchecker configuration in Solr's example `solrconfig.xml`.

Processing the q parameter

We've not yet discussed the parameters of a search with the spellchecker component enabled. But at this point of the configuration discussion, understand that you have the choice of just letting the user query q get processed or you can use `spellcheck.q`.

When a user query (q parameter) is processed by the `spellcheck` component to look for spelling errors, Solr needs to determine what words are to be examined. This is a two-step process. The first step is to pull out the queried words from the query string, ignoring any syntax, such as AND. The next step is to process the words with an analyzer so that, among other things, lowercasing is performed.

The analyzer chosen is through a field type specified directly within the search component configuration with `queryAnalyzerFieldType`. It really should be specified, but it's actually optional. If left unspecified, there would be no text analysis, which would in all likelihood be a misconfiguration.

 This algorithm is implemented by a spellcheck **query converter**—a Solr extension point. The default query converter, known as `SpellingQueryConverter`, is probably fine.

Processing the spellcheck.q parameter

If the `spellcheck.q` parameter is given (which really isn't a query per se), then the string is processed with the text analysis referenced by the `fieldType` option of the spellchecker being used. If a file-based spellchecker is being used, then you should set this explicitly. Index-based spellcheckers will sensibly use the field type of the referenced indexed spelling field.

 The dichotomy of the ways in which the analyzer is configured between both q and `spellcheck.q` arguably needs improvement.

Building index- and file-based spellcheckers

If the spellchecker you are using is `IndexedBasedSpellChecker` or `FileBasedSpellChecker` (or, technically, `Suggester`), then it needs to be *built*, which is the process in which the dictionary is read and is built into the `spellcheckIndexDir`. If it isn't built, then no corrections will be offered, and you'll probably be very confused. You'll be even more confused when troubleshooting the results if it was built once but is far out of date and so needs to be built again.

Generally, building is required if it has never been built before, and it should be built periodically when the dictionary changes. It need not necessarily be built for every change, but it obviously won't benefit from any such modifications.

 Using `buildOnOptimize` or `buildOnCommit` is a low-hassle way to keep the spellcheck index up to date. However, most apps never optimize or optimize too infrequently to make use of this, or they commit too frequently. So instead (or in addition to `buildOnOptimize`), issue build commands manually on a suitable time period and/or at the end of your data loading scripts. Furthermore, setting `spellcheckIndexDir` will ensure the built spellcheck index is persisted between Solr restarts.

In order to perform the build of a spellchecker, simply enable the component with `spellcheck=true`, add a special parameter called `spellcheck.build`, and set it to true: `http://localhost:8983/solr/mbartists/select?&qt=mb_artists&rows=0&spellcheck=true&spellcheck.build=true&spellcheck.dictionary=a_spell`.

The other spellcheck parameters will be explained shortly. There is an additional related option similar to `spellcheck.build` called `spellcheck.reload`. This doesn't rebuild the index, but it basically re-establishes connections with the index—both `sourceLocation` for index-based spellcheckers and `spellcheckIndexDir` for all types. If you've decided to have some external process build the dictionary or simply share built indexes between spellcheckers, then Solr needs to know to reload it to see the changes—a quick operation.

Issuing spellcheck requests

At this point, we've covered how to configure a spellchecker but not how to issue requests that actually use it. In summary, all that you are required to do is add `spellcheck=true` to a standard search request, but it is more likely that you will set other options, once you start experimenting.

It's important to be aware that there are effectively three mutually exclusive internal modes that this component places itself in:

- The default mode is only to offer suggestions for query terms that find no results. This is intuitive, but sometimes a term that finds results was an indexed typo.

- If `spellcheck.onlyMorePopular=true`, then the spellcheck component will not only try to offer suggestions for query terms that find no results, it will also do so for the other terms, provided it can offer a suggestion that occurs more frequently in the index. Now Solr is working harder and intuitively, this should help fix cases when the query is an indexed typo. However, the erroneous query term might not be an indexed typo (for example, June versus Jane); can Solr still try harder? Yes...

- If `spellcheck.alternativeTermCount` is set, then it will try to find suggestions for all terms, and the suggestions need not occur more frequently.

Despite these progressively aggressive spellcheck modes, there might still be no suggestions or fewer than the number asked for if it simply can't find anything suitable.

Let's now explore the various request parameters recognized by the spellchecker component:

- `spellcheck`: This refers to a Boolean switch that must be set to `true` to enable the component in order to see suggested spelling corrections.

- `spellcheck.dictionary`: This is the named reference to a dictionary (spellchecker) to use configured in `solrconfig.xml`. It defaults to `default`. This can be set multiple times and Solr will merge the suggestions.

- `spellcheck.q` or `q`: The string containing words to be processed by this component can be specified as the `spellcheck.q` parameter, and if not present, then the `q` parameter. Please look for the information presented earlier on how these are processed.

Which should you use: spellcheck.q or q?

Assuming you're handling user queries for Solr that might contain some query syntax, then the default `q` is right, as Solr will then know to filter out possible uses of Lucene/Solr's syntax, such as AND, OR, `fieldname:word`, and so on. If not, then `spellcheck.q` is preferred, as it won't go through that unnecessary processing. This also allows its parsing to be different on a spellchecker-by-spellchecker basis, which we'll leverage in our example.

- `spellcheck.count`: This refers to the maximum number of corrections to offer per word. The default is `1`. Corrections are ordered by those closest to the original, as determined by the `distanceMeasure` algorithm.

Although counter-intuitive, raising this number affects the suggestion ordering—the results get better! The internal algorithm sees ~10 times as many as this number and then it orders them by closest match. Consequently, use a number between `5` and `10` or so to get quality results.

- `spellcheck.extendedResults`: This is a Boolean switch that adds frequency information, both for the original word and for the suggestions. It's helpful when debugging.

- `spellcheck.collate`: This is a Boolean switch that adds a revised query string to the output that alters the original query (from `spellcheck.q` or `q`) to use the top recommendation for each suggested word. It's smart enough to leave any other query syntax in place. The following are some additional options for use when collation is enabled:

- ○ spellcheck.maxCollations: This specifies the maximum number of collations to return, defaulting to 1.

- ○ spellcheck.maxCollationTries: This specifies the maximum number of collations to *try* (verify it yields results), defaulting to 5. If this is non-zero, then the spellchecker will not return collations that yield no results.

- ○ spellcheck.maxCollationEvaluations: This specifies the maximum number of word correction combinations to rank before the top candidates are tried (verified). Without this limit, queries with many misspelled words could yield a combinatoric explosion of possibilities. The default is 10000, which should be fine.

- ○ spellcheck.collateExtendedResults: This is a Boolean switch that adds more details to the collation response. It adds the collation hits (number of documents found) and a mapping of misspelled words to corrected words.

- ○ spellcheck.collateParam.xx: This will allow parameter override, where xx is the parameter you want to override; for example, to override mm from a low value to a high value so that the spellchecker is truly verifying that the replacement (collation) terms exist together in the same document. This is similar to local-params, but is applied to the collated query string verification when maxCollationTries is used.

 Enable spellcheck.collate as a user interface will most likely want to present a convenient link to use the spelling suggestions. Furthermore, ensure the collation is verified to return results by setting spellcheck.maxCollationTries to a small non-zero number—perhaps 5.

- spellcheck.onlyMorePopular: This is a Boolean switch that will offer spelling suggestions for queried terms that *were* found in the index, provided that the suggestions occur more often. This is in addition to the normal behavior of only offering suggestions for queried terms *not* found in the index. To detect when this happens, enable extendedResults and look for origFreq being greater than 0. This is disabled, by default.

- spellcheck.alternativeTermCount: This specifies the maximum number of suggestions to return for each query term *that already exists in the index/dictionary*. Normally, the spellchecker doesn't offer suggestions for such query terms, and so setting this triggers the spellchecker to try to find suggestions for all query terms. The configured number essentially overrides spellcheck.count for such terms, giving the opportunity to use a more conservative (lower) number, since it's less likely one of these query terms was actually misspelled.

- `spellcheck.maxResultsForSuggest`: This specifies the maximum number of results the request can return in order to both generate spelling suggestions and set the `correctlySpelled` element to `false`. This acts as an early short-circuit rule in the spellchecker if you set it, otherwise there is no rule. This option is only applicable when `spellcheck.onlyMorePopular` is `true` or `spellcheck.alternativeTermCount` is set, because only those two options can trigger suggestions for queries that return results.

 We recommend that you experiment with various options provided by the `SpellChecker` component, with the real data that you are indexing so that you can find out what options work best for your requirements.

Example usage for a misspelled query

We'll try out a typical spellcheck configuration that we've named a_spell. We've disabled showing the query results with `rows=0` because the actual query results aren't the point of these examples. In this example, it is imagined that the user is searching for the band Smashing Pumpkins, but with a misspelling.

Here are the search results for Smashg Pumpkins, using the a_spell dictionary:

```xml
<?xml version="1.0"?>
<response>
<lst name="responseHeader">
    <int name="status">0</int>
    <int name="QTime">124</int>
    <lst name="params">
    <str name="spellcheck">true</str>
    <str name="indent">on</str>
    <str name="spellcheck.extendedResults">true</str>
    <str name="spellcheck.collateExtendedResults">true</str>
    <str name="spellcheck.maxCollationTries">5</str>
    <str name="spellcheck.collate">true</str>
    <str name="rows">0</str>
    <str name="echoParams">explicit</str>
    <str name="q">Smashg Pumpkins</str>
    <str name="spellcheck.dictionary">a_spell</str>
    <str name="spellcheck.count">5</str>
    <str name="qt">/mb_artists</str>
    </lst>
</lst>
```

```xml
<result name="response" numFound="0" start="0"/>
<lst name="spellcheck">
  <lst name="suggestions">
    <lst name="smashg">
      <int name="numFound">5</int>
      <int name="startOffset">0</int>
      <int name="endOffset">6</int>
      <int name="origFreq">0</int>
      <arr name="suggestion">
        <lst>
          <str name="word">smash</str>
          <int name="freq">36</int>
        </lst>
        <lst>
          <str name="word">smashing</str>
          <int name="freq">4</int>
        </lst>
        <lst>
          <str name="word">smashign</str>
          <int name="freq">1</int>
        </lst>
        <lst>
          <str name="word">smashed</str>
          <int name="freq">5</int>
        </lst>
        <lst>
          <str name="word">smasher</str>
          <int name="freq">2</int>
        </lst>
      </arr>
    </lst>
    <bool name="correctlySpelled">false</bool>
    <lst name="collation">
      <str name="collationQuery">smashing Pumpkins</str>
      <int name="hits">1</int>
      <lst name="misspellingsAndCorrections">
        <str name="smashg">smashing</str>
      </lst>
    </lst>
  </lst>
</lst>
</response>
```

In this scenario, we intentionally chose a misspelling that is closer to another word: "smash". Were it not for `maxCollationTries`, the suggested collation would be "smash Pumpkins", which would return no results. There are a few things we want to point out regarding the spellchecker response:

- Applications consuming this data will probably only use the collation query, despite the presence of a lot of other information.

- The suggestions are ordered by the so-called *edit-distance* score (closest match), which is not displayed. It may seem here that it is ordered by frequency, which is a coincidence.

 There is an extension point to the spellchecker to customize the ordering—search Solr's wiki on `comparatorClass` for further information. You could write one that orders results based on a formula, fusing both the suggestion score and document frequency.

- `startOffset` and `endOffset` are the index into the query of the spellchecked word. This information can be used by the client to display the query differently, perhaps displaying the corrected words in bold.

- `numFound` is always the number of suggested words returned, not the total number available, if `spellcheck.count` were raised.

- `correctlySpelled` is intuitively `true` or `false`, depending on whether all of the query words were found in the dictionary or not.

Query complete/suggest

One of the most effective features of a search user interface is automatic/instant-search or completion of query input in a search input box. It is typically displayed as a drop-down menu that appears automatically after typing. There are several ways this can work:

- **Instant-search**: Here, the menu is populated with search results. Each row is a document, just like the regular search results are, and as such, choosing one takes the user *directly* to the information instead of a search results page. At your discretion, you might opt to consider the last word partially typed. Examples of this are the URL bar in web browsers and various person search services. This is particularly effective for quick lookup scenarios against identifying information such as a name/title/identifier. It's less effective for broader searches. It's commonly implemented either with edge n-grams or with the Suggester component.

- **Query log completion**: If your application has sufficient query volume, then you should perform the query completion against previously executed queries that returned results. The pop-up menu is then populated with queries that others have typed. This is what Google does. It takes a bit of work to set this up. To get the query string and other information, you could write a custom search component, or parse Solr's log files, or hook into the logging system and parse it there. The query strings could be appended to a plain query log file, or inserted into a database, or added directly to a Solr index. Putting the data into a database before it winds up in a Solr index affords more flexibility on how to ultimately index it in Solr. Finally, at this point, you could index the field with an `EdgeNGramTokenizer` and perform searches against it, or use a `KeywordTokenizer` and then use one of the approaches listed for query term completion below. We recommend reading this excellent article by Jay Hill on doing this with `EdgeNGrams` at `http://lucidworks.com/blog/auto-suggest-from-popular-queries-using-edgengrams/`.

Monitor your user's queries!

Even if you don't plan to do query log completion, you should capture useful information about each request for ancillary usage analysis, especially to monitor which searches return no results. Capture the request parameters, the response time, the result count, and add a timestamp.

- **Query term completion**: The last word of the user's query is searched within the index as a prefix, and other indexed words starting with that prefix are provided. This type is an alternative to query log completion and it's easy to implement. There are several implementation approaches: facet the word using `facet.prefix`, use Solr's Suggester feature, or use the Terms component. You should consider these choices in that order.

- **Facet/Field value completion**: This is similar to query term completion, but it is done on data that you would facet or filter on. The pop-up menu of choices will ideally give suggestions across multiple fields with a label telling you which field each suggestion is for, and the value will be the exact field value, not the subset of it that the user typed. This is particularly useful when there are many possible filter choices. We've seen it used at `Mint.com` and elsewhere to great effect, but it is under-utilized in our opinion. If you don't have many fields to search, then the Suggester component could be used with one dictionary per field. Otherwise, build a search index dedicated to this information that contains one document per field and value pair, and use an edge n-gram approach to search it.

There are other interesting query completion concepts we've seen on sites too, and some of these can be combined effectively. First, we'll cover a basic approach to instant-search using edge n-grams. Next, we'll describe three approaches to implementing query term completion—it's a popular type of query completion, and these approaches highlight different technologies within Solr. Lastly, we'll cover an approach to implement field-value suggestions for one field at a time, using the `Suggester` search component.

Instant-search via edge n-grams

As mentioned in the beginning of this section, instant-search is a technique in which a partial query is used to suggest a set of relevant *documents*, not terms. It's great for quickly finding documents by name or title, skipping the search results page.

Here, we'll briefly describe how you might implement this approach using edge n-grams, which you can think of as a set of token prefixes. This is much faster than the equivalent wildcard query because the prefixes are all indexed. The edge n-gram technique is arguably more flexible than other suggest approaches: it's possible to do custom sorting or boosting, to use the highlighter easily to highlight the query, to offer infix suggestions (it isn't limited to matching titles left-to-right), and it's possible to filter the suggestions with a filter query, such as the current navigation filter state in the UI. It should be noted, though, that this technique is more complicated and increases indexing time and index size. It's also not quite as fast as the Suggester component.

One of the key components to this approach is the `EdgeNGramFilterFactory` component, which creates a series of tokens for each input token for all possible prefix lengths. The field type definition should apply this filter to the *index* analyzer only, not the *query* analyzer. Enhancements to the field type could include adding filters such as `LowerCaseFilterFactory`, `TrimFilterFactory`, `ASCIIFoldingFilterFactory`, or even a `PatternReplaceFilterFactory` for normalizing repetitive spaces. Refer to *Chapter 3, Text Analysis*, for detailed information on analysis components such as `EdgeNGramFilterFactory`. Furthermore, you should set `omitTermFreqAndPositions=true` and `omitNorms=true` in the field type since these index features consume a lot of space and won't be needed.

 The Solr Admin Analysis tool (covered in *Chapter 3, Text Analysis*) can really help with the design of the perfect field type configuration. Don't hesitate to use this tool!

A minimalist query for this approach is to simply query the n-grams field directly; since the field already contains prefixes, this just works. It's even better to have only the last word in the query search this field while the other words search a field indexed normally for keyword search. Here's an example: assuming `a_name_wordedge` is an n-grams based field and the user's search text box contains `simple mi`: `http://localhost:8983/solr/mbartists/select?defType=edismax&qf=a_name&q.op=AND&q=simple a_name_wordedge:mi`.

The search client here inserted `a_name_wordedge:` before the last word.

The combination of field type definition flexibility (custom filters and so on), and the ability to use features such as DisMax, custom boosting/sorting, and even highlighting, really make this approach worth exploring.

Query term completion via facet.prefix

Most people don't realize that faceting can be used to implement query term completion, but it can. This approach has the unique and valuable benefit of returning completions filtered by filter queries (such as faceted navigation state) and by query words prior to the last one being completed. This means the completion suggestions should yield matching results, which is *not* the case for the other techniques. However, there are limits to its scalability in terms of memory use and inappropriateness for real-time search applications.

Faceting on a tokenized field is going to use an entry in the **field value cache** (based on `UnInvertedField`) to hold all words in memory. It will use a hefty chunk of memory for many words, and it's going to take a non-trivial amount of time to build this cache on every commit during the auto-warming phase. For a data point, consider MusicBrainz's largest field: `t_name` (track name). It has nearly 700K words in it. It consumes nearly 100 MB of memory and it took 33 seconds to initialize on my machine. The mandatory initialization per commit makes this approach unsuitable for real-time-search applications (See *Chapter 10, Scaling Solr*, for more information).

> Measure this for yourself. Perform a trivial query to trigger its initialization and measure how long it takes. Then search Solr's statistics page for **fieldValueCache**. The size is given in bytes next to **memSize**. This statistic is also logged quite clearly.

For this example, we have a search box searching track names and it contains the following:

```
michael ja
```

All of the words here except the last one become the main query for the term suggest. For our example, this is just `michael`. If there isn't anything, then we'd want to ensure that the request handler used would search for all documents. The faceted field is `a_spell`, and we want to sort by frequency. We also want there to be at least one occurrence, and we don't want more than five suggestions. We don't need the actual search results, either. This leaves the `facet.prefix` faceting parameter to make this work. This parameter filters the facet values to those starting with this value.

Remember that facet values are the final result of text analysis, and therefore are probably lowercased for fields you might want to do term completion on. You'll need to pre-process the prefix value similarly, or else nothing will be found.

We're going to set this to `ja`, the last word that the user has partially typed. Here is the URL for such a search `http://localhost:8983/solr/mbartists/select?q=michael&df=a_spell&wt=json&omitHeader=true&indent=on&facet=on&rows=0&facet.limit=5&facet.mincount=1&facet.field=a_spell&facet.prefix=ja`.

When setting this up for real, we recommend creating a request handler just for term completion with many of these parameters defined there, so that they can be configured separately from your application.

In this example, we're going to use Solr's JSON response format. Here is the result:

```
{
  "response":{"numFound":1919,"start":0,"docs":[]},
  "facet_counts":{
    "facet_queries":{},
    "facet_fields":{
      "a_spell":[
        "jackson",17,
        "james",15,
        "jason",4,
        "jay",4,
        "jacobs",2]},
    "facet_dates":{},
    "facet_ranges":{}}}
```

This is exactly the information needed to populate a pop-up menu of choices that the user can conveniently choose from.

However, there are some issues to be aware of with this feature:

- You may want to retain the case information of what the user is typing so that it can then be re-applied to the Solr results. Remember that `facet.prefix` will probably need to be lowercased, depending on text analysis.

- If stemming text analysis is performed on the field at the time of indexing, then the user might get completion choices that are clearly wrong. Most stemmers, namely Porter-based ones, stem off the suffix to an invalid word. Consider using a minimal stemmer, if any. For stemming and other text analysis reasons, you might want to create a separate field with suitable text analysis just for this feature. In our example here, we used `a_spell` on purpose because spelling suggestions and term completion have the same text analysis requirements.

- If you would like to perform term completion of multiple fields, then you'll be disappointed that you can't do so directly. The easiest way is to combine several fields at index time. Alternatively, a query searching multiple fields with faceting configured for multiple fields can be performed. It would be up to you to merge the faceting results based on ordered counts.

Query term completion via the Suggester

A high-speed approach to implement term completion, called the Suggester, was introduced in Version 3 of Solr. Until Solr 4.7, the Suggester was an extension of the spellcheck component. It can still be used that way, but it now has its own search component, which is how you should use it. Similar to spellcheck, it's not necessarily as up to date as your index and it needs to be *built*. However, the Suggester only takes a couple of seconds or so for this usually, and you are not forced to do this per commit, unlike with faceting. The Suggester is generally very fast—a handful of milliseconds per search at most for common setups. The performance characteristics are largely determined by a configuration choice (shown later) called `lookupImpl`, in which we recommend `WFSTLookupFactory` for query term completion (but not for other suggestion types). Additionally, the Suggester uniquely includes a method of loading its dictionary from a file that optionally includes a sorting weight.

We're going to use it for MusicBrainz's artist name completion. The following is in our `solrconfig.xml`:

```
<requestHandler name="/a_term_suggest" class="solr.SearchHandler"
startup="lazy">
  <lst name="defaults">
    <str name="suggest">true</str>
    <str name="suggest.dictionary">a_term_suggest</str>
    <str name="suggest.count">5</str>
```

```
    </lst>
    <arr name="components">
      <str>aTermSuggester</str>
    </arr>
  </requestHandler>

  <searchComponent name="aTermSuggester"
  class="solr.SuggestComponent">
    <lst name="suggester">
      <str name="name">a_term_suggest</str>
      <str name="lookupImpl">WFSTLookupFactory</str>
      <str name="field">a_spell</str>
      <!-- <float name="threshold">0.005</float> -->
      <str name="buildOnOptimize">true</str>
    </lst>
  </searchComponent>
```

The first part of this is a request handler definition just for using the Suggester. The second part of this is an instantiation of the `SuggestComponent` search component. The dictionary here is loaded from the `a_spell` field in the main index, but if a file is desired, then you can provide the `sourceLocation` parameter. The document frequency threshold for suggestions is commented here because MusicBrainz has unique names that we don't want filtered out. However, in common scenarios, this threshold is advised.

The Suggester needs to be built, which is the process of building the dictionary from its source into an optimized memory structure. If you set `storeDir`, it will also save it such that the next time Solr starts, it will load automatically and be ready. If you try to get suggestions before it's built, there will be no results. The Suggester only takes a couple of seconds or so to build and so we recommend building it automatically on startup via a `firstSearcher` warming query in `solrconfig.xml`. If you are using Solr 5.0, then this is simplified by adding a `buildOnStartup` Boolean to the Suggester's configuration.

To be kept up to date, it needs to be rebuilt from time to time. If commits are infrequent, you should use the `buildOnCommit` setting. We've chosen the `buildOnOptimize` setting as the book dataset is optimized after it's completely indexed; and then, it's never modified. Realistically, you may need to schedule a URL fetch to trigger the build, as well as incorporate it into any bulk data loading scripts you develop.

Now, let's issue a request to the Suggester. Here's a completion for the incomplete query string `sma` `http://localhost:8983/solr/mbartists/a_term_suggest?q=sma&wt=json`.

And here is the output, indented:

```
{
  "responseHeader":{
    "status":0,
    "QTime":1},
  "suggest":{"a_term_suggest":{
    "sma":{
      "numFound":5,
      "suggestions":[{
        "term":"sma",
        "weight":3,
        "payload":""},
      {
        "term":"small",
        "weight":110,
        "payload":""},
      {
        "term":"smart",
        "weight":50,
        "payload":""},
      {
        "term":"smash",
        "weight":36,
        "payload":""},
      {
        "term":"smalley",
        "weight":9,
        "payload":""}]}}}}
```

If the input is found, it's listed first; then suggestions are presented in weighted order. In the case of an index-based source, the weights are, by default, the document frequency of the value.

For more information about the Suggester, see the Solr Reference Guide at `https://cwiki.apache.org/confluence/display/solr/Suggester`. You'll find information on `lookupImpl` alternatives and other details. However, some secrets of the Suggester are still undocumented, buried in the code. Look at the factories for more configuration options.

Query term completion via the Terms component

The Terms component is used to expose raw indexed term information, including term frequency, for an indexed field. It has a lot of options for paging into this voluminous data and filtering out terms by term frequency.

The Terms component has the benefit of using no Java heap memory, and consequently, there is no initialization penalty. It's always up to date with the indexed data, like faceting but unlike the Suggester. The performance is typically good, but for high query load on large indexes, it will suffer compared to the other approaches. An interesting feature unique to this approach is a regular expression term match option. This can be used for case-insensitive matching, but it probably doesn't scale to many terms.

For more information about this component, visit the Solr Reference Guide at `https://cwiki.apache.org/confluence/display/solr/The+Terms+Component`.

Field-value completion via the Suggester

In this example, we'll show you how to suggest complete field values. This might be used for instant-search navigation by a document name or title, or it might be used to filter results by a field. It's particularly useful for fields that you facet on, but it will take some work to integrate into the search user experience. This can even be used to complete multiple fields at once by specifying `suggest.dictionary` multiple times.

To complete values across many fields at once, you should consider an alternative approach than what is described here. For example, use a dedicated suggestion index of each name-value pair and use an edge n-gram technique or shingling.

We'll use the Suggester once again, but using a slightly different configuration. Using `AnalyzingLookupFactory` as the `lookupImpl`, this Suggester will be able to specify a field type for query analysis and another as the source for suggestions. Any tokenizer or filter can be used in the analysis chain (lowercase, stop words, and so on). We're going to reuse the existing `textSpell` field type for this example. It will take care of lowercasing the tokens and throwing out stop words.

For the suggestion source field, we want to return complete field values, so a string field will be used; we can use the existing `a_name_sort` field for this, which is close enough.

Here's the required configuration for the suggest component:

```
<searchComponent name="aNameSuggester"
class="solr.SuggestComponent">
  <lst name="suggester">
    <str name="name">a_name_suggest</str>
    <str name="lookupImpl">AnalyzingLookupFactory</str>
    <str name="field">a_name_sort</str>
    <str name="buildOnOptimize">true</str>
    <str name="storeDir">a_name_suggest</str>
    <str name="suggestAnalyzerFieldType">textSpell</str>
  </lst>
</searchComponent>
```

And here is the request handler and component:

```
<requestHandler name="/a_name_suggest" class="solr.SearchHandler"
startup="lazy">
  <lst name="defaults">
    <str name="suggest">true</str>
    <str name="suggest.dictionary">a_name_suggest</str>
    <str name="suggest.count">5</str>
  </lst>
  <arr name="components">
    <str>aNameSuggester</str>
  </arr>
</requestHandler>
```

We've set up the Suggester to build the index of suggestions after an `optimize` command. On a modestly powered laptop, the build time was about 5 seconds. Once the build is complete, the /a_name_suggest handler will return field values for any matching query. Here's an example that will make use of this Suggester: http://localhost:8983/solr/mbartists/a_name_suggest?wt=json&omitHeader=true&q=The smashing,pum.

Here's the response from that query:

```
{
  "spellcheck":{
    "suggestions":[
      "The smashing,pum",{
        "numFound":1,
        "startOffset":0,
        "endOffset":16,
        "suggestion":["Smashing Pumpkins, The"]},
      "collation","(Smashing Pumpkins, The)"]}}
```

As you can see, the Suggester is able to deal with the mixed case. Ignore The (a stop word) and also the , (comma) we inserted, as this is how our analysis is configured. *Impressive!* It's worth pointing out that there's a lot more that can be done here, depending on your needs, of course. It's entirely possible to add synonyms, additional stop words, and different tokenizers to the analysis chain.

There are other interesting lookupImpl choices. FuzzyLookupFactory can suggest completions that are *similarly* typed to the input query; for example, words that are similar in spelling, or just typos. AnalyzingInfixLookupFactory is a Suggester that can provide completions from matching prefixes anywhere in the field value, not just the beginning. Other ones are BlendedInfixLookupFactory and FreeTextLookupFactory. See the Solr Reference Guide for further information.

The QueryElevation component

At times, you may desire to make editorial/manual modifications to the search results of particular user queries. This might be done as a solution to a popular user query that doesn't score an expected document sufficiently high—if it even matched at all. The query might have found nothing at all, perhaps due to a common misspelling. The opposite may also be true: the top result for a popular user query might yield a document that technically matched according to your search configuration, but certainly isn't what you were looking for. Another usage scenario is implementing a system akin to paid keywords for certain documents to be on top for certain user queries.

This feature isn't a general approach to fix queries not yielding effective search results; it is a Band-Aid for that problem. If a query isn't returning an expected document scored sufficiently high enough (if at all), then use Solr's query debugging to observe the score computation. You may end up troubleshooting text analysis issues too if a search query doesn't match an expected document— perhaps by adding a synonym. The end result may be tuning the boosts or applying function queries to incorporate other relevant fields into the scoring. When you are satisfied with the scoring and just need to make an occasional editorial decision, this component is for you.

Configuration

This search component is not in the standard component list and so it must be registered with a handler in `solrconfig.xml`. Here, we'll add it to the `/mb_artists` request handler definition, just for this example, anyway:

```
<requestHandler name="/mb_artists" class="solr.SearchHandler">
  <lst name="defaults">
  ...
  </lst>
  <arr name="last-components">
    <str>elevateArtists</str>
  </arr>
</requestHandler>

<searchComponent name="elevateArtists"
    class="solr.QueryElevationComponent">
  <str name="queryFieldType">text</str>
  <str name="config-file">elevateArtists.xml</str>
  <str name="forceElevation">false</str>
</searchComponent>
```

This excerpt also reveals the registration of the search component using the same name as that referenced in `last-components`. A name was chosen to reflect the fact that this elevation configuration is only for artists. There are three named configuration parameters for a query elevation component, and they are explained as follows:

- `config-file`: This is a reference to the configuration file containing the editorial adjustments. It is resolved relative to both Solr's `conf` directory, and if that fails, then Solr's `data` directory.

 When it's in the `data` directory (usually a sibling to `conf`), it will be reloaded when Solr commits.

- `queryFieldType`: This is a reference to a field type in `schema.xml`. It is used to normalize both a query (the `q` parameter) and the query text attribute found in the configuration file, for comparison purposes. A field type might be crafted just for this purpose, but it should suffice to simply choose one that at least performs lowercasing. By default, there is no normalization.

- `forceElevation`: The query elevation component fools Solr into thinking the specified documents matched the user's query and scored the highest. However, by default, it will not violate the desired sort as specified by the `sort` parameter. In order to force the elevated documents to the top no matter what `sort` is, set this parameter to `true`.

A new option in Solr 4.7 is the ability for a request to specify which docs to elevate (or exclude) via the `elevateIds` and `excludeIds` (comma delimited unique key IDs) request parameters, which overrides the config file.

Let's take a peek at `elevateArtists.xml`:

```
<elevate>
  <query text="corgan">
    <doc id="Artist:11650" /><!--the Smashing Pumpkins-->
    <doc id="Artist:510" /><!-- Green Day -->
    <doc id="Artist:35656" exclude="true" /><!-- Starchildren -->
  </query>
  <!-- others queries... -->
</elevate>
```

In this elevation file, we've specified that when a user searches for `corgan`, the Smashing Pumpkins then Green Day should appear in the top two positions in the search results and that the artist `Starchildren` is to be excluded. Note that query elevation kicks in when the configured query text matches the user's query exactly, while taking into consideration configured text analysis. Thus, a search for `billy corgan` would not be affected by this configuration. It shouldn't be surprising that the documents are listed by ID in this file, but those IDs may not be clear alone to whoever reads this file, so we suggest using some comments to clarify the intent of the changes as seen here.

This component is quite simple with unsurprising results, so an example of this in action is not given. The only thing notable about the results when searching for `corgan` with the preceding configuration is that the top two results, `the Smashing Pumpkins` and `Green Day`, have scores of `1.72` and `0.0`, respectively, yet the `maxScore` value in the result element is `11.3`. Normally, a default sort results in the first document having the same score as the maximum score, but in this case that happens at the third position, as the first two were inserted by the query elevation component. Moreover, normally a result document has a score greater than `0`, but in this case one was inserted by this component that never matched the user's query.

The MoreLikeThis component

Have you ever searched for something and found a link that wasn't quite what you were looking for but was reasonably close? If you were using an Internet search engine such as Google, then you may have tried the "more like this…" link next to a search result. Some sites use other language like "find similar…" or "related documents…" As these links suggest, they show you pages similar to another page. Solr supports **more like this (MLT)** too.

The MLT capability in Solr can be used in the following three ways:

- **As a search component**: The MLT search component performs MLT analysis on each document returned in a search. This is not usually desired and so it is rarely used.

- **As a request handler**: The MLT request handler gives MLT results that are based on a specific indexed document. This is commonly used in reaction to a user clicking a "more like this" link on existing search results. The key input to this option is a reference to the indexed document that you want similar results for.

- **As a request handler with externally supplied text**: The MLT request handler can give MLT results based on text posted to the request handler. For example, if you were to send a text file to the request handler, then it would return the documents in the index that are most similar to it. This is atypical, but an interesting option nonetheless.

- **As a query parser**: Solr 5 includes a query parser named mlt that can more easily be combined with other queries or relevancy boosting than the other options. See the Solr Reference Guide for further information.

The essences of the internal workings of MLT operate like this:

1. Gather all of the terms with frequency information from the input document:

   ○ If the input document is a reference to a document within the index, then loop over the fields listed in mlt.fl, and then the term information needed is readily there for the taking if the field has termVectors enabled. Otherwise, get the stored text and reanalyze it to derive the terms (slower).

   ○ If the input document is posted as text to the request handler, then analyze it to derive the terms. The analysis used is that configured for the first field listed in mlt.fl.

2. Filter the terms based on configured thresholds. What remains are only the *interesting terms*.

3. Construct a Boolean OR query with these interesting terms across all of the fields listed in mlt.fl.

Configuration parameters

In the following configuration options, the input document is either each search result returned if MLT is used as a component, or it is the first document returned from a query to the MLT request handler, or it is the plain text sent to the request handler. It simply depends on how you use it.

Parameters specific to the MLT search component

Using the MLT search component adorns an existing search with MLT results for each document returned.

- `mlt`: You must set this to `true` to enable MLT when using it as a search component. It defaults to `false`.

- `mlt.count`: This refers to the number of MLT results to be returned for each document returned in the main query. It defaults to `5`.

Parameters specific to the MLT request handler

Using the MLT request handler is more like a regular search, except that the results are documents similar to the input document. Additionally, filters (the `fq` parameter) are applied.

- `q`, `start`, and `rows`: The MLT request handler uses the same standard parameters for the query start offset, and row count as used for querying. But in this case, `start` and `rows` is for paging into the MLT results instead of the results of the query. The query is typically one that simply references one document, such as `id:12345` (if your unique field looks like this). `start` defaults to `0` and `rows` to `10`.

- `mlt.match.offset`: This parameter is the offset into the results of `q` to pick which document is the input document. It defaults to `0` so that the first result from `q` is chosen. As `q` will typically search for one document, this is rarely modified.

- `mlt.match.include`: The input document is normally included in the response if it is in the index (see the `match` element in the output of the example) because this parameter defaults to `true`. Set this parameter to `false` to exclude it, if that information isn't needed.

- `mlt.interestingTerms`: If this is set to `list` or `details`, then the so-called *interesting terms* that MLT uses for the similarity query are returned with the results in an `interestingTerms` element. If you enable `mlt.boost`, then specifying `details` will additionally return the query boost value used for each term. The default, `none`, disables this. Aside from diagnostic purposes, it might be useful to display these in the user interface, either listed out or in a tag cloud.

 Use `mlt.interestingTerms` while experimenting with the results to get an insight into why the MLT results matched the documents it did.

- `facet, ...`: The MLT request handler supports faceting the MLT results. See the previous chapter on how to use faceting.

 Additionally, remember to configure the MLT request handler in `solrconfig.xml`. An example of this is shown later in the chapter.

Common MLT parameters

These parameters are common to both the search component and request handler. Some of the thresholds here are to tune which terms are *interesting* to MLT. In general, expanding thresholds (that is, lowering minimums and increasing maximums) will yield more useful MLT results at the expense of performance. The parameters are explained as follows:

- `mlt.fl`: This provides a comma- or space-separated list of fields to consider in MLT. The *interesting terms* are searched within these fields only. These field(s) must be indexed. Furthermore, assuming the input document is in the index instead of supplied externally (as is typical), then each field should ideally have `termVectors` set to `true` in the schema (best for query performance, although index size is larger). If that isn't done, then the field must be stored so that MLT can re-analyze the text at runtime to derive the term vector information. It isn't necessary to use the same strategy for each field.

- `mlt.qf`: Different field boosts can optionally be specified with this parameter. This uses the same syntax as the `qf` parameter that is used by the DisMax query parser (for example: `field1^2.0 field2^0.5`). The fields referenced should also be listed in `mlt.fl`. If there is a title or similar identifying field, then this field should probably be boosted higher.

- `mlt.mintf`: This parameter specifies the minimum number of times (frequency) a term must be used within a document (across those fields in `mlt.fl` anyway) for it to be an *interesting term.* The default is 2. For small documents, such as in the case of our MusicBrainz dataset, try lowering this to 1.

- `mlt.mindf`: This specifies the minimum number of documents that a term must be used in for it to be an *interesting term.* It defaults to 5, which is fairly reasonable. For very small indexes, as little as 2 is plausible, and maybe larger for large multi-million document indexes with common words.

- `mlt.maxdf`: This specifies the maximum number of documents that a term must be used in for it to be an *interesting term.* There is no limit, by default.

- `mlt.minwl`: This is used to specify the minimum number of characters in an *interesting term*. It defaults to `0`, effectively disabling the threshold. Consider raising this to 2 or 3.

- `mlt.maxwl`: This parameter specifies the maximum number of characters in an *interesting term*. It defaults to `0` and disables the threshold. Some really long terms might be flukes in input data and are out of your control, but most likely this threshold can be skipped.

- `mlt.maxqt`: This specifies the maximum number of *interesting terms* that will be used in an MLT query. It is limited to `25` by default, which is plenty.

- `mlt.maxntp`: Fields without `termVectors` enabled take longer for MLT to analyze. This parameter sets a threshold to limit the number of terms to consider in an input field to further limit the performance impact. It defaults to `5000`.

- `mlt.boost`: This Boolean toggles whether or not to boost each *interesting term* used in the MLT query differently, depending on how interesting the MLT module deems it to be. It defaults to `false`, but try setting it to `true` and evaluating the results.

Usage advice

For ideal query performance, ensure that `termVectors` is enabled for the field(s) referenced in `mlt.fl`, particularly in the larger fields. In order to further increase performance, use fewer fields, perhaps just one that is dedicated for use with MLT. Using the `copyField` directive in the schema makes this easy. The disadvantage is that the source fields cannot be boosted differently with `mlt.qf`. However, you might have two fields for MLT as a compromise. Use a typical full complement of text analysis including lowercasing, synonyms using a stop list (such as `StopFilterFactory`), and aggressive stemming in order to normalize the terms as much as possible. The field needn't be stored if its data is copied from some other field that is stored. During an experimentation period, look for *interesting terms* that are not so interesting for inclusion in the stop word list. Lastly, some of the configuration thresholds that scope the interesting terms can be adjusted based on experimentation.

The MLT results example

Firstly, an important disclaimer on this example is in order.

> The MusicBrainz dataset is not conducive to applying the MLT feature, because it doesn't have any descriptive text. If there was perhaps an artist description and/or widespread use of user-supplied tags, then there might be sufficient information to make MLT useful. However, to provide an example of the input and output of MLT, we will use MLT with MusicBrainz anyway.

We'll be using the request handler method — the recommended approach. The MLT request handler needs to be configured in `solrconfig.xml`. The important bit is the reference to the class, the rest of it is our prerogative.

```
<requestHandler name="/mlt_tracks" class="solr.MoreLikeThisHandler">
  <lst name="defaults">
    <str name="mlt.fl">t_name</str>
    <str name="mlt.mintf">1</str>
    <str name="mlt.mindf">2</str>
    <str name="mlt.boost">true</str>
  </lst>
</requestHandler>
```

This configuration shows that we're basing the MLT on just track names. Let's now try a query for tracks similar to the song "The End is the Beginning is the End" by The Smashing Pumpkins. The query was performed with `echoParams` to clearly show the options used:

```
<?xml version="1.0" encoding="UTF-8"?>
<response>
<lst name="responseHeader">
  <int name="status">0</int>
  <int name="QTime">2</int>
  <lst name="params">
    <str name="mlt.mintf">1</str>
    <str name="mlt.mindf">2</str>
    <str name="mlt.boost">true</str>
    <str name="mlt.fl">t_name</str>
    <str name="rows">5</str>
    <str name="mlt.interestingTerms">details</str>
    <str name="indent">on</str>
    <str name="echoParams">all</str>
    <str name="fl">t_a_name,t_name,score</str>
```

```
            <str name="q">id:"Track:1810669"</str>
        </lst>
    </lst>
    <result name="match" numFound="1" start="0"
        maxScore="16.06509">
        <doc>
            <float name="score">16.06509</float>
            <str name="t_a_name">The Smashing Pumpkins</str>
            <str name="t_name">The End Is the Beginning Is the End</str>
        </doc>
    </result>
    <result name="response" numFound="855211" start="0"
        maxScore="6.3063927">
        <doc>
            <str name="t_name">End Is the Beginning</str>
            <str name="t_a_name">In Grey</str>
            <float name="score">6.3063927</float></doc>
        <doc>
            <str name="t_name">Is the End the Beginning</str>
            <str name="t_a_name">Mangala Vallis</str>
            <float name="score">5.6426353</float></doc>
        <doc>
            <str name="t_name">The End Is the Beginning</str>
            <str name="t_a_name">Royal Anguish</str>
            <float name="score">5.6426353</float></doc>
        <doc>
            <str name="t_name">The End Is the Beginning</str>
            <str name="t_a_name">Ape Face</str>
            <float name="score">5.6426353</float></doc>
        <doc>
            <str name="t_name">The End Is the Beginning Is the
                    End</str>
            <str name="t_a_name">The Smashing Pumpkins</str>
            <float name="score">5.0179915</float></doc>
    </result>
    <lst name="interestingTerms">
        <float name="t_name:end">1.0</float>
        <float name="t_name:is">0.7513826</float>
        <float name="t_name:the">0.6768603</float>
        <float name="t_name:beginning">0.62302685</float>
    </lst>
</response>
```

The `<result name="match">` element is there due to `mlt.match.include` defaulting to `true`. The `<result name="response" ...>` element has the main MLT search results. The fact that so many documents were found is not material to any MLT response; all it takes is one interesting term in common. The *interesting terms* were deliberately requested so that we can get an insight on the basis of the similarity. The fact that `is` and `the` were included shows that we don't have a stop list for this field—an obvious thing to fix to improve the results. Nearly any stop list is going to have such words.

> For further diagnostic information on the score computation, set `debugQuery` to `true`. This is a highly advanced method but it exposes information invaluable to understand the scores. Doing so in our example shows that the main reason the top hit was on top was not only because it contained all of the interesting terms as did the others in the top 5, but also because it is the shortest in length (a high `fieldNorm`).

The Stats component

The **stats** component calculates some mathematical statistics of fields in the index. The main requirement is that the field be indexed. The following statistics are computed over the non-null values (except `missing` which counts the nulls):

- `min`: The smallest value
- `max`: The largest value
- `sum`: The sum
- `count`: The quantity of non-null values accumulated in these statistics
- `missing`: The quantity of records skipped due to missing values
- `sumOfSquares`: The sum of the square of each value; this is probably the least useful and is used internally to compute `stddev` efficiently
- `mean`: The average value
- `stddev`: The standard deviation of the values
- `distinctValues`: A list of *all* distinct (non-duplicating) values
- `countDistinct`: The size of distinctValues

If you calculate stats on a string or date field, then only `min`, `max`, `count`, `missing`, `distinctValues`, and `countDistinct` are calculated. The `distinctValues` and `countDistinct` are only present if `stats.calcdistinct` is enabled.

Configuring the stats component

This component is simple to configure and can be done as follows:

- `stats`: Set this to `true` in order to enable the component. It defaults to `false`.
- `stats.field`: Set this to the name of the indexed field to calculate statistics on. It is required. This field must be indexed or preferably have DocValues. This parameter can be added multiple times in order to calculate statistics on more than one field. And like `facet.field`, it can be preceded with a filter query exclusion in local-params syntax; for example, `&stats.field={!ex=t_duration}t_duration&fq={!tag=t_duration}t_duration:1000`.
- `stats.calcdistinct`: A Boolean option to include a list of all distinct (non-duplicating) values for this field. Be judicious about using this! Using it on some fields could trigger an `OutOfMemoryError` easily. Solr 5.2 has a scalable option to provide an estimated count.
- `stats.facet`: Optionally, set this to the name of the field in which you want to facet the statistics over. Instead of the results having just one set of stats (assuming one `stats.field`), there will be a set for each value in this field, and those statistics will be based on that corresponding subset of data. This is analogous to the GROUP BY syntax in SQL. This parameter can be specified multiple times to compute the statistics over multiple fields' values. In addition, you can use the field-specific parameter name syntax for cases when you are computing stats on different fields and you want to use a different facet field for each statistic field. For example, you can specify `f.t_duration.stats.facet=tracktype` assuming a hypothetical field `tracktype` to categorize the `t_duration` statistics on. The field should be indexed or have DocValues and not tokenized.

 Due to the bug SOLR-1782, a `stats.facet` field should *not* be multivalued, and it should be limited to a string. If you don't heed this advice, then the results are in question and you may get an error!

Statistics on track durations

Let's look at some statistics for the duration of tracks in MusicBrainz at `http://localhost:8983/solr/mbtracks/mb_tracks?rows=0&indent=on&stats=true&stats.field=t_duration`.

And here are the results:

```
<?xml version="1.0" encoding="UTF-8"?>
<response>
```

```
<lst name="responseHeader">
  <int name="status">0</int>
  <int name="QTime">5202</int>
</lst>
<result name="response" numFound="6977765" start="0"/>
<lst name="stats">
  <lst name="stats_fields">
    <lst name="t_duration">
      <double name="min">0.0</double>
      <double name="max">36059.0</double>
      <double name="sum">1.543289275E9</double>
      <long name="count">6977765</long>
      <long name="missing">0</long>
      <double name="sumOfSquares">5.21546498201E11</double>
      <double name="mean">221.1724348699046</double>
      <double name="stddev">160.70724790290328</double>
    </lst>
  </lst>
</lst>
</response>
```

This query shows that on average, a song is 221 seconds (or 3 minutes 41 seconds) in length. An example using `stats.facet` would produce a much longer result, which won't be given here in order to leave space for other components. However, there is an example at `http://wiki.apache.org/solr/StatsComponent`.

The Clustering component

The clustering component groups documents into similar **clusters** using sophisticated statistical techniques. Each cluster is identified by a few words from the documents that were used to distinguish the documents in that cluster from the other clusters. As with the `MoreLikeThis` component, which also uses statistical techniques, the quality of the results is hit or miss. This component resides in its own *contrib module* and it provides an extension point to integrate a clustering engine.

The primary means of navigation/discovery of your data should generally be search and faceting. For so-called *unstructured text* use cases, there are, by definition, few attributes to facet on. Clustering search results and presenting tag clouds (a visualization of faceting on words) are generally exploratory navigation methods of last resort in the absence of more effective document metadata.

Presently, there are two **search-result clustering** algorithms available as part of the Carrot2 open source project that this module has adapters for; other commercial options exist too. Solr ships with the needed third-party libraries—JAR files. The clustering component has an extension point to support **full-index clustering** (offline clustering) via the `clustering.collection` parameter, but no implementation has materialized yet.

To get started with exploring this feature, we'll direct you to the Solr Reference Guide at `https://cwiki.apache.org/confluence/display/solr/Result+Clustering`. There is quick-start set of instructions in which you'll be clustering Solr's example documents in under five minutes. It should be easy to copy the necessary configuration to your Solr instance and modify it to refer to your document's fields. As you dive into the technology, Carrot2's powerful GUI workbench should be of great help in tuning it to get more effective results. For a public demonstration of Carrot2's clustering, visit `http://search.carrot2.org/stable/search`.

Collapsing and expanding

The collapse query parser and expand search component are two related features that arrived in Solr 4.7 as an alternative to Solr's Result Grouping feature (`group=true`). First, we'll describe these two features and then compare it to result grouping.

The Collapse query parser

The collapse query parser filters search results so that only one document is returned out of all of those for a given field's value. Said differently, it collapses search results to one document per group of those with the same field value. This query parser is a special type called **post-filter**, which can only be used as a filter query because it needs to see the results of all other filter queries and the main query. In order to pick which document of a set is chosen to be the one returned, it by default it picks the highest scoring one, but it can be configured to choose based on the document with the highest or lowest value of a field or function query.

An excerpt of the query in action is this filter query: `fq={!collapse field=t_a_id}`. A complete example will be shown soon. There are only a few parameters:

- `field`: This refers to the field to group documents by, which should be single-valued and ideally have *DocValues* enabled—the same requirement and recommendation for a field that you sort on.

- `min` or `max`: This is either a field or function query that yields a ranking value used to choose which document to return in a grouped set. For `min`, the document with the smallest value is chosen, and for `max`, the largest. If your function query needs to be computed based on the document's score, refer to that via `cscore()`.

- `nullPolicy`: This refers to the policy on how to treat blank/null values for the group field. It can be `ignore`, `collapse`, or `expand`. By default, documents having no value are ignored (filtered out). If `nullPolicy` is set to `collapse`, the documents with no value in this field are treated as one group and therefore one document will be chosen from them. If this parameter is `expand` then all of these documents are returned (they aren't collapsed).

The Expand component

The expand search component augments the response to return more documents from the groups that were collapsed. It can also be used without collapsing by similarly returning other documents that share the field values found in the main search results. This information is in its own part of Solr's response format, quite unlike the Result Grouping format. Here are the parameters:

- `expand`: This is set to `true`. Generally, it's the only required parameter.

- `expand.field`: This is the field to expand search results for documents in the main result list. It's inferred if you use the collapse query parser; otherwise it is required.

- `expand.sort`: This overrides the `sort` parameter for use in expanding.

- `expand.rows`: This defines how many rows to return for each group. Defaults to `5`.

- `expand.q`: This overrides the `q` parameter for the expanded results.

- `expand.fq`: This overrides the `fq` parameters for the expanded results.

An example

Here's a quick example using MusicBrainz track data collapsing by artist. The query is *Cherub Rock* (a song/track name). We expand to show one additional document in each group:

```
http://localhost:8983/solr/mbtracks/mb_tracks?wt=json
&q="Cherub+Rock"&fl=score,id,t_a_id,t_a_name,t_name,t_r_name
&rows=2
&fq={!collapse field=t_a_id}
&expand=true&expand.rows=1
```

And here's the response:

```
{
  "responseHeader":{
    "status":0,
    "QTime":20},
  "response":{"numFound":22575,"start":0,"maxScore":15.757925,"docs":[
    {
      "id":"Track:414903",
      "t_name":"Cherub Rock",
      "t_a_id":11650,
      "t_a_name":"The Smashing Pumpkins",
      "t_r_name":"Cherub Rock",
      "score":15.757925},
    {
      "id":"Track:6855353",
      "t_name":"Cherub Rock",
      "t_a_id":33677,
      "t_a_name":"Razed in Black",
      "t_r_name":"Cherub Rock: A Gothic-Industrial Tribute to the
              Smashing Pumpkins",
      "score":14.348505}]
  },
  "expanded":{
    "33677":{"numFound":1,"start":0,"maxScore":0.13129683,"docs":[
      {
        "id":"Track:4034054",
        "t_name":"Share This Poison",
        "t_a_id":33677,
        "t_a_name":"Razed in Black",
        "t_r_name":"Rock Sound: Music With Attitude, Volume 52",
        "score":0.13129683}]
    },
    "11650":{"numFound":91,"start":0,"maxScore":12.960967,"docs":[
      {
        "id":"Track:7413518",
        "t_name":"Cherub Rock",
        "t_a_id":11650,
        "t_a_name":"The Smashing Pumpkins",
        "t_r_name":"Guitar Hero™ III: Legends of Rock Companion
                Pack",
        "score":12.960967}]
  }}}
```

The effect of collapsing is generally straightforward, and there is no impact to the response format. Interpreting the expanded section can be confusing. Firstly, as you can see, the ordering of the expanded groups isn't significant—it's not the same as the main results. Next, understand that each part underneath the expanded section is a mini result list keyed by the group field value. The first one shown is for field value 33677, and it says numFound is 1. But since the main result list has one document already, you can interpret this as that there are a total of two documents matching the query that have this field value. Likewise, 92 (91 + 1) documents have the field value 11650.

Compared to Result grouping

Result grouping, also known as **field collapsing** or simply **grouping**, has been around since Solr 3 and is *somewhat* obsoleted by collapse and expand. It's technically built into the query component instead of being its own component. For comparison purposes, here is a group query equivalent to the previous example:

```
http://localhost:8983/solr/mbtracks/mb_tracks?wt=json
&q="Cherub+Rock"
&fl=score,id,t_a_id,t_a_name,t_name,t_r_name&rows=2
&group=true&group.field=t_a_id&group.ngroups=true&group.limit=2
```

And here is the result:

```
{
    "responseHeader":{
        "status":0,
        "QTime":49},
    "grouped":{
        "t_a_id":{
            "matches":105155,
            "ngroups":22575,
            "groups":[{
                "groupValue":11650,
                "doclist":{"numFound":92,"start":0,
                        "maxScore":15.757925,"docs":[
                    {
                        "id":"Track:414903",
                        "t_name":"Cherub Rock",
                        "t_a_id":11650,
                        "t_a_name":"The Smashing Pumpkins",
                        "t_r_name":"Cherub Rock",
                        "score":15.757925},
                    {
```

```
                    "id":"Track:7413518",
                    "t_name":"Cherub Rock",
                    "t_a_id":11650,
                    "t_a_name":"The Smashing Pumpkins",
                    "t_r_name":"Guitar Hero™ III: Legends of Rock
                              Companion Pack",
                    "score":12.960967}]
            }},
        {
            "groupValue":33677,
            "doclist":{"numFound":2,"start":0,
                    "maxScore":14.348505,"docs":[
                {
                    "id":"Track:6855353",
                    "t_name":"Cherub Rock",
                    "t_a_id":33677,
                    "t_a_name":"Razed in Black",
                    "t_r_name":"Cherub Rock: A Gothic-Industrial
                              Tribute to the Smashing Pumpkins",
                    "score":14.348505},
                {
                    "id":"Track:4034054",
                    "t_name":"Share This Poison",
                    "t_a_id":33677,
                    "t_a_name":"Razed in Black",
                    "t_r_name":"Rock Sound: Music With Attitude,
                              Volume 52",
                    "score":0.13129683}]
            }}]}}}
```

We've highlighted the beginning part of the grouping, which reflects that a grouped response has a fairly different response structure than a regular one. The `matches` number is `105155`, which is equivalent to `numFound` if grouping weren't enabled — the number of matching documents. `ngroups` is `22575`, which is the number of groups found. Each group begins by showing the group's value and then a document list structure that looks just like normal search results.

Result grouping is often much slower than collapse and expand, particularly when the number of possible groups is high in relation to the number of documents, as in the preceding example. It's even more dramatic if you only need the top document since you needn't use the expand component. Nevertheless, Result grouping is not quite obsolete because it has some unique features over collapse and expand:

- One request can group results multiple times for different fields
- One request can hold multiple queries to independently get results for (`group.query`)

- It can group based on the value returned from a function query versus being limited to a field's value

- It can instruct the faceting component to facet on the leading document as if it had all field values in its group (group.facet)

If you'd like to learn more about Result Grouping and its parameters, see the Solr Reference Guide at https://cwiki.apache.org/confluence/display/solr/Result+Grouping.

The TermVector component

This component is used to expose the raw **term vector** information for fields that have this option enabled in the schema—termVectors set to true. It is false by default. The term vector is per field and per document. It lists each indexed term in order with the offsets into the original text, term frequency, and document frequency. It's not that useful, so I'll refer you to the wiki for further information, which can be found at https://cwiki.apache.org/confluence/display/solr/The+Term+Vector+Component.

Summary

Consider what you've seen with Solr search components: highlighting search results, suggesting search spelling corrections, query autocomplete, editorially modifying query results for particular user queries, suggesting documents "more like this", calculating mathematical statistics of indexed numbers, and grouping/collapsing search results. By now, it should be clear why the text search capability of your database is inadequate for all but basic needs. Even Lucene-based solutions don't necessarily have the extensive feature set that you've seen here. You may have once thought that searching was a relatively basic thing, but Solr search components really demonstrate how much more there is to it.

The chapters thus far have aimed to show you the majority of the features in Solr and to serve as a reference guide for them. The remaining chapters don't follow this pattern. In the next chapter, you're going to see numerous ways that applications integrate with Solr. That includes client APIs as well as things like a crawler and Hadoop.

9
Integrating Solr

As the saying goes, *if a tree falls in the woods and no one hears it, did it make a sound?* Similarly, if you have a wonderful search engine, but your users can't access it, do you really have a wonderful search engine? Fortunately, Solr is very easy to integrate into a wide variety of client environments via its modern, easy-to-use, REST-like interface and multiple data formats. In this chapter, we will:

- Quickly prototype a search UI using Solritas (the `/browse` UI)
- Look at accessing Solr results through various language-based clients, including Java, Ruby, and PHP
- Learn how to build a dynamic JavaScript-based interface for Solr using AJAX calls
- Briefly cover building our own Google-like search engine by crawling the `MusicBrainz.org` site with the Nutch web crawler
- Leverage Hadoop to build Solr indexes using multiple machines
- Translate search results into the OpenSearch XML standard via XSLT
- Review ManifoldCF, a framework for syncing content from external repositories that respects the access rules of external documents

There are so many possible topics we could have covered in this chapter, but only so much space is available. We have put a page together on the Solr community wiki page that pulls all the options for working with Solr, from language-specific client libraries, such as .NET and Python, to options for using document processing pipelines, various Solr compatible crawlers, monitoring tools, and more. Visit `http://wiki.apache.org/solr/SolrEcosystem` for the latest listings.

> **In a hurry?**
>
> This chapter covers a wide variety of integrations with Solr. If you are in a hurry, jump to the next section, *Inventory of examples*, to find the source code that you can immediately start using. Then read the sections that apply to the environment you are working in.

We will be using our MusicBrainz dataset to power these examples. You can download the full sample code for these integrations from our website `http://www.SolrEnterpriseSearchServer.com`. This includes a prebuilt Solr and scripts to load the collections *mbtracks* with seven million records and *mbartists* with 400,000 records. When you have downloaded the zipped file, you should follow the setup instructions in the `README.txt` file.

Working with the included examples

We have included a wide variety of sample integrations that you can run as you work through this chapter. The examples stored in `./examples/9/` of the downloadable ZIP file are as self-contained as we could make them. They are detailed in this chapter, and you shouldn't run into any problems making them work. Check the support section of the book website for any errata.

Inventory of examples

The following is a quick summary of the various examples of using Solr, available unless otherwise noted in `./examples/9/`:

- **ajaxsolr**: This is an example of building a fully featured Solr Search UI using just JavaScript.
- **php**: This is a bare bones example of the PHP integration with Solr.
- **solr-php-client**: This is a richer example of integrating Solr results into a PHP-based application.
- **Solritas**: This a web search UI using the template files in `/cores/mbtypes/conf/velocity`.
- **jquery_autocomplete**: This is an example of using the jQuery Autocomplete library to provide search suggestions based on Solr searches.
- **myfaves**: This is a Ruby on Rails application using the Ruby Solr client library Sunspot to search for music artists.
- **nutch**: This is a simple example of the Nutch web crawler integrated with Solr.

- **manifoldcf**: This is a crawler document ingestion framework with connectors to many systems such as SharePoint.

- **solrj**: This is an example of a SolrJ-based Java client.

- **solr-map-reduce-example**: This shows using Hadoop and the MapReduce paradigm to build Solr indexes using multiple machines.

- **heritrix-2.0.2**: This is an example of web crawling with Heritrix. The output files in `heritrix-2.0.2/jobs/` are used in the SolrJ example.

Solritas – the integrated search UI

The contrib module, `velocity`, nicknamed **Solritas**, is a simple template engine that lets you build user interfaces directly in Solr using **Apache Velocity**, a very simple macro language to generate the HTML. It's similar to JSP or PHP, but with a simpler syntax consisting of just a handful of commands. It is very simple to pick up, as you can see in the following snippet of code, for rendering the HTML that displays the ID and name of an artist pulled from the first Solr document in a list of results:

```
#set($doc = $response.results.get(0))
#set($id = $doc.getFieldValue("id"))
<div>ID: $id</div>
<div>Name: #field('a_name')</div>
```

When a Velocity template is invoked, Solritas places some objects, indicated with a $ character, into a rendering context that you can use, such as $response and $request. In the preceding example, you can see that the first result in the response is assigned to the $doc object variable using the #set command. Java methods such as getFieldValue() are easily called in Velocity, allowing you to access the full power of Java within a scripting environment that is evaluated at runtime. Velocity also supports building your own functions, such as the #field() function for displaying a field from a document.

You can try out an interface optimized for searching for MusicBrainz artists by browsing to `http://localhost:8983/solr/mbartists/browse`. This web interface supports faceted browsing, autocompletion of queries, boosting of artists based on how recent the release is, "More Like This" based on artist name, and even "Did You Mean" spell checking!

When the browser invokes the URL, Solr hands the request off to a request handler with the name, /browse, which is a search request handler that works like any other. The point where the request takes a different turn is in rendering the response, which in Solr is configured with the wt parameter. Short for **writer type**, the choices are better known as **response writers**. Instead of letting it default to XML, it's set to velocity. The Velocity response writer uses the v.layout and v.template parameters to determine which template file to use for the overall page layout as well as what template for the specific page to render. The templates are located in conf/velocity/ relative to the Solr core, and they end in .vm. To use another directory, set the v.base_dir parameter. Note that the use of parameters to choose the template allows you to override it in the URL if desired.

```xml
<?xml version="1.0"?>
<requestHandler name="/browse" class="solr.SearchHandler">
<lst name="defaults">
  <str name="wt">velocity</str>
  <str name="v.template">browse</str>
  <str name="v.layout">layout</str>
  <str name="title">MusicBrainz</str>

  <str name="defType">edismax</str>
  <str name="mm">1</str>
  <str name="q.alt">*:*</str>
  <str name="rows">10</str>
  <str name="fl">*,score</str>
  <str name="qf">a_name^1.5 a_member_name^1.0</str>
  <str name="pf">a_name^1.5 a_member_name^1.0</str>

  <str name="mlt.qf">a_name^1.5 a_member_name^1.0</str>
  <str name="mlt.fl">a_name,a_member_name</str>
  <int name="mlt.count">3</int>
  <int name="mlt.mintf">1</int>
  <int name="mlt.mindf">2</int>
  <str name="mlt.boost">true</str>

  <str name="facet">on</str>
  <str name="facet.field">a_type</str>
  <str name="facet.field">type</str>
  <str name="facet.mincount">1</str>
  <str name="facet.range">a_release_date_latest</str>
  <str name="f.a_release_date_latest.facet.range.start">
    NOW/YEAR-10YEARS</str>
  <str name="f.a_release_date_latest.facet.range.end">NOW</str>
```

```
    <str name="f.a_release_date_latest.facet.range.gap">+1YEAR</str>
    <str name="f.a_release_date_latest.facet.range.other">
      before</str>
    <str name="f.a_release_date_latest.facet.range.other">
      after</str>

    <str name="spellcheck">on</str>
    <str name="spellcheck.dictionary">a_spell</str>
    <str name="spellcheck.collate">true</str>

    <str name="hl">on</str>
    <str name="hl.fl">a_name a_member_name</str>
    <str name="f.a_name.hl.fragsize">0</str>
    <str name="f.a_name.hl.alternateField">a_name</str>
  </lst>
  <arr name="last-components">
    <str>spellcheck</str>
  </arr>
  </requestHandler>
```

The pros and cons of Solritas

Although it is good to impress your boss by quickly building a remarkably full-featured search interface using Solritas, there are some cons to keep in mind:

- While many of the various Velocity files are fairly agnostic about the structure of the data being rendered, there are enough places where you have to both configure some parameters in solrconfig.xml and hardcode them in the Velocity template and that means you'll have to customize the templates to fit your schema. This can be a bit of a gotcha!

- Using Velocity to render a UI for a high volume website isn't a good idea as you are putting the entire search and render load on the same server, and Solr isn't optimized for serving up assets such as CSS or JavaScript files.

- Building a web application based only on a collection of page templates, no matter whether the technology is Velocity, JSP, or PHP, gets harder to maintain and comprehend as it grows in complexity. Arguably, the /browse out-of-the-box interface has reached that complexity point since there is no strong MVC model to follow.

- Integrating a Velocity-driven UI into a larger system isn't simple since you can't easily add your own business logic without modifying Solr itself.

However, some aspects of what I really love about Solritas are:

- The ability to quickly prototype an interface. I find that most end users don't know what fields they want searchable until they have something they can play with. Quickly prototyping a search interface for the business stakeholders is powerful.

- If you need to emit a small chunk of HTML to integrate Solr into another application, or even other text formats such as JSON or custom XML, then this can be a simple yet powerful integration method. The query `http://localhost:8983/solr/mbartists/select?limit=1&q=corgan&qt=mb_artists&wt=velocity&v.template=fragment` returns a small fragment of HTML rendered by the completely standalone Velocity template `fragment.vm`:

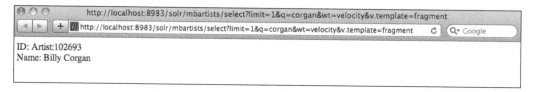

To learn more about building your own Velocity-based interface, look at the example code in `/configsets/mbtype/conf/velocity`. The example application that ships with Solr also has some good examples of exposing Solr features, such as spatial search using Velocity. You can get more information about the list of tools and objects added to the rendering context from the Solr wiki at `http://wiki.apache.org/solr/VelocityResponseWriter`. More information about Velocity is available at `http://velocity.apache.org/`.

SolrJ – Solr's Java client API

SolrJ is Solr's Java client API that insulates you from the dirty details of parsing and sending messages back and forth between your application and Solr. More than just a client API, it is also the way to run Solr embedded in your code instead of communicating to one remotely over HTTP—more on that later.

Although you don't have to use SolrJ to communicate with Solr, it's got some great performance features that may even tempt non-Java applications to use a little Java (or run on a JVM) in order to use it. The following are the features:

- It communicates with Solr via an efficient and compact binary message format (still over HTTP) called **javabin**. It can still do standard XML if desired (useful if your client and your server are different versions).

- It streams documents to Solr asynchronously in multiple threads for maximizing indexing throughput. This is not the default but it's easy to configure it this way.

- It routes documents and search requests to a SolrCloud cluster intelligently by examining the cluster state in ZooKeeper. A document can be delivered directly to the leader of the appropriate shard, and searches are load-balanced against available replicas, possibly obviating the need for an independent load balancer. Read more about SolrCloud in *Chapter 10, Scaling Solr*.

Aside from performance, SolrJ has some other nice qualities too. It can automatically map Solr documents to your Java class, and vice versa, simply by following JavaBean naming conventions and/or using annotations. And it has API convenience methods for most of Solr's search and response format options that are more often absent in other client APIs.

The sample code – BrainzSolrClient

To illustrate the use of SolrJ, we've written some sample code in `./examples/9/ solrj/` to index and search the web pages downloaded from `MusicBrainz.org`. The web pages were crawled with **Heritrix**, an open source web crawler used by the Internet Archive. Heritrix is included with the code supplement to the book at `./examples/9/crawler/heritrix-2.0.2/`, as well as an **ARC** archive file of a crawl deep within the `jobs/` subdirectory.

Most of the code is found in `BrainzSolrClient.java`, which has a `main` method. There is also a JUnit test that calls `main()` with various arguments. You will notice that BrainzSolrClient demonstrates different ways of connecting to Solr and different ways of searching and indexing for documents.

Dependencies and Maven

Many Java projects are built with Apache Maven, and even if yours isn't, the information here is adaptable. Solr's artifacts and required dependencies are all published to Maven Central with decent POMs. Over time, the dependency information has gotten better but nonetheless it is subject to change and you might find it necessary to add exclusions related to logging or something else. For example, SolrJ 4.8 declares a dependency on Log4j even though it doesn't use it directly; SolrJ 4.9 doesn't declare this dependency.

 Run `mvn dependency:tree` to see what your project's dependencies are and look for problems, such as incompatible or missing logging jars.

If your code needs SolrJ to communicate remotely to Solr, then declare a dependency on SolrJ:

```
<dependency>
  <groupId>org.apache.solr</groupId>
  <artifactId>solr-solrj</artifactId>
  <version>${solr.version}</version>
  <scope>compile</scope>
</dependency>
```

Due to transitive dependency resolution, this will automatically inherit SolrJ's dependencies: `commons-io`, `httpclient`, `httpcore`, and `httpmime` (from the Apache HttpComponents project), `zookeeper` (only used for SolrCloud), `noggit`, and `wstx-asl`. SolrJ 4.8 erroneously includes Log4j too. The `wstx-asl` dependency (Woodstox) isn't actually needed; it has been included with SolrJ since the days of Java 1.6 when Java's built-in XML processing implementation was substantially slower than Woodstox. Speaking of which, SolrJ 4.7 and onwards requires Java 7.

 SolrJ has additional logging dependencies that won't transitively resolve, `jcl-over-slf4j` (commons-logging) and an SLF4J target logger. See the next subsection on logging.

If you wish to use `EmbeddedSolrServer` for embedding Solr, then add the `solr-core` artifact as well instead. Note that this brings in a ton of transitive dependencies since you're running Solr in-process; some of these might have incompatible versions with the ones your application uses.

If you wish to write plugins to Solr and test Solr using Solr's excellent test infrastructure, then add a test dependency on the artifact `solr-test-framework` *before* `solr-core` or other Lucene/Solr artifacts. If the ordering is wrong, then you should see a helpful error.

Declaring logging dependencies

Unfortunately, the world of logging in Java is a mess of frameworks. Java includes one but few use it for a variety of reasons. What just about any Java application should do (particularly the ones built with Maven or that produce a POM to publish dependency metadata) is explicitly declare the logging dependencies; don't leave it to transitive resolution. If you prefer Log4j, the most popular one, then the dependency list is `slf4j-api`, `jcl-over-slf4j`, `slf4j-log4j`, and finally `log4j`.

If the project is a direct plugin into Solr, then declare none, except perhaps for testing purposes, since the plugin will inherit Solr's. If the project is a library/module that doesn't wish to insist that its clients use a particular framework, then just depend on `slf4j-api` and `jcl-over-slf4j` and then declare any others as `optional` or scope them to `test` scope so that they aren't transitively required.

The SolrServer class

The first class in SolrJ's API to learn about is the `SolrServer` class (package `org.apache.solr.client.solrj`). In Solr 5, it was renamed as `SolrClient`, with its subclasses following suit. As its name suggests, it represents an instance of Solr. Usually it's a client to a remote instance but, in the case of `EmbeddedSolrServer`, it's the real thing. `SolrServer` is an abstract class with multiple implementations to choose from:

- `HttpSolrServer`: This is generally the default choice for communicating to Solr.
- `ConcurrentUpdateSolrServer`: This wraps `HttpSolrServer`, handling document additions asynchronously with a buffer and multiple concurrent threads that independently stream data to Solr for high indexing throughput. It is ideal for bulk-loading data (that is, a re-index), even for SolrCloud. In Solr 3, this class was named `StreamingUpdateSolrServer`.

 Don't forget to override `handleError()`; `add()` usually won't throw an error if something goes wrong.

- `LBHttpSolrServer`: This wraps multiple `HttpSolrServers` with load-balancing behavior using a round-robin algorithm and temporary host blacklisting when connection problems occur. It's usually inappropriate for indexing purposes.
- `CloudSolrServer`: This wraps `LBHttpSolrServer` but communicates to the ZooKeeper ensemble that manages a SolrCloud cluster to make intelligent routing decisions for both searching and indexing. Compared to `HttpSolrServer`, this reduces latency and has enhanced resiliency when a replica becomes unavailable. If you are using SolrCloud, this is the implementation to use.
- `EmbeddedSolrServer`: This is a real local Solr instance without HTTP, and less (but some) message serialization. More on this later.

Remember to call `shutdown()` or `close()` on the SolrServer when finished to properly release resources.

With the exception of `EmbeddedSolrServer`, they are easy to instantiate with simple constructors. Here's how to instantiate `HttpSolrServer`, whose only parameter is the URL to the Solr instance, to include the core or collection name:

```
public SolrServer createRemoteSolr() {
    return new HttpSolrServer("http://localhost:8983/solr/crawler");
}
```

Using javabin instead of XML for efficiency

SolrJ uniquely supports the ability to communicate with Solr using a custom binary format it calls **javabin**, which is more compressed and efficient to read and write than XML. However, the javabin format has changed on occasion, and when it does, it can force you to use the same (or sometimes newer) version on the client. By default, SolrJ sends requests in XML and it asks for responses back in javabin. Here's a code snippet to consistently toggle XML versus javabin for both request and responses:

```
if (useXml) {// xml, very compatible
    solrServer.setRequestWriter(new RequestWriter());//xml
    solrServer.setParser(new XMLResponseParser());
} else {//javabin, sometimes Solr-version sensitive
    solrServer.setRequestWriter(new BinaryRequestWriter());
    solrServer.setParser(new BinaryResponseParser());
}
```

 We recommend that you make the XML / javabin choice configurable as we saw earlier, with the default being javabin. During an upgrade of Solr, your Solr client could be toggled to use XML temporarily.

Searching with SolrJ

Performing a search is very straightforward:

```
SolrQuery solrQuery = new SolrQuery("Smashing Pumpkins");
solrQuery.setRequestHandler("/select");
QueryResponse response = solrServer.query(solrQuery);
SolrDocumentList docList = response.getResults();
```

`SolrQuery` extends `SolrParams` to add convenience methods around some common query parameters. `SolrDocumentList` is a `List<SolrDocument>` plus the numFound, start, and maxScore metadata. For an alternative to working with a `SolrDocument`, see the *Annotating your JavaBean – an alternative* section ahead. A little known alternative to the query method is `queryAndStreamResponse`, which takes a callback SolrJ call for each document it parses from the underlying stream. It can be used to more efficiently stream large responses from Solr to reduce latency and memory, although it only applies to the returned documents, not to any other response information.

Here's another example of adding faceting to find out the most popular hosts and paths indexed by the crawler:

```
SolrQuery solrQuery = new SolrQuery("*:*");
solrQuery.setRows(0);//just facets, no docs
solrQuery.addFacetField("host","path");//facet on both
solrQuery.setFacetLimit(10);
solrQuery.setFacetMinCount(2);
QueryResponse response = solr.query(solrQuery);
for (FacetField facetField : response.getFacetFields()) {
  System.out.println("Facet: "+facetField.getName());
  for (FacetField.Count count : facetField.getValues()) {
    System.out.println(" " +
        count.getName()+":"+count.getCount());
  }
}
```

The `QueryResponse` class has a lot of methods to access the various aspects of a Solr search response; it's pretty straightforward. One method of interest is `getResponse`, which returns a `NamedList`. If there is some information in Solr's response that doesn't have a convenience method, you'll have to resort to using that method to traverse the response tree to get the data you want.

Indexing with SolrJ

To index a document with SolrJ, you need to create a `SolrInputDocument`, populate it, and give it to the `SolrServer`. What follows is an excerpt from the code for the book that indexes a web-crawled document:

```
void indexAsSolrDocument(ArchiveRecordHeader meta,
    String htmlStr) throws Exception {
  SolrInputDocument doc = new SolrInputDocument();
  doc.setField("url", meta.getUrl(), 1.0f);
  doc.setField("mimeType", meta.getMimetype(), 1.0f);
  doc.setField("docText", htmlStr);
```

```
URL  = new URL(meta.getUrl());
doc.setField("host", url.getHost());
doc.setField("path", url.getPath());
solrServer.add(doc); // or could batch in a collection
}
```

If one of these fields were multivalued, then we would call `addField` for each value instead of `setField`, as you can see in the preceding code.

Depending on your commit strategy, you may want to call `commit()`. The semantics of committing documents are described in *Chapter 4, Indexing Data*.

 Unless you are using `ConcurrentUpdateSolrServer`, you will want to do some amount of batching. This means passing a Java Collection of documents to the add method instead of passing just one at a time. In the *Sending data to Solr in bulk* section of *Chapter 10, Scaling Solr*, there is more information showing how much it improved performance in a benchmark.

Deleting documents

Deleting documents is simple with SolrJ. In this query, we'll delete everything (`*:*` is the query to match all documents):

```
solrServer.deleteByQuery( "*:*" );
```

To delete documents by their ID, call `deleteById`. As with the add method, it's overloaded to take `commitWithin` a number of milliseconds.

Annotating your JavaBean – an alternative

If you already have a class holding the data to index under your control (versus a third-party library), you may prefer to annotate your class's setters or fields with SolrJ's `@Field` annotation instead of working with `SolrInputDocument` and `SolrDocument`. It might be easier to maintain and less code, if a little slower. Here's an excerpt from the book's sample code with an annotated class `RecordItem`:

```
package solrbook;
import org.apache.solr.client.solrj.beans.Field;

public class RecordItem {
  //@Field("url")   COMMENTED to show you can put the annotation on
    a setter
  String id;
```

```
@Field String mimeType;

@Field("docText") String html;

@Field String host;

@Field String path;

public String getId() { id; }

@Field("url") void setId(String id) { this.id = id; }

//... other getter's and setters
}
```

To search and retrieve a `RecordItem` instance instead of a `SolrDocument`, you simply call this method on `QueryResponse`:

```
List<RecordItem> items = response.getBeans(RecordItem.class);
```

Indexing `RecordItem` is simple too:

```
solrServer.addBean(item);
```

Embedding Solr

One of the most interesting aspects of SolrJ is that, because Solr and SolrJ are both written in Java, you can instantiate Solr and interact with it directly instead of starting up Solr as a separate process. This eliminates the HTTP layer and serializing the request too. The response is serialized; however, the returned documents can avoid it by using `queryAndStreamResponse` as mentioned earlier. We'll describe further why or why not you might want to embed Solr, but let's start with a code example. As you can see, starting up an embedded Solr is more complex than any other type:

```
public static SolrServer createEmbeddedSolr(String instanceDir)
    throws Exception {
  String coreName = new File(instanceDir).getName();
  // note: this is more complex than it should be. See SOLR-4502
  SolrResourceLoader resourceLoader =
      new SolrResourceLoader(instanceDir);
  CoreContainer container = new CoreContainer(resourceLoader,
      ConfigSolr.fromString(resourceLoader, "<solr />"));
  container.load();
  Properties coreProps = new Properties();
  //coreProps.setProperty(CoreDescriptor.CORE_DATADIR,
```

```
    dataDir);//"dataDir"  (optional)
  CoreDescriptor descriptor = new CoreDescriptor(
    container, coreName, instanceDir, coreProps);
  SolrCore core = container.create(descriptor);
  container.register(core, false);//not needed in Solr 4.9+
  return new EmbeddedSolrServer(container, coreName);
}
```

 A nonobvious limitation of instances of EmbeddedSolrServer is that it only enables you to interact with one SolrCore. Curiously, the constructor takes a core container, yet only the core named by the second parameter is accessible.

Keep in mind that your application embedding Solr will then take on all of Solr's dependencies, of which there are many.

When should you use embedded Solr? Tests!

In my opinion, a great use case for embedding Solr is unit testing!. Starting up an embedding Solr configured to put its data into memory in RAMDirectoryFactory is efficient and it's much easier to incorporate into tests then awkwardly attempting to use a real Solr instance. Note that using EmbeddedSolrServer in tests implies that your application shouldn't hardcode how it instantiates its SolrServer since tests will want to supply it. If you wish to test while communicating with Solr over HTTP then take a look at JettySolrRunner, a convenience class in the same package as EmbeddedSolrServer, with a main method that starts Jetty and Solr. Depending on how you use this class, this is another way to embed Solr without having to manage another process. Yet another option to be aware of is mostly relevant when testing custom extensions to Solr. For that case, you won't use a SolrServer abstraction, your test will extend SolrTestCaseJ4, which embeds Solr and has a ton of convenience methods. For more information on this, review a variety of Solr's tests that use that class and learn by example.

What about using it in other places besides tests? No application *needs* to embed Solr, but some apps may find it preferable. Fundamentally, embedded Solr is in-process (with the application) and doesn't listen on a TCP/IP port. It's easy to see that standalone Java-based desktop applications may prefer this model. Another use case seen in Solr's MapReduce contrib module and, in at least a couple of open source projects in the wild, is to decouple index building from the search server. The process that produces the document indexes it to disk with an embedded Solr instead of communicating remotely to one. Communicating to a standalone Solr process would of course also work but it's operationally more awkward.

After the index is built, it's copied to where a standalone Solr search process is running (this can be skipped for shared filesystems). If the index needs to get merged into an existing index instead of replacing or updating one, then it is merged with the MERGEINDEXES core admin command. A final commit to the search process will make the new index data visible in search results.

One particular case that people seek to embed Solr is for an anticipated performance increase, particularly during indexing. However, there is rarely a convincing performance win in doing so because the savings are usually negligible compared to all the indexing work that Solr has to do, such as tokenizing text, inverting documents, and of course writing to disk. Nonetheless, there are always exceptions (such as when leveraging Hadoop as a builder), and you might have such a case.

An alternative way to achieve in-process indexing is to write a custom RequestHandler class (possibly extending ContentStreamHandlerBase) that fetches and processes your data to your liking. It could be more convenient than using EmbeddedSolrServer depending on your use case.

Using JavaScript/AJAX with Solr

During the Web 1.0 epoch, JavaScript was primarily used to provide basic client-side interactivity such as a roll-over effect for buttons in the browser for what were essentially static pages generated by the server. However, in today's Web 2.0 environment, AJAX has led to JavaScript being used to build much richer web applications that blur the line between client-side and server-side functionality. Solr's support for the **JavaScript Object Notation (JSON)** format for transferring search results between the server and the web browser client makes it simple to consume Solr information by modern Web 2.0 applications. JSON is a human-readable format for representing JavaScript objects, which is rapidly becoming a de facto standard for transmitting language-independent data with parsers available to many languages. The JSON.parse() function will safely parse and return a valid JavaScript object that you can then manipulate:

```
var json_text = ["Smashing Pumpkins","Dave Matthews Band","The
    Cure"];
var bands = JSON.parse('(' + json_text + ')');
alert("Band Count: " + bands.length()); // alert "Band Count: 3"
```

While JSON is very simple to use in concept, it does come with its own set of quirks related to security and browser compatibility. To learn more about the JSON format, the various client libraries that are available, and how it is and is not like XML, visit the homepage at http://www.json.org.

As you may recall from the discussion on query parameters in *Chapter 4, Indexing Data*, you change the format of the response from Solr from the default XML to JSON by specifying the JSON writer type as a parameter in the URL via wt=json. Here is the result with indent=on:

```
{
  "responseHeader":{
  "status":0,
  "QTime":1,
  "params":{
    "q":"hills rolling",
    "wt":"json",
    "indent":"on"}},
  "response":{"numFound":44,"start":0,"docs":[
    {
    "a_name":"Hills Rolling",
    "a_release_date_latest":"2006-11-30T05:00:00Z",
    "a_type":"2",
    "id":"Artist:510031",
    "type":"Artist"}
  ...
    ]
 }}
```

Solr can be configured to change the way it structures certain parts of the response, most notably for field value faceting. This affects JSON, Ruby, and Python response formats: json.nl. Yes, it's not just for JSON, and it technically affects the output of Solr's so-called NamedList internal data, but only in rare circumstances. The default choice, flat, is inconvenient to work with despite its succinctness, so other options are available. Note that the map choice does not retain the ordering once it is materialized in memory. Here is a table showing the effects of each choice on faceting on the MusicBrainz artist type:

Choice	Effect
flat	"a_type":["person",126,"group",71,"0",0]
map	"a_type":{"person":126,"group":71,"0":0}
arrarr	"a_type":[["person",126],["group",71],["0",0]]
arrmap	"a_type":[{"person":126},{"group":71},{"0":0}]

You will find that you run into difficulties while parsing JSON in various client libraries, as some are stricter about the format than others. Solr does output very clean JSON, such as quoting all keys and using double quotes and offers some formatting options for customizing the handling of lists of data. If you run into difficulties, a very useful website for validating your JSON formatting is http://www.jsonlint.com/. This can be invaluable for finding issues such as an errant trailing comma.

Wait, what about security?

If requests to Solr come from a web browser, then you must consider security. You will learn in *Chapter 11, Deployment*, that one of the best ways to secure Solr is to limit what IP addresses can access your Solr install through firewall rules. Obviously, if users on the Internet are accessing Solr through JavaScript, then you can't do this. However, this chapter describes how to expose a read-only request handler that can be safely exposed to the Internet without exposing the complete admin interface. Also, make sure that any filters that *must* be applied to your data, such as a filter query enforcing only active products, are shown as appends parameters in your request handler. Additionally, you might proxy Solr requests to ensure the parameters meet a whitelist, to include their values. This can be where you apply various business rules, such as preventing a malicious user from passing parameters such as rows=1000000!

Building a Solr-powered artists autocomplete widget with jQuery and JSONP

Now, it's well established in the search industry that some form of query autocompletion remarkably improves the effectiveness of a search application. There are several fundamentally different types of autocompletion—be sure to read about them in *Chapter 8, Search Components*. Here is a screenshot of Google showing completions based on search queries it has seen before:

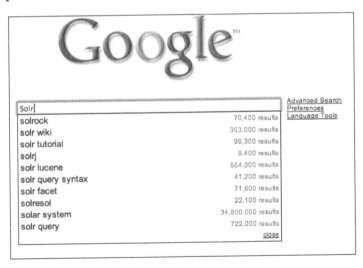

Building an autocomplete textbox powered by Solr is very simple by leveraging the JSON output format and the very popular jQuery JavaScript library's Autocomplete widget.

jQuery is a fast and concise JavaScript library that simplifies HTML document traversing, event handling, animating, and AJAX interactions for rapid web development. It has gone through explosive usage growth in 2008 and is one of the most popular AJAX frameworks. jQueryUI is a subproject that provides widgets such as Autocomplete. You can learn more about jQuery at `http://www.jquery.com` and `http://www.jqueryui.com`.

A working example using search-result-based completions (versus query log completion or term completion) is available at `/examples/9/jquery_autocomplete/index.html` that demonstrates suggesting an artist as you type in his or her name. You can read the doc and see a live demo of various autocompletions online at `http://jqueryui.com/demos/autocomplete/`.

There are three major sections to the HTML page:

- The JavaScript script `import` statements at the top
- The jQuery JavaScript that actually handles the events around the text being input
- A very basic HTML page for the form at the bottom

We start with a very simple HTML form that has a single text input box with the `id="artist"` attributes:

```
<div class="ui-widget">
  <label for="artist">Artist: </label>
  <input id="artist" />
</div>
```

We then add a function that runs, after the page has loaded, to turn our basic input field into a text field with suggestions:

```
$( "#artist" ).autocomplete({
  source: function( request, response ) {
    $.ajax({
      url: "http://localhost:8983/solr/mbartists/
        artistAutoComplete?wt=json&json.wrf=?",
      dataType: "jsonp",
      data: {
        q: request.term,
        rows: 10,
        fq: "type:Artist"
      },
      success: function( data ) {
```

```
            response( $.map(data.response.docs,function(doc) {
              return {
                label: doc.a_name,
                value: doc.a_name,
              }
            }));
          }
        });
      },
      minLength: 2,
      select: function( event, ui ) {
        log( ui.item ?
          "Selected: " + ui.item.label :
          "Nothing selected, input was " + this.value);
      },
      open: function() {
        $( this ).removeClass( "ui-corner-all" ).addClass
                                            ( "ui-corner-top" );
      },
      close: function() {
        $( this ).removeClass( "ui-corner-top" ).addClass
                                            ( "ui-corner-all" );

      }
    });
```

The `$("#artist").autocomplete()` function takes in the URL of our data source, in our case Solr, and an array of options and custom functions and ties it to the input form element. The `source: function( request, response )` function supplies the list of suggestions to display via a `$.ajax` callback. The `dataType: "jsonp"` option informs jQuery that we want to retrieve our data using JSONP. **JSONP** stands for **JSON with Padding**, an admittedly not very intuitive name! This means when you call the server for JSON data, the server wraps its typical JSON response in a call to a function provided by jQuery. This allows you to work around the web browser cross-domain scripting issues of running Solr on a different URL and/or port from the originating web page. jQuery takes care of all of the low level plumbing to create the callback function, which is supplied to Solr through the `json.wrf=?` URL parameter. If you look at the Solr logs, you will see the name of a function passed in: `json.wrf=jQuery15104412757297977805_1309313922023`.

Notice the `data` structure:

```
data: {
  q: request.term,
  rows: 10,
  fq: "type:Artist"
},
```

These items are tacked onto the URL as query parameters to Solr.

Following the best practices, we have created a Solr request handler called `/artistAutoComplete`, which is configured with the DisMax query parser to search over all of the fields in which an artist's name might show up: `a_name`, `a_alias`, and `a_member_name`, so arguably this is more of an instant search than word autocompletion. It's nice to use different request handlers for different search types rather than using `/select` for absolutely everything.

The `response()` function is called to convert the JSON result data from Solr into the format Autocomplete requires. It consists of a `map()` function that takes the returned JSON data structure for the documents returned and calls an anonymous function for each document. The anonymous function parses out the value to use as the label and value, in our case just the artist name.

Once the user has selected a suggestion, the `select()` function is called, and the name of the selected artist is appended to the `<div id="log">` div.

One thing that we haven't covered is the pretty common use case for an Autocomplete widget that populates a text field with an identifier for the suggestion used to take the user to a detail page on it—typical of instant-search type completion. For example, in order to store a list of artists, I would want the Autocomplete widget to simplify the process of looking up the artists, but would need to store the list of selected artists in a database. You can still leverage Solr's superior search ability, but tie the resulting list of artists to the original database record through a primary key ID, which is indexed as part of the Solr document.

If you try to lookup the primary key of an artist using the name of the artist, then you might run into problems, such as having multiple artists with the same name or unusual characters that don't translate cleanly from Solr to the web interface to your database record.

Instead, a hidden field stores the primary key of the artist and is used in your server-side processing in place of the text typed into the search box:

```
<input type="hidden" id="artist_id"/>
<input id="artist" />
```

We use the `change()` function to ensure freeform text that doesn't result in a match is ignored by clearing out the `artist_id` form field and returning `false` from the function:

```
change: function( event, ui ) {
  if (!ui.item){
    log("term " + $( this ).val() + " was not found, clearing");
```

```
      $( this ).val( "" );
      return false;
   } else {
      log("hidden field artist_id:" + ui.item.id);
      $( "#artist_id").val( ui.item.id);
      return true;
   }
}
```

Look at /examples/9/jquery_autocomplete/index_with_id.html for a complete example. Change the field artist_id from input type="hidden" to type="text" so that you can see the ID changing more easily as you select different artists. Make sure you click away from the suggestion box to see the change occur!

> **Where should I get my results to display as suggestions?**
>
> There are many approaches for supplying the list of suggestions for autocomplete, and even the nomenclature of autosuggest, autocomplete, or suggest-as-you-type have loosely defined meanings. This important subject is covered in the *Query complete/suggest* section in *Chapter 8, Search Components*.

AJAX Solr

AJAX Solr is an excellent Solr search UI framework for building AJAX-based search interfaces. It is an off-shoot of an older project called **SolrJS**, which is now defunct. AJAX Solr adds some interesting visualizations of result data, including widgets for displaying the tag clouds of facets, plotting country code-based data on a map of the world using the Google Chart API, and filtering results by date fields. When it comes to integrating Solr into your web application, if you are comfortable with JavaScript, then this can be a very effective way to add a really nice AJAX view of your search results without changing the underlying web application. If you're working with an older web framework that is brittle and hard to change, such as IBM's Lotus Notes or ColdFusion frameworks, then this keeps the integration from touching the actual business objects, and keeps the modifications in the client layer via HTML and JavaScript.

The AJAX Solr project's homepage is at `https://github.com/evolvingweb/ajax-solr` and provides a great demo of searching Reuter's business news wire results:

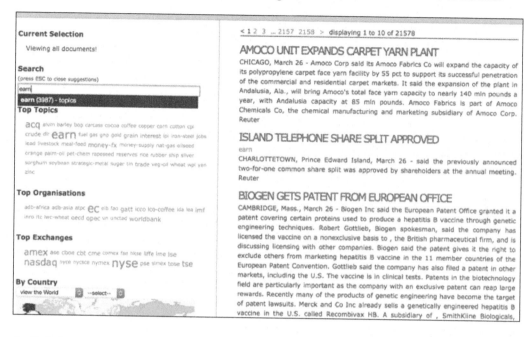

A slightly tweaked copy of the demo is at `/examples/9/ajaxsolr/reuters.html`. Note that if you try to access the demo and see no content, then most likely the Internet-accessible demo Solr instance is offline.

AJAX Solr provides rich UI functionality through widgets—small blocks of JavaScript that render a specific UI component. It comes with widgets, such as an autocompletion of field values, a tag cloud, a facet view, a country code, and calendar-based date ranges, as well as displaying the results with paging. They all inherit from an `AbstractWidget` and follow pretty much the same pattern. They are configured in `reuters/js/reuters.js` by passing in a set of options. Here is an example of configuring the autocomplete widget to populate the search box with autocomplete suggestions drawn from the topics, organizations, and exchanges fields:

```
Manager.addWidget(new AjaxSolr.AutocompleteWidget({
id: 'text',
target: '#search',
field: 'allText',
fields: [ 'topics', 'organisations', 'exchanges' ]
    }));
```

A central `AjaxSolr.Manager` object coordinates the event handling between the various widgets, makes the queries to Solr, and messages the widgets. The preceding code shows the call to add the widget to the `AjaxSolr.Manager` object. Working with AJAX Solr and creating new widgets for your specific display purposes comes easily to anyone who comes from an object-oriented background.

 The various widgets that come with AJAX Solr serve more as a foundation and source of ideas rather than as a finished set of widgets. You'll find yourself customizing them extensively to meet your specific display needs.

We've developed a MusicBrainz-based example at `./examples/9/ajaxsolr/mbtracks.html` for browsing track data. It is based on the Reuters example with a custom widget for term autocompletion using the `facet.prefix` technique. We did not configure Solr to load these facets via Solr's `firstSearcher` event in `solrconfig.xml` because this is the only demo that uses it, and it takes up to 30 seconds to load given the large index. Therefore, be patient while waiting for the first completion results.

Using XSLT to transform XML search results

A relatively unknown, but powerful way to integrate with Solr is via its support for **XSLT (eXtensible Stylesheet Language Transformations)**. XSLT is a specification for transforming XML documents into other XML formats, which includes HTML. There are various implementations of this specification and Java includes one. Solr provides a query response writer that executes a provided XSLT stylesheet to transform Solr's XML search results into some other format. Solr comes with a couple of examples in `./conf/xslt/`. Here is an example of transforming search results into an RSS feed:

```
http://localhost:8983/solr/mbartists/select/
?q=marley&wt=xslt&tr=example_rss.xsl
```

The `wt` parameter triggers the use of XSLT, and the `tr` parameter supplies the name of the stylesheet to be used.

There are some caveats to keep in mind for XSLT support. Internally, XSLT files are compiled before they are used, and while Solr will cache the last compiled XSLT for a period of time, configured in the `queryResponseWriter` via the `xsltCacheLifetimeSeconds` parameter, it only caches a single one. So, if you use more than one XSLT stylesheet, then you are likely to find degraded performance. Additionally, because Solr has to have the entire XML document in memory first to render the XSLT stylesheet, you may run into memory issues if you are returning large numbers of results.

> For a practical example of Solr's XSLT support, see SOLR-2143, which adds support for the **OpenSearch** specification to Solr. OpenSearch is a collection of simple formats and standards for search engine interoperability. It's most useful in federated search.

> **Need a debugger for Solr queries?**
>
> Want to understand how Solr determined the score for the documents you returned? You can use `example.xsl` to quickly transform your results to HTML and expose the query debugging information in an easy-to-read format. Just make sure you specify the score field to be returned so that you get the toggle for the scoring info: `http://localhost:8983/solr/mbartists/select/?q=smashing&wt=xslt&tr=example.xsl&fl=*,score&debugQuery=true`.

Accessing Solr from PHP applications

There are a number of ways to access Solr from PHP, and none of them seem to have taken hold of the market as the single best approach. So keep an eye on the wiki page at `http://wiki.apache.org/solr/SolPHP` for new developments.

Adding the URL parameter, `wt=php`, produces simple PHP output in a typical array data structure:

```
array(
  'responseHeader'=>array(
  'status'=>0,
  'QTime'=>0,
  'params'=>array(
    'wt'=>'php',
    'indent'=>'on',
    'rows'=>'1',
    'start'=>'0',
    'q'=>'Pete Moutso')),
```

```
    'response'=>array('numFound'=>523,'start'=>0,'docs'=>array(
array(
    'a_name'=>'Pete Moutso',
    'a_type'=>'1',
    'id'=>'Artist:371203',
    'type'=>'Artist'))
  ))
```

The same response using the Serialized PHP output specified by `wt=phps` URL parameter is a much less human-readable format that is more compact to transfer over the wire:

```
a:2:{s:14:"responseHeader";a:3:{s:6:"status";i:0;s:5:"QTime";i:1;s
:6:"params";a:5:{s:2:"wt";s:4:"phps";s:6:"indent";s:2:"on";s:4:"ro
ws";s:1:"1";s:5:"start";s:1:"0";s:1:"q";s:11:"Pete
Moutso";}}s:8:"response";a:3:{s:8:"numFound";i:523;s:5:"start";i:0
;s:4:"docs";a:1:{i:0;a:4:{s:6:"a_name";s:11:"Pete
Moutso";s:6:"a_type";s:1:"1";s:2:"id";s:13:"Artist:371203";s:4:"ty
pe";s:6:"Artist";}}}}
```

> **Think twice before using the PHP writer types**
>
> Un-serializing potentially untrusted data can increase security vulnerability. Additionally, the future of these writer types is in some doubt as PHP client abstraction projects such as solr-php-client and Solarium both use JSON in preference to the PHP writer types.

solr-php-client

A richer option for PHP integration is the solr-php-client. It is available at `http://code.google.com/p/solr-php-client/`. Interestingly enough, this project leverages the JSON writer type to communicate with Solr instead of the PHP writer type, showing the prevalence of JSON for facilitating interapplication communication in a language-agnostic manner. The developers chose JSON over XML because they found that JSON parsed much quicker than XML in most PHP environments. Moreover, using the native PHP format requires using the `eval()` function, which has a performance penalty and opens the door for code injection attacks.

The solr-php-client can both create documents in Solr as well as perform queries for data. In `/examples/9/solr-php-client/demo.php`, there is a demo on how to create a new artist document in Solr for the singer Susan Boyle, and then performing some queries. Installing the demo in your specific local environment is left as an exercise for the reader. On a Macintosh, you should place the `solr-php-client` directory in `/Library/WebServer/Documents/`.

An array data structure of key value pairs that match your schema can be easily created and then used to create an array of `Apache_Solr_Document` objects to be sent to Solr. Notice that we are using the artist ID value -1. Solr doesn't care what the ID field contains, just that it needs to be present. Using -1 ensures that we can find Susan Boyle by ID later!

```
$artists = array(
 'susan_boyle' => array(
  'id' => 'Artist:-1',
  'type' => 'Artist',
  'a_name' => 'Susan Boyle',
  'a_type' => 'person',
  'a_member_name' => array('Susan Boyle')
 )
);
```

The value for `a_member_name` is an array, because `a_member_name` is a multivalued field.

Sending the documents to Solr and triggering the commit and optimize operations is as simple as follows:

```
$solr->addDocuments( $documents );
$solr->commit();
$solr->optimize();
```

If you are not running Solr on the default port, then you will need to tweak the `Apache_Solr_Service` configuration:

```
$solr = new Apache_Solr_Service( 'localhost', '8983',
  '/solr/mbartists' );
```

Queries can be issued using one line of code; the variables `$query`, `$offset`, and `$limit` contain what you would expect them to:

```
$response = $solr->search( $query, $offset, $limit );
```

Displaying the results is very straightforward as well. Here we are looking for Susan Boyle based on her ID of -1, highlighting the result using a blue font:

```
foreach ( $response->response->docs as $doc ) {

    $output = "$doc->a_name ($doc->id) <br />";

    // highlight Susan Boyle if we find her.
```

```
    if ($doc->id == 'Artist:-1') {
      $output = "<em><font color=blue>" . $output . "</font></em>";
    }

    echo $output;
}
```

Successfully running the demo creates Susan Boyle and issues a number of queries. Notice that if you know the ID of the artist, it's almost like using Solr as a relational database to select a single specific row of data. Instead of `select * from artist where id=-1`, we did `q=id:"Artist:-1"`, but the result is the same!

Solarium may be what you want!

Solarium (`http://www.solarium-project.org/`) attempts to improve on other PHP client libraries by not just abstracting away the HTTP communication layer but also more fully modeling the concepts expressed by Solr. It has objects that allow you to easily build complex filter queries and faceting logic.

Drupal options

Drupal is a very successful open source **Content Management System (CMS)** that has been used for building everything from the `WhiteHouse.gov` site to political campaigns and university websites. Drupal's built-in search has always been considered adequate, but not great, so the option of using Solr to power search is very popular.

The Apache Solr Search integration module

The Apache Solr Search integration module, hosted at `http://drupal.org/project/apachesolr`, builds on top of the core search services provided by Drupal, but provides extra features such as faceted search and better performance by offloading servicing search requests to another server. The module has had significant adoption and is the basis of some other Drupal search-related modules.

In order to see the Apache Solr module in action, just visit `Drupal.org` and perform a search to see the faceted results.

Hosted Solr by Acquia

Acquia is a company providing commercially supported Drupal distributions, and also offers hosted Solr search for Drupal sites that want better search than the built-in MySQL-based search. Acquia's adoption of Solr as a better solution for Drupal than Drupal's own search shows the rapid maturing of the Solr community and platform.

Acquia maintains *in the cloud,* a large infrastructure of Solr servers saving individual Drupal administrators from the overhead of maintaining their own Solr server. A module provided by Acquia is installed into your Drupal and monitors for content changes. Every five or ten minutes, the module sends content that either hasn't been indexed, or needs to be re-indexed, up to the indexing servers in the Acquia network. When a user performs a search on the site, the query is sent up to the Acquia network, where the search is performed, and then Drupal is just responsible for displaying the results. Acquia's hosted search option supports all of the usual Solr goodies, including faceting. Drupal has always been very database intensive, with only moderately complex pages performing hundreds of individual SQL queries to render! Moving the load of performing searches off one's Drupal server into the cloud, drastically reduces the load of indexing and performing searches on Drupal.

Acquia has developed some slick integration beyond the standard Solr features based on their tight integration into the Drupal framework, which include the following:

- The **Content Construction Kit** (CCK) allows you to define custom fields for your nodes through a web browser. For example, you can add a particular field onto a blog node such as oranges/apples/peaches. Solr understands these CCK data model mappings and actually provides a facet of oranges/apples/peaches for it.

- Turn on a single module and instantly receive content recommendations giving you more-like-this functionality based on results provided by Solr. Any Drupal content can have recommendation links displayed with it.

- Multisite search is a strength of Drupal and provides the support of running multiple sites on a single codebase, such as `drupal.org`, `groups.drupal.org`, and `api.drupal.org`. Currently, part of the Apache Solr module is the ability to track where a document came from when indexed, and as a result, add the various sites as new filters into the search interface.

Acquia's hosted search product is a great example of **Platform as a Service** (**PaaS**), and hosted Solr search is a very common integration approach for many organizations that don't wish to manage their own Java infrastructure or need to customize the behavior of Solr drastically. For a list of all the companies offering hosted Solr search, visit `http://wiki.apache.org/solr/SolrHostingProviders`.

Ruby on Rails integrations

There has been a lot of churn in the Ruby on Rails world for adding Solr support, with a number of competing libraries attempting to support Solr in the most Rails-native way. Rails brought to the forefront the idea of **Convention over Configuration**, the principle that sane defaults and simple rules should suffice in most situations versus complex configuration expressed in long XML files. The various libraries for integrating Solr in Ruby on Rails applications establish conventions in how they interact with Solr. However, there are often a lot of conventions to learn, such as suffixing String object field names with _s to match up with the dynamic field definition for String in Solr's `schema.xml`.

Solr's Ruby response writer

The Ruby hash structure looks very similar to the JSON data structure with some tweaks to fit Ruby, such as translating nulls to nils, using single quotes for escaping content, and the Ruby => operator to separate key/value pairs in maps. Adding a `wt=ruby` parameter to a standard search request, returns results that can be `eval()` into a Ruby hash structure like this:

```
{
  'responseHeader'=>{
  'status'=>0,
  'QTime'=>1,
  'params'=>{
    'wt'=>'ruby',
    'indent'=>'on',
    'rows'=>'1',
    'start'=>'0',
    'q'=>'Pete Moutso'}},
  'response'=>{'numFound'=>523,'start'=>0,'docs'=>[
    {
    'a_name'=>'Pete Moutso',
    'a_type'=>'1',
    'id'=>'Artist:371203',
    'type'=>'Artist'}]
}}
```

 Beware—running `eval()` has security implications!

The sunspot_rails gem

The `sunspot_rails` gem hooks into the lifecycle of the ActiveRecord model objects and transparently indexes them in Solr as they are created, updated, and deleted. This allows you to do queries that are backed by Solr searches, but still work with your normal ActiveRecord objects. Let's go ahead and build a small Rails application that we'll call `myFaves`, which allows you to store your favorite MusicBrainz artists in a relational model and also to search for them using Solr.

Sunspot comes bundled with a full install of Solr as part of the gem, which you can easily start by running `rake sunspot:solr:start`, running Solr on port 8982. This is great for quickly doing development since you don't need to download and set up your own Solr. Typically, you are starting with a relational database already stuffed with content that you want to make searchable. However, in our case, we already have a fully populated index of artist information, so we are actually going to take the basic artist information out of the *mbartists* index of Solr and populate our local `myfaves` database used by the Rails application. We'll then fire up the version of Solr shipped with Sunspot, and see how `sunspot_rails` manages the lifecycle of ActiveRecord objects to keep Solr's indexed content in sync with the content stored in the relational database. Don't worry, we'll take it step by step! The completed application is at `/examples/9/myfaves` for your reference.

Setting up the myFaves project

This example assumes you have Rails 3.x already installed. We'll start with the standard plumbing to get a Rails application set up with our basic data model:

```
>>rails new myfaves
>>cd myfaves
>>./script/generate scaffold artist name:string group_type:string
  release_date:datetime image_url:string
>>rake db:migrate
```

This generates a basic application backed by a SQLite database. Now, we need to specify that our application depends on Sunspot. Edit `Gemfile` and add the following code:

```
gem 'sunspot_rails', '~> 1.2.1'
```

Next, update your dependencies and generate the `config/sunspot.yml` configuration file:

```
>>bundle install
>>rails generate sunspot_rails:install
```

We'll also be working with roughly 399,000 artists, so obviously we'll need some page pagination to manage that list, otherwise pulling up the artists' /index listing page will timeout. We'll use the popular will_paginate gem to manage pagination. Add the will_paginate gem declaration to your Gemfile and re-run bundle install:

```
gem "will_paginate", "~> 3.0.pre4"
```

Edit the ./app/controllers/artists_controller.rb file, and replace the call to @artists = Artist.all in the index method with:

```
@artists = Artist.paginate :page => params[:page], :order =>
  'created_at DESC'
```

Also, add a call to the view helper at ./app/views/artists/index.html.erb to generate the page links:

```
<%= will_paginate @artists %>
```

Start the application using ./script/rails start, and visit the page http://localhost:3000/artists/. You should see an empty listing page for all of the artists. Now that we know that the basics are working, let's go ahead and actually leverage Solr.

Populating the myFaves relational database from Solr

Step one will be to import data into our relational database from the mbartists Solr index. Add the following code to ./app/models/artist.rb:

```
class Artist < ActiveRecord::Base
  searchable do
    text :name, :default_boost => 2
    string :group_type
    time :release_date
  end
end
```

The searchable block maps the attributes of the Artist ActiveRecord object to the artist fields in Solr's schema.xml. Since Sunspot is designed to store any kind of data in Solr that is stored in your database, it needs a way of distinguishing among various types of data model objects. For example, if we wanted to store information about our User model object in Solr, in addition to the Artist object, then we would need to provide a field in the schema to distinguish the Solr document for the artist with the primary key of 5 from the Solr document for the user, which also has the primary key of 5. Fortunately, the mbartists schema has a field named type that stores the value Artist, which maps directly to our ActiveRecord class name of Artist.

There is a simple script called `populate.rb` at the root of `/examples/9/myfaves` that you can run, which will copy the artist data from the existing Solr `mbartists` index into the myFaves database:

```
>>./populate.rb
```

The `populate.rb` is a great example of the types of scripts you may need to develop to transfer data in and out of Solr. Most scripts typically work with some sort of batch size of records that are pulled from one system and then inserted into Solr. The larger the batch size, the more efficient the pulling and processing of data typically is at the cost of more memory being consumed, and the slower the commit and optimize operations are. When you run the `populate.rb` script, play with the batch size parameter to get a sense of resource consumption in your environment. Try a batch size of `10` versus `10000` to see the changes. The parameters for `populate.rb` are available at the top of the script:

```
MBARTISTS_SOLR_URL = 'http://localhost:8983/solr/mbartists'
BATCH_SIZE = 1500
MAX_RECORDS = 100000
```

There are roughly 399,000 artists in the `mbartists` index, so if you are impatient, then you can set `MAX_RECORDS` to a more reasonable number to complete running the script faster.

The connection to Solr is handled by the `RSolr` library. A request to Solr is simply a hash of parameters that is passed as part of the GET request. We use the `*:*` query to find all of the artists in the index and then iterate through the results using the `start` parameter:

```
rsolr = RSolr.connect :url => MBARTISTS_SOLR_URL
response = rsolr.select({
:q => '*:*',
:rows=> BATCH_SIZE,
:start => offset,
:fl => ['*','score']
})
```

In order to create our new Artist model objects, we just iterate through the results of `response['response']['docs']`, parsing each document in order to preserve our unique identifiers between Solr and the database and creating new `ActiveRecord` objects. In our MusicBrainz Solr schema, the ID field functions as the primary key and looks like `Artist:11650` for The Smashing Pumpkins. In the database, in order to sync the two, we need to insert the Artist with the ID of `11650`. We wrap the insert statement `a.save!` in a `begin/rescue/end` structure so that if we've already inserted an artist with a primary key, then the script continues. This allows us to run the populate script multiple times without erroring out:

```
response['response']['docs'].each do |doc|
  id = doc["id"]
  id = id[7..(id.length)]
  a = Artist.new(
  :id => id,
  :name => doc["a_name"],
  :group_type => doc["a_type"],
  :release_date => doc["a_release_date_latest"]

  begin
    a.save!
  rescue ActiveRecord::StatementInvalid => err
    raise err unless err.to_s.include?("PRIMARY KEY must be
      unique") # sink duplicates
  end
end
```

We've successfully migrated the data we need for our myFaves application out of Solr and we're ready to use the version of Solr that's bundled with Sunspot.

Solr configuration information is listed in ./myfaves/config/sunspot.yml. Sunspot establishes the convention that development is on port 8982, unit tests that use Solr connect on port 8981, and then production connects on the traditional 8983 port:

```
development:
  solr:
    hostname: localhost
    port: 8982
```

Start the included Solr by running `rake sunspot:solr:start`. To shut down Solr, run the corresponding `rake` command, `sunspot:solr:stop`. On the initial startup, `rake` will create a new top level ./solr directory and populate the conf directory with default configuration files for Solr (including schema.xml, stopwords.txt, and so on) pulled from the Sunspot gem.

Building Solr indexes from a relational database

Now, we are ready to trigger a full index of the data from the relational database into Solr. sunspot provides a very convenient rake task for this with a variety of parameters that you can learn about by running `rake -D sunspot:reindex`:

```
>>rake sunspot:solr:start
>>rake sunspot:reindex
```

Browse to `http://localhost:8982/solr/admin/schema.jsp` to see the list of dynamic fields generated by following the **Convention over Configuration** pattern of Rails applied to Solr. Some of the conventions that are established by Sunspot and expressed by Solr in `./solr/conf/schema.xml` are as follows:

- The primary key field of the model object in Solr is always called `id`.

- The type field that stores the disambiguating class name of the model object is called `type`.

- Heavy use of the dynamic field support in Solr. The data type of ActiveRecord model objects is based on the database column type. Therefore, when `sunspot_rails` indexes a model object, it sends a document to Solr with the various suffixes to leverage the dynamic column creation. In `./solr/conf/schema.xml`, the only fields defined outside of the management fields are dynamic fields:

  ```
  <dynamicField name="*_text" type="text" indexed="true"
  stored="false"/>
  ```

- The default search field is called `text`. However, you need to define what fields are copied into the text field. Sunspot's DSL is oriented towards naming each model field you'd like to search from Ruby.

The document that gets sent to Solr for our Artist records creates the dynamic fields such as `name_text`, `group_type_s` and `release_date_d`, for a text, string, and date field, respectively. You can see the list of dynamic fields generated through the schema browser at `http://localhost:8982/solr/admin/schema.jsp`.

Now we are ready to perform some searches. Sunspot adds some new methods to our `ActiveRecord` model objects such as `search()` that lets us load `ActiveRecord` model objects by sending a query to Solr. Here we find the group *Smash Mouth* by searching for matches to the word `smashing`:

```
% ./script/rails console
Loading development environment (Rails 3.0.9)
>>search= Artist.search{keywords "smashing"}
=><Sunspot::Search:{:fq=>["type:Artist"], :q=>"smashing",
:fl=>"* score", :qf=>"name_text^2", :defType=>"dismax", :start=>0,
:rows=>30}>
>>search.results.first
=>[#<Artist id: 93855, name: "Smashing Atoms", group_type: nil,
release_date: nil, image_url: nil, created_at: "2011-07-21 05:15:21",
updated_at: "2011-07-21 05:15:21">]
```

The raw results from Solr are stored in the `search.hits` variable. The `search.results` variable returns the `ActiveRecord` objects from the database.

Let's also verify that Sunspot is managing the full lifecycle of our objects. Assuming `Susan Boyle` isn't yet entered as an artist; let's go ahead and create her:

```
>>Artist.search{keywords  'Susan Boyle', :fields => [:name]}.hits
=>[]
>>susan = Artist.create(:name => "Susan Boyle", :group_type =>'1',
    :release_date => Date.new)
=> #<Artist id: 548200, name: "Susan Boyle", group_type: 1,
    release_date: "-4712-01-01 05:00:00", created_at: "2011-07-22
21:05:53"", updated_at: "2011-07-22 21:05:53"">
```

Check the log output from your Solr running on port 8982, and you should also have seen an update query triggered by the insert of the new Susan Boyle record:

```
INFO: [] webapp=/solr path=/update params={} status=0 QTime=24
```

Now, delete Susan's record from your database:

```
>>susan.destroy
=> #<Artist id: 548200, name: "Susan Boyle", group_type: 1,
    release_date: "-4712-01-01 05:00:00", created_at: "2009-04-21
    13:11:09", updated_at: "2009-04-21 13:11:09">
```

As a result, there should be another corresponding update issued to Solr to remove the document:

```
INFO: [] webapp=/solr path=/update params={} status=0 QTime=57
```

You can verify this by doing a search for Susan Boyle directly, which should return no rows at `http://localhost:8982/solr/select/?q=Susan+Boyle`.

Completing the myFaves website

Now, let's go ahead and put in the rest of the logic for using our Solr-ized model objects to simplify finding our favorite artists. We'll store the list of favorite artists in the browser's session space for convenience. If you are following along with your own generated version of the myFaves application, then the remaining files you'll want to copy over from `/examples/9/myfaves` are as follows:

- `./app/controller/myfaves_controller.rb`: This contains the controller logic for picking your favorite artists.

- `./app/views/myfaves/`: This contains the display files for picking and showing the artists.

- `./app/views/layouts/myfaves.html.erb`: This is the layout of the myFaves views. We use the Autocomplete widget again so that this layout embeds the appropriate JavaScript and CSS files.

- `./public/stylesheets/jquery.autocomplete.css` and `./public/stylesheets/indicator.gif`: They are stored locally in order to fix pathing issues with the `indicator.gif` showing up when the autocompletion search is running.

The only other edits you need to make are:

- Edit `./config/routes.rb` by adding `resources :myfaves` and `root :to => "myfaves#index"`.

- Delete `./public/index.html` to use the new `root` route you just defined.

- Copy the index method out of `./app/controllers/artists_controllers.rb` because we want the index method to respond with both HTML and JSON response types.

- Run `rake db:sessions:create` to generate a sessions table, then `rake db:migrate` to update the database with the new sessions table. Edit `./config/initializers/session_store.rb` and change to using `:active_record_store` for preserving the session state.

You should now be able to run `./script/rails start` and browse to `http://localhost:3000/`. You will be prompted to enter the search by entering the artist's name. If you don't receive any results, then make sure you have started Solr using `rake sunspot:solr:start`. Also, if you have only loaded a subset of the full 399,000 artists, then your choices may be limited. You can load all of the artists through the `populate.rb` script and then run `rake sunspot:reindex`, although it will take a long time to complete. This is something good to do just before you head out for lunch or home for the evening!

If you look at `./app/views/myfaves/index.rhtml`, then you can see that the jQuery autocomplete call is a bit different:

```
$("#artist_name").autocomplete( '/artists.json?callback=?', {
```

The URL we are hitting is `/artists.json`, with the `.json` suffix telling Rails that we want the JSON data back instead of normal HTML. If we ended the URL with `.xml`, then we would have received XML-formatted data about the artists. We provide a slightly different parameter to Rails to specify the JSONP callback to use. Unlike the previous example, where we used `json.wrf`, which is Solr's parameter name for the callback method to call, we use the more standard parameter name `callback`. We changed the `ArtistController` index method to handle the `autocomplete` widget's data needs through JSONP. If there is a `q` parameter, then we know that the request was from the `autocomplete` widget, and we ask Solr for `@artists` to respond with. Later on, we render `@artists` into JSON objects, returning only the `name` and `id` attributes to keep the payload small.

We also specify that the JSONP callback method is what was passed when using the `callback` parameter:

```
def index
if params[:q]
    @artists = Artist.search{ keywords params[:q] }.results
else
    @artists = Artist.paginate :page => params[:page], :order =>
        'created_at DESC'
end

respond_to do |format|
format.html # index.html.erb
format.xml { render :xml => @artists }
format.json { render :json => @artists.to_json(:only => [:name,
        :id]), :callback => params[:callback] }
end
end
```

At the end of all of this, you should have a nice autocomplete interface for quickly picking artists.

When you are selecting Sunspot as your integration method, you are implicitly agreeing to the various conventions established for indexing data into Solr. If you are used to working with Solr directly, you may find understanding the Sunspot DSL for querying a bit of an obstacle. However, if your background is in Rails, or you are building very complex queries, then learning the DSL will pay off in productivity and the ability to maintain complex expressive queries.

Which Rails/Ruby library should I use?

The two most common high-level libraries for interacting with Solr are `acts_as_solr` and Sunspot. However, in the last couple of years, Sunspot has become the more popular choice, and comes in a version designed to work explicitly with Rails called `sunspot_rails` that allows Rails' `ActiveRecord` database objects to be transparently backed by a Solr index for full text search.

For lower-level client interface to Solr from Ruby environments, there are two libraries duking it out to be the client of choice: `solr-ruby`, a client library developed by the Apache Solr project and `rsolr`, which is a reimplementation of a Ruby-centric client library. Both of these solutions are solid and act as great low-level API libraries. However, `rsolr` has gained more attention, has better documentation, and some nice features such as a direct embedded Solr connection through JRuby. `rsolr` also has support for using `curb` (Ruby bindings to `curl`, a very fast HTTP library) instead of the standard `Net::HTTP` library for the HTTP transport layer.

In order to perform a select using `solr-ruby`, you need to issue the following code:

```
response = solr.query('washington', {
 :start=>0,
 :rows=>10
 })
```

In order to perform a select using `rsolr`, you need to issue the following code:

```
response = solr.select({
 :q=>'washington',
 :start=>0,
 :rows=>10
 })
```

So you can see that doing a basic search is pretty much the same in either library. Differences crop up more as you dig into the details on parsing and indexing records. You can learn more about `solr-ruby` on the Solr wiki at `http://wiki.apache.org/solr/solr-ruby` and learn more about `rsolr` at `http://github.com/mwmitchell/rsolr/`.

Think whether you really need another layer of abstraction between you and Solr. Making a call to Solr using `wt=ruby` and evaluating the results may be the simplest solution.

Nutch for crawling web pages

A very common source of data to search is content in web pages, either from the Internet or inside the firewall. The long-time popular solution for crawling and indexing web pages, especially for millions of them, is **Nutch**, a former Lucene subproject. If you need to scale to millions of pages up, then consider Nutch or Heritrix. For smaller scales, there are many options (that are also simpler), including `ManifoldCF`, which is discussed later.

What about Heritrix?

In the previous editions of the book, we highlighted Heritrix—a crawler sponsored by the Internet Archive that was arguably a more scalable crawler than Nutch. The output files from the crawler are used in the SolrJ example, and there is an example in `/examples/9/heritrix-2.0.2/`. However, Nutch has shown more development activity than Heritrix in the past couple of years, and thus, we are focusing only on it in this edition.

Nutch is an Internet scale web crawler similar to Google with components such as the web crawler itself, a link graphing database, and parsers for HTML and other common formats found on the Internet. Nutch is designed to scale horizontally over multiple machines during crawling using the big data platform, **Hadoop**, to manage the work.

 The Nutch project is the progenitor of the BigData/Search world! Nutch was developed by Doug Cutting and Mike Cafarella in 2002, a few years after Doug developed Lucene (the underpinnings of Solr). To scale it, they built the **Nutch Distributed File System** (**NDFS**), which became HDFS. To parse data, they used MapReduce, which spun off to become Hadoop!

Nutch has gone through varying levels of activity and community involvement and has two lines of development—1.x which is very stable and mature, and 2.x which is less but has a more flexible architecture. Previously, Nutch used its own custom search interface based on Lucene, but now, it leverages Solr for search in the 1.9 codebase. This allows Nutch to focus on web crawling, while Solr provides a powerful dedicated search platform with features such as query spellcheck and faceting that Nutch previously didn't have. Nutch natively understands web relevancy concepts such as the value of links towards calculating a page rank score, and how to factor in what an HTML <title/> tag is, when building the scoring model to return results. In the 2.0 version, it leverages more standard open source components, such as HBase for the link database instead of its own internal technology. While a better approach, it has more dependencies, so the demo uses the 1.9 codebase.

Nutch uses a seed list of URLs that tells it where to start finding web pages to crawl. The directory at ./examples/9/nutch/ contains a configured copy of Nutch for crawling through a list of Wikipedia pages for the 300 most popular artists according to MusicBrainz's count of track lookups. Look at the seed_urls.rb script to see the logic used for building the URL seed list wikipedia_seed_urls.txt. To crawl the Internet for a handful of documents, starting from the seed list and index into Solr run from ./examples/9/nutch/ directory:

```
>> ./apache-nutch-1.8/bin/crawl wikipedia_seed_urls.txt testCrawl/
http://127.0.0.1:8983/solr/nutch/ 1
```

Browse to http://localhost:8983/solr/nutch/select?q=*:*&fl=url,title and you will see some wiki pages crawled and indexed by Nutch into Solr.

The `sizeFetchlist=10` parameter in the `./apache-nutch-1.8/bin/crawl` bash script tells Nutch how many documents to crawl. We have hardcoded it to 10 to make sure the example crawl doesn't consume all your resources. Once you are satisfied that Nutch is working the way you want, uncomment the line `sizeFetchlist=`expr $numSlaves * 50000``, and trigger the crawl again to index each of the wiki pages listed in the `wikipedia_seed_urls.txt` file.

The schema file (at `./cores/nutch/conf/schema.xml`) that Nutch uses is very selfexplanatory. The biggest change you might make is to set `stored="false"` on the content field to reduce the index size if you are doing really big crawls and need to save space.

For more information about the plugins that extend Nutch, and how to configure Nutch for more sophisticated crawling patterns, look at the documentation at `http://nutch.apache.org`.

Solr and Hadoop

Apache Hadoop and the big data ecosystem have exploded in popularity and most developers are at least loosely familiar with it. Needless to say, there are many pieces of the Hadoop ecosystem that work together to form a big data platform. It's mostly an a-la-carte world in which you combine the pieces you want, each having different uses, or makes different trade-offs between ease-of-coding and performance. What does Solr have to do with Hadoop, you may ask? Read on.

HDFS

As an alternative to a standard filesystem, Solr can store its indexes in **Hadoop Distributed File System (HDFS)**. HDFS acts like a shared filesystem for Solr, somewhat like how networked storage is (for example, a SAN), but is implemented at the application layer instead of at the OS or hardware layer. HDFS offers almost limitless growth, and you can increase storage incrementally without restarting or reconfiguring the server processes supporting it. HDFS has redundancy too, although this is extra-redundant with SolrCloud replication. Ideally, Solr nodes should be running on the same machines as HDFS data nodes. If you already have HDFS for other purposes, be it for MapReduce jobs or whatever, then this may be particularly appealing, but otherwise, it is probably more complex than it's worth. Solr's HDFS integration is built into Solr—see the Solr Reference Guide for the details and read it thoroughly. If you've already got HDFS running, it's really quite easy to get Solr to use it.

A nice bonus of using HDFS is the option of using the `autoAddReplicas` feature in Solr 4.10. With this feature, Solr will respond to a node failure by automatically adding replacement replicas on other nodes to maintain the desired `replicationFactor`. Although it may work with any shared filesystem, only HDFS is supported right now. A *planned* benefit of shared filesystems is having leaders and replicas use the same index, thereby saving space and freeing replicas from much of the impact of concurrent indexing activity. See SOLR-6237 (`https://issues.apache.org/jira/browse/SOLR-6237`) for the current status. Once that feature is released, using HDFS will be far more compelling!

Indexing via MapReduce

Solr includes a contrib module named `map-reduce` that provides Hadoop MapReduce components for indexing documents into new Solr indexes stored on HDFS. It includes a cool **go-live** feature that will then merge those generated indexes into Solr's existing indexes in HDFS without experiencing any downtime. This module provides the most value when your data is already in HDFS and there is a lot of data and/or CPU-intensive work in generating the resulting Solr input documents, such as doing text extraction from common document formats. Using the MapReduce paradigm, this work is parallelized across a cluster of Hadoop nodes in a fault-tolerant manner, and even the resulting Solr indexes get built from this process. Even if you are doing trivial text processing on tweets, you can benefit from this module by leveraging your large Hadoop cluster to index all of your data faster than you would be able to with just your Solr cluster. Furthermore, your search performance is not going to be heavily impacted by the ongoing indexing activity because it is separated.

To learn more about the `map-reduce` module, start with **MapReduceIndexerTool**, a command-line program and façade to the nuts and bolts here. It's not documented in Solr's Reference Guide; instead Google it and you will wind up looking at its documentation within the documentation for *Cloudera Search*: `http://www.cloudera.com/content/cloudera/en/documentation/cloudera-search/v1-latest/Cloudera-Search-User-Guide/csug_mapreduceindexertool.html`.

Morphlines

This module and two other related contrib modules use an **Extract Transform Load** (ETL) framework called **Morphlines**, open sourced by Cloudera. However, unlike some other popular ETLs, this one is lightweight and developer friendly (no IDE!) and has a data model matching Lucene/Solr—String keys supporting multiple values. Morphlines enables MapReduceIndexerTool to support any input format and custom transformations just by editing a configuration file. If the numerous built-in Morphline commands aren't sufficient, you can of course write your own commands to plug in. Morphlines does not require Hadoop or even Solr, though you will see strong associations with both. If you have non-trivial steps to construct a Solr input document for indexing, then you should definitely check it out. The best source of information for this is available at `http://kitesdk.org/docs/current/kite-morphlines/index.html`.

Running a Solr build using Hadoop

The source code for this example is available at `/examples/9/solr-map-reduce-example`.

> The original code was published by SolrCloud lead developer Mark Miller: `https://github.com/markrmiller/solr-map-reduce-example`.

Make sure you don't have any Solr or Hadoop processes running before you start performing the following steps:

1. Start the example via the `./run-example.sh` script. You'll see that the Hadoop and Solr distributions are downloaded, and various processes related to them are run.

2. When it completes, browse to `http://127.0.0.1:8042` and you'll see the Hadoop WebApp. Assuming all went well, you can query some Twitter data via `http://localhost:8983/solr/collection1/select?q=*:*`.

Looking at the storage

So what makes this special, or different than a traditional SolrCloud setup? Well, first off, the Lucene data files aren't stored on your local filesystem, instead they are on a locally running HDFS cluster. If you browse to one of the shards at `http://localhost:8983/solr/#/collection1`, you will see that the filesystem implementation is listed as `org.apache.solr.core.HdfsDirectoryFactory`, and that the data is being stored on the HDFS cluster:

```
Data:   hdfs://127.0.0.1:8020/solr1/collection1/core_node2/data

Index:  hdfs://127.0.0.1:8020/solr1/collection1/core_node2/data/index

Impl:   org.apache.solr.core.HdfsDirectoryFactory
```

How did that happen? If you dig around in `run-example.sh`, you'll see that when Solr was started, some additional HDFS-related parameters were passed in:

```
-Dsolr.directoryFactory=solr.HdfsDirectoryFactory -
Dsolr.lock.type=hdfs -Dsolr.hdfs.home=hdfs://127.0.0.1:8020/solr1
-Dsolr.hdfs.confdir=$hadoop_conf_dir
```

The `solr.directoryFactory` parameter told Solr to change the default `<directoryFactory/>` setting in `solrconfig.xml` to be a HDFS directory factory instead of the traditional filesystem one. Additionally, `solr.lock.type` overrides the native lock type to enable HDFS, own semantics around locking.

HDFS works very similar to the Unix filesystem that you are already used to, except instead of the `solr.home` parameter pointing to a local directory, the `solr.hdfs.home` parameter is the URL of the directory in HDFS. In this case, the data is stored in `/solr1/` at the root of the HDFS server running locally on port 8020. Since we are running two Solrs in our local environment, if you look at `run-example.sh`, you'll see that the second Solr has started with the same parameters except for the HDFS location to store the second shard:

```
-Dsolr.hdfs.home=hdfs://127.0.0.1:8020/solr2
```

Let's take a look at the HDFS cluster. From the root of `./examples/9/solr-map-reduce-example`, run the command to list the command of all the files and directories on our HDFS cluster:

```
./hadoop-2.2.0/bin/hadoop fs -fs hdfs://127.0.0.1:8020 -ls /
```

The command is pretty selfexplanatory; we are using the Hadoop client to make a file listing call. The location of the filesystem is passed in as a url starting with `hdfs://`, which means you can see how HDFS is meant, from the ground up, to be used in a distributed manner. The command we wish to run is to list all the files in the root directory. The output should be something like this:

```
Found 5 items
drwxr-xr-x   - epugh supergroup          0 2014-11-12 09:53 /indir
drwxr-xr-x   - epugh supergroup          0 2014-11-12 09:54 /outdir
drwxr-xr-x   - epugh supergroup          0 2014-11-12 09:53 /solr1
drwxr-xr-x   - epugh supergroup          0 2014-11-12 09:53 /solr2
drwxr-xr-x   - epugh supergroup          0 2014-11-12 09:53 /tmp
```

Ignore /indir and /outdir for now. As you can see, we have two filesystems rooted on the HDFS cluster at /solr1 and /solr2. With HDFS, as the size of the data in these filesystems grow, you just add more hardware to the HDFS cluster, and HDFS manages distributing the additional data to the new hardware. Let's look in a bit more detail at the data files stored in HDFS:

```
hadoop-2.2.0/bin/hadoop fs -fs hdfs://127.0.0.1:8020 -ls
/solr1/collection1/core_node2/data/index
```

As you can see, we have our write lock file, but this time in HDFS, as well as some Lucene segment files. (To save space, I have only listed the first couple of files):

```
Found 13 items
-rw-r--r--   1 epugh supergroup          0 2014-11-12 09:53
/solr1/collection1/core_node2/data/index/HdfsDirectory@798a0aac
lockFactory=org.apache.solr.store.hdfs.HdfsLockFactory@5ef215db-
write.lock
-rwxr-xr-x   1 epugh supergroup      42943 2014-11-12 09:54
/solr1/collection1/core_node2/data/index/_0.fdt
-rwxr-xr-x   1 epugh supergroup         89 2014-11-12 09:54
/solr1/collection1/core_node2/data/index/_0.fdx
-rwxr-xr-x   1 epugh supergroup       2951 2014-11-12 09:54
/solr1/collection1/core_node2/data/index/_0.fnm
```

So let's see if we can use the power of HDFS to quickly add another Solr process. We've added a script called add-third-solr.sh that fires up another Solr server process, and add it to the cluster of Solrs supporting collection1. List out the root directory in HDFS and you'll see that the data is now being stored in HDFS in /solr3. Look at the log file in the solr-4.10.1/example3/example3.log file to see the behavior. Keen-eyed readers will notice, however, that the /solr3 directory is a complete copy of the original /solr1 or /solr2 directory that has the leader's data. As we mentioned in the intro, once SOLR-6237 is wrapped up, this will drastically reduce the amount of disk storage required, making HDFS a much more compelling option over the traditional SolrCloud.

One last thing to keep in mind when looking at using HDFS is that HDFS is primarily oriented towards the storage of fewer larger files that can be split up and stored on multiple servers versus many small files that are rapidly changing. If you have a near real-time scenario, with many small incremental changes to your data, then you will want to make sure that the overhead of HDFS isn't prohibitive. On the other hand, if you periodically build an index, optimize it, and leave it alone, then the strengths of HDFS may meet your needs perfectly.

The data ingestion process

This demo uses source Twitter data stored in a format called **Avro**. Apache Avro is a powerful data serialization framework, like Thrift and ProtoBuf. What makes Avro great is that each `.avro` file includes the schema that describes the data that is stored inside that file. This means that you can interrogate any `.avro` file and figure out how to read back the data. This makes this data format very stable, with none of the stubs required by Thrift or ProtoBuf for writing and reading the data. Go ahead and open the `sample-statuses-20120906-141433-medium.avro` file with a text editor. You'll see the schema for the data listed in the binary file as shown here:

```
{"type":"record","name":"Doc","doc":"adoc","fields":[{"name":"id",
"type":"string"},{"name":"user_friends_count","type":["int","null"
]},{"name":"user_location","type":["string","null"]},{"name":"user
_description","type":["string","null"]},{"name":"user_statuses_cou
nt","type":["int","null"]},{"name":"user_followers_count","type":[
"int","null"]},{"name":"user_name","type":["string","null"]},{"nam
e":"user_screen_name","type":["string","null"]},{"name":"created_a
t","type":["string","null"]},{"name":"text","type":["string","null
"]},{"name":"retweet_count","type":["int","null"]},{"name":"retwee
ted","type":["boolean","null"]},{"name":"in_reply_to_user_id","typ
e":["long","null"]},{"name":"source","type":["string","null"]},{"n
ame":"in_reply_to_status_id","type":["long","null"]},{"name":"medi
a_url_https","type":["string","null"]},{"name":"expanded_url","typ
e":["string","null"]}]}
```

Remember how we performed a `ls` command on the HDFS cluster? Similar commands in `run-example.sh` are used to insert the sample data into the cluster:

```
samplefile=sample-statuses-20120906-141433-medium.avro
$hadoop_distrib/bin/hadoop --config $hadoop_conf_dir fs -mkdir
hdfs://127.0.0.1/indir
$hadoop_distrib/bin/hadoop --config $hadoop_conf_dir fs -put
$samplefile hdfs://127.0.0.1/indir/$samplefile
```

Want to try it yourself? The following command will upload a copy of the sample data into `/indir`, which is the staging directory for in-bound data for processing using Hadoop:

```
./hadoop-2.2.0/bin/hadoop fs -fs hdfs://127.0.0.1:8020 -put sample-
statuses-20120906-141433-medium.avro hdfs://127.0.0.1/indir/sample-
statuses-20120906-141433-medium2.avro
```

Once the data is loaded, we are ready to run the Morphline process in our Hadoop cluster to import the data into Solr. The files stored in the HDFS cluster under /indir will be processed into Lucene indexes that are placed into /outdir in HDFS. Let's look at /outdir to see one of the segment files:

```
./hadoop-2.2.0/bin/hadoop fs -fs hdfs://127.0.0.1:8020 -ls
/outdir/results/part-00000/data
```

Morphlines works by taking a configuration file that describes the steps in the data processing pipeline. Open up the readAvroContainer.conf file in your text editor. You can see that this is DSL for data processing. And yes, it's **YAFF (Yet Another File Format)** called **HOCON (Human-Optimized Config Object Notation)**, so it may take you a bit to get used to it.

The key bit to understand is that the file declares a set of commands:

- readAvroContainer, extractAvroPaths, convertTimestamp, sanitizeUnknownSolrFields, and finally loadSolr. Each of these commands is documented in the readAvroContainer.conf file; however, you can guess from the names that the first step of the Morphline is to read records from our .avro files that where uploaded into the /indir directory.

- The second step, extractAvroPaths is interesting, as it uses a basic path expression, akin to XPath, to map the fields in the Avro document to the names of the fields in Solr. In this simple example, it's pretty redundant since there is a 1-to-1 mapping between field names in Avro and in the Solr schema, but you can see how this would be useful in mapping Avro documents to an existing Solr schema.

- convertTimestamp is a nice example of the types of manipulations that you always have to do when importing data into Solr. Solr is very fussy about getting all dates in the full ISO standard format of yyyy-MM-dd'T'HH:mm:ss'Z', and this function makes it easy.

- sanitizeUnknownSolrFields takes advantage of the RESTful APIs added to Solr to query the schema service for the list of fields that Solr knows about, and then filters the documents being sent to drop any fields that Solr doesn't know about.

- Lastly, the loadSolr command pops the documents into your Solr. The amazing thing is that what you think of as complex process turns out to be the easiest step:

  ```
  loadSolr {
    solrLocator : ${SOLR_LOCATOR}
  }
  ```

Unfortunately, like many things with Hadoop, the command line to invoke loading data with Morphlines is quite intimidating. To make things simpler, look at the `run-just-morphline.sh` script, it only runs the Morphline. It assumes you've already run the `run-example.sh` script to start up the Hadoop and Solr processes. Most of the parameters are pretty selfexplanatory. The really interesting parameter is the `--go-live` parameter. What this tells the Morphline process to do is to take all the index data generated by the Morphline process in `/outdir`, and uses the information in ZooKeeper to deploy this new data into the right locations in HDFS for the Solr servers (for us that's `/solr1` and `/solr2`), and then merge them into the live indexes.

Look at the console output from running the script, you can see the MapReduce jobs running all the steps of the Morphline. It gives you a sense of how MapReduce works! If you are debugging the Morphline, add the `-dry-run` parameter to the command. When you run the Morphline, it will output to the console the documents that it would have otherwise inserted into Solr, giving you a way of debugging what is going on.

Want to know it's working? Look at the Gen value in the Solr admin for one of your shards, and then rerun the Morphline process. You will see the Gen value increment by one. One thing to note is that while the number of live documents in the index won't go up, remaining at 2104, the total number of documents in the index will continue to go up because new segment files are being appended constantly. This can be a bit confusing since Solr considers the shard to be optimized, despite the existence of ostensibly deleted documents in the index!

ManifoldCF – a connector framework

Apache **ManifoldCF** (**CF** meaning **Connector Framework**) provides a framework for extracting content from multiple repositories, enriching it with document-level security information, and outputting the resulting document into Solr based on the security model found in Microsoft's Active Directory platform. Working with ManifoldCF requires an understanding of the interaction between extracting content from repositories via a **Repository Connector**, outputting the documents and security tokens via an **Output Connector** into Solr, listing a specific user's access tokens from an **Authority Connector**, and finally performing a search that filters the document results based on the list of tokens. ManifoldCF takes care of ensuring that, as content and security classifications for content are updated in the underlying repositories, it is synched to Solr, either on a scheduled basis or a constantly monitoring basis. Finally, it has a convenient web UI to manage the connector states.

Connectors

ManifoldCF provides **connectors** that index into Solr content from a number of enterprise content repositories, including SharePoint, Documentum, Meridio, LiveLink, and FileNet. Competing with DataImportHandler and Nutch, ManifoldCF also crawls web pages, RSS feeds, JDBC databases, and remote Windows shares and local filesystems, while adding the document-level security tokens, where applicable. Also of note is its MediaWiki connector. The most compelling use case for ManifoldCF is leveraging ActiveDirectory to provide access tokens for content indexed in Microsoft SharePoint repositories, followed by just gaining access to content in the other enterprise-content repositories.

Putting ManifoldCF to use

While the sweet spot for using ManifoldCF is with an authority like ActiveDirectory, we're going to reuse our `MusicBrainz.org` data and come up with a simple scenario for playing with ManifoldCF and Solr. We will use our own `MusicBrainzConnector` class to read in data from a simple CSV file that contains a MusicBrainz ID for an artist, the artist's name, and a list of music genre tags for the artist:

```
4967c0a1-b9f3-465e-8440-4598fd9fc33c,Enya,folk,pop,irish
```

The data will be streamed through Manifold and out to our `/manifoldcf` Solr core with the list of genres used as the access tokens. To simulate an Authority service that translates a username to a list of access tokens, we will use our own `GenreAuthority`. It will take the first character of the supplied username, and return a list of genres that start with the same character. So a call to ManifoldCF for the username `paul@example.com` would return the access tokens *pop* and *punk*. A search for "Chris" would match on "Chris Isaak" since he is tagged with *pop*, but "Chris Cagle" would be filtered out since he plays only *American* and *country* music.

Browse the source for both `MusicBrainzConnector` and `GenreAuthority` in `./examples/9/manifoldcf/connectors/` to get a better sense of how specific connectors work with the greater ManifoldCF framework.

To get started, we need to add some new dynamic fields to our schema in `cores/manifoldcf/conf/schema.xml`:

```
<dynamicField name="allow_token_*" type="string" indexed="true"
stored="true" multiValued="true"/>
<dynamicField name="deny_token_*" type="string" indexed="true"
stored="true" multiValued="true"/>
```

These rules will allow the Solr output connector to store access tokens in the fields such as `allow_token_document` and `deny_token_document`.

Now we can start up ManifoldCF. The version distributed with this book is a stripped-down version, with just the specific connectors required for this demo! In a separate window from `./examples/9/manifoldcf/example` run the following code:

```
>>java -jar start.jar
```

ManifoldCF ships with Jetty as a servlet container, hence the very similar start command to the one Solr uses!

Browse to `http://localhost:8345/mcf-crawler-ui/` to access the ManifoldCF user interface which exposes the following main functions:

- **List Output Connections**: This provides a list of all the recipients of the extracted content. It is configured to store content in the `manifoldcf` Solr core.

- **List Authority Connections**: This translates user credentials to a list of security tokens. You can test that our GenreAuthority is functioning by calling the API at `http://localhost:8345/mcf-authority-service/ UserACLs?username=paul@example.com` and verifying you receive a list of genre access tokens starting with the letter p.

- **List Repository Connections**: This is the only repository of content we have is the CSV file of author/genre information. The other repositories, such as RSS feeds or SharePoint sites would be listed here. When you create a repository, you associate a connector and the Authority you are going to use, in our case, GenreAuthority.

- **List All Jobs**: This lists all the combinations of input repository and output Solrs.

- **Status and Job Management**: This very useful screen allows you to stop, start, abort, and pause the jobs you have scheduled, and provide a basic summary of the number of documents that have been found in the repository as well as those processed in Solr.

Go ahead and choose the **Status** and **Job Management** screen and trigger the indexing job. Click on **Refresh** a couple of times, and you will see the artist's content being indexed into Solr. To see the various genres being used as access tokens, browse to:

```
http://localhost:8983/solr/manifoldcf/select?q=*:*&facet=true&face
t.field=allow_token_document&rows=0.
```

At the time of writing, neither ManifoldCF nor Solr have a component that hooked ManifoldCF-based permissions directly into Solr. However, based on the code from the *ManifoldCF in Action* manuscript, available at http://code.google.com/p/ manifoldcfinaction/, you can easily add a Search Component to your request handler. Add the following code to solrconfig.xml:

```
<requestHandler name="standard" class="solr.SearchHandler"
                default="true">
  <arr name="components">
    <str>manifoldcf</str>
  </arr>
</requestHandler>

<searchComponent name="manifoldcf" class="org.apache.manifoldcf.
                examples.ManifoldCFSecurityFilter">
  <str name="AUTHENTICATED_USER_NAME">username</str>
</searchComponent>
```

You are now ready to perform your first query! Do a search for *Chris*, specifying your username as paul@example.com and you should see only *pop* and *punk* music artists being returned!

```
http://localhost:8983/solr/manifoldcf/select?q=Chris&username=paul
@example.com
```

Change the username parameter to courtney@example.com and Chris Cagle, *country* singer should be returned! As documents are added/removed from the CSV file, ManifoldCF will notice the changes and reindex the updated content.

Document-level security

A frequent requirement for search engines is to maintain document-level security. While a public search engine may expose all documents to all users, many intranet-oriented search engines maintain information that it is accessible to only a subset of users. Historically, the solution to maintaining document-level security has been a roll-your-own with the most common approaches being listed here:

1. Hopefully your requirements allow you to enrich your indexed document with access tokens that can be searched for using a filter query based on the current user's access tokens. For a simplistic example, to allow only documents marked as accessible to the marketing department, or unclassified, you might add this parameter: fq=group_label:(marketing_department OR UNCLASSIFIED) to your query. However, there will be syncing challenges if the authorization lists per document are managed elsewhere. ManifoldCF helps with that and uses this general approach to document security.

2. Write a custom Solr post-filter QParser. This isn't too hard to work correctly but it's fundamentally difficult to scale when an external service must be consulted. This is because it operates on every document the search matches, not just the top X results.

3. Separate from Solr, implement a postprocessing filter on the document result set that removes documents that the user shouldn't see. This approach is convenient because you can just wrap your calls to Solr with your own proprietary security model. However, this approach is often flawed, particularly when faceting is used, since the facet counts can't be based on the access control rules.

Summary

As you've seen, Solr offers a plethora of integration options, from its ability to customize its output using the various query response writers, to clients for specific languages, to frameworks that enable powerful frontends for both indexing content as well as providing a jump start in developing the search user interface. The simplicity of using HTTP GET to request actions to be performed by Solr and responding with simple documents makes it very straightforward to integrate Solr-based search into your applications regardless of what your preferred development environment is.

Don't forget to explore all the integration options available for your favorite language, framework, or other needs at `http://wiki.apache.org/solr/SolrEcosystem`.

In the next chapter, we are going to look at how to scale Solr to meet the growing demand by covering approaches for scaling an individual Solr server as well as scaling out by leveraging multiple Solr servers working cooperatively.

10
Scaling Solr

You've deployed Solr, and the world is beating a path to your door, leading to a sharp increase in the number of queries being issued, and meanwhile you've indexed tenfold the amount of information you originally expected. You discover that Solr is taking longer to respond to queries and index new content. When this happens, it's time to start looking at what configuration changes you can make to Solr to support more load. We'll look at a series of changes/optimizations that you can make, starting with the simplest changes that give the most bang for your buck to more complex changes that require thorough analysis of the impact of the system changes.

In this chapter, we will cover the following topics:

- Tuning complex systems
- Testing Solr performance with SolrMeter
- Optimizing a single Solr server – scale up
- Configuring Solr for near real-time search
- Moving to multiple Solr servers (scale wide with SolrCloud)

In a hurry?

If you flipped to this chapter because you need to speed up Solr queries, look at the *Solr caching* section. If you have lots of data, or want near real-time search, then jump down to SolrCloud in the Scale Wide section.

Tuning complex systems is hard

Tuning any complex system, whether it's a database, a message queuing system, or the deep dark internals of an operating system, is something of a black art. Researchers and vendors have spent decades figuring out how to measure the performance of systems and coming up with approaches for maximizing the performance of those systems. For some systems that have been around for decades, such as databases, you can just search online for *tuning tips for X database* and find explicit rules that suggest what you need to do to gain performance. However, even with those well-researched systems, it still can be a matter of trial and error.

In order to measure the impact of your changes, you should look at a couple of metrics and optimize for these three parameters:

- **Transactions Per Second (TPS)**: In the Solr world, how many search queries and document updates are you able to perform per second? You can get a sense of that by using the **Plugins / Stats** page and looking at the `avgTimePerRequest` and `avgRequestsPerSecond` parameters of your request handlers.

- **CPU usage**: This is used to quickly gain a sense of the CPU usage of Solr using JConsole. You can also use OS-specific tools such as **PerfMon** (Windows) and **top** (Unix) to monitor your Java processes, which can be helpful if you have a number of services running on the same box that are competing for resources (not recommended for maximum scaling).

- **Memory usage**: When tuning for memory management, you are looking to ensure that the amount of memory allocated to Solr doesn't constantly grow. While it's okay for the memory consumption to go up a bit, letting it grow unconstrained eventually means you will receive out-of-memory errors! As a result, you need to have balanced increases in memory consumption with significant increases in TPS. You can use JConsole to keep an eye on memory usage.

In order to get a sense of what the **Steady State** for your application is, you can gather the statistics by using the SolrMeter load testing tool to put your Solr deployment under load. We'll discuss in the next section how to build a load testing script with SolrMeter that accurately mirrors your real-world interactions with Solr. This effort will give you a tool that can be run repeatedly and allows more of an apple-to-apple comparison of the impact of the changes to your configuration.

Solr's architecture has benefited from its heritage as the search engine developed in-house from 2004 to 2006 to power CNET.com, a site that, at the time of writing, is ranked 86th for traffic by Alexa.com. Solr, out-of-the-box, is already very performant, with extensive effort spent by the community to ensure that there are minimal bottlenecks. Additional tuning will trade-off increases in search performance at the expense of disk index size, indexing speed, and/or memory requirements (and vice versa). The approaches are as follows:

- **Scale up**: This is the optimization of a single instance of Solr, which looks at caching and memory configuration. Run Solr on a dedicated server (no virtualization) with very fast CPUs and SSD drives with lots of RAM if you can afford it. In the scale up approach, you are trying to maximize what you can get out of a single server.

- **Scale horizontally**: This looks at moving to multiple Solr servers using SolrCloud. If your queries run quickly with an acceptable avgTimePerRequest, but have too many incoming requests, then replicate your complete index across multiple Solr nodes. If your queries take too long to complete due to the complexity or size of the index, then use sharding to share the load of processing a single query across multiple sharded Solr servers.

Use SolrMeter to test Solr performance

One of the biggest challenges when conducting performance testing is to know when you've accomplished your goals. SolrMeter, available at http://code.google.com/p/solrmeter/, makes it very easy to test your Solr configuration. When performance testing Solr, you are typically tweaking configuration values such as cache sizes and query parameters in response to two ongoing activities: the pace of the documents being indexed into Solr, and the pace of the queries being issued to Solr. SolrMeter makes it very easy to control the pace of these two activities through a simple GUI tool. SolrMeter brings together both basic load testing functionality with some visualization and analytics of your Solr instance. A typical example is looking at your cache rates. While you can use the Solr Admin **Plugins / Stats** page to pull back these results, you are only seeing a snapshot in time.

In the following screenshot, you can see a visualization of the `queryResultCache` over time:

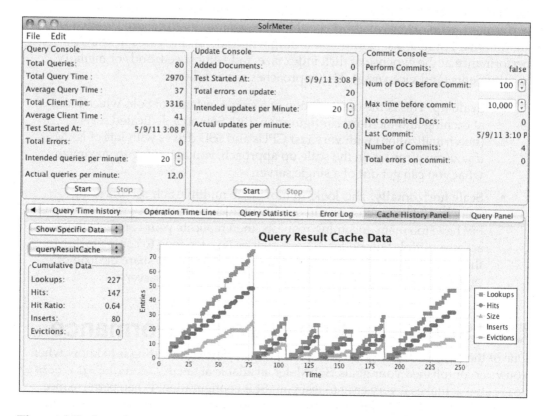

The middle four slopes were created because I began the **Update Console** 75 seconds after starting to index new data. You can easily see the impact of commits on the caches. This type of visualization can help you go beyond just using the default caching configurations.

Start SolrMeter with the embedded configuration for the `mbartists` core by running from `./examples/10/solrmeter`:

```
>>java –Dsolrmeter.configurationFile=./mbartists.smc.xml-jar
solrmeter-0.2.0-jar-with-dependencies_3_1_4_0.jar
```

`mbartists.smc.xml` specifies to SolrMeter which data files to use to power the queries to be made and the data to be indexed. SolrMeter takes in separate data files to randomly build combinations of queries with filters, faceting, and updates applied.

If you are already using Solr and logging the queries, then you should instead provide an `externalQueries.txt` file that has the full set of query parameters:

```
q="Maxtor Corp"+OR+Belkin&rows=5&fq=inStock:true&
facet=true&facet.field=price
```

Just extract the entire line after the ? character logged by the GET requests in the Solr log. This is great for repeating the same set of queries, so you are doing A/B testing as you are tweaking the various settings. SolrMeter also supports exporting the query time and a histogram of the query time in the CSV format to make your own graphs.

You can also use SolrMeter to place a "base" load on a Solr, and then use other testing tools that offer more scripting or analytics options to ensure that what works just fine when Solr isn't under load continues to meet expectations when Solr is under load, for example, you might want to set up 60 updates per minute and 300 queries per minute as a base load. Using SolrMeter, you can quickly set this scenario up, and then use another tool like JMeter that drives your frontend search user interface to ensure your application meets your expected SLA when Solr is under load. Alternatively, you can easily change settings, such as cache configurations or faceting settings, and see the impact that these changes have on performance. Finally, SolrMeter now runs as a command-line application, so you can use it as the heart of automated performance tests.

I like to build my list of queries for load testing by extracting a day's worth of queries from the existing search engine log or the HTTP web server log files. This gives me a realistic set of data, so I am tuning to what my users actually search for, not what I *think* they are searching for! SolrMeter can be used for this.

Optimizing a single Solr server – scale up

There are a large number of different options that Solr gives you for enhancing the performance of a specific Solr instance, and for most of these options, deciding to modify them depends on the specific performance result you are trying to tune for. This section is structured from the most generally useful optimizations to more specific optimizations.

Configuring JVM settings to improve memory usage

Solr runs inside a **Java Virtual Machine (JVM)**, an environment that abstracts your Java-based application from the underlying operating system. JVM performance improves with every release, so use the latest version. There are many different parameters that you can tune the JVM for. However, most of them are "black magic", and changing them from the defaults can quickly cause problems if you don't know what you're doing. Additionally, the folks who write the JVMs spend a lot of time coming up with sophisticated algorithms that mean the JVM will usually tune itself better than you can. However, there is a fairly simple configuration change that most Java server applications benefit from (not just Solr), which is to set the initial and maximum heap memory allocated to the JVM to the same value and to specify that you are running a server application, so the JVM can tune its optimization strategy for a long running process:

```
java( )-Xms2G -Xmx2G -server -jar start.jar
```

Of course, the question now is how much memory should be allocated to the Java heap. If you specify too little, then you run the risk of getting an `OutOfMemoryException`. If you specify the largest practical value, which is the actual memory you have, less some for the operating system and other processes, this is a suboptimal configuration too. Operating systems make use of available memory as a cache for disk access, and Solr searches benefit substantially from this, while indexing does not, especially since Solr 4.0 was released. I recommend measuring how much heap you need by picking some high value, then running a full battery of representative queries against Solr so that all its caches get filled, then using JConsole to perform a full garbage collection. At that point, you can see how much memory it's using. With that figure, provide some breathing room of 20 percent.

 With 8 GB of RAM available, I typically set Solr to use 4 GB. I don't go above 6 or 8 GB without a very good reason because the impact of garbage collection starts to be very appreciable. Add `-XX:+PrintGC ApplicationStoppedTime` to your startup to see GC pause.

The ultimate figure is of course highly dependent on the size of your Solr caches and other aspects of the Solr configuration; therefore, *tuning the heap size should be one of the later steps.*

 Jump forward to *Chapter 11, Deployment,* for a discussion about enabling JMX to work with JConsole.

Using MMapDirectoryFactory to leverage additional virtual memory

If you have plenty of virtual memory relative to your index size, then using memory-mapped I/O via `MMapDirectoryFactory` should be faster than `StandardDirectoryFactory` for interacting with the filesystem on 64-bit JVMs. This is set via the `<directoryFactory />` tag in `solrconfig.xml`, and is chosen by default on 64-bit Solaris and Linux JVMs. The memory used is outside of the Java heap, so you do not need to modify any JVM startup options. This is one of the reasons that even if you have 32 or 64 GB of memory, your Solr instance may only be set to use 8 GB.

Enabling downstream HTTP caching to reduce load

Solr has great support for using HTTP caching headers to enable downstream HTTP software to cache results. Frequently, you may have the same search being issued over and over, even though the results are always the same. Placing an intermediate caching server, such as Squid, in front of Solr should reduce the load on Solr and potentially reduce Solr's internal "query cache" requirements, thus, freeing up more RAM. When a request uses certain caching headers, Solr can then indicate whether the content has changed by either sending back an HTTP 200 status code if it has, or a *304 Not Modified* code when the content hasn't changed since the last time the request asked for it.

In order to specify that you want Solr to do HTTP caching, you need to configure the `<httpCaching/>` stanza in `solrconfig.xml`. By default, Solr is configured to never return a 304 code, instead it always returns a 200 response (a normal non-cached response) with the full body of the results. In `./examples/configsets/mbtype/solrconfig.xml`, uncomment the "production" `httpCaching` stanza and restart Solr:

```
<httpCachinglastModifiedFrom="openTime"
    etagSeed="SolrMusicBrainz" never304="false">
  <cacheControl>max-age=43200, must-revalidate</cacheControl>
</httpCaching>
```

We have specified that sending back 304 messages is okay. We have also specified in `cacheControl` that the max time to store responses is 43,200 seconds, which is half a day. We've also specified through `must-revalidate` that any *shared cache*, such as a Squid proxy, needs to check back with Solr to see whether anything has changed, even checking to see whether the `max-age` has expired, which acts as an extra check.

During development, leave never304="true" to ensure that you are always looking at the results of fresh queries and aren't misled by looking at cached results, unless you are using eTags and the browser properly honors them.

By running curl with the mbartists core, we can see additional cache-related information in the header. For your typing convenience, these curl commands are available in ./examples/10/http_cache_commands.txt:

```
>>curl -v "http://localhost:8983/solr/mbartists
/mb_artists?q=Smashing+Pumpkins"
< HTTP/1.1 200 OK
< Cache-Control: max-age=43200, must-revalidate
< Expires: Tue, 08 Oct 2013 05:42:20 GMT
< Last-Modified: Mon, 07 Oct 2013 17:42:14 GMT
<ETag: "NDgwMDAwMDAwMDAwMDAwMFNvbHJNdXNpY0JyYWlueg=="
```

So, let's look at what we get back if you pass a last modified header specifying that we have downloaded the content after the previously returned last modified time:

```
>>curl -v -z "Mon, 07 Oct 2013 17:42:15 GMT"
   http://localhost:8983/solr/mbartists/mb_artists?q=Smashing+Pumpkins
* About to connect() to localhost port 8983 (#0)
*    Trying ::1... connected
* Connected to localhost (::1) port 8983 (#0)
> GET /solr/mbartists/select/?q=Smashing+Pumpkins HTTP/1.1
> Host: localhost:8983
> Accept: */*
>If-Modified-Since: Mon, 07 Oct 2013 17:42:14 GMT
>
< HTTP/1.1 304 Not Modified
< Cache-Control: max-age=43200
< Expires: Tue, 08 Oct 2013 05:45:23 GMT
< Last-Modified: Mon, 07 Oct 2013 17:42:14 GMT
<ETag: "NDgwMDAwMDAwMDAwMDAwMFNvbHJNdXNpY0JyYWlueg=="
```

Specifying an If-Modified-Since time just one second after the Last-Modified time means that Solr gives us back a 304 Not Modified code and doesn't have to execute the search nor send a large response to the client, leading to a faster response time and less load on the server.

Entity tags are a newer method that are more robust and flexible than using the `Last-Modified` date. An `ETag` is a string that identifies a specific version of a component. In the case of Solr, they are generated by combining the current version of the index with the `etagSeed` value. Every time the index is modified, the current `ETag` value will change. If we add the fake artist "The Eric Band" to the `mbartists` index, and then run our previous query, we'll see that the `ETag` has changed because the version of the Solr index has changed:

```
>>curl 'http://localhost:8983/solr/mbartists/update?commit=true' -H
  "Content-Type: text/xml" --data-binary '<add><doc><field name=
  "a_name">The Eric Band</field><field name="id">Fake:99999
  </field><field name="type">Artist</field></doc></add>'

>>curl -v -z "Tue, 03 May 2011 09:36:36 GMT GMT"
  http://localhost:8983/solr/mbartists/select/?q=Smashing+Pumpkins
>
< HTTP/1.1 304 Not Modified
< Cache-Control: max-age=43200
<Expires: Sat, 07 May 2011 02:17:02 GMT
<Last-Modified: Fri, 06 May 2011 14:16:55 GMTGMT
<ETag: "NTMyMzQwMzhmNDgwMDAwMFNvbHJNdXNpY0JyYWluueg=="
< Server: Jetty(6.1.3)
```

To take advantage of the HTTP protocol level caching supplied by Solr, you need to make sure your client respects the caching directives returned by Solr. Two very popular caches that understand `ETags` are Varnish (`http://www.varnish-cache.org`) and Squid (`http://www.squid-cache.org`).

 Remember, the fastest query possible from Solr's perspective is the query that it doesn't have to make!

Solr caching

Caching is a key part of what makes Solr fast and scalable, and the proper configuration of caches is a common topic on the `solr-user` mailing list! Solr uses multiple in-memory caches. The caches are associated with individual **Index Searchers**, which represent a snapshot view of the data. Following a commit, new index searchers are opened and then auto-warmed. **Auto-warming** is when the cached queries of the former searcher are rerun to populate the new searcher. Following auto-warming, predefined searches are run as configured in `solrconfig.xml`. Put some representative queries in the `newSearcher` and `firstSearcher` listeners, particularly for queries that need sorting on fields. Once complete, the new searcher will begin servicing new incoming requests.

Each auto-warming query and predefined search increases the commit time, so make sure those searches are actually increasing the cache hit ratio and don't over do it!

There are a number of different caches configured in `solrconfig.xml`, which are as follows:

- **filterCache**: This stores unordered lists of documents that match a query. It is primarily used for storing filter queries (the `fq` parameter) for reuse, but it's also used in faceting under certain circumstances. It is arguably the most important cache. The filter cache can optionally be used for queries (the `q` parameter) that are not score-sorted if `useFilterForSortedQuery` is enabled in `solrconfig.xml`. However, unless testing reveals performance gains, it is best left disabled — the default setting.

- **queryResultCache**: This stores ordered lists of document IDs from searches. The order is defined by any sorting parameters passed. This cache should be large enough to store the results of the most common searches, which you can identify by looking at your server logs. This cache doesn't use much memory, as only the ID of the documents is stored in the cache. The `queryResultWindowSize` setting allows you to preload document IDs into the cache if you expect users to request documents that fall within the ordered list. So, if a user asks for products 20 through 29, then there is a good chance they will next look for 30 through 39. If the `queryResultWindowSize` is `50`, then the initial request will cache the first 50 document IDs. When the user asks for 30 through 39, they will retrieve the cached data and won't have to access the Lucene indexes.

- **documentCache**: This caches field values that have been defined in `schema.xml` as being stored, so that Solr doesn't have to go back to the filesystem to retrieve the stored values. Fields are stored by default.

 The documented wisdom on sizing this cache is to be larger than the *max results * max concurrent queries* being executed by Solr to prevent documents from being re-fetched during a query. As this cache contains the fields being stored, it can grow large very quickly.

These caches are all configured the same way, which is explained as follows:

- **class**: This specifies the cache implementation Java class name. Solr comes with LRUCache, FastLRUCache, and LFUCache. The current wisdom is that for caches that don't have a high hit ratio, and, therefore, have more churn use LRUCache, because the cache is evicting content frequently. If you have a high hit ratio, then the benefits of FastLRUCache kick in because it doesn't require a separate thread for managing the removal of unused items. You want a high hit ratio to maximize FastLRUCache because storing data is slower as the calling thread is responsible for making sure that the cache hasn't grown too large.

- **size**: This defines the maximum items that the cache can support and is mostly dependent on how much RAM is available to the JVM.

- **autowarmCount**: This specifies how many items should be copied from an old search to a new one during the auto-warming process. Set the number too high and you slow down commits; set it too low and the new searches following those commits won't gain the benefits of the previously cached data. Look at the warmupTime statistic on Solr's admin screen to see how long the warm up takes. There are some other options too, such as initialSize, acceptableSize, minSize, showItems, and cleanupThread specific to FastLRUCache, but specifying these are uncommon. There is a wealth of specific information available on the wiki at http://wiki.apache.org/solr/SolrCaching that covers this topic.

Tuning caches

Monitoring the **Plugins / Stats** admin page for caches, you can get a sense of how large you need to make your caches. If the hit ratio for your caches is low, then it may be that they aren't caching enough to be useful. However, if you find that the caches have a significant number of evictions, then it implies that they are filling up too quickly and need to be made larger. Caches can be increased in size as long as Solr has sufficient RAM to operate in.

> If your hit ratio for a cache is very low, then you should consider shrinking its size, and perhaps turning it off altogether by commenting out the cache configuration sections in solrconfig.xml. This will reduce the memory footprint and may help improve performance by removing the overhead of checking the caches and auto-warming the caches during commits.

Indexing performance

There are several aspects of Solr tuning that increase indexing performance. We'll start with optimizing the schema, then look at sending data to Solr in bulk, and then finish with Lucene's merge factor and optimization.

Designing the schema

Good schema design is probably one of the most important things you can do to enhance the scalability of Solr. You should refer to *Chapter 2, Schema Design*, for a refresher on many of the design questions that are inextricably tied to scalability. The easiest schema issue to look at for maximizing scalability is, "Are you storing the minimum information you need to meet the needs of your users?" There are a number of attributes in your schema field definitions, which inform us about what is being indexed and are discussed here:

- `indexed`: Some fields are purely there to be returned in search results — not to be searched (used in a query like q or fq). For such fields, set `indexed="false"`. If the field is not needed for search but is needed for faceting or a variety of other features, then see the last bullet, `docValues`, instead.

- `stored`: Storing field values in the index simplifies and speeds up search results because results need not be cross-referenced and retrieved from original sources. It is also required for features such as highlighting. However, storing field values will obviously increase the index size and indexing time. A quick way to see what fields are stored is to do a simple search with `fl=*` as a parameter; the fields in the result are the stored fields. You should only store fields that you actually display in your search results or need for debugging purposes. It is likely that your index has some data repeated but indexed differently for specialized indexing purposes such as faceting or sorting — only one of those, if any, needs to be stored.

- `docValues`: If a field is sorted, faceted, or used in a function query, grouping, collapsing, or stats, then you should usually set `docValues="true"`. Those features require either indexed or docValues, but `docValues` is ideal. So-called `"DocValues"` data reduces Java heap memory requirements by memory mapping field data for certain features, and reduces commit latency, making it almost a necessity for real-time search.

> If you need faster indexing, see if you can reduce the text analysis you perform in `schema.xml` to just what you need, for example, if you are certain the input is plain ASCII text, then don't bother mapping accented characters to ASCII equivalents.

Sending data to Solr in bulk

Indexing documents into Solr is often a major bottleneck due to the volume of data that needs to be indexed initially compared to the pace of ongoing updates. The best way to speed up indexing is to index documents in batches. Solr supports sending multiple documents in a single add operation, and this will lead to a drastic speedup in performance.

However, as the size of your individual documents increase, performance may start to decrease. A reasonable rule of thumb is doing document add operations in batches of 10 for large documents, and in batches of 100 for small documents.

To see the impact of batching, I indexed some data using the script `examples/10/batch/simple_test.rb` and documented the time it took. Take a look at the following table:

Scenario	Time
Single process adding documents one at a time	24m13.391s
Single process adding documents in batches of 100	5m43.492s
Single process adding documents in batches of 500	5m51.322s

You can see the impact that moving from sending one document at a time to a batch of 100 had an almost five-fold reduction in time. However, after a certain point, increasing the batch size doesn't decrease the overall time, instead, it may increase it.

SolrJ can load data the fastest

The fastest client approach to load data into Solr is SolrJ's `ConcurrentUpdateSolrServer` Java class. It places documents to be added into a queue that is consumed by multiple threads that each have a separate HTTP connection to Solr. Furthermore, it uses the compact javabin format. Due to the asynchronous nature of its use, the `ConcurrentUpdateSolrServer.handleError()` method must be extended to implement a callback to respond to errors. Also, with this client, you needn't add documents in batches, as it will only waste memory.

Disabling unique key checking

By default, if you specify a **uniqueKey** for your schema, when indexing content, Solr checks the uniqueness of the document being indexed so that you don't end up with multiple documents sharing the same primary key. If you know you have unique keys and don't have those documents in the index when doing a bulk load of data, then you can disable this check. For an update request in any format supported by Solr, add `overwrite=false` as a request parameter in the URL.

Index optimization and mergeFactor settings

When you add a document to Lucene, they get added to an in-memory write buffer that has a limited size—see `ramBufferSizeMB` in `solrconfig.xml`. When it gets full or if a commit happens (to include gracefully shutting down Solr), the buffer is flushed into a new Lucene **segment** on disk. A segment comprises about 11 files or so, and it's read-only. Deleted documents get flagged as such but aren't actually purged right away. As the number of segments increase, Lucene periodically *merges* them together into larger segments, which purges deleted documents as a side effect too. A key setting controlling this is the `mergeFactor` in `solrconfig.xml`, which is basically how many segments get merged into one at once.

 Check out this great blog post (with illustrated video) at `http://blog.mikemccandless.com/2011/02/ visualizing-lucenes-segment-merges.html` by Mike McCandless, the author of *Lucene in Action*, that visualizes what happens during segment merging. This really helped me understand the behavior of Solr during commits.

The rule of thumb is that the more static your content is (that is, the less frequent you need to commit data), the lower the merge factor you want. If your content is changing frequently, or if you have a lot of content to index, then a higher merge factor allows for faster indexing throughput at the expense of search performance. So, if you have infrequent index updates, then a low merge factor of 2 will have fewer segments, which leads to faster searching. However, if you expect to have large indexes, significantly above 10 GB, then having a higher merge factor like 20 will help with the indexing time, but then dial it back once you are done with bulk indexing.

After indexing a lot of documents (or perhaps at off-peak hours), it's sometimes beneficial to issue an **optimize** command. Optimize forces the merging of Lucene's segments down to one (or whatever the optional `maxSegments` parameter is), which increases search performance, and it also purges wasted space from deleted documents.

 You can see the number of segments on the **Overview** screen's **Statistics** section. You can also issue an optimize from this screen.

Optimizing your index is no longer quite as important as it used to be, and indeed the optimize command might eventually be renamed to `forceMerge` to make it less attractive to invoke by unsuspecting users. Optimization consumes significant CPU, temporary disk space, disk I/O, and will mean index replication must replicate larger segments, *so it's not something to invoke often*. If you do optimize, consider setting `maxSegments` as a trade-off.

> Consider having two strategies for indexing your content—the first strategy that is used during bulk loads that minimizes commits and merging to allow for the highest indexing throughput possible, and then a second strategy used during day-to-day routine operations that indexes documents and commits as needed to make them visible, and does some merging to keep the segment count in-check (via either a low `mergeFactor` or optimize).

Enhancing faceting performance

There are a few items to look at when ensuring that faceting performs well. First of all, faceting and filtering (the `fq` parameter) go hand-in-hand, thus, monitoring the filter cache to ensure that it is adequately sized. The filter cache is used for faceting itself as well. In particular, any `facet.query` or `facet.range` based facets will store an entry for each facet count returned. You should ensure that the resulting facets are as reusable as possible from query to query. For example, it's probably not a good idea to have direct user input involved in either a `facet.query` or in `fq` because of the variability. As for dates, try to use fixed intervals that don't change often or round off NOW relative dates to a chunkier interval (for example, NOW/DAY instead of just NOW). For text faceting (for example, `facet.field`), the `filterCache` is not used unless you explicitly set `facet.method` to enum. You should do this when the total number of distinct values in the field is somewhat small, say less than 50. Finally, you should add representative faceting queries to `firstSearcher` in `solrconfig.xml` so that when Solr executes its first user query, the relevant caches are already warmed up.

Using term vectors

A **term vector** is a list of terms resulting from the text analysis of a field's value. It optionally contains the term frequency, document frequency, and numerical offset into the text. Without them, the same information can be derived at runtime but that's slower. While disabled by default, enabling term vectors for a field in `schema.xml` enhances:

- MoreLikeThis queries, assuming that the field is referenced in `mlt.fl` and the input document is a reference to an existing document (that is not externally passed in).

- By highlighting search results with the standard or FastVector highlighter

By enabling term vectors for a field increases the index size and indexing time, and isn't required to perform MoreLikeThis queries or highlight search results; however, typically, if you are using these features, then the enhanced performance gained is worth the longer indexing time and greater index size.

Improving phrase search performance

For indexes reaching a million documents or more, phrase searches can be slow. If you are using the automatic phrase boosting features of the DisMax query parser (excellent for relevancy), then more phrase queries are occurring than you may be aware of. What slows down phrase searches are the presence of terms in the phrase that show up in a lot of documents. In order to ameliorate this problem, particularly common and uninteresting words such as "the" can be filtered out through a stop filter. But this thwarts searches for a phrase such as "to be or not to be" and prevents disambiguation in other cases where these words, despite being common, are significant. Besides, as the size of the index grows, this is just a band-aid for performance as there are plenty of other words that shouldn't be considered for filtering out, yet are common.

Shingling (sometimes called word-grams) is a clever solution to this problem, which combines pairs of consecutive terms into one so-called shingle. The original terms still get indexed, but only the shingles are used in phrase queries. Shingles naturally have a very low frequency relative to single words. Consider the text "The quick brown fox jumped over the lazy dog". The use of shingling in a typical configuration would yield the indexed terms (shingles) "the quick", "quick brown", "brown fox", "fox jumped", "jumped over", "over the", "the lazy", and "lazy dog" in addition to all of the original nine terms. Since so many more terms are indexed, naturally there is a commensurate increase in indexing time and resulting index size. **Common-grams** is a more selective variation of shingling that only shingles when one of the consecutive words is in a configured list. Given the preceding sentence using an English stop word list, the indexed terms would be "the quick", "over the", "the lazy", and the original nine terms.

 As a side benefit, these techniques also improve search relevancy since the TF and IDF factors are using coarser units (the shingles) than the individual terms.

In our MusicBrainz dataset, there are nearly seven million tracks, and that is a lot! These track names are ripe for either shingling or common-grams. Despite the high document count, the documents are small and so the actual index is only a couple gigabytes. Both the approaches are quite plausibly appropriate given different trade-offs. Here is a variation of the MusicBrainz title field called `title_commonGrams`:

```
<fieldType name="title_commonGrams" class="solr.TextField"
    positionIncrementGap="100"">
  <analyzer type="index">
    <tokenizer class="solr.StandardTokenizerFactory"/>
    <filter class="solr.LowerCaseFilterFactory"/>
    <filter class="solr.EnglishMinimalStemFilterFactory"/>
    <filter class="solr.CommonGramsFilterFactory"
            words="commongrams.txt" ignoreCase="true"/>"/>
  </analyzer>
  <analyzer type="query">
    <tokenizer class="solr.StandardTokenizerFactory"/>
    <filter class="solr.LowerCaseFilterFactory"/>
    <filter class="solr.EnglishMinimalStemFilterFactory"/>
    <filter class="solr.CommonGramsQueryFilterFactory"
            words="commongrams.txt" ignoreCase="true""/>
  </analyzer>
</fieldType>
```

 Notice that the filter's class name varies from index to query time, which is very unusual.

To come up with a list of common words for common-grams, use stop words and add some of the **Top Terms** list in Solr's schema browser as a guide for the field in question. You could try a more sophisticated methodology, but this is a start. Shingle filters go in the same position, but they are configured a little differently:

```
<!-- index time ...-->
<filter class="solr.ShingleFilterFactory"
  maxShingleSize="2" outputUnigrams="true"/>
<!-- query time -->
<filter class="solr.ShingleFilterFactory"
  maxShingleSize="2" outputUnigrams="false"
  outputUnigramsIfNoShingles="true"/>
```

You might choose to save additional index space and search performance by adding a stop filter after shingling or common-grams for typical stop-words so long as they don't need to be searchable by themselves. This wasn't done here for MusicBrainz song titles since we didn't feel it was worth it on name data.

Evaluating the search performance improvement of shingling proved to be tricky for the limited time I gave it. Some rough (nonscientific) testing showed that a search for *Hand in my Pocket* against the shingled field versus the nonshingled field was two to three times faster. I've seen very compelling search performance numbers using common-grams from others online, but I didn't evaluate it.

Shingling and common-grams increase phrase search performance at the expense of indexing speed and disk use. In the following table, I present the relative cost of these two techniques on the track name field in MusicBrainz compared to the cost of doing typical text analysis. These percentages may look high and might scare you away, but remember that these are based purely on one aspect (the index portion) of one field. The overall index time and disk use didn't change dramatically, not even with shingling. You should try it on your data to see the effects.

	Indexing time increase %	Disk space increase %
Common-grams	220%	25%
Shingling	450%	110%

The use of either is recommended for most applications

Given that shingling takes over five times as long and uses twice as much disk space, it makes more sense on small-to-medium scale indexes, where phrase boosting is used to improve relevancy. Common-grams is a relative bargain for all other applications.

Configuring Solr for near real-time search

Real-time search is the ability to search for content immediately after adding/ updating it. A typical scenario is that a user is performing some sort of add/update action on content, then the system is able to process the change fast enough so that if the user then searches for that immediately, they will always be able to see the latest changes applied. **Near real-time search** (often abbreviated to NRT) allows for a larger time window—most would say less than 5 seconds. This time window, however big or small it is, is also known as the **index latency**. Solr 4's commits are faster than before, and it has a new even faster soft commit ability. As a result, all apps can have NRT search, and with some tuning, some can commit so fast that you can reasonably say you have real-time search!

Here are a series of tips to consider in your quest for the holy grail of real-time search with Solr:

- Use soft commits with `autoCommit`! Solr's default example configuration ships this way; the only thing you need to do is supply a `commitWithin` time (perhaps 1 or 2 seconds) on the commits you issue from a client, which will trigger a soft commit sometime within that window. Ensure that your window is large enough for how long a soft commit takes. Test this simply by using `softCommit=true` in your URL to update Solr. The indexing chapter has some more information on the subject. The `autoCommit` window in `solrconfig.xml` should be somewhere between 15 seconds and a minute or so.

- If your query load is high enough that you need replicas, you should use SolrCloud and definitely not the old master/slave replication setup. Near real-time search at scale is one of SolrCloud's main features.

- Minimize warming, which hugely affects how long commits, especially soft ones, take. Reduce the `autowarmCount` of your caches and reduce the amount of work your queries do in the `newSearcher` listener. Keep those queries to their essentials—a query that uses sorting, faceting, and function queries on applicable fields.

- Use docValues on any field that you sort on, facet on, or some other features. This was explained earlier in this chapter.

- Follow any previous guidance on performance tuning, especially schema-related advice to minimize indexing time.

- Use SSD disks if you can afford it. Definitely avoid virtualization.

- Spread the documents over more shards so that the shards are smaller, which will query faster. In striving for NRT search, many configuration choices slow down searches, and so, smaller shards help balance those effects.

- Consider reducing the ratio of Solr shards on a machine per number of CPU cores so that more machine resources are available for the frequent commit rate and warming activity.

Use SolrCloud to go big – scale wide

Once you've optimized Solr running on a single server, and reached the point of diminishing returns for optimizing further, the next step is to shard your single index over multiple Solr nodes, and then share the querying load over many Solr nodes. The ability to scale wide is a hallmark of modern scalable Internet systems, and Solr shares this.

Arguably the biggest feature in Solr 4, **SolrCloud** provides a self-managing cluster of Solr servers (also known as *nodes*) to meet your scaling and near real-time search demands. SolrCloud is conceptually quite simple, and setting it up to test is fairly straightforward. The challenge typically is keeping all of the moving pieces in sync over time as your data set grows and you add and remove nodes.

> **What about master/slave replication?**
>
> In the past years, our data volumes were small enough that we could store all our data in a single index, and use a master/slave replication process to create many copies of our index to deal with query volume, at the cost of introducing more latency to the update process. SolrCloud, however, deals with the twin problems of massive data volumes that require sharding to support them, and minimizing latency to support near real-time search.

SolrCloud uses Apache **ZooKeeper** to keep your nodes coordinated and to host most of the configuration files needed by Solr and your collections. ZooKeeper is not unique to Solr; other projects such as Apache Hadoop and Kafka use it too. ZooKeeper is responsible for sharing the configuration information and, critically, the state of the cluster's nodes. SolrCloud uses that state to intelligently route index and search requests around the cluster. ZooKeeper is a compact piece of server software installed on a few of the hosts in your cluster, although you can use an embedded version that ships with Solr for development. You don't want to use embedded ZooKeeper in production because if you take down a Solr node that is running ZooKeeper, then you might also paralyze your SolrCloud cluster if the number of ZooKeeper nodes falls below a **quorum**. See more about ZooKeeper in *Chapter 11, Deployment*.

> Handling failover automatically is a huge benefit of SolrCloud, particularly as the node count increases.

This new way of managing Solr clusters comes with some new and modified terminology. Let's take a look at the terms you'll need to understand.

SolrCloud glossary

The first step in learning SolrCloud is understanding the subtle changes to the definition of terms we've used with Solr in the past. For example, cores and shards were often treated as interchangeable in simple Solr installations. In SolrCloud, they live on two separate tiers of the architecture; one represents a logical concept while the other represents a physical container for data.

We've broken down our SolrCloud terms by layer. Collections and shards comprise the logical layer. The physical layer contains the implementation details that make the logical layer possible such as cores, leaders, replicas, and clusters.

Logical layout	
collection	This is a logical container for a set of documents. They share the same schema and configuration. If a collection is large enough to warrant it, it is further divided into multiple shards.
shard	This is a logical slice of a collection. There may be one or more shards for each collection. A shard has one or more physical Solr cores assigned to the shard that are replicas of each other for durability and for handling higher load for the shard. The replicas for a shard are generally distributed across multiple nodes / machines.
Physical layer	
core, replica	A core is a replica of a shard of a collection, it's an index with all of the documents assigned to that shard and so do the other cores/replicas assigned to the same shard. In SolrCloud, all cores are assigned to a shard and thus a collection. And unlike a core before SolrCloud, the configuration is in ZooKeeper linked via the collection; it's *not* read from the filesystem.
leader	This is a replica designated to additionally be responsible for managing new or updated documents. Exactly one of the replicas for the shard always has this designation. When new or updated documents are submitted to a replica, it is forwarded to the leader if that replica doesn't have that role. The leader then propagates the document to all replicas. SolrCloud manages assigning and changing leadership roles among the cores; *you generally don't have to concern yourself with who is the leader.*
node	This is a single running Solr Java process in SolrCloud mode. Solr is in SolrCloud mode by virtue of configuring the ZooKeeper information at startup (for example, -DzkHost=...). Typically, you'll have one node running on each server, but this isn't always true for bigger hardware.
cluster	This is a group of nodes configured with the same ZooKeeper information. A cluster hosts document collections.

Now, let's look at a diagram of how these various components map to each other:

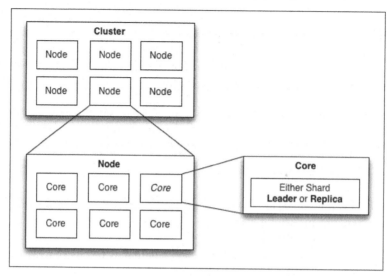

Physical tier of SolrCloud

Launching Solr in SolrCloud mode

We can leverage the techniques covered in *Chapter 11, Deployment,* to host SolrCloud but we'll also need to include a few arguments to Java, as well as planning a strategy for running ZooKeeper.

At minimum the zkHost system property will need to be included and should contain a list of ZooKeeper URIs separated with a semicolon. These URIs will almost always include the port that ZooKeeper is running on. The root key for this specific cluster is sometimes included as well when a ZooKeeper instance is shared by multiple SolrClouds.

Here's an example of launching Solr from a command prompt with two ZooKeeper hosts named zk1.example.com and zk2.example.com:

```
>> java -DzkHost=zk1.example.com:2181;zk2.example.com:2181 …
```

 In Solr 5, and optionally in Solr 4.10, you will instead do this:
```
bin/solr -z zk1.example.com:2181;zk2.example.com:2181
```

Note that this command will throw an error if none of the ZooKeeper hosts listed here are alive and responding to requests, or if you haven't created a configuration for your collection in ZooKeeper already.

The simplest way around these requirements is passing the `bootstrap_conf` and `zkRun` parameters. Note that neither of these are recommended for a production cluster. The `zkRun` parameter causes Solr to start an embedded instance of ZooKeeper and the `bootstrap_conf` parameter requires that the node have its own copy of the configuration files for the collection. These options might be useful for a trivial or learning implementation, but might interfere with availability and manageability for all but the smallest clusters.

As a general rule, keep your Solr startup parameters for each node as simple as possible. Anything that can be managed by the collections API or ZooKeeper (both discussed later) should *not* be included in the launch config for individual nodes. A good node configuration might just include the `zkHost` parameter and any required JVM tuning settings. Most SolrCloud tutorials outside of this book will have you clearly violating our advice, but we recommend sticking to this, even when getting started. Otherwise, it confuses collection configuration with Solr startup—things that should have nothing to do with each other.

Managing collections and configurations

"Apache ZooKeeper is a centralized network service for maintaining configuration information, naming, providing distributed synchronization, and providing group services.", as defined on ZooKeeper's website. A simpler way to understand it, as seen by a developer is, that it appears as *a distributed in-memory filesystem*. It was designed specifically to help manage the data about a distributed application, and to be clustered and highly available in the face of inevitable failures. The index data does *not* go in ZooKeeper.

SolrCloud uses ZooKeeper as a system of record for the cluster state, for centralized configuration, and to coordinate leader election.

As mentioned earlier, we don't want to rely on the `bootstrap_conf` option when we are launching nodes. So the first thing we need to do with ZooKeeper is upload the configuration for one of our collections. The SolrCloud documentation includes a great example of how to create a configuration. We'll include it here for convenience.

This next set of examples is based on the all-in-one SolrCloud script in `./examples/10/start-musicbrainz-solrcloud.sh`. When you run the script it will:

1. Download the Solr distribution from the book website.

2. Unpack it and copy it multiple times, once for each node you want to start up.

3. Load, using the following command line, the `mbtypes` general purpose configuration into ZooKeeper:

```
>> java -classpath example/solr-webapp/WEB-INF/lib/*
org.apache.solr.cloud.ZkCLI -cmd upconfig -zkhost
localhost:2181 -confdir configsets/mbtype/conf -confname
mbtypes -solrhome example/solr
```

 In Solr 5, replace everything before `-cmd` with a bash script reference to `server/scripts/cloud-scripts/zkcli.sh`.

4. Start up multiple separate Solr processes. The first one runs on port 8983, the subsequent ones start on port 8985,8986, and so on.

Eventually, you will want to update the configuration files in SolrCloud. We recommended keeping these files in some type of source control system such as Git or SVN; that way anyone can check them out and make adjustments. Once changes have been made, they will need to be posted back to ZooKeeper using the same `upconfig` command we saw earlier.

If you'd like finer control, you can post individual files or even arbitrary data to be treated like a configuration file as well as deleting, linking, and even bootstrapping multiple configuration sets. See the Solr *Command Line Utilities* documentation at `https://cwiki.apache.org/confluence/display/solr/Command+Line+Utilities` for specifics.

Stand up SolrCloud for our MusicBrainz artists index

So let's start up SolrCloud for our MusicBrainz dataset that we have played with in previous chapters. We've provided an example script that downloads Solr, unpacks it, and runs as many servers as you want. I recommend 2 to 4 nodes on a typical multicore laptop.

Under `/examples/10`, run the script to stand up your SolrCloud nodes:

```
>>./start-musicbrainz-solrcloud.sh 2 2
```

Refresh the **Admin Cloud Graph** view and you will have something like the following diagram:

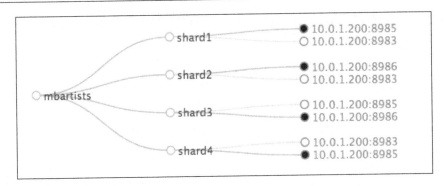

The script takes two parameters, the number of nodes you want and the number of shards for your default index, called `collection1`. This script is heavily influenced by the `/cloud-dev` scripts that are in the Solr source tree, a resource worth looking at.

Once the script has downloaded Solr and fired up the various Solr nodes, pull up the Cloud admin panel, and you will see the default **collection1** created. As part of the script, it loaded the `mbtype` configuration files into ZooKeeper. You can see them listed under `/configs` in the Tree view. Inspect the shell script to see the exact command we used to upload the configuration files to ZooKeeper.

To monitor the progress of the various nodes, you can easily tail the logs:

```
>> tail -f solrcloud-working-dir/example*/example*.log
```

To create the collections, just call the collections API:

```
>> curl 'http://localhost:8983/solr/admin/collections?action=CREATE&
name=mbartists&numShards=2&replicationFactor=1&maxShardsPerNode=2&col
lection.configName=mbtypes'
```

Once the command finishes, refresh the cloud view in the Solr admin. Play with the `numShards`, `replicationFactor`, and `maxShardsPerNode` settings, to visually get a sense of how SolrCloud distributes shards. Go big, try `numShards` of 8, `replicationFactor` of 4, and `maxShardsPerNode` of 30 to see the possibilities of SolrCloud.

Once you have the configuration you want, back up to `/examples` and reindex the MusicBrainz data:

```
>> ant index:mbartists
```

In my experiments, even running all the nodes on my local laptop, the time to index the `mbartists` dataset dropped by 25 percent due to the sharding of the dataset over multiple processes compared to not using SolrCloud.

Choosing the replication factor and number of shards

When you create a collection, you specify the degree to which its documents are replicated (copied) and sharded (divided) using the `replicationFactor` and `numShards` parameters, respectively.

The number of shards tells SolrCloud how many different logical slices the documents are to be divided into. Each additional shard improves indexing performance and usually increases query performance. Each search will internally be a distributed search among the shards. If a collection has too many shards, there will be diminishing returns due to coordinating and merging so many requests.

One way to think about the number of shards versus the replication factor is to imagine you are ordering a set of encyclopedias to share with your family. In this example, we'll say each volume in the encyclopedia set is a shard containing a number of articles (that is, Solr documents). We'll assume one volume per letter in the alphabet, so `numShards=26`. This keeps each volume small enough that it's easy to read and we don't need to "scale up" our desk or bookshelf. And for our first illustrated example, we'll use a `replicationFactor` of 1 — just one copy of the data. In SolrCloud terms, each physical volume is the only replica (also known as core) for its shard since the `replicationFactor` is 1. If I want to read or "update" the entry for Antelope, I'll need the "A" volume.

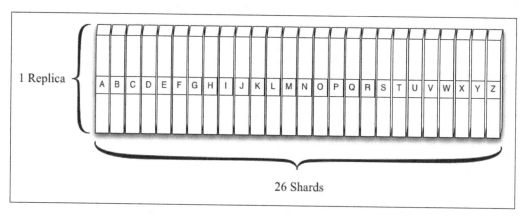

If we were buying encyclopedias for a local library, we might find that the volume of requests was high enough that people were lingering by the shelves waiting for a volume to become free (note that Solr isn't going to queue the requests but replicas will slow down if overwhelmed with concurrent load). Assuming we have plenty of room on our shelves, we could order two more sets of the same encyclopedia; now we have a numShards of 26 and a replicationFactor of 3. Even more importantly, this means if one of the replicas were to become corrupt or if a library patron loses a copy, the library now has other copies and it can replicate them when needed. We have **durability** now.

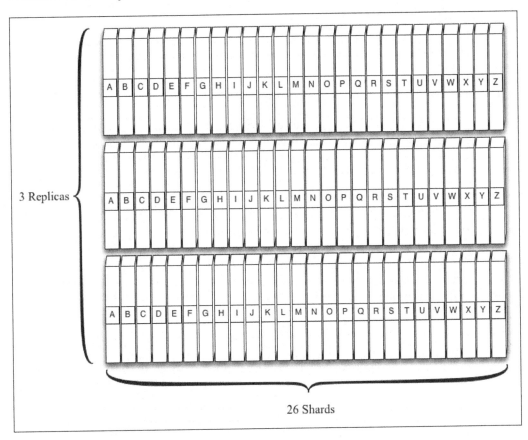

Creating and deleting collections

Collections are managed using the collections or core admin APIs — RESTful APIs invoked via simple URLs. This is a big difference compared to pre-SolrCloud approaches in which you usually pre-position cores where Solr expects to see them or refer to them in `solr.xml`. Just send a request to the collections API on *any* node in our cluster, and SolrCloud will manage that change across all the nodes.

Assuming you have started a SolrCloud cluster using `./examples/10/start-musicbrainz-solrcloud.sh`, then to add a new collection named `musicbrainz` with data split into 4 shards, each with 2 replicas (8 cores total), we run:

```
>> curl 'http://localhost:8983/solr/admin/collections?action=CREATE
&name=musicbrainz&numShards=4&replicationFactor=2&collection.configNa
me=mbtype'
```

A few other parameters the CREATE action accepts are as follows:

- `collection.configName`: This allows you to specify which named configuration to use for the collection if it doesn't have the same name as the collection. The configuration must be uploaded into ZooKeeper before creating the collection.

- `createNodeSet`: This takes a comma-separated list of nodes, and limits the new collection to only those nodes. It lets you deploy a collection on a subset of SolrCloud nodes. It becomes more important if you are deploying many collections on a single SolrCloud cluster, and want to make sure you are controlling the distribution of load across the cluster. SolrCloud doesn't know which nodes are heavily taxed and which are not, or which nodes are on the same rack when it provisions replicas, but you can tell it where to provision them.

- `maxShardsPerNode`: This sets the maximum number of shards that a node supporting this collection can contain. The preceding example needs 8 cores across the cluster, which will default to requiring 8 nodes. Setting `maxShardsPerNode=4` will only require 2 nodes; each one will be hosting 4 replicas. SolrCloud is smart enough to divide the shards evenly among the available nodes to reduce single-points-of-failure when that's possible. Furthermore, you should generally have at least as many CPU cores on these nodes as there are Solr cores since each search will result in one concurrent search thread per shard.

Replicas and leaders

Each shard has one or more copies of itself in the cloud at any point in time. SolrCloud will strive to make sure that each shard has a number of replicas at least equal to the replicationFactor specified for that collection. Any of these replicas can be used during a search query.

Update queries must be handled by a leader for that shard. Leaders are responsible for managing changes to all the documents in their shard. At any given time there will be exactly one leader for a given shard. Imagine, if, instead of encyclopedias like in the precious example, we were keeping a list of all the telephone numbers for people in a company. We could break that list up by department (sharding) as well as making a copy for each person in that department (replication). Then we appoint one person in each department to keep the list up to date and send updated copies to everyone else. If they leave, we appoint someone else to the job. The leaders in SolrCloud operate the same way. For each shard/department in our analogy, we appoint one node to process all changes for that shard. If that node disappears, a new leader is elected.

 A new leader is elected when the existing leader disconnects from ZooKeeper.

If a client issues an update to any node in the cloud, it will be automatically routed to the leader for the appropriate shard. While this is very efficient, it's worth noting that the SolrJ library takes an even more efficient route. The CloudSolrServer SolrJ client connects to the ZooKeeper server, and is able to always send requests to the node that's acting as the leader for a shard without routing through a middleman.

Document routing

Out of the box, SolrCloud uses a hash of the document's IDs to determine which shard it belongs to. Most of the time, this is fine; it will result in equal shard sizing. However, sometimes you need more control over which documents are colocated. For example, if you are using result grouping (also known as field collapsing), then all documents in the same group must be on the same shard. And to optimize search over huge collections, you can sometimes identify useful groupings of the documents that you keep together on certain shards such that when you do a search you can sometimes specify a subset of the shards to search. There are a couple options that SolrCloud has beyond the default.

The primary option is enabled by what's called the `compositeId` router—the default mechanism a collection uses. Basically, you tell SolrCloud what piece of data in a document it should take the hash on to determine which shard it belongs to. There are two ways to do this: by configuring the collection to use a certain field via `router.field` (a parameter supplied when creating the collection) which has this data, or by prefixing the ID with the data using `!` as a delimiter. If you use `router.field`, then the specified field is now required. As an example, if we had a set of products in our search index that could be easily categorized into departments, we could use the department instead of the ID to control sharding without adjusting the configuration. Provide the department as a prefix to the document ID, separated by `!` (for example, `"housewares!12345"`). Later, if we know a user is searching within that specific department, we can limit the query to only that shard by passing `_route_=housewares` in our search query. This can greatly increase search speed on a large index, and in some cases may help improve relevancy precision.

```
>> curl http://localhost:8983/solr/collection1/select?
collection=collection1&_route_=housewares
```

The other option is to use the **implicit router**, otherwise known as **manual sharding**. It's used when the desired mapping of documents to shards doesn't match the preceding description. For example, what if all your data is time-stamped (like Twitter tweets or log data) and you only want to keep the last year of data on an on-going basis. The most efficient way to do this is to divide the past year into shards, perhaps by month, and then when a new month starts, you simply remove the oldest shard (month) and you add a new one. This is really fast since only one shard is being indexed to. To use the implicit router, you create the collection without specifying `numShards` (not very intuitive, ehh?). When in this mode, your indexing client is responsible for sending the document to the correct shard; Solr won't route it.

 The `compositeId` router is definitely the simplest to use, and it's harder to use shard splitting with the implicit router.

Shard splitting

As of Solr 4.3.1, you can split a shard into two smaller shards, even while indexing and searching—this is a very important feature. Over the life of a collection, you may need to split your shards to maintain search performance as the size of the index grows. If you customized how documents are routed, some specific shards may be larger or receive more traffic and thus might need to be split without necessarily splitting the others.

After SolrCloud finishes the split, the old shard will still exist but be in an inactive state, so you'll want to delete it afterwards. Sending the following command to any SolrCloud node will result in `shard1` being split and replaced with `shard1_0` and `shard1_1`:

```
>> curl 'http://localhost:8983/solr/admin/collections?
action=SPLITSHARD&collection=mbartists&shard=shard1'
```

Now check that it finished successfully. When it has, delete the original shard:

```
>> curl 'http://localhost:8983/solr/admin/collections?
action=DELETESHARD&collection=mbartists&shard=shard1'
```

Dealing with long running collection tasks

Added in Solr 4.8 is the ability to submit long running tasks in an asynchronous mode. For example, splitting a shard or creating a collection that is highly sharded and has many replicas may take a long time. To support this, just supply the `async` parameter with a unique ID that you want to refer the operation by. Let's create a collection asynchronously:

```
>> curl 'http://localhost:8983/solr/admin/collections?
action=CREATE&name=massive_sharding&numShards=6&replicationFactor=6&m
axShardsPerNode=40&collection.configName=mbtype&async=99'
```

The `async=99` parameter is determined by you, and needs to track this operation. The response will come back immediately, and then you can check the status by using a `REQUESTSTATUS` command:

```
>> curl 'http://localhost:8983/solr/admin/collections?
Action=REQUESTSTATUS&requestid=99'
```

Oddly enough, the parameter is called `async` when you create it, and `requestid` when you go back to look it up. It will give you status information; however, if the operation is failing, you might not get the same level of debugging. For example, if you try to create a collection with the same name as an existing collection, the `REQUESTSTATUS` command just tells you that the command failed.

To clear out the history of requests, call `REQUESTSTATUS` with a `requestid` of `-1`:

```
>> curl 'http://localhost:8983/solr/admin/collections?
Action=REQUESTSTATUS&requestid=-1'
```

Adding nodes

New nodes can be added to SolrCloud at anytime just by launching Solr and providing the zkHost parameter that points to your ZooKeeper ensemble:

```
>> java -DzkHost=zk1.example.com:2181
```

This new node will then become available to host replicas for any of the collections registered with ZooKeeper. You can then use the ADDREPLICA command to create new replicas that are hosted by the newly added node. To add a new node to our MusicBrainz cluster, run the script ./examples/10/add-musicbrainz-node.sh and pass in an unused port number for Jetty:

```
>>./add-musicbrainz-nodes.sh 8989
```

Then you can add more replicas using the following code:

```
>> curl 'http://localhost:8983/solr/admin/collections?
Action=ADDREPLICA&collection=mbartists&shard=shard2&node=10.0.1.200:8
989_solr'
```

Notice that the node name is a very specific pattern. It is the name that is assigned to it when the node joined ZooKeeper, and you can find it listed in the Cloud Tree view under /live_nodes. When you add a new replica, it will start, using replication under the covers, to copy all the data from the leader to the newly added replica. Refresh the Cloud Graph view and you will see the node go from Recovering to Active state.

Summary

Solr offers many knobs and levers for increasing performance; the biggest challenge can be figuring out which knobs and levers to use! Make sure you budget your time to try a number of approaches, and take a step-wise approach to trying different approaches out. From turning the simpler knobs for enhancing the performance of a single server, to pulling the big levers of scaling wide through using SolrCloud, performance and scalability with appropriate hardware are issues that can be solved fairly easily, and Solr provides almost linear scaling. The SolrCloud codebase has evolved quickly over the course of 4.x, so if you are on an older version, especially prior to 4.7.1, you will find many enhancements and stability fixes to encourage you to upgrade.

11
Deployment

Now that you have identified the information you want to make searchable, built the Solr schema to support your expected queries, and made the tweaks to the configuration you need, you're ready to deploy your Solr-based search platform into production. While the process of deployment may seem simple after all the effort you've gone through in development, it brings its own set of challenges. In this chapter, we'll look at the issues that come up when going from "Solr runs on my desktop" to "Solr is ready for the enterprise".

We'll cover the following topics in this chapter:

- Implementation methodology
- Installing Solr into a Servlet container
- Configuring logging
- A SearchHandler per search interface
- Solr cores, and the new admin features
- Setting up ZooKeeper for SolrCloud
- Monitoring Solr
- Securing Solr

Deployment methodology for Solr

There are a number of questions that you need to ask yourself in order to inform the development of a smooth deployment strategy for Solr. The deployment process should ideally be fully scripted and integrated into the existing **Configuration Management (CM)** process of your application.

Configuration Management is the task of tracking and controlling changes in the software. CM attempts to make the changes that occur in software knowable as it evolves to mitigate mistakes caused due to those changes.

Questions to ask

The list of questions that you'll want to answer to work in conjunction with your operations team includes:

- How similar is my deployment environment to my development and test environments? Can I project that if one Solr instance was enough to meet my load requirements in test, then it is also applicable to the load expected in production based on having similar physical hardware?

- Do I need multiple Solr servers to meet the projected load or for failover? If you do, look back at *Chapter 10, Scaling Solr*.

- Do I have an existing build tool such as Ant/MSBuild/Capistrano with which to integrate the deployment process? Even better, does my organization use a deployment tool such as Puppet or Chef that I can leverage?

- How will I import the initial data into Solr? Is this a one-time-only process that might take hours or days to perform and needs to be scheduled ahead of time? Is there a nightly process in the application that will perform this step? Can I trigger the load process from the deploy script?

- Have I changed the source code required to build Solr to meet my own needs? Do I need to version it in my own source control repository? Can I package my modifications to Solr as discrete components instead of changing the source of Solr and rebuilding?

- Do I have full access to the data in production, or do I have to coordinate with an operations team who are responsible for controlling access to production? If operations is performing the indexing tasks, are the steps required properly documented and automated?

- Have I defined acceptance tests for ensuring Solr is returning the appropriate results for a specific search before moving to production?

- What are the defined performance targets, such as requests per second, time to index data, time to perform query that Solr needs to meet? Are these documented as a **Service Level Agreement (SLA)**?

- Into what kind of servlet container (Tomcat, Jetty, or JBoss) will Solr be deployed? Does how I secure Solr change depending on the servlet container?

- What is my monitoring strategy for making sure Solr is performing properly? This isn't just about Solr's response time or error monitoring but critically includes the user queries. The single best tool for improving your search relevance is to look at your user queries. A reasonable user query that is returning zero results directly points to how you can improve your relevancy.

- Do I need to store index data directories separately from application code directories, for instance, on a separate hard drive? If I have small enough indexes to fit in RAM, can I use a memory-based filesystem? Can I use SSDs?

- What is my backup strategy for my indexes, if any? If the indexes can be rebuilt quickly from another data source, then backups may not be needed. However, if the indexes are the "Gold Master", such as from crawling the Web for data that can't be re-crawled, or the time to rebuild an index is too great, then frequent backups are crucial.

- Are any scripted administration tasks required, for example, performing index optimizations, old backups removal, deletion of stale data, or rebuilding spell check dictionaries?

- Am I better off with an externally hosted Solr capability? There are a number of companies that have launched SaaS offerings for Solr, from Acquia offering hosted Solr search specifically for Drupal websites to WebSolr providing a generic Solr hosting option.

Installing Solr into a Servlet container

Solr is deployed as a simple **WAR** (Web application archive) file that packages up the servlet, JavaScript files, code libraries, and all of the other bits that are required to run Solr. Therefore, Solr can be deployed into any Java EE Servlet container that meets the Servlet 2.4 specification, such as Apache Tomcat, JBoss, and GlassFish, as well as Jetty, which by default ships with Solr.

Differences between Servlet containers

The key thing to resolve when working with Solr and the various Servlet containers is that technically you are supposed to compile a single WAR file and deploy that into the Servlet container. It is the container's responsibility to figure out how to unpack the components that make up the WAR file and deploy them properly. For example, with Jetty, you place the WAR file in `/webapps`, but when you start Jetty, it unpacks the WAR file in `/work` as a subdirectory, with a somewhat cryptic name that looks something like `Jetty_0_0_0_0_8983_solr.war__solr__k1kf17`.

In contrast, with Apache Tomcat, you place the `solr.war` file into `/webapp`. When you either start up Tomcat, or Tomcat notices the new `.war` file, it unpacks it into `/webapp`. Therefore, you will have the original `/webapp/solr.war` and the newly unpacked (exploded) `/webapp/solr` version. The Servlet specification carefully defines what makes up a WAR file. However, it does not define exactly how to unpack and deploy the WAR files, so your specific steps will depend on the Servlet container you are using. For information specific to various servlet containers, see Solr's wiki at `http://wiki.apache.org/solr/SolrInstall`. If you are not strongly predisposed to choosing a particular Servlet container, then choose Jetty, which is a remarkably lightweight, stable, and fast Servlet container. It is what Solr is developed against, and is the least likely to give you problems. Note that, in Solr 5, the need for a servlet container to host Solr will be removed, and Solr will run in it's own process, like MySQL or any other server process does, using the installation and start scripts. For more information, refer to the following wiki pages: `https://cwiki.apache.org/confluence/display/solr/Taking+Solr+to+Production#TakingSolrto Production-ServiceInstallationScript` and `https://cwiki.apache.org/confluence/display/solr/Solr+Start+Script+Reference`.

Defining the solr.home property

Probably the biggest thing that trips up folks deploying into different containers is specifying the `solr.home` property. Solr stores all of its configuration information outside of the deployed webapp, separating the **data** part from the **code** part for running Solr. In the example app, while Solr is deployed and running from a subdirectory in `/work`, the `solr.home` directory is pointing to the top level `/solr` directory, where all of the data and configuration information is kept. You can think of `solr.home` as being analogous to where the data and configuration is stored for a relational database such as MySQL. You don't package your MySQL database as part of the WAR file, and nor do you package your Lucene indexes.

By default, Solr expects the `solr.home` directory to be a subdirectory called `/solr` in the current working directory as defined by the Servlet container. With both Jetty and Tomcat you can override that by passing in a JVM argument that is somewhat confusingly namespaced under the `solr` namespace as `solr.solr.home`:

```
-Dsolr.solr.home=/Users/epugh/solrbook/solr
```

Alternatively, you might find it easier to specify the `solr.home` property by appending it to the JAVA_OPTS system variable. On Unix systems, you would do the following:

```
>>export JAVA_OPTS=\"$JAVA_OPTS -
Dsolr.solr.home=/Users/epugh/solrbook/solr"
```

Alternatively, lastly, you might choose to use JNDI with Tomcat to specify the `solr.home` property as well as where the `solr.war` file is located. **JNDI (Java Naming and Directory Interface)** is a very powerful, if somewhat difficult to use, directory service that allows Java clients such as Tomcat to look up data and objects by name.

By configuring the stanza appropriately, we were able to load up the `solr.war` file and home directory from the example configuration shipped with Jetty using Tomcat instead. The following stanza went in the `/apache-tomcat-6-0.18/conf/Catalina/localhost` directory that we downloaded from `http://tomcat.apache.org`, in a file called `solr.xml`:

```
<Context docBase="/Users/epugh/solr_src/example/webapps/solr.war"
   debug="0" crossContext="true" >
<Environment name="solr/home" type="java.lang.String"
            value="/Users/epugh/solr_src/example/solr"
            override="true" />
</Context>
```

We had to create the `./Catalina/localhost` subdirectories manually.

> Note the somewhat confusing JNDI name for `solr.home` is `solr/home`. This is because JNDI is a tree structure, with the home variable being specified as a node of the Solr branch of the tree. By specifying multiple different context stanzas, you can deploy multiple separate Solr instances in a single Tomcat instance.

Configuring logging

Solr's logging facility provides a wealth of information, from basic performance statistics, to what queries are being run, to any exceptions encountered by Solr. The log files should be one of the first places you look when you want to investigate any issues with your Solr deployment. There are two types of logs:

- The HTTP server request style logs, which record the individual web requests made to Solr.

- The Solr application logging that uses SLF4J (Simple Logging Framework for Java, a logging façade), which uses the built-in Java JDK logging facility to log the internal operations of Solr.

HTTP server request access logs

The HTTP server request logs record the requests that come in and are defined by the Servlet container in which Solr is deployed. For example, the default configuration for managing the server logs in Jetty is defined in `jetty.xml`:

```
<Ref id="RequestLog">
  <Set name="requestLog">
    <New id="RequestLogImpl"
      class="org.mortbay.jetty.NCSARequestLog">
    <Arg><SystemProperty name="jetty.logs"
      default="./logs"/>/yyyy_mm_dd.request.log</Arg>
    <Set name="retainDays">90</Set>
    <Set name="append">true</Set>
    <Set name="extended">false</Set>
    <Set name="LogTimeZone">GMT</Set>
    </New>
  </Set>
</Ref>
```

The log directory is created in the subdirectory of the Jetty directory. If you have multiple drives and want to store your data separately from your application directory, then you can specify a different directory. Depending on how much traffic you get, you should adjust the number of days to preserve the log files.

We recommend you keep the log files for as long as possible by archiving them. The search request data in these files is some of the best data available to help you improve the relevancy of your search results. By using web analytics tools such as the open source AWStats package to parse your request logs, you can quickly visualize how often different queries are run, and what search terms are frequently being used. This leads to a better understanding of what your users are searching for.

Tailing the HTTP logs is one of the best ways to keep an eye on a deployed Solr. You'll see each request as it comes in and can gain a feel for what types of transactions are being performed, whether it is frequent indexing of new data, or different types of searches being performed. A pause in the logging will quickly highlight garbage collection issues!

The request time data will let you quickly see performance issues. Here is a sample of some requests being logged. You can see that the first request is a POST to the `/solr/update` URL from a browser running locally (`127.0.0.1`) with the date. The request was successful, with a 200 HTTP status code being recorded. The POST took 149 milliseconds. The second line shows a request for the admin page being made, which also was successful and took a slow 3,816 milliseconds, primarily because in Jetty, the JSP page is compiled the first time it is requested.

The last line shows a search for `dell` being made to the `/solr/select` URL.
You can see that up to 10 results were requested and that it was successfully
executed in 378 milliseconds.

On a faster machine with more memory and a properly "warmed" Solr cache,
you can expect a few tens of milliseconds result time. Unfortunately, you don't
get to see the number of results returned, as this log only records the request.

```
127.0.0.1 - - [25/02/2015:22:57:14 +0000] "POST /solr/update
HTTP/1.1" 200 149
127.0.0.1 - - [25/02/2015:22:57:33 +0000] "GET /solr/admin/
HTTP/1.1" 200 3816
127.0.0.1 - - [25/02/2015:22:57:33 +0000] "GET /solr/admin/
            solr-admin.css
        HTTP/1.1" 200 3846
127.0.0.1 - - [25/02/2015:22:57:33 +0000] "GET
            /solr/admin/favicon.ico
        HTTP/1.1" 200 1146
127.0.0.1 - - [25/02/2015:22:57:33 +0000] "GET /solr/admin/
            solr_small.png
        HTTP/1.1" 200 7926
127.0.0.1 - - [25/02/2015:22:57:33 +0000] "GET
            /solr/admin/favicon.ico
        HTTP/1.1" 200 1146
127.0.0.1 - - [25/02/2015:22:57:36 +0000] "GET
            /solr/select/?q=dell%0D%0A&version=2.2&
            start=0&rows=10&indent=on
        HTTP/1.1" 200 378
```

While you may not see things quite the same way Neo did in the movie *The Matrix*,
you will get a good gut feeling of how Solr is performing!

> AWStats is a full-featured open source request log file analyzer
> under the GPL license and is available from `http://awstats.`
> `sourceforge.net`.

Solr application logging

Logging events is a crucial part of any enterprise system. Veteran Java programmers
know that the history of Java and logging is complicated, resulting in a fragmented
landscape. However, logging in Solr has long been a fraught situation, with various
approaches to logging, from Java's built-in logging (also known as JDK logging) to
Log4J competing with each other.

As of Version 1.4, Solr standardized on using the **Simple Logging Facade for Java (SLF4J)** package, which logs to another target logging package selected at runtime instead of at compile time, but to do this, you have to change the logging JAR files inside the WAR file, a nonobvious process! So in Solr 4.3, all the logging files were removed from the Solr WAR file. Instead, you are to provide your own logging files for your chosen implementation. If you use the default Jetty-based Solr package, you'll see that the SLF4J, Log4J, and related jars are in ./lib/ext/. If you want to change what logging you use, change the jar files there, without repackaging Solr. There is more information on the wiki at https://wiki.apache.org/solr/SolrLogging; however, hopefully, logging is a solved topic for the Solr community from here on out. Logging has been, as Erik Hatcher in a post to the solr-dev mailing list memorably called it: a *JARmageddon*.

Configuring logging output

By default, Solr sends its logging messages to the standard error stream:

```
0    [main] INFO  org.eclipse.jetty.server.Server  - jetty-
8.1.10.v20130312
```

Obviously, in a production environment, Solr will be running as a service, and you will want the messages to be recorded to a log file instead. Here is an example of setting up logging to a file using JDK logging. Create a logging.properties file (an example is at examples/11/logging.properties) with the following content:

```
# Default global logging level:
.level = INFO

# Write to a file:
handlers = java.util.logging.ConsoleHandler,
java.util.logging.FileHandler

# Write log messages in human readable format:
java.util.logging.FileHandler.formatter =
java.util.logging.SimpleFormatter
java.util.logging.ConsoleHandler.formatter =
java.util.logging.SimpleFormatter

# Log to the logs subdirectory, with log files named solrxxx.log
java.util.logging.FileHandler.pattern = ./logs/solr_log-%g.log
java.util.logging.FileHandler.append = true
java.util.logging.FileHandler.count = 10
java.util.logging.FileHandler.limit = 10000000 #Roughly 10MB
```

When you start Solr, you need to pass the location of the `logging.properties` file:

```
>>java -Djava.util.logging.config.file=logging.properties -jar
    start.jar
```

By specifying two log handlers, you can send the output to the console as well as log files. The `FileHandler` logging is configured to create up to 10 separate logs, each with 10 MB of information. The log files are appended, so that you can restart Solr and not lose previous logging information. Note, if you are running Solr as a service, it is probably going to redirect the STDERR output from `ConsoleHandler` to a log file as well. In that case, you will want to remove `java.util.ConsoleHandler` from the list of handlers. Another option is to reduce how much is considered as output by specifying `java.util.logging.ConsoleHandler.level = WARNING`.

Jetty startup integration

Regardless of which logging solution you go with, you don't want to make the startup arguments for Solr more complex. You can leverage Jetty's configuration to specify the system properties during startup. Edit `jetty.xml` and add the following stanza to the outermost `<Configure id="Server" class="org.mortbay.jetty.Server"/>` element:

```
<Call class="java.lang.System" name="setProperty">
<Arg>log4j.configuration</Arg>
<Arg>file:/Users/epugh/log4j.properties</Arg>
</Call>
```

This is also how you can configure other system properties that you might pass in via -D parameters.

Managing log levels at runtime

Sometimes you need more information than you are typically logging to debug a specific issue, so Solr provides an admin interface to change the logging verbosity of the components in Solr.

While you can't change the overall setup of your logging strategy, such as the appenders or file rollover strategies at runtime, you can change the level of detail to log without restarting Solr. If you change a component like `org.apache.solr.core.SolrCore` to FINE level of logging, then make a search request to see more detailed information. One thing to remember is that these customizations are NOT retained through restarts of Solr. If you find that you are reapplying log configuration changes after every restart, then you should change your default logging setup to specify custom logging detail levels.

Even if you adjust the logging levels here to something more detailed, you probably still won't see the messages in the console. By default, `ConsoleHandler` has an INFO level threshold. You can lower it with this in your `logging.properties`: `java.util.logging.ConsoleHandler.level = FINE`.

One of the challenges with logging is that you need to log enough details to troubleshoot issues, but not so much that your log files become ridiculously large and you can't winnow through the information to find what you are looking for.

Tools have arisen to manage those log files and make actionable decisions on the information stored within. Splunk and Loggly are commercial options; however, recently, LucidWorks has paired LogStash for collecting logs, Kibana for visualization, and Solr for storing, and powering the interface has become available. You can download the tool, and the open source components, from `http://www.lucidworks.com/lucidworks-silk/`.

A RequestHandler per search interface

There are two questions to answer early on when configuring Solr and thinking about who the consumers of the search services are—"Are you providing generic search services that may be consumed by a variety of end user clients?" or "Are you providing search to a specific application?"

If you are providing generic search functionality to an unknown set of clients, then you might just have a single request handler handling search requests at `/solr/select`, which provides full access to the index. However, it is likely that Solr is powering interfaces for one or more applications that you know are going to make certain specific kinds of searches.

For example, say you have an e-commerce site that supports searching for products. In that case, you may want to only display products that are available for purchase. A specifically named request handler that always returns the stock products (using `appends`, as `fq` can be specified multiple times) and limits the rows to 50 (using `invariants`) would be appropriate:

```
<requestHandler name="/products" class="solr.SearchHandler" >
  <lst name="invariants">
    <int name="rows">50</int>
  </lst>
  <lst name="appends">
    <str name="fq">inStock:true</str>
```

```
    </lst>
  </requestHandler>
```

However, the administrators of the same site would want to be able to find all products, regardless of whether they are in stock or not. They would be using a different search interface and so you would provide a different request handler that returns all of the information available about your products:

```
<requestHandler name="/allproducts" class="solr.SearchHandler" />
```

Later on, if your site needs to change, or if the internal searching site changes, particularly with respect to tuning search relevancy, you can easily modify the appropriate request handler without impacting other applications interacting with Solr. In particular, if you have complex query parsing logic, you can hide much of that behind the request handler, so that your clients can work with a simpler query structure.

> You can always add new request handlers to meet new needs by requiring the qt request parameter to be passed in the query like this: /solr/select?qt=/allproducts. However, this doesn't look quite as clean as having specific URLs like /solr/allproducts. A fully named request handler can also have access to them controlled by the use of Servlet *security* (see the *Securing Solr from prying eyes* section later in this chapter).

Leveraging Solr cores

Recall from *Chapter 2, Schema Design*, that you can either put different types of data into a single index or use separate indexes. Up to this point, the only way you would know how to use separate indexes is to actually run multiple instances of Solr. However, adding another complete instance of Solr for each type of data you want to index is rather time consuming and unnecessary.

A Solr server instance supports multiple separate indexes (cores) to exist within a single Solr server instance as well as bringing features like hot core reloading and swapping that make administration easier. In fact, the MusicBrainz setup with this book has 6 cores. The core name immediately follows the /solr/ part and precedes the request handler (for example, /select). In SolrCloud mode, this spot is the collection name. In this URL, we search the mbartists core like this:

```
http://localhost:8983/solr/mbartists/select?q=dave%20matthews
```

Other than the introduction of the core name in the URL, you still perform all of your management tasks, searches, and updates in the same way as you always did in a single core setup.

Configuring solr.xml

Since Solr started supporting multiple cores, `solr.xml`, located in the `solr.home` directory has been how Solr would find all the cores. Starting in 4.4, Solr auto discovers cores as an alternative mechanism. At startup, Solr will look through all the subdirectories below `solr.home`, and in each subdirectory, no matter how many levels deep, if it finds a file named `core.properties`, then it knows it has found a directory with configuration information on a core to be loaded. The `core.properties` file only has to exist, it doesn't have to have any content, although it can contain core-specific configuration parameters. In Solr 5.0, `solr.xml` will no longer list cores; it will only contain properties related to running Solr such as SolrCloud-related properties. We have included the old style `solr.xml` in the example code in `./cores/solr_legacy.xml`; this will look familiar to folks who have used earlier versions of Solr. The `./cores/solr.xml` reflects the new approach. You might remember a property called `persistent="true"` in `solr.xml`, it has been removed as this file is now immutable.

Some of the configuration options are:

- `sharedLib="lib"`: This specifies the path to the `lib` directory containing shared JAR files for all the cores. On the other hand, if you have a core with its own specific JAR files, then you would place them in the `core/lib` directory. For example, the karaoke core uses Solr Cell (see *Chapter 4, Indexing Data*) for indexing rich content, so the JARs for parsing and extracting data from rich documents are located in `./examples/cores/karaoke/lib/`.

- `shareSchema`: This allows you to use a single in-memory representation of the schema for all the cores that use the same `instanceDir`. This will cut down on your memory use and startup time, especially in situations where you have many cores. I have seen Solr run with dozens of cores with no issues beyond increased startup time as each index is opened.

- `solrCloud`: This is a stanza of XML for configuring SolrCloud across all collections deployed in SolrCloud. There are a number of options such as `distribUpdateConnTimeout`, `distribUpdateSoTimeout`, `leaderVoteWait`, `leaderConflictResolveWait`, and `zkClientTimeout` that are all related to managing timeouts. In general, the defaults should be fine, but if your SolrCloud has many collections, is running on a slow network, or your nodes are on multiple networks, then you may need to increase the timeouts.

- `shardHandler`: This is a stanza that also deals with the HTTP layer and has options that expose the Apache HTTP Client library settings such as `socketTimeout` and `connTimeout` that you may need to change.

Each core is configured via a fairly obvious set of properties provided in `core.properties`. This file is mutable, and you should put your custom properties into it:

- `name`: This specifies the name of the core, and therefore what to put in the URL to access the core.

- `configSet`: This specifies the name of a shared configuration that you want to use for the core. See *Chapter 10, Scaling Solr* for more about using configuration sets.

- `instanceDir`: This specifies the path to the directory that contains the `conf` directory for the core, and `data` directory too, by default. A relative path is relative to `solr.home`. In a basic single-core setup, this is typically set to the same place as `solr.home`. In the preceding example, we have three cores using the same configuration directory, and two that have their own specific configuration directories.

- `dataDir`: This specifies where to store the indexes and any other supporting data, like spell check dictionaries. If you don't define it, then by default each core stores its information in the `<instanceDir>/data` directory.

- You can also provide your own properties just by defining them in the file, and then referencing them in your solr configuration.

Some of the most interesting properties in the `core.properties` file are the `loadOnStartup` and the `transient` properties. If you have a Solr node with hundreds or thousands of cores, for example, if you have one core per user interacting with the system, then you would only want to load the cores of the people who are actively using your system, otherwise, Solr will run out of memory. By default, `loadOnStartup` is true so that each core will load, but in this use case you would want it to be false, and only load the core when the user logs in. The inverse, setting the `transient` property to true allows Solr to start unloading cores if too many users are logged on at the same time. You must be wondering how to load the core in response to the user login action, check the RELOAD command (see the *Managing cores* section later in this chapter) that is part of the Solr Core Admin API.

Property substitution

Property substitution allows you to externalize configuration values, which can be very useful for customizing your Solr install with environmental specific values. For example, in production, you might want to store your indexes on a separate solid state drive, then you would specify it as a property: `dataDir="${ssd.dir}"`. You can also supply a default value to use if the property hasn't been set as well: `dataDir="${ssd.dir:/tmp/solr_data}"`. This property substitution works in `solr.xml`, `solrconfig.xml`, `schema.xml`, and DIH configuration files.

Properties can be defined in `core.properties` or as Java system properties. To set a Java system property, use the `-D` parameter like this: `-Dssd.dir=/Volumes/ssd`.

Include fragments of XML with XInclude

XInclude stands for **XML Inclusions** and is a W3C standard for merging a chunk of XML into another document. Solr has support for using XInclude tags in `solrconfig.xml` to incorporate a chunk of XML at load time.

In `./examples/cores/karaoke/conf/solrconfig.xml`, we have externalized the `<query/>` configuration into three flavors: a default query cache setup, a no caching setup, and a big query cache setup:

```
<xi:includehref="cores/karaoke/conf/${karaoke.xinclude.query}"
  parse="xml" xmlns:xi="http://www.w3.org/2001/XInclude">
  <xi:fallback>
    <xi:include href="cores/karaoke/conf/solrconfig-query-default.
      xml"/>
  </xi:fallback>
</xi:include>
```

The `${karaoke.xinclude.query}` property is defined in the core definition:

```
<core name="karaoke" instanceDir="karaoke"
  dataDir="../../cores_data/karaoke">
<property name="karaoke.xinclude.query"
  value="solrconfig-query-nocache.xml"/>
</core>
```

If the XML file defined by the `href` attribute isn't found, then the `xi:fallback` included file is returned. The fallback metaphor is primarily if you are including XML files that are loaded via HTTP and might not be available due to network issues.

Managing cores

While there isn't a nice GUI for managing Solr cores the way there is for some other options, the URLs you use to issue commands to Solr cores are very straightforward, and they can easily be integrated into other management applications. The response by default is XML, but you can also return results in JSON by appending `wt=json` to the command.

We'll cover a couple of the common commands using the example Solr setup in `./examples`. The individual URLs listed here are stored in plain text files in `./examples/11/` to make it easier to follow along in your own browser:

- STATUS: Getting the status of the current cores is done through `http://localhost:8983/solr/admin/cores?action=STATUS`. You can select the status of a specific core, such as `mbartists` through `http://localhost:8983/solr/admin/cores?action=STATUS&core=mbartists`. The STATUS command provides a nice summary of the various cores, and it is an easy way to monitor statistics showing the growth of your various cores.

- CREATE: You can generate a new core called `karaoke_test` based on the karaoke core, on the fly, using the CREATE command through `http://localhost:8983/solr/admin/cores?action=CREATE&name=karaoke_test&instanceDir=karaoke&config=solrconfig.xml&schema=schema.xml&dataDir=./examples/cores_data/karaoke_test`. If you create a new core that has the same name as an old core, then the existing core serves up requests until the new one is generated, and then the new one takes over.

- RENAME: Renaming a core can be useful when you have fixed names of cores in your client, and you want to make a core fit that name. To rename the `mbartists` core to the more explicit core name `music_brainz_artists`, use the URL `http://localhost:8983/solr/admin/cores?action=RENAME&core=mbartists&other=music_brainz_artists`. This naming change only happens in memory, as it doesn't update the filesystem paths for the index and configuration directories.

- SWAP: Swapping two cores is one of the key benefits of using Solr cores. Swapping allows you to have an offline "on deck" core that is fully populated with updated data. In a single fast-atomic operation, you can swap out the current live core that is servicing requests with your freshly populated "on deck" core. As it's an atomic operation, there isn't any chance of mixed data being sent to the client. As an example, we can swap the `mbtracks` core with the `mbreleases` core through `http://localhost:8983/solr/admin/cores?action=SWAP&core=mbreleases&other=mbtracks`. You can verify the swap occurred by going to the `mbtracks` admin page and verifying that Solr home is displayed as `cores/mbreleases/`.

- RELOAD: As you make minor changes to a core's configuration through `solrconfig.xml`, `schema.xml`, and supporting files you don't want to be stopping and starting Solr constantly. In an environment with even a couple of cores, it can take some tens of seconds to restart all the cores during which Solr is unavailable. By using the RELOAD command, you can trigger a reload of just one specific core without impacting the others. An example of this is if you use `synonyms.txt` for query time synonym expansion. If you modify it, you can just reload the affected core! A simple example for `mbartists` is `http://localhost:8983/solr/admin/cores?action=RELOAD&core=mbartists`.

- UNLOAD: Just like you would expect, the unload action allows you to remove an existing core from Solr. Currently running queries are completed, but no new queries are allowed. A simple example for `mbartists` is `http://localhost:8983/solr/admin/cores?action=UNLOAD&core=mbartists`.

- MERGEINDEXES: (For advanced users) The merge command allows you to merge one or more indexes into yet another core. This can be very useful if you've split data across multiple cores and now want to bring them together without re-indexing the source data all over again. It can also be used as the final step of an off-line indexing step in which index data is added (merged) into a live index. You need to issue commits to the individual indexes that are sources for data. After merging, issue another commit to make the searchers aware of the new data. This all happens at the Lucene index level on the filesystem, so functions such as deduplication that work through update request processors are not invoked. The full set of commands using curl is listed in `./11/MERGE_COMMAND.txt`.

Some uses of multiple cores

Solr's support of multiple cores in a single instance enables you to serve multiple indexes of data in a single Solr instance. Multiple cores also address some key needs for maintaining Solr in a production environment:

- **Rebuilding an index**: While Solr has a lot of features to handle, such as doing sparse updates to an index with minimal impact on performance, occasionally you need to bulk update significant amounts of your data. This invariably leads to performance issues, as your searchers are constantly being reopened. By supporting the ability to populate a separate index in a bulk fashion, you can optimize the offline index for updating content. Once the offline index has been fully populated, you can use the SWAP command to take the offline index and make it the live index.

- **Testing configuration changes**: Configuration changes can have very differing impacts depending on the type of data you have. If your production Solr has massive amounts of data, moving that to a test or development environment may not be possible. By using the CREATE and the MERGE commands, you can make a copy of a core and test it in relative isolation from the core being used by your end users. Use the RELOAD command to restart your test core to validate your changes. Once you are happy with your changes, you can either SWAP the cores or just reapply your changes to your live core and RELOAD it.

- **Merging separate indexes together**: You will find that over time you have more separate indexes than you need, and you want to merge them together. You can use the MERGEINDEXES command to merge two cores together into a third core. However, note that you need to do a commit on both cores and ensure that no new data is indexed while the merge is happening.

- **Renaming cores at runtime**: You can build multiple versions of the same basic core and control which one is accessed by your clients using the RENAME command to rename a core to match the URL the clients are connecting to.

You can learn more about Solr core related features at https://cwiki.apache. org/confluence/display/solr/Core+Admin and https://cwiki.apache.org/ confluence/display/solr/Core-Specific+Tools.

Setting up ZooKeeper for SolrCloud

ZooKeeper is the technology that keeps all the nodes in SolrCloud in sync, and in *Chapter 10, Scaling Solr,* we discussed how to leverage it. However, for convenience, we told Solr to run the ZooKeeper service internally (embedded, in-process) by passing the zkRun parameter to Solr on startup. While you could do that in production, you usually shouldn't because then you tie your ZooKeeper service to your Solr nodes. So imagine the scenario where you want to stop and restart Solr? Running embedded ZooKeeper means that you also take down one of your ZooKeeper nodes when you stop a Solr node. ZooKeeper has the concept of a **quorum** of servers that all host the exact same configuration file, and to have a valid quorum, at least half of the ZooKeeper processes must be functioning. If you have three Solr nodes running embedded ZooKeeper, and you restart two of the Solr nodes, you no longer have a quorum of 2 out of 3 servers, a situation called **split brain**, and your SolrCloud cluster goes down. Since your Solr nodes are much more volatile in nature than your ZooKeeper nodes, you hamstring the reliability of your ZooKeeper service.

Folks are often concerned when you spec out a set of servers for SolrCloud and mention that you need an additional three or five servers to run your ZooKeeper service on, beyond the servers hosting Solr. However, since ZooKeeper, in the context of providing configuration management to a cluster of SolrCloud servers, is pretty lightly used, and therefore doesn't generate much load. It has two tasks: store the configuration files for a Solr collection, including the locations of all the nodes making up each collection, and send messages to all the Solr nodes when the state changes for one of them like a node going up or down, or a new collection being defined. When a message about a state change is sent to Solr, then each Solr node queries back to ZooKeeper about the state change, and adjusts accordingly. That adjustment may be downloading a new synonyms.txt or a solrconfig.xml and restarting the core to load the new configuration.

Neither of these tasks requires extensive disk space, CPU, or memory, so it's very reasonable to run your ZooKeeper nodes on virtual machines. All the heavy work of indexing data, performing queries, is done on the Solr nodes, so they should be sized appropriately.

Installing ZooKeeper

Installing ZooKeeper by hand is pretty straightforward, though it's a great thing to automate with tools like Puppet since you have to repeat the same basic steps multiple times!

Solr pretty much keeps up with the latest ZooKeeper; check the release notes for your specific Solr download. Download the ZooKeeper package and unzip to a reasonable directory like /opt/ZooKeeper. In the unzipped directory, there will be a sample configuration file at ./conf/zoo_sample.cfg, copy it to zoo.cfg. Edit the file and add two parameters that point to where the ZooKeeper data and transaction logs are store. In very high performance situations, you might want dedicated disks for that, but in most cases, with SolrCloud, you can have both sets of data stored on the same disk. Also, provide a list of all the servers that are in the **ensemble** of ZooKeeper servers:

```
dataDir=/var/lib/zookeeperdata
dataLogDir=/var/log/zookeeper
# servers in the ensemble
server.1=zk1.mycompany.com:2888:3888
server.2=zk2.mycompany.com:2888:3888
server.3=zk3.mycompany.com:2888:3888
```

There is one odditiy in ZooKeeper in which you provide a magic file called `myid` that specifies the name of the server at the root of `dataDir`: `/var/lib/zookeeperdata/myid`. On `zk1.mycompany.com`, that would be the value 1, on `zk2.mycompany.com`, it would be 2, and so on. You can then start ZooKeeper by running the following code:

```
>> ./bin/zkServer.sh ../conf/start zoo.cfg
```

Repeat these steps on each server, changing the `myid` file.

Administering Data in ZooKeeper

There are two ways of interacting with ZooKeeper, one is the SolrCloud centric script called `zkcli.sh` that comes with Solr. Assuming you have a local SolrCloud running using `./examples/10/start-musicbrainz-solrcloud.sh`, navigate to `./examples/10/solrcloud-working-dir/example/scripts/cloud-scripts`. To list out the contents of the data in ZooKeeper, run the list command:

```
>> ./zkcli.sh -zkhost localhost:9983 -cmd list
```

You can upload a specific file using the `put` command or just push up, or pull down a complete set of configuration files using the `upconfig` or `downconfig` commands.

However, if you want to treat the ZooKeeper data as a simple Unix filesystem with commands such as `ls` or `rm`, then you need to use the command-line client that comes with ZooKeeper. To make things more confusing, it is called `zkCli.sh`, just one character case off of the Solr version called `zkcli.sh`.

```
>> ./zookeeper-3.4.6/bin/zkCli.sh -server 127.0.0.1:9983
```

Notice that we pass in the IP address and port of the ZooKeeper ensemble we want to connect to. You can now list out all the config files that belong to the `mbtypes` collection:

```
>> ls /configs/mbtypes
```

To see all the commands available for interacting with the data in ZooKeeper, run help:

```
>> help
```

Monitoring Solr performance

Ensuring that Solr is meeting the SLA expectations for performance is the goal of monitoring. Solr provides both RESTful and JMX hooks to allow you to integrate Solr into your enterprise monitoring platform.

 Don't have your own monitoring platform? There are two offerings, available from New Relic (http://newrelic.com) and Sematext (http://sematext.com/spm/) that provide a comprehensive monitoring solution. Both are cloud based (SaaS) and communicate via a small agent installed into Solr that provides a wealth of statistics and analysis about the JVM, as well as Solr specific metrics such as request response time and throughput, cache hit rate, and indexing performance.

Stats Admin interface

From the admin interface, when you click on the **Plugins / Stats** link, you get a list of all the plugins for Solr, and can drill down by plugin and get detailed information, including any custom components you develop! However, what isn't immediately obvious is that this information is actually being served up to the browser as JSON data that is consumed by the Admin page. This means, if you perform a GET request, you can return the data in whichever format you want, based on the wt parameter:

```
>>curl "http://localhost:8983/solr/mbartists/admin/mbeans?stats=true&
cat=CACHE&wt=xml&indent=true"
```

Open the downloaded file and you will see all the data as XML. The following is an excerpt of the statistics available for the cache that stores individual documents and the standard request handler, where the metrics you might want to monitor are highlighted:

```
<entry>
  <name>documentCache</name>
  <class>org.apache.solr.search.LRUCache</class>
  <version>1.0</version>
  <description>LRU Cache(maxSize=512,
    initialSize=512)</description>
  <stats>
    <stat name="lookups">3251</stat>
    <stat name="hits">3101</stat>
    <stat name="hitratio">0.95</stat>
```

```
        <stat name="inserts">160</stat>
        <stat name="evictions">0</stat>
        <stat name="size">160</stat>
        <stat name="warmupTime">0</stat>
        <stat name="cumulative_lookups">3251</stat>
        <stat name="cumulative_hits">3101</stat>
        <stat name="cumulative_hitratio">0.95</stat>
        <stat name="cumulative_inserts">150</stat>
        <stat name="cumulative_evictions">0</stat>
      </stats>
  </entry>
  <entry>
    <name>standard</name>
    <class>org.apache.solr.handler.component.SearchHandler</class>
    <version>$Revision: 1052938 $</version>
    <description>Search using components:
      org.apache.solr.handler.component.QueryComponent,
      org.apache.solr.handler.component.FacetComponent
    </description>
    <stats>
        <stat name="handlerStart">1298759020886</stat>
        <stat name="requests">359</stat>
        <stat name="errors">0</stat>
        <stat name="timeouts">0</stat>
        <stat name="totalTime">9122</stat>
        <stat name="avgTimePerRequest">25.409472</stat>
        <stat name="avgRequestsPerSecond">0.446995</stat>
    </stats>
  </entry>
```

While integrating into each monitoring system will be different, as an example, you can look at ./examples/11/check_solr.rb for a simple Ruby script that queries a core and checks whether the average hit ratio and the average time per request are above certain thresholds:

```
>> ./check_solr.rb -w 13 -c 20 -I mbartists
CRITICAL - Average Time per request more than 20 milliseconds old:
39.5
```

Monitoring Solr via JMX

Java Management Extensions (JMX) is a Java standard API for monitoring and managing applications and network services. Originally meant to help with server administration, it was added to J2SE Version 5. JMX-enabled applications and services expose information and available operations for resources such as **MBeans (Managed Bean)**. MBeans can be managed remotely by a wide variety of management consoles such as the JConsole GUI that comes with Java and the web-based JMX Console that comes with the JBoss application server. Here is a screenshot of a nice sawtooth pattern of memory usage that you want from Solr; as you can see, garbage collection kicks in on a regular basis:

Solr exposes information about its components through MBeans. However, actual management operations, such as re-indexing information, are not exposed through JMX. You can leverage JMX to monitor the status of Solr, such as finding out how many documents have been indexed. In large enterprise environments, the JMX standard simplifies integrating monitoring tasks into existing monitoring platforms.

> The information exposed via JMX Mbeans is now exposed as XML as well as other formats by appending a wt parameter: http://localhost:8983/solr/mbartists/admin/ mbeans?stats=true&wt=json. This is an easier way to quickly query for JMX information.

Starting Solr with JMX

In solrconfig.xml, the <jmx/> tag needs to be uncommented to enable JMX support. In order to actually start up with JMX, you need to provide some extra parameters to support remote connections, including the port to be connected to:

```
>>java -Dcom.sun.management.jmxremote -
Dcom.sun.management.jmxremote.port=3000 -
Dcom.sun.management.jmxremote.ssl=false -
Dcom.sun.management.jmxremote.authenticate=false -jar start.jar
```

However, this configuration is totally insecure. In a production environment, you would want to require usernames and passwords for access. For more information, please refer to the JMX documentation at http://java.sun.com/j2se/1.5.0/ docs/guide/management/agent.html#remote.

J2SE ships with JConsole, a GUI client for connecting to JMX servers. In order to start it, run the following command:

```
>> [JDK_HOME]/bin/jconsole
```

In order to connect to Solr, choose the **Remote** tab, and enter localhost for **Host or IP** and 3000 for **Port**. As we have started without requiring authentication, you do not need to enter a username and password.

For Solr, the key tabs to use in JConsole are **Memory** and **MBeans**. **Memory** provides a visual charting of the consumption of memory and can help you monitor low memory situations and when to start optimizing your indexes (as discussed in *Chapter 9, Integrating Solr*).

You can also monitor the various components of Solr by choosing the **MBeans** tab. In order to find out how many documents you've indexed, you would look at the `SolrIndexSearch` Mbean. Select **solr** from the tree listing on the left, and drill down to the `searcher` folder and select the `org.apache.solr.search.SolrIndexSearcher` component. You will see information such as the number of documents, and how many are marked deleted (it's the difference between `maxDocs` and `numDocs`). While you can pull this type of information out of the admin statistics web page, the JMX standard provides a much simpler method that can be easily integrated into other tools.

In order to save yourself typing in the extra startup parameters, see the previous *Jetty startup integration* section for how to add these JMX startup parameters, such as `-Dcom.sun.management.jmxremote` to your Jetty configuration.

Securing Solr from prying eyes

Solr, by default, comes completely open. Anyone can make search requests, anyone can upload documents, anyone can access the administration interface, and anyone can delete data. However, it isn't difficult to lock down Solr for use in any kind of environment. We can do this by making use of the standard practices that you would apply to any kind of web application or server software.

Limiting server access

The single biggest thing you can do to secure Solr is to lock down who has access to the server. Using standard firewall techniques, you can control what IP addresses are allowed to connect to the Solr through the 8983 port.

Unless you have very unusual needs, you won't expose Solr to the Internet directly; instead users will access Solr through some sort of web application, that in turn forwards requests to Solr, collects the results, and displays them to your users. By limiting the IP addresses that can connect to Solr to just those belonging to your web farm, you've ensured that random Internet users and internal users don't mess with Solr.

 If you lock down access via IP addresses, then don't forget that if you have external processes uploading content, you need to make sure those IP addresses are added.

Using IP addresses to control access is crude and basic; it doesn't help if someone is connecting to Solr from one of the valid IP addresses. Fortunately, Solr is just a WAR file deployed in a Servlet container, so you can use all of the capabilities of Servlet containers to control access. In order to limit access to /solr/update* and /solr/ admin/* in Jetty by requiring BASIC authentication from your users, you merely edit the web.xml in your Solr WAR adding the following stanza at the bottom:

```
<security-constraint>
  <web-resource-collection>
    <web-resource-name>Solr Admin</web-resource-name>
    <url-pattern>/admin/*</url-pattern>
  </web-resource-collection>
  <auth-constraint>
    <role-name>admin</role-name>
  </auth-constraint>
</security-constraint>
<security-constraint>
  <web-resource-collection>
    <web-resource-name>Solr Update</web-resource-name>
    <url-pattern>/update*</url-pattern>
  </web-resource-collection>
  <auth-constraint>
    <role-name>admin</role-name>
    <role-name>content_updater</role-name>
  </auth-constraint>
</security-constraint>

<login-config>
  <auth-method>BASIC</auth-method>
  <realm-name>Test Realm</realm-name>
</login-config>
```

This specifies that access to the /update* URLs is limited to anyone in the roles of admin or content_updater, although only admin users can access the /admin/* URLs. The realm-name is what ties the security constraints to the users configured in Jetty.

Customizing web.xml in Jetty

Sometimes cracking open a WAR file just to customize web.xml can be a pain. However, if you are a Jetty user, then you can put the changes into ./etc/webdefault.xml and Jetty will apply the changes to any WAR file deployed. This is a nice trick if you have just a single webapp in the Jetty container. See ./examples/ solr/etc/webdefault.xml and ./examples/solr/etc/ jetty.xml for example.

Edit the `jetty.xml` file and uncomment the `<Set name="UserRealms"/>` stanza so that it looks like the following:

```
<Set name="UserRealms">
    <Array type="org.mortbay.jetty.security.UserRealm">
        <Item>
            <New class="org.mortbay.jetty.security.HashUserRealm">
                <Set name="name">Solr Realm</Set>
                <Set name="config">
                    <SystemProperty name="jetty.home" default="."/>/etc/
                    realm.properties
                </Set>
            </New>
        </Item>
    </Array>
</Set>
```

The `./etc/realm.properties` file contains a list of users with their passwords and roles to which they belong. We've specified that the user named `administrator` has the roles of `content_updater` and `admin`, and therefore can access any `/update` and `/admin` URLs. However, the user `eric` can only access the `/update` URLs as shown in the following code:

```
administrator: $ecretpa$$word,content_updater,admin
eric: mypa$$word, content_updater
guest: guest,read-only
```

Adding authentication introduces an extra roadblock for automated scripts that need to interact with Solr to upload information. However, if you use BASIC authentication, then you can easily pass the username and password as part of the URL request. The only downside is that the password is being transmitted in cleartext, and you should wrap the entire request in SSL for maximum security:

```
http://USERNAME:PASSWORD@localhost:8080/solr/update
```

 Normally, you wouldn't want to store passwords in plain text on the server in a file such as `realm.properties` that isn't encrypted. More information is available at `http://docs.codehaus.org/display/JETTY/Realms`.

Put Solr behind a Proxy

Another approach to securing Solr is to lock it down via firewall rules and run a proxy that mediates access to the locked down Solr. If you specify that port 8983 isn't accessible to the public, but only accessible on the local box, then you can deploy a proxy on the same server that controls access. There are a some Solr-specific proxy servers available: `https://github.com/o19s/solr_nginx`, and a **NodeJS** option: `https://github.com/dergachev/solr-security-proxy`.

Let's try out the NodeJS option. Assuming that you have Node Package Manager `npm` installed, run the following code:

```
>> npm install solr-security-proxy
```

Then, to start the proxy that allows access to the `mbartists` and `mbtracks` cores, but none of the other cores on port 9090, run the startup script in `/examples/11` as follows:

```
>> ./start-solr-security-proxy.sh
```

You can verify access by trying to access the `mbartists` core at `http://localhost:9090/solr/mbartists/select?q=*:*`, but being denied access to the karoke core at `http://localhost:9090/solr/mbartists/select?q=*:*`. Go ahead, try out some attacks like trying to trigger commits or access the admin control panel!

To administer the protected Solr, you will either need to be on the local box, or set up the firewall to allow access to your specific IP address.

Securing public searches

Although, typically, you access Solr through an intermediate web application, you may want to expose Solr directly to the Internet, albeit in a limited way. One scenario for this is exposing a search in an RSS/Atom feed made possible with Solr's XSLT support (see *Chapter 5, Searching*, for more on XSLT). Another is using JavaScript, AJAX, and JSONP callbacks from the browser to directly connect to Solr and issue searches. There may be other scenarios where firewall rules and/or passwords might still be used to expose parts of Solr, such as for modifying the index, but some search requests must be exposed to direct Internet access. In this case, you need to configure the exposed request handlers with `invariants` and/or `appends` clauses as applicable. For a limited example of this, see the *A RequestHandler per search interface* section earlier in this chapter.

If there are certain records that need to be excluded from public access, then you'll need to specify an appropriate `fq` (filter query). If there are certain fields on documents that need to be kept private, then this can be problematic to completely secure, especially if you are working with sensitive data. It's simple enough to specify `fl` (field list) through `invariants`, but there are a good number of other parameters that might expose the data (for example, highlighting, maybe faceting) in ways you didn't realize:

```
<lst name="invariants">
  <int name="fl">public_id,public_description</int>
  <str name="fq">public:true</int>
</lst>
```

Therefore, if you are working with sensitive data, exposing Solr in this way is not recommended.

Controlling JMX access

If you have started Solr with JMX enabled, then you should also have a JMX username and password configured. While, today, the JMX interface only exposes summary information about the Solr components and memory consumption, in the future versions, actual management options such as triggering optimizing indexes will most likely be exposed through JMX. So, putting JMX access under lock and key is a good idea.

Securing index data

One of the weaknesses of Solr, due to the lack of a built-in security model, is that there aren't well-defined approaches for controlling which users can manipulate the indexes by adding, updating, and deleting documents, and who can search which documents. Nevertheless, there are some approaches for controlling access to documents.

Controlling document access

You can start off with some of the ideas talked about in the *A RequestHandler per search interface* section to control search access to your index. However, if you need to control access to documents within your index and must control it based on the user accessing the content, then one approach is to leverage the faceted search capabilities of Solr. You may want to look back at *Chapter 7, Faceting*, to refresh your memory on faceting. For example, you may have a variety of documents that have differing visibility depending on whether someone is a member of the public or an internal publicist.

The public can only see a subset of the data, but a publicist can see more information, including information that isn't ready for public viewing. When indexing documents, you should store the roles in a separate `multiValued` field that a user must belong to in order to gain access to the document:

```
<field name="roles" type="text" indexed="true" stored="true"
  multiValued="true" />
```

A document that was for everyone would be indexed with the role values Public and Publicist. Another document that was for internal use would just have the Publicist role. Then, at query time, you could append extra request parameters to limit what is returned depending on the roles that someone belonged to by treating the roles as a facet:

```
/solr/select/?q=music&start=0&facet=on&facet.field=roles&fq=role%3
Apublic
```

In the preceding example, we are querying for `music` that is accessible by anyone with the role `public`. Obviously, this requires significant logic to be implemented on the client side interfacing with Solr, and is not as robust a solution as we may wish.

Other things to look at

Remote streaming is the ability to give Solr the URL to a remote resource or local file and have Solr download the contents as a stream of data. This can be very useful when indexing large documents as it reduces the amount of data that your updating process needs to move around. However, it means that if you have the `/debug/dump` request handler enabled, then the contents of any file can be exposed. Here is an example of displaying to anyone my `authorized_keys` file:

```
http://localhost:8983/solr/mbartists/debug/dump?stream.file=/Users
/epugh/.ssh/authorized_keys
```

If you have this turned on, then make sure that you are monitoring the log files, and also that access to Solr is tightly controlled. *The example application has this function turned on by default.*

In addition, in a production environment, you want to comment out the `/debug/dump` request handler, unless you are actively debugging an issue.

Just as you need to be wary of a SQL injection attack for a relational database, there is a similar concern for Solr. Solr should not be exposed to untrusted clients if you are concerned about the risk of a denial of service attack. This is also a concern if you are lax in how your application acts as a broker to Solr. It's fairly easy to bring down Solr by asking it to sort by every field in the schema, which would result in sudden exorbitant memory usage. There are other similar attacks if an attacker can submit an arbitrary function query as part of their query.

Summary

We briefly covered a wide variety of the issues that surround taking a Solr configuration that works in a development environment and getting it ready for the rigors of a production environment. Solr's modular nature and stripped down focus on search allows it to be compatible with a broad variety of deployment platforms. Solr offers a wealth of monitoring options, from log files to HTTP request logs to JMX options. Nonetheless, for a really robust solution, you must define what the key performance metrics are that concern you, and then implement automated solutions for tracking them.

Assuming you haven't already built your application, look back at *Chapter 9, Integrating Solr*, to see how easily you can integrate Solr search through various client libraries. Otherwise, just enjoy the stability and performance of the most popular search engine, helping your users find what they are looking for!

Quick Reference

This chapter is a convenient reference for common search-related request parameters. It is assumed that you have already read the related material in the book and are just looking for something to jog your memory.

You can find an electronic PDF version of this chapter at `http://www.solrenterprisesearchserver.com`. Having it printed makes it quite convenient.

 The third column indicates whether a parameter can be specified only once (single) or multiple times (multi).

Core search

The following parameters are commonly used in most search queries. These are also covered in *Chapter 5, Searching*:

Parameter	Description	Single/ multi
`qt=/select`	A named request handler.	single
`q`	The query string. Usually, as entered by an end user.	single
`defType=lucene`	The query parser for q. The recommended one is `edismax` (or `dismax`).	single
`fq`	A filter query.	multi
`start=0`	The index into the search results to start returning documents.	single
`rows=10`	The number of search result document rows to return.	single
`fl=*`	The field list to retrieve, comma separated. To get scores: `*,score`	multi

Parameter	Description	Single/multi
sort=score desc	The sort order. A comma-separated list with asc or desc.	single
wt=xml	The writer type for the response format. One of xml, json, python, php, phps, ruby, javabin, csv, xslt, or velocity.	single

Other parameters are: version=2.2, omitHeader=off, and timeAllowed=-1.

Diagnostic

Diagnostic parameters covered in *Chapter 5, Searching*, are: indent=off, debugQuery=off, explainOther (a query for one doc), debug.explain. structured=off, echoParams=explicit (none/explicit/all), and echoHandler=off.

[Use wt=xslt&tr=example.xsl&debugQuery=true&fl=*,score.]

Lucene query parser

The following table shows parameters for the Lucene query parser. These are covered in *Chapter 5, Searching*:

Parameter	Description	Single/multi
df	The default field to search.	single
q.op=OR	The default query operator. One of AND or OR.	single

DisMax query parser

The following table shows parameters for the DisMax query parser. These are covered in *Chapter 5, Searching*, and *Chapter 6, Search Relevancy*:

Parameter	Description	Single/multi
q.alt	This is an alternate query to run when q is absent. The recommended one is: *:* (all docs)	single

Parameter	Description	Single/multi
qf	This stands for query fields, including optional boosts, for example, id^5.0 name^2.0 body.	multi
mm=100%	This is the min-should-match specification. It is used to change to all-optional, use 0%	single
qs=0	This is the query slop for phrases explicitly in the query string.	single
pf	This stands for phrase fields for automatic phrase boosting. This is same as qf syntax.	single
ps=0	This is the phrase slop for pf.	single
tie=0	This is the score tie-breaker. The recommended one is 0.1.	single
bq	This is a boost query. The boost is added.	multi
bf	This is a boost function. The boost is added.	multi
boost	This is a boost function. The boost is multiplied. Works for edismax only.	multi

The other edismax additions are lowercaseOperators=on, pf2, pf3, ps2, ps3, stopwords=on, and uf.

Lucene query syntax

Lucene query syntax, covered in *Chapter 5, Searching*, has the following Boolean operators: AND, OR, NOT, &&, and || with leading + or -. Here is an example:

```
{!lucene df=title q.op=$myop} "phrase query slop"~2 w?ldcard*
fuzzzy~0.7 -(updatedAt:[* TO NOW/DAY-2YEAR] +boostMe^5)
```

Faceting

The following parameters are commonly used in facet queries, and are covered in *Chapter 7, Faceting*:

- **Field specific parameter**: (Works for highlighting too) f.myfieldname. facet.mincount=1

- **Field value faceting**: facet=on, facet.field=myfieldname, facet. sort=count (count, index), facet.limit=100, facet.offset=0, facet.mincount=0, facet.missing=off, facet.prefix, facet.method (enum, fc, or fcs)

- **Range faceting**: `facet=on`, `facet.range=myfieldname`, `facet.range.start`, `facet.range.end`, `facet.range.gap` (for example, `+1DAY`), `facet.range.hardend=off`, `facet.range.other=off`, `facet.range.include=lower` (`lower upper`, `edge`, `outer`, or `all`)
- **Facet queries**: `facet=on`, `facet.query`
- **Facet pivots**: `facet.pivot=field1,field2,field3`
- **Facet keys**: `facet.field={!key=Type}r_type`
- **Filter exclusion**: `fq={!tag=r_type}r_type:Album&facet.field={!ex=r_type}r_type`

Highlighting

The following parameters are applicable to the highlighting component, covered in *Chapter 8, Search Components*: `hl=off`, `hl.fl`, `hl.requireFieldMatch=off`, `hl.usePhraseHighlighter=off`(the recommended one is `on`), `hl.highlightMultiTerm=off`, `hl.snippets=1`, `hl.fragsize=100`, and `hl.mergeContiguous=off`.

Spell checking

These parameters are applicable These parameters are applicable to the spellcheck component, detailed in to the spellcheck component, detailed in *Chapter 8, Search Components*: `spellcheck=off`, `spellcheck.dictionary=default`, `spellcheck.q` (alternative to q), `spellcheck.count=1`, `spellcheck.onlyMorePopular=off`, `spellcheck.extendedResults=off`, `spellcheck.collate=off`, `spellcheck.maxCollations=1`, `spellcheck.maxCollationTries=0`, `spellcheck.maxCollationEvaluations=10000`, and `spellcheck.collateExtendedResults=off`.

Miscellaneous nonsearch

- **Commit**: `/update?commit=true` (`optimize=true` to optimize)
- **Delete**: `/update?stream.body=<delete><query>*:*</query></delete>`
- **Reload config**: `/admin/cores?action=RELOAD&core=mycorename`

Index

C

Thank you for buying
Apache Solr Enterprise Search Server
Third Edition

About Packt Publishing

Packt, pronounced 'packed', published its first book, *Mastering phpMyAdmin for Effective MySQL Management*, in April 2004, and subsequently continued to specialize in publishing highly focused books on specific technologies and solutions.

Our books and publications share the experiences of your fellow IT professionals in adapting and customizing today's systems, applications, and frameworks. Our solution-based books give you the knowledge and power to customize the software and technologies you're using to get the job done. Packt books are more specific and less general than the IT books you have seen in the past. Our unique business model allows us to bring you more focused information, giving you more of what you need to know, and less of what you don't.

Packt is a modern yet unique publishing company that focuses on producing quality, cutting-edge books for communities of developers, administrators, and newbies alike. For more information, please visit our website at www.packtpub.com.

About Packt Open Source

In 2010, Packt launched two new brands, Packt Open Source and Packt Enterprise, in order to continue its focus on specialization. This book is part of the Packt Open Source brand, home to books published on software built around open source licenses, and offering information to anybody from advanced developers to budding web designers. The Open Source brand also runs Packt's Open Source Royalty Scheme, by which Packt gives a royalty to each open source project about whose software a book is sold.

Writing for Packt

We welcome all inquiries from people who are interested in authoring. Book proposals should be sent to author@packtpub.com. If your book idea is still at an early stage and you would like to discuss it first before writing a formal book proposal, then please contact us; one of our commissioning editors will get in touch with you.

We're not just looking for published authors; if you have strong technical skills but no writing experience, our experienced editors can help you develop a writing career, or simply get some additional reward for your expertise.

PUBLISHING

open source
community experience distilled

Apache Solr 4 Cookbook

ISBN: 978-1-78216-132-5   Paperback: 328 pages

Over 100 recipes to make Apache Solr faster, more reliable, and return better results

1. Learn how to make Apache Solr search faster, more complete, and comprehensively scalable.

2. Solve performance, setup, configuration, analysis, and query problems in no time.

3. Get to grips with, and master, the new exciting features of Apache Solr 4.

Apache Solr High Performance

ISBN: 978-1-78216-482-1   Paperback: 124 pages

Boost the performance of Solr instances and troubleshoot real-time problems

1. Achieve high scores by boosting query time and index time, implementing boost queries and functions using the Dismax query parser and formulae.

2. Set up and use SolrCloud for distributed indexing and searching, and implement distributed search using Shards.

3. Use GeoSpatial search, handling homophones, and ignoring listed words from being indexed and searched.

Please check **www.PacktPub.com** for information on our titles

[PACKT] open source ✻
PUBLISHING   community experience distilled

Apache Solr Beginner's Guide

ISBN: 978-1-78216-252-0   Paperback: 324 pages

Configure your own search engine experience with real-world data with this practical guide to Apache Solr

1. Learn to use Solr in real-world contexts, even if you are not a programmer, using simple configuration examples.

2. Define simple configurations for searching data in several ways in your specific context, from suggestions to advanced faceted navigation.

3. Teaches you in an easy-to-follow style, full of examples, illustrations, and tips to suit the demands of beginners.

Apache Solr PHP Integration

ISBN: 978-1-78216-492-0   Paperback: 118 pages

Build a fully-featured and scalable search application using PHP to unlock the search functions provided by Solr

1. Understand the tools that can be used to communicate between PHP and Solr, and how they work internally.

2. Explore the essential search functions of Solr such as sorting, boosting, faceting, and highlighting using your PHP code.

3. Take a look at some advanced features of Solr such as spell checking, grouping, and auto complete with implementations using PHP code.

Please check **www.PacktPub.com** for information on our titles

CPSIA information can be obtained
at www.ICGtesting.com
Printed in the USA
FSOW03n2153200915
11340FS